Finlay J. Macdonald, whose radio talks were a regular delight, enjoyed a long and successful career as a BBC talks producer, and then as a television director.

'It is one of the delights one gets in reading Finlay J. Macdonald that he can take the ordinary everyday events of life and clothe them with wit, verve and humour. Of course, nostalgia abounds, but it is tinged with just the right leaven of realism which makes the reader-ever aware of the fact that life, even in its happier moments, is often veneered with sharp barbs.'
Books in Scotland

The Finlay J. Macdonald Omnibus

Crowdie and Cream
Crotal and White
The Corncrake and the Lysander

WARNER BOOKS

A *Futura* Book

First published in three volumes:
Crowdie and Cream © Finaly J. Macdonald 1982
First published in Great Britain in 1982 by
Macdonald & Co (Publishers) Ltd, London & Sydney.
First Futura edition 1983, reprinted 1986, 1988, 1990.
Crotal and White © Finlay J. Macdonald 1983
First published in Great Britain in 1983 by
Macdonald & Co (Publishers) Ltd, London & Sydney.
First Futura edition 1984, reprinted 1986, 1990.
The Corncrake and the Lysander © Finlay J. Macdonald 1985
First published in Great Britain in 1985 by
Macdonald & Co (Publishers) Ltd, London & Sydney.
First Futura edition 1986, reprinted 1988, 1991 (twice)
This edition published by Warner Books in 1994.

ISBN 0 7515 1348 2

Printed in England by Clays Ltd, St Ives plc

Warner Books
A Division of
Little, Brown and Company (UK)
Brettenham House
Lancaster Place
London WC2E 7EN

BOOK ONE
CROWDIE AND CREAM

For Kathleen

Chapter One

'Big pee wet pussy' was, on the indisputable authority of my mother, the first reasonably coherent sentence that I ever uttered. If, nowadays, in translation it sounds like one of those dubious apothegms so indiscriminately attributed to Confucius, that is not, necessarily, further proof of my constant assertion that English is a very imprecise language compared with my own. At the time – given even that I was attempting to talk in our own native language – it was still only my mother's own complicity in the plot that made it possible for her to deduce from my apoplectic infant Gaelic that, despite all precautions, I had caught my father in the act of drowning the family cat in the peaty pool which he had fondly imagined to be out of sight of the house and of me.

My first sentence, unlike volumes of subsequent ones over the years, was a gross understatement. By the time I had scrambled my tearful way to the water's edge 'big pee' had not just 'wet pussy' but had rendered her very dead, and no amount of smooth baby-talk on my father's part would convince me that she was happier 'down among the lovely big water lilies' than she had been on his favourite chair or on my grandmother's knee. And it took me a long time to forgive my father, far less understand that in the commotion upon which we were embarking a cat of indeterminate pedigree was an encumbrance which he could well do without. In vain he tried to explain to me that the ducks and the drake, and the hens and the

5

cockerel, and even Fanny, the sheep-dog, had to take precedence over the cat because they were going to help us make our way in our new life. Not that it mattered any more. By the time he finished talking the bubbles had slowed down and stopped . . .

We were, in fact, on the eve of uprooting and moving to a new world – a land bland and beckoning with promise – albeit only sixteen miles south. But, in those sixteen miles, a relentless rocky moorland gave way to flat green pasture fringed with golden beaches, and my parents were fortunate to be given the chance to make a new start with the best of their lives still ahead of them. Or so they must have thought.

I grew up with the legend that the Good Lord made the world in six days, and despite what people like Charles Darwin and David Attenborough have had to say on the subject that's the way that the bit of me I like best likes to believe it. If only for the tail end of the legend which goes on to say that when God was resting, as everybody should, on the seventh day, he suddenly discovered that he had completely forgotten to use one last handful of jewels which he had meant to place in some exotic area like the Caribbean. However, rather than break the Sabbath more than was necessary, he just opened a window in heaven and threw the jewels out without even bothering to watch where they fell. Some cynics claim that he still doesn't know but that, in fact, they strung themselves out along the north-west coast of Scotland forming the long line of islands now known as The Outer Hebrides.

I was born in the second island from the top. At least we call Harris an island, and even the Post Office calls it 'The Isle of Harris', but, geographically, it is only a tall mountain range which separates it from what is called, also inaccurately, the Island of Lewis. Be that as it may, a Harrisman is a Harrisman, and a Lewisman is a Lewisman, and neither would have it differently! Up till the end of the eighteenth century, Harris belonged to the Clan MacLeod whose Chiefs to this day call themselves the MacLeods of

6

Harris although their base is Dunvegan Castle in Skye. When the Clan system began to disintegrate during the eighteenth and nineteenth centuries Harris, like most of the other Clan Lands, was broken up and sold off to incomer landlords whose interests were either Sporting (in the hunting, salmon fishing or shooting sense) or Financial in terms of farming or commercial fishing.

Over the years the population was ruthlessly hounded off the rich arable land of the south-west and crowded on to the rocky heather shores of the northern and eastern coasts where the people squeezed bare livelihoods from thin soil and the sea. Their housing was primitive, consisting largely of thatched 'black houses' completely devoid of sanitation and custom designed for the encouragement of tuberculosis which was the inevitable death of one person out of three at the beginning of this century. Such cash as there was came from a haphazard cottage industry in Harris Tweed, and from family members who found work on the mainland or from the large numbers of men who went into the merchant navy.

Just after the First World War Harris received a rare injection of optimism when the whole island was bought by Lord Leverhulme, the multi-millionaire soap magnate, who had plans for the injection of massive capital into the island and its creation into the hub of a huge fish and tweed empire. Leverhulme's entrepreneurial genius had amassed him a fortune in the Congo, and the model town of Port Sunlight in Lancashire is still a monument to the enlightenment of his thinking and planning. Lord Leverhulme had already attempted to found mammoth fishing and agricultural projects in Lewis, but the deep-rooted suspicion of landlord intentions had denied him access to the free manipulation of the land resources which he regarded as fundamental to the integrated developments he envisaged. Frustrated by what he regarded as short-sighted intransigence, he abandoned Lewis and attempted to make a fresh start in Harris where the local population, who had had more time to study the 'Leverhulme vision', were much more willing to co-operate. Unfortunately Leverhulme died in the year that I was born and my father, who had been a staunch believer in him, was one of the many ex-servicemen who found themselves bogged down in the unrelenting past from which they had thought themselves to be escaping. After Leverhulme's death Harris was, once again, segmented into job lots of smaller estates and sold off to the highest bidders and it looked as if the old dreary pattern was about to be stamped once again on a community whose morale had suffered yet another collapse. But it wasn't to be quite like that. Although I – barely past the toddling period – could scarcely be expected to be aware of it, a whole new chapter of local history was beginning to be written around me, and it is typical of the innocent values of childhood that my vague awareness of it hinged on the drowning of a cat whose name or colour I can't even remember.

In 1919 a host of island soldiers and sailors had returned from the First World War eager to make a new start and get for themselves a share of the land fit for heroes to live in' which Lloyd George or someone in the elevated realms of government had promised them. That was all they wanted – for each a bit of land. They had been prepared to await the outcome of the Leverhulme experiment but when that bubble burst the old land hunger began to gnaw at them again. But too late. By the mid 1920s the nation's gratitude was beginning to ebb, and the new landlords who succeeded Leverhulme were not over-anxious to have their estates divided up among raggle-taggle warriors who didn't look nearly as impressive in threadbare pullovers and dungarees as they had done in uniform. And, come to think of it, they weren't nearly as necessary as they had been between 1914 and 1918 now that all the Peace Treaties were signed and sealed and more or less in the process of being ratified. But, over the years, a powerful 'crofter lobby' had been built up, and at last the Board of Agriculture in Edinburgh, which had already begun to show its teeth elsewhere, began to take a tentative interest in our neck of the woods.

My father and seven others were lucky. The landlord of a large and lush estate on the Atlantic coast of South Harris was prevailed upon to let a sizeable hunk of his territory be divided and rented out as eight crofts for which he would get annual rental while retaining to himself the fishing and shooting rights and, of course, the mineral rights should somebody stumble across gold. All the men had to do was pay their small rentals of about seven pounds a year, build themselves a village, and build, each to himself, a family of children and a flock of sheep in whichever order he chose. Much like Abraham and Jacob and Laban and those other forebears in another age and in another clime.

I wish I could remember and record some of the impact that my arrival, as the first boy of the new village, made on me. But, alas, all I can remember is that the two-hour journey in the little seven-seater bus which contained everything that we possessed in the world was punctuated by frequent stops for my mother to be sick. Poor woman! It was an affliction that was to bedevil her for years on the rare occasion that she made the journey. Nor was she by any means the only sufferer. The fact that the bus, with the springing of half a century ago, took two hours to complete a journey that is now comfortably achieved in a quarter of an hour is ample testimony to the state of a road which, in all fairness, was originally carved through the mountains for the occasional convenience of the traveller by horse and trap. But, over the years, it also became fairly obvious that my mother's upsets were always more pronounced on the journey south. Her heart never really left the Northlands, perhaps because her roots there were deeper than my father's. For someone of his strongly romantic nature the achievement of a place of his own in South Harris represented something akin to the emotion of the Jew returning to Israel; he was one of those people whose fairly immediate ancestors had been uprooted from

9

the South during the evictions of the previous century and his sense of history could easily be manipulated to conjure up an imagery of an Israelite far, far older than the Jew. He was not to know that he was not escaping from bondage but, rather, going into it.

For me, the new village wove a spiritual and physical magic as I grew up with it. It was carved out from what had been the granary of the Clan MacLeod in the old days of that Clanship. The Atlantic thundered or shimmied according to its mood on mile upon mile of shell-white beach which, in its turn, was selvedge to rolling green meadowland intended, surely, by the Almighty in those early days of creation as a golf course. The machair, as it was called in Gaelic, was set aside as winter grazing for the township's sheep.

That was 'below the road', on the setting sun side. Above the road were the crofts themselves, each consisting of thirteen or fourteen acres of arable land stretching up to an infinity of heather moorland which was too rough and sour for cultivation but ideal for summer pasture. And the whole panorama was contained in a crescent swathe of tall mountains whose names, while ringing out like a peal of bells in Gaelic, in reality bore testimony to the Viking occupation of those lands a thousand years before. If it all sounds idyllic it's because it was to the boy who was I. And the land is still there for me to see when time allows me back to relive the years when it was moulding my life for me.

Our croft was probably the best of the eight in that the soil was a perfect blend of sand and peat through which the plough could shear an uninterrupted quarter-mile furrow; it was not by accident that the estate owners from the MacLeod Chiefs onwards had situated their vegetable gardens there. I know that only because Great Aunt Rachel once pointed out to me where the 'kale garden' as she called it had been, and Great Aunt Rachel would know because she was a relic of the indigenous population which had once thronged that coastline. She was my father's aunt, and by virtue of the fact that her people had

10

been 'clerics' or clerks to the church there as far back as the eighteenth century, when the vast majority of the popu- lation had been shunted off to the Northlands during the evictions, her family had been allowed to stay on, on the moorland fringe of the church's land, in a 'grace and favour hovel of stone and marram thatch. With that devout loyalty which the real 'Downstairs' has for the true blue 'Upstairs' Great Aunt Rachel never concealed the fact that she thought the nation to have fallen on evil days when fat rich lands were parcelled out to the peasantry.

In theory, thirteen acres of arable land, well cultivated, should provide enough vegetables and potatoes for the table and enough fodder for the cattle beasts in winter and they, in turn, should provide enough milk for drinking and for butter and cheese. By the same token the grazing outruns should maintain enough sheepstock to provide wool to make our clothes, mutton for the table and a small cash income from the sale of wethers and cast ewes to pay the rent. In addition to all that, our moorland grazing contained underneath it millions of tons of peat which would provide fuel for the crofting community for cen- turies and for free. Doubtless some ex-colonial bureaucrat, who had moved his desk from one of the crumbling outposts of Empire to Edinburgh, would add to all that bounty fish from the sea and rabbits from the machair for supplementary white meat and consider that a grateful government had done well by eight men returning from the trenches or the navy. And to a certain extent he would be right. Had our allocated corner of Utopia been in that particular bare-foot area of the Pacific for which God had meant those legendary jewels in the first place, then life for the settlers would have been superlatively good. For me and for the generation coming off the production lines it was good beyond measure in the early years, and when hardship came along – as it did – we were still too young to know it for what it was, and it's the *knowing* that makes the difference come joy, come sorrow.

11

Chapter Two

The view which opened up for us as we topped the Back of Scarista Hill on that first day can have done little to lift my mother's morale or confirm her faith in my father's optimism. As far as the eye could see there was nothing but beautiful emptiness save for the solid schoolhouse, built in 1892 when a rash of schools erupted through the West Highlands to conform to the Education Act of twenty years earlier, and an incongruously large church and manse dating back to the middle of the eighteenth century before the land had been cleared of its people. A few wisps of peat smoke from the moorland might have betrayed the well-camouflaged black houses of the few cottars who had been allowed to stay on in landless penury because they had proved too troublesome to evict or because they were useful as a supply of casual labour on the big estates. Finally, in the far distance ahead, there stood out in solitary splendour the small manorial homestead of Scaristaveg – the neighbouring estate which had escaped being crofterized. It was owned by a superficially benign old gentleman who had, at least, the virtue of being a Gaelic speaker from the mainland Highlands. But if those wisps of smoke from the moorland were visible from his drawing-room window he must have known that time was running out – fast!

Till such time as my father could get our house built we were to live with his Aunt Rachel – that redoubtable descendant of the clerics who had got out of her little moorland cottage by dint of marrying a widower who had been himself employed by the church in some capacity or other in the days when part of the minister's 'living' was the sizeable swatch of prize agricultural land known as the glebe. Being allegedly committed to delving full time in Jehovah's vineyards the minister invariably employed at least one man to supervise the more earthly tillage. If Alastair was, indeed, such an employee he did very well out of it because he was able to provide Rachel with a large and comfortable home in a village only a few miles away from our new land. He appeared to make few demands on her – apparently not of the kind that resulted in a family anyway – and in exchange for looking after his daughter by his previous marriage, he indulged her to the extent of allowing her to bring our family to live under his roof for free and for as long as it might take my father to build a house. I have forgotten almost all of that period with the exception of our benefactress whom I was to come to love like a third grandmother.

Like all the women on the distaff side of my father's family, Great Aunt Rachel was built like a Churchill tank with a personality to match. She was also literate in that she could write and read English, which was not all that usual in her generation in our part of the world. And that, in itself, was enough to set her apart. She claimed to have met Lord Macaulay, which seemed to make a huge impression on people even though they had never heard of the great writer, and she could produce two crystal goblets which he had given her. All of which would seem to be perfectly feasible since the said Lord Macaulay's great grandfather had been minister of her old parish (the one we were about to enter into) and that reverend gentleman had carved himself a niche in eighteenth-century history by being the only man who tried to betray Bonnie Prince Charlie when the latter was being hunted in the Western Isles after Culloden. That particular bit of the story seemed to have escaped Aunt Rachel's capacious memory!

13

The crystal goblets were strictly for display and were only brought out to be polished or to be exhibited to some special visitor. They couldn't possibly be of any more practical use anyway in an environment as morally and economically stringent as hers, and they would have looked absurd with the thick black tea to which she was so thoroughly addicted.

No ancient or modern brewer of real ale was more devoted to his tipple than Aunt Rachel was to her tea. And no alchemist took greater care with the blending of his potions. She never used a teapot. She used a little black pan which she filled to within an inch of the top with fresh spring water and placed on the open fire so that it could absorb the flavour of the peat smoke that curled up around it as it came to the boil. When it began to bubble she added half a fistful of tea from a large caddy sporting a fading picture of Queen Victoria, whom, come to think of it, she resembled in more ways than one, and the brew was made to boil vigorously while she knitted a measured knuckle of sock which she had calculated long ago took her ten minutes. The fact that she got arthritic and slower as she got older didn't alter anything. As far as she was concerned an inch and a half of sock was still ten minutes, and that was the duration for which tea boiled. The tea got blacker as Great Aunt Rachel's hair got whiter, and she lived to be very old. Latterly her fainter-hearted visitors used to conjure up all sorts of excuses to get out of having to partake of her hospitality, and it was useless for her sister or her stepdaughter, who guessed at the reason for the reluctance, to suggest a milder distillation. But it was only well behind her back that anybody dared smile at the old lady's oft-quoted assertion – in which the pun evaded her innocence in both her languages – 'When I make tea I make tea, and when I make water I make water.'

Great Aunt Rachel was the repository of the history of her branch of our family – the only branch that counted in her reckoning – and it was she who told me, later on in life, how we all began and why I look the way I do.

14

It all went back to a sea battle between the English and the Spaniards away down in the south' according to her. And the English routed the Spaniards, which was just as it should be since there were no Scots in the opposing team. 'Round about the end of the sixteenth century' was the nearest she would come to putting a date on it. Anyway, the Spanish fleet was defeated and tried to escape back home by the long way round the north of Scotland, but they ran into heavy weather and most of their galleys foundered in the Orkneys and the Western Isles.

Round about that time a spinster fore-runner of ours was dragging out a lonely existence in a house on the very spot of moorland where Aunt Rachel's own home had stood before she married her widower, above what was to be our new village. The lady was approaching the age when matrimony seemed to be passing her by and she had to rely on her neighbours to cut her peat for her and keep her supplied with her minimal requirements of food in the way of milk and meat and oatmeal. She augmented her store of fuel by beachcombing when the wind was in the west, and it was after one particularly bad storm that she went down to the sands and found what she took at first to be a corpse bobbing in the ebb. 'She turned the thing over with her foot,' to use Great Aunt Rachel's own words, 'and, lo and behold, he stirred and groaned.' Being a kindly soul she took him home and dried him out, and he turned out to be – again I quote – 'a little sallow sailor from foreign parts who couldn't speak any Gaelic'. Which is not surprising if, as Aunt Rachel seemed to imply, he was a lone survivor from the ill-fated Armada of King Philip II of Spain! Anyway, the two got married and from them descended my Great Aunt Rachel and, in due course, me.

It was a great pedigree for a romantically inclined young boy like me to grow up with, and for years I was happy to attribute to it a complexion that is decidedly off-white and a *mañana* attitude to dead-lines. It was only recently that

15

– having been caught up in the frenetic slip-stream of *Roots* – I decided to put my past to the test and tentatively approached the distinguished Scottish genealogist, Bill Lawson, and asked him to confirm the legend. Bill is a man of infinite kindliness and nothing would have delighted him more than to give me a chart straight back to Mount Ararat, but his professional integrity would allow him only to confirm that my first known ancestor was one Murdo MacKay (*floruit* 1780) who was indeed shipwrecked on Toe-Head – a wild headland jutting into the Atlantic in front of our village. But that was two centuries after the Spanish Armada, and Murdo MacKay is one of the less likely Spanish names. What is more credible is that he was a survivor from the wreck of one of the ships bound for America with a cargo of the victims of one of the early infamous Sutherland Clearances – perhaps, indeed, a sole survivor. For sure there was such a man, and, having escaped with only a broken leg, he decided out of gratitude to the Almighty to devote his services to the church and he became the 'cleric' from whom Aunt Rachel was descended.

Since that encounter with the reality, I have become increasingly aware that every by-ordinar living being in the West Highlands, from unsociable marmalade tom-cats to the most vicious midges, are invariably debited, one way or another, to some form of flotsam from the Spanish Armada.

And Lord Macaulay's crystal goblets . . .? Well, they're there all right. But, even without recourse to any form of historian or other authority, I can deduce with reasonable certainty that Lord Macaulay was dead by the time Great Aunt Rachel was born. But I have noticed that always, somewhere, there was a grain of history in her fictions and, at worst, I like to think that she had a vivid imagination.

My father did not inherit the forcefulness of personality of 'the clerics'. He was a mild-mannered man who despite of – or, perhaps, because of – five gruelling years in the

16

trenches would go out of his way to avoid trouble or even an argument, choosing to take a quizzical view of life through the wrong end of the telescope. What he did inherit from them was a strong streak of imagination and poetry – qualities which were not, necessarily, the best assets for a man beginning to carve out a new living from raw croft land.

The pattern of procedure was that each new crofter built, on his land, a corrugated iron shack into which he moved with his wife and the beginnings of his family while he was building up his stock of sheep and cattle. My father started off in due course with one jet black cow, inexplicably called Daisy, and about twenty sheep donated by his own parents and his in-laws. The theory was that they would multiply and keep on multiplying till he achieved the regulation quota or 'souming' of sixty sheep and two cows and their followers. One only had to thumb back through Holy Writ to the Book of Genesis and the story of Noah to be reassured that spectacular results could be achieved with a considerably smaller, if more varied, investment of breeding stock than even my father had. And Noah didn't have the patronage of the Board of Agriculture for Scotland which had pledged itself to the provision of a pedigree bull who would be changed every two years to avoid any danger of incest.

Our 'pattern of procedure', however, seemed to be taking an unduly long time to establish itself and our new house a long time to materialize, although, by all the laws, we were enviably placed in that my mother came of a long line of carpenters – the extant members of which had volunteered to give of their services. In fact, for the first few years of our life in the south, we were to discover that our vaguest relatives from the Northlands were more than willing to come and share in our toils, particularly in summer, in much the same way as the modern city-dweller discovers clouds of unsuspected friends the moment he acquires a cottage in the country.

In the end, with another spring descending on us and

17

only the foundations of the new house laid, it was decided that it might be better to live on location, and so, along with another family, we moved into the residential end of the school building which was initially planned for the head-teacher's family, but which was vacant for reasons that I shall bring myself to describe later. We weren't to know that our short sojourn in the schoolhouse was to give us a ringside seat for events which were to reverberate throughout Scotland and raise echo in the Mother of Parliaments in Westminster.

Chapter Three

There is a highly distinctive odour of which whiffs may still, very occasionally, be detected in the corridors of the House of Lords, although never at Ascot. Like the most exclusive perfumes it is a harmonization of many essences and, nowadays, at the higher end of the olfactory register one may detect contributions from the distinguished palaces of Givenchy or Dior. But pervasively, and unmistakably to the cognoscenti, there comes through, on humid days in particular, the inter-reaction of wool and urine. To say that one is more likely to come across it among the older representatives of the aristocracy is not to suggest a higher incidence of incontinence among the hereditary members of the Upper Chamber. It is just that by virtue of their age and tradition they are more likely to be still the wearers of the real hand-spun, hand-woven, 'never-left-the-croft' Harris Tweed which was the mainstay of the primitive economy of the island at the time of which I write.

It was Lady Dunmore, the wife of one of the more enlightened former proprietors of Harris, who had seen the potential of the rough, tough, cloth made from the wool of the local black-face sheep as ideal cladding for the hunting, fishing and shooting fraternity which was beginning to discover the Western Isles at the beginning of the century. And she had encouraged the wives of her tenants to make tweed surplus to their own domestic requirements, and she had helped them to market it. In my young days we were still only in the early stages of adapting to a 'money economy' and the wives of cottars and crofters alike were just beginning to exploit their home-made tweeds as a source of hard cash to pay the rent and the increasing luxuries of imported food and clothes. Although my grandfather, on my father's side, was a weaver it was only after we had moved south that I became conscious of the paraphernalia of the trade – important among which was the pee-tub, to which I had first been introduced during our stay with Great Aunt Rachel.

When hand-spun Harris Tweed comes out of the loom it is very rough indeed, and very loose and greasy. It has to be shrunk to a pre-ordained width beyond which it is guaranteed to shrink no further on the wearer's back. Otherwise the results might be highly uncomfortable, if not strangulating in sundry places. The roughness is an acceptable, and indeed desirable, characteristic of the cloth since it contributes to the wearer's warmth and to his (or her) 'man-among-the-heather' image. But the greasy oiliness, which was part of the essential rain-proofing of a Hebridean sheep, was always considered more than even the most dedicated stalker or salmon fisher could tolerate, and it was partially removed during the shrinking and washing process.

The substance most effective for removing the oiliness was ammonia and – far removed as we were from hardware and chandlers' shops – the best available source of ammonia was matured human urine. Not only did it clean the tweed but it gave it that distinctive aroma about which the gentry from the Home Counties used to rave, and which, as I've said, may still be found to cling to those members of the monied classes who are aristocratic enough to be able to boast of old suits in which the *nouveau riche* would not be seen dead.

Anyway, for some time after we became established in the new village it was common for every household to save up its spent pennies, as it were, in large tubs in the byre or some sheltered place where the rain would not dilute the collection too much and interrupt its maturing. Every household contributed to its own tub as did friendly visitors who were doubly welcome if they happened to be breaking their journey on the long road home after a night on the beer. 'Where do you keep your tub?' was our nearest genteelism to 'Where can I wash my hands?' – that absurd euphemism which I have known to land many a bewildered tourist in a bedroom equipped with a ewer and a wash hand basin which far from fulfilled his most urgent need. In more sophisticated parts of the nation specialists in porcelain were making fortunes evolving quick methods for disposing of what we were struggling to save, but it was to be several years before they were to find a market with us.

During the few months of our stay in the schoolhouse we didn't have a pee-tub of our own, partly because my mother couldn't settle down to the business of spinning for a tweed till we got settled into our new house, and, largely, I suspect because the lady whose sub-tenants we were in a way would almost certainly have objected. For some reason best known to herself, the Headmistress, as she was called, although she was the sole representative of the Education Authority in the parish, chose to live in lodgings rather than in the schoolhouse which had been designed for a man with a family. For all I know the Authority may have moved her out in order to make room, temporarily, for us and the other family whose own house wasn't yet ready for occupation. In any case Miss Dalbeith roared out of the morning and into the evening on a motor-bicycle causing stampedes among the villagers' small herd of cows and horses which had not yet become accustomed to their new surroundings, far less the petrol-ized age and female motor-cyclists.

At that stage, mercifully, I had nothing to do with Miss Dalbeith nor, even more mercifully, had Miss Dalbeith anything to do with me. We heard a lot of her – through the schoolhouse wall – but, except for her arrivals and departures, we saw little of her apart from her once-daily visit to inspect the house presumably to ensure that we weren't breaking up and burning the doors or the floorboards for fuel. Once or twice my father tried to engage her in conversation on the strength of being able to speak English and having himself once had a motor-bicycle, but he got short shrift and was left muttering to my mother that the lady was better suited to a broomstick. When she took to riding through the village occasionally on a Sunday, all the elders could do was wish that she were a member of the kirk so that she could be excommunicated. Miss Dalbeith would have been above the law even if the occupant of the Manse had been the Ayatollah Kerr instead of the Reverend . . .

I suspect that the only reason why I didn't stumble more across the path of my future 'Headmistress' was that I was revelling in the freedom of the wide-open spaces of the new village. Having lived till then amidst the sheltered rocky bays and inlets of the north, the explosion of space was overwhelming. I remember as if it were yesterday instead of half a century ago, standing alone – a minuscular fluff of infancy on an infinity of sand – staring at a sea horizon far out and above my eye level, picking up a distant swelling in the water which would move seemingly slowly and gently towards me but gathering weight and volume and power as it came, till, at last, it seemed to hang high above me with a white angry fringe forming on its top. And then it would crash down with a roar that picked up an echo from somewhere, and suddenly, as if defeated or tamed, it would end up like a fold of deckled creamy linen at my feet and then crease back whence it came. Often and often my mother would have to trek the whole width of the beach to drag me back home because no shouting voice could carry against the waves even on the quietest day. Poor woman! She had been brought up beside a sea without waves, and she never lost her fear of the Atlantic. Nor I my respect for it.

Some days I would set off in the other direction and

22

up towards the little black houses of the old population – old in the sense that their people had been there on the moor's edge for generations. In terms of years, the menfolk were only slightly older than my father. Although my father's people had been of their stock, they seemed different from us. Or perhaps the legend which surrounded them made them seem different to the little boy. Two of them had been in prison and, although I didn't know it, they were preparing to go again. One of them was a tall black shepherd who sang songs that he composed himself, and the other was alleged to be a joiner, although I never knew him to practise a trade. Their crime had been an attempt to stake out land for themselves from the small estate which lay adjacent to the one which had been allotted to us. And when they were arrested they had shown contempt not only for the law but also for the Court – in words and ribald song. They had been sentenced to four months in Porterfield Prison in Inverness, but Labour M.P.s led by Tom Johnstone (later to be Secretary of State for Scotland) created such a row that they had been allowed home after two months, and they had returned as folk heroes and utterly unrepentant.

I used to spend hours listening to the Black Shepherd telling his stories as he puffed incessantly at an evil-looking stubby pipe which he kept re-filling from a long rope of thick black tobacco sliced and rubbed to the correct texture between palms that rasped like two pieces of sandpaper. His wife was a tea maker of only marginally lower calibre than Great Aunt Rachel, and she plied it with a generosity which would have taxed the bladder of a seasoned drinker of Somerset cider than which there is no more impatient brew. Whenever I got up at nature's insistence I was reminded to be sure to 'use the tub now'. That tub had stood for so long that its fumes would have brought tears to the eyes of a seaman, and it was on the point of becoming the subject of a song which is now, to the best of my knowledge, in the archives of Edinburgh University.

The Black Shepherd was, in theory at least, an employee of the landlord who owned the estate which had been the centre of the troubles earlier on, but I suspect that he had been made redundant – to use a word which had not then acquired such common currency – following on his encounters with the law. Certainly he was never a guest in the house of the landlord who was basically a gentle character with only two passions in life – trout fishing and a card-game called 'catch-the-ten', which was a modified form of whist in which the object was to capture the ten-spot card of whichever suit was trump, or, as the landlord called it, 'trumph'. His guests, in the main, were chosen from among his more docile tenants and the incomer crofters because he wasn't sufficiently 'upper-crust' to merit the attention of the belted knights who were his fellow estate owners. Nor was 'catch-the-ten' sufficient intellectual challenge for the doctor and the minister. In any case he preferred his cronies to be 'trusties' whom he could depend upon to let him win, and who in their turn knew that if they didn't their chances of going home with a few plump trout were considerably diminished.

Up on the moor the Black Shepherd and his friends were getting restive. It says much for them – either that or it underlines a defeatism born of generations of repression – that they had accepted their reverses with so little rancour towards us, the incomers. They had watched the fat land on their doorsteps being parcelled out among strangers. They had seen the newcomers appearing to begin to prosper. They had seen one season of corn ripening and being harvested by men who had, perhaps, less claim to that particular land than themselves. And they were now beginning to see new houses going up while they were confined to their hovels. At last, while the spring nights were still long enough for the card sessions to be in progress the men from the moors decided to deal themselves a fresh hand and they were determined that they were going to deal themselves some trumps.

Over the weeks they had quietly procured some sacks of

grain, and one fine spring morning they went out and parcelled out some of the landlord's best fields among themselves and began to plough and sow. This time they had acted without warning, and there was no policeman on hand to stop them. Previously they had merely staked out claims to land, marking their claims with assorted little pegs, but now they they were planting seed. Needless to say, the landlord couldn't stand by and nod approval while his best green fields turned black under a plough of his own which had been commandeered from behind his steadings overnight, and, in those pre-telephone days, there was nothing he could do except drum up a regiment, in the shape of some reluctant farm hands, to drive off 'raiders' who were, in all probability, their own kith and kin. The farm hands, directed by the landlord waving a silver mounted walking-stick, went into action. But they had reckoned without the women!

Up on the hillside, the women-folk saw their men being 'attacked' by the landlord and his henchmen and they decided to take a hand. They formed a loose-knit human chain stretching from the pee-tubs to the landlord, and pail after pail of malodorous urine passed down the line to be generously thrown over the landlord who, alone, attempted to hold his ground. But not for long. Soaking wet, and with smarting eyes, he too was forced to retreat leaving the ploughmen to sow their grain to the last handful, cheered on by the school-children whom even Miss Dalbeith could not control. The law, of course, had to move against the 'raiders' once again, and, once again, the ringleaders went to prison to even greater press and parliamentary outcry than before. It would be nice to tell that the 'raiders' came out of jail to find fields of golden corn awaiting them. But, alas, no. And it was just as well for them that their sentences were in no way timed to the harvest.

In the short term nobody won. The landlord, having washed and disinfected himself, rubbed his hands glee-fully and proclaimed that his fields had been sown for him without cost to himself, and he set about the business of catching trout and playing 'catch-the-ten' with great content. What he didn't know – any more than they themselves knew – was that the cottars had lost their agricultural know-how somewhere along the line and what they had bought and sown by some inexplicable mischance was a large quantity of sago which did not flourish in our climate and our soil. The winter's imported cattle food cost the landlord dear.

There was one sad side-effect resulting in a change which, I suppose, would have come sooner or later anyway. As a result of the 'battle of the pails' there was an acute shortage of matured urine for tweed that year and an enterprising shop-keeper somewhere cashed in on it by importing bottled ammonia for the first time. For the pee-tub time was trickling out.

In those days, visitors to the village were few and far between. There were only a dozen or so cars on the whole island, and when during the daylight hours one or other of them ventured along the coastal track which was only then being carved out as a single track road, its noise could be heard approaching from a mile away. There was always a rush to windows and doors to see it pass, and it was good for half an hour's speculation as to who was in it and where it was going and why. If it happened to be the doctor's then the speculation would continue into the next day till it was established whether he was on his way to fish or to death. Speculation would end only on the arrival of Calum the Post who, whether he was delivering or collecting the mail, could be depended on to be carrying a greater volume of news in his head than in his van.

Occasionally, word would get round the community that 'men from the Board were coming round'. By what form of bush telegraph the news got round I do not know but, presumably, the visitors from the mainland would have had to make arrangements for the hiring of a car from Stornoway or Tarbert and the driver of the car would be an islander who had a sister who had a cousin who had a friend in the long line of word of mouth communication which has been the bush telegraph in rural areas the world over since tribal barriers were broken down and men could trust each other to pass on messages more accurately than smoke signals could do. Not so very long ago an old man who had been a boy on the remote island of Scarp, off the north-west coast of Harris, assured me that, before the First World War, at times when Scarp was cut off from the mainland of Harris by winter storms, news would reach Scarp of events which had taken place in the very south of Harris within twenty-four hours. It is no more puzzling than the fact that in our own micro-chip age there is still nothing that excels the speed of rumour.

The 'men from the Board' were dapper gentlemen who travelled in pairs and wore knickerbockers and brushed their teeth. They represented the Board of Agriculture which had been set up in 1912 with powers to acquire, compulsorily if necessary, some of the vast West Highland estates and divide them into crofts to satisfy the insatiable land hunger which was sweeping the whole of the north of Scotland. Its task was what an earlier Irish politician had described in similar circumstances as the 'unshirkable duty to strive towards undoing the unnatural divorce between the people and the land'. 'The people' were the contemporaries of my grandparents and parents in the north of Scotland as in Ireland – ordinary men and women as opposed to 'the lairds' or 'the landed gentry' who had been for generations their exploiters and oppressors to a degree unparalleled today save in the totalitarian states of South America.

'What is that floating in the ebb?' the old Highlander asked his crony. 'It looks like a board of wood or something.'

'If it is moving fast,' was the reply, 'it will *be* a plank of wood. If it's moving slowly it'll be the Board of Agriculture.'

The Board had, perforce, moved slowly over the twenty-five years or so of its existence, hampered less perhaps by

27

the interpolation of two wars than by the intransigence of landlords whose credo was 'to have and to hold', and who, in the upholding of that credo, were prepared to exploit every avenue of legality and appeal.

But, slowly, on the Highland mainland and in Skye and some of the other Hebridean islands the Board of Agriculture had inched on against the opposition and had created some two and a half thousand new crofts and enlarged more than five thousand previously established small - very small - holdings. In all, about three quarters of a million acres of land had had the 'unnatural divorce' healed and been given to the people. In the process, of course, the Board of Agriculture had, in the British fashion, inbred itself into a bureaucracy with its own laws and laws to safeguard its own laws, so that by the time our men, at the tail end of the line, were given their bit of land, a croft had, indeed, become 'a piece of land surrounded by regulations'. It was in the supervision of these regulations that the knickerbockered twosomes always planned to arrive on us unexpectedly.

It may well have been a Hebridean who coined the phrase: 'When the Good Lord made time, he made plenty of it.' And if it was, why not? But the chestnut has been hung round his neck to imply that the islander will not willingly do today what can be put off till tomorrow, and I am certainly not living proof to the contrary. But, in those boyhood days about which I'm writing, it was difficult, if not pointless, to cultivate a sense of urgency when life was governed by time and tide, by season and weather, and by communication and transport. Every stick of wood and every sheet of corrugated iron and every piece of ancillary hardware from shelf brackets to nails had to be imported – invariably from Glasgow or from Greenock, because it was from there that the venerable coasters *The Dunara Castle* and *The Hebrides* sailed on their Odysseys round the myriad islands of the west coast with us at the tail end. Certain shops and firms in those faraway places had near monopolies of our community's trade by virtue of the fact that they could interpret the islanders' needs as expressed in rough sketches and fractured English, and acted on them as expeditiously as the schedules of the two ships allowed. Some of those firms won themselves trust and loyalty which were to help swell their prestige and their profits for decades, and their names became part of the vernacular. For years I had to pause and think whether Peter Fisher was the Galilean apostle or the Glasgow supplier of paints and wallpapers.

But it mattered not how efficient the suppliers, their deliveries were still governed by the schedules of *The Dunara* and *The Heb*, and their schedules, in turn, were governed by tide and weather because, in those days, they had to unload at some very exposed rough jetties or even ferry their cargoes ashore in dribs and drabs by rowing boat. It could well be a month before an order despatched from our village was finally delivered, and it could well be that when it was delivered the weather had turned so stormy that only an idiot would attempt to manoeuvre a six-foot sheet of plywood or corrugated iron; or else the materials would appear on the very first day of a spell of dry weather which had to be seized upon for the cutting of the peat or the shearing of the sheep – whichever chore was seasonal at the time.

These were factors not always appreciated by the bureaucrats in Edinburgh whose morning coffees and afternoon teas arrived on their desks at the pre-ordained times regardless of whether or not *The Dunara Castle* was being held up in Castlebay for nine days by a force ten gale. And so, when the days were sufficiently lengthened and the salmon were deemed to be running well in the Outer Islands, the men from the Board tore themselves away from their offices and their wives and set out on their pilgrimages to check on the progress being made by the new crofters on the new land which had been bestowed upon them.

While the men from Edinburgh may not have understood the problems governing the tempo of island life, the men of the islands understood the official mentality fine.

As soon as news came that an inspection was imminent all the proper seasonal work was temporarily abandoned, and work on the new houses was resumed with vigour even if it meant stripping off some sarking or corrugated iron that had already been laid, and going through the motions of nailing it back on again. By whatever means, every man jack in the village was busy as the government's hired car jolted its way down the road, stopping here and there to justify its journey. Since a tour of the crofting communities was a coveted 'perk' for the office-bound officials, they came round in strict rotas so that, in fact, the same pair never came on successive occasions, making it extremely difficult for one delegation to decide whether or how much advance had been made on what had been seen by the previous one. The crofters, who could modulate the fluency of their English as the occasion demanded, were always cautiously reassuring. And, at the end of the inspection, they always wished the officials 'a nice holiday'. At which the men from the Board flashed uncertain little white smiles and continued their journey towards the hotel where, I am sure, they coined new aphorisms on the theme of God making plenty of time.

Chapter Four

Up till now I have written as if we were just three in our family. But we weren't. We were, in fact, four. Just before we left the Northlands my mother had – with consummate timing – provided my father with a second son and me with a first brother, three years to the day and almost to the hour after she had brought me into the world in unconscious celebration of America's Independence Day. He is now a hirsute hunk of middle-age whose arrival in a community, far less a room, can scarce pass unnoticed, but in the days of our transit encampment in the school-house he was too immobile to be of consequence or companionship.

My earliest companion was, in fact, a girl of neither kith nor kin. If I was the first of the incomer boys in the new village, then she was the first girl – older than me by a whiff of years which chivalry now forbids me measure publicly. Like me, she had been born furth of the village, and, like me, she was in a state of suspended domiciliation in the schoolhouse while her father, who treasured time as laconically as my own, was building their new temporary house on a croft two miles along the road. There were four in her family too, and to this day I cannot figure out how eight people managed to crowd into the tiny schoolhouse. But we did. And during the long summer holiday when she was free from the moils of Miss Dalbeith's classroom Molly and I became intermittently firm friends. It says much for the soothing of time that we are friends still despite the fact that she is the only person who, to my knowledge, set out deliberately to poison me!

We had come from different but equally harsh and rocky areas of the island, and the freedom of the flat green miles and the white beaches must have been as overwhelming for her as for me. The lush coastal land had never known a chemical, nor predator worse than a leisurely cow, and so in summer it erupted with buttercups, daisies, speedwell, groundsel, yarrow, forget-me-nots and ones I've long since forgotten, or whose names I have never known in English. It is an occasionally regretted fact of life for me that I have two strictly limited botanical horizons. There is a vast flora with which I was familiar in boyhood, the terminology of which never seemed to merit being translated into the English area of my vocabulary upon which there always seemed to be more pressing demands, with the result that I can walk through the Chelsea Flower Show in exalted company and in moronic silence because a prize Iris Reticulata is, to me, common marshland 'sealasdair' which, when boiled with wool, gives a very distinctive black in the making of Harris Tweed. A foot in two cultures can be fulfilling at times and chastening at others.

But when one talks of cultures one is admitting to an awareness which is sometimes the very negation of culture in the real sense, and what Molly and I were revelling in was just the simple business of enjoying being alive in a good world to which we knew no alternative. In those days neither of us, nor any of our kind, wore shoes from May till September and there are few tingles that linger in the sub-conscious more delicately than those skiffing runs through the morning with daisy and buttercup heads clipping off between toes cold in the dew. To the boy and the girl those were the Eden days before the apple blushed.

I suspect that Molly's seniority occasionally made her impatient with the unrelieved company of a mere boy. Maybe deep below her own comprehendings there were

32

the stirrings of the old primeval instinct to which the boy as yet held no key. Maybe the boy was just the surrogate rag doll – easy to pick up but difficult to discard at whim. Anyway, at times she would tire of me and on occasion she tried to lose me by using the superior speed of her lanky legs to strand me in the sand dunes far from the sight of home. But I had the homing instinct of a retriever pup and I was quick to learn that if I kept out of sight for a while and then arrived at the door looking bedraggled and blubbering and feigning terror I would get cuddled while Molly would get clouted for abandoning me to dangers which I have still to discover in that bland and empty land. Till one day she decided to get rid of me once and for all.

We were, she assured me, going to visit a secret place far beyond the limits of our normal peregrinations, and I was to tell no one. It was always flattering to be invited on an excursion with Molly and, in my innocence, it never dawned on me that the invitations came only at week-ends and during the school holiday when the two or three girls that there were of her own age retreated to their own patches all of three miles away. She had a sister who was in the same age relationship to her as my brother was to me, and, by that token the same age as me, but her sister was of a much less tom-boyish nature than Molly and, in any case, was more resistant to Molly's blandishments and blackmails because she had grown up in their shadow. So, we were given permission to set off with the usual warnings from the two mothers to Molly to look after me and to make sure that she didn't let me out of her sight. The warnings were as routine as were their disregardings.

We headed, as usual, in the direction of the beach and as soon as we reached the broad belt of marram grass that separated the grazing land from the shore Molly began to lengthen her considerable stride. This was an old dodge, but I always fell for it. As soon as I began to pump furiously to keep pace, the marram tips whipped at my bare calves like a myriad needles till I was gritting my

33

teeth against the tears. And the more my vision blurred the more likely I came to stubbing my toes against the marram roots and stumbling. And the more I stumbled the more Molly taunted me with my footlessness and cried me on. I knew it was useless to shout 'Wait for me' and so I blundered on careful only to dodge the rabbit holes which I knew could wrench a knee or an ankle. Time blurred. But the anticipation of a 'secret place' spurred me on, and eventually I tumbled over the rim of a large green hollow at the bottom of which Molly sat laughing and panting. 'You managed!' she gasped. Which was more than another young lady was going to be able to say in that same green hollow a good few years later on.

Those big soft craters punctuate the Atlantic seaboard like giant dimples in a swathe of seersucker. Aeons ago vast storms spooned out the sand and piled it elsewhere at their whim and left it to the marram roots to bind the huge heaps into sand dunes which, in turn, turned fortress against further attacks by the wind from the west. Perhaps it was the same great holocaust that buried Stone Age Skara Brae that wrought its pattern on our shoreline too, and maybe swept away a civilization instead of petrifying it for subsequent revelation as it did in Orkney. In the lea of the dunes the seabirds and the gentler winds duly seeded the hollows and quilted them with burdock and bluebell and heliotrope, and the shimmering yellow dandelions which gave Molly her inspiration that day on the machair.

She was a great teller of tales, and even now it is to her that I most frequently turn if I need to be refreshed on some area of local lore or legend. Which is not surprising because she is descended from a long line of poets and songmakers. I didn't know that then, nor did it cross my infant mind to wonder how she – an incomer like myself – knew that, long ago, an army of warriors from a foreign land had come ashore on the beach and had set about plundering and pillaging the land as they had done up and down the whole of the rest of our coast. But here, in this very hollow, they had come face to face with a host of little people – fairies who, instead of fighting the foreigners, made them welcome and made them sit down and rest and eat and drink their fairy food. And as the fierce Norsemen nibbled the tid-bits their tiredness and their fierceness left them, and they began to hear the most beautiful music that they had ever heard in their lives and they began to dream dreams of unsurpassed beauty. One by one the warriors fell asleep and when the last of them had nodded off the fairies pulled them down into their own world on top of which we were sitting now. It was a world of music and milk and honey and the wild men had liked it so much that they never came back from it again, and never again troubled the people of Harris.

'Here! You taste this and you'll be able to go down and see them for yourself.'

I hadn't the faintest desire to consort with fairies even in their connotation of those days, but so persuasive was Molly that I couldn't refuse to taste the dandelion leaf she offered me.

It was disappointing. Not fragrant on the palate like the young primroses we used to pick at, nor honey sweet like *bainne nan gamhna* whose trumpet-shaped pistils my father had taught me to suck with dire warnings (now forgotten) not to put any plant whatsoever in my mouth without checking on its edibility with my mother or himself. Compared with those the dandelion leaves were tasteless for the first half dozen or so, and then they began to develop a tartness on the tongue which was not at all unpleasant to the child whose palate had not yet been tuned to artificial sweetness. I admitted to Molly that they 'weren't bad' (reasonable praise in Gaelic) and thus encouraged she continued to ply me with more and more and more. I didn't notice the self-satisfied smirk on her face, nor that she was being singularly abstemious herself. The promise of the trip to fairyland was forgotten for a while, and when I remembered Molly taunted me with my

35

ignorance and pointed out that I hadn't got on to the yellow petals yet.

I have no idea how many dandelions – stamens, pistils, sepals, the lot – I had consumed when Molly sprang to her feet and announced that she was going home, and off she went like a roe-deer through the marram. Nor have I any idea how long I sat and whimpered and called after her, although old experience should have told me that that was in vain, before I staggered to my feet and set off after her.

Often, in the unrestorable years of the 'local', I have fumbled home by way of quagmire and lamppost and the rest, but rarely with more difficulty than that day. The bent stroked my legs where it had whipped them before, and a great sleepiness kept pulling at my consciousness. My stomach managed to stay in place till I reached the front door behind which I could hear the blurred voices of the two mothers interrogating Molly as to where she had left me this time. The shrillness of the voices suggested that Molly's mother was both alarmed and angry and, in a woman of her calibre, the combination can be pretty fearsome. My own mother was more timid by nature, and the fact that she was on the offensive against another woman's child was proof that her anxiety – which was never far from the surface in the earlier years of her motherhood – was being fanned by intimations of disaster. I don't know whether, through the hullabaloo, she heard me scrabbling at the door, or if she suddenly decided to set out on one of her habitual forays in search of me. In any case she plucked the front door open at the precise moment at which my innards capitulated and cascaded a pool of luteous bile over the doorstep and her feet. And into it, I collapsed!

It required little medical or botanical skill to diagnose my problem. Even the robust digestive system of a Hebridean infant doesn't cope all that readily with a couple of dozen dandelions, and, as the concern for my safety took a dramatic upward turn, so the hapless Molly found the charge against her being upgraded from one of child neglect to one of homicide either culpable or attempted. Because, in the fabular pharmacopoeia in our small corner, dandelions were reckoned to be deadly poisonous!

Dandelions are not, of course, lethal or there wouldn't be any wealthy herbalists left at large. But their various constituents are individually emetic, diuretic or soporific, depending on how, and in what proportions, they are prescribed. Administered in the haphazard and frenzied way in which they had been force-fed to me they produced all the known responses at the same time and a few more for good measure.

Once they got over their initial fright the two mothers swung into galvanic action, with a firm aside to Molly to the effect that she would be attended to when they had finished with me. The one pummelled me to keep me awake while the other plied me with cups of warm salt water which I dutifully swallowed and then, in due course, rejected – each ejection becoming gratifying less bilious. At long last they must have come to the conclusion that I would survive, and as I was allowed to slip into a deep sleep I was hazily aware that my mother was removing my trousers while her mother was removing Molly's knickers for totally different reasons. If perchance I fell asleep with a smile on my face it must have been at the thought that Molly wouldn't be able to sit comfortably for a while because her mother had the muscular arms of the Harriswoman who has waulked innumerable tweeds.

When I woke up my father was back home and was being tartly complimented on once again managing to be absent when there was a crisis in the home – that most recurrent of themes in the unfinished symphony of marital disaccord, in which, paradoxically, there is nothing more infuriating than the failure of one partner (invariably the male) to rise to either taunt or insult. My father was a man of infinite patience. He was deeply in love with my mother in a fraternity where that emotion, once promulgated, was neither flaunted nor flouted. But I suspect that the maturity which had ripened in the trenches, coupled with a decade of seniority, made it sometimes appear to her as if he were treating her crises as her imaginings. Which they frequently were, because, in her early years, she could find a worry in a blessing. 'I could sometimes smash that pipe of his to bitlets', I once heard her confess to a neighbour, referring to my father's habit of venting his argument on the stem of his 'Lovat' while appearing to smile into the middle distance with his eyes. I still feel that 'There's no use talking to you', isn't the real end of an argument unless it's accompanied by a clattering of plates . . .

'So you've been eating the fairies, boy!' That was enough to snap me out of the remains of my torpor.

'Down in one of the hollows at the Blue Skerry, eh? Well, well.' I waited while he examined the stem of his pipe for a crack, and tamped it and got it going again.

Long ago, apparently, the machair of Harris had no people as we know them now. Instead, the land was inhabited by 'the little folks' or the fairies and they lived a life of love and laughter and the sun always shone. The merest whiff of rain was miracled by the sun into a rainbow, and out of the rainbow the little folk spun threads of many colours for their clothes. It was a gay and carefree world until there came along men in boots, with their heads so high from the ground that they didn't even notice the earth upon which they were stamping nor the life they were trampling underfoot. So the fairies went underground – all of them except the ones who couldn't face a life without the sun, and who stayed above and turned themselves into flowers, the proudest of which was the Notched Flower of St Bridget as the dandelion is called in Gaelic. High up above it all, the sun watched what was happening with sorrow. Where it had twinkled down on the earth all day long before, it now took to closing its eyes at night, and, in sympathy, the dandelion took to closing and opening its eyes with it, so that, to this day, even when the clouds are hiding the sun you can tell its rising and its setting by watching the Flower of St Bridget!

38

'I hope the new house is coming along as well as the stories are doing!'

I could tell by the twinkle in my mother's voice that her tension had vanished, and the relief of it closed the file on the Dandelion in my mind.

It was to be many years later, when a furious sand-storm laid bare Stone Age coffins and skeletons in that same hollow by the Blue Skerry, that it dawned on me that there had been a subtle thread common to the two folk legends that Molly and my father, in their very different ways, had brought to life for me that day.

'The house is coming along fine,' said my father as he put his pipe in his pocket and went to the table. 'I was burning a few sticks to test the chimney just before I came home. We must be thinking of ordering a grate soon.' He rubbed his eyes quickly with his knuckles and yawned – the token gesture to the Almighty to which he had reduced the traditional grace before meat – and began to eat, little knowing that in those casual few sentences about the chimney he had laid the foundations of the one and only phobia which was to obsess him for the rest of his life.

Chapter Five

I have no diaries to consult. No letters. None of the tools of the trade of the historian or the hagiographer of which I am neither anyway. Nor have I the awesome memory of my old friend, the late Sir Compton MacKenzie who – in his mid eighties – used to regale me with recollections of the Victorian scene as viewed from his perambulator. Far less have I the self-confident talent of a revered uncle of mine who, in the face of the unimpeachable evidence of no less expert a witness than his own mother and my devout grandmother, would graphically recall not only the looks but the conversations and peccadillos of people who were dead long before he was born.

All I have are the milestones of childhood – occasions, mishaps and moments which were momentous of their time and in their place – that have remained only because, at the beginning of each new day, they seemed to be promising a great adventure which, in the end, turned out to be just another life. Such a milestone was the Day of the Dandelions, and it's only because I remember *it* that I'm now able to remember the day which followed it.

The evening of the Day of the Dandelions had passed sullenly, and even our regular visitor didn't arrive to break the monotony. Wee Barabel, as she was called, lived on her own in a tumbledown thatched cottage on the edge of the moor. Like all the others who lived there she was a relic of the old population who had survived the several evictions and population shifts, but unlike Great Aunt

Rachel, she did not have the self-confidence of a long pedigree and an education. In fact she was a simple old soul who, under today's social conditions and observances, would have been taken into care of some sort or other, because she lived in her one little room in conditions of squalor even for those times. She claimed that she had no idea how old she was, but she must have convinced somebody at some stage or other that she had enough years to merit the weekly pension for which she thanked 'Loy George and the Lord' in that order in the garbled prayers into which she was liable to launch at the drop of a hat and in totally unpredictable circumstances. Despite her occasionally embarrassing outbursts of devotion she had the reputation of being a witch, but that did not deter the few teenage lumps of boys who lived in her vicinity from teasing her mercilessly although, secretly, they were scared of her and wouldn't dare offend her openly. The older people were sorry for her and made sure that she never lacked for milk or fuel, and though they might inwardly groan when they saw her appearing, the womenfolk always reached for the kettle and plied her with tea and scones when she arrived.

My father was very fond of Wee Barabel because she was full of stories of life in the olden days. She would retail – with what accuracy I know not – lurid accounts of soldiers coming round and clearing people out of their homes at the landlords' behest to make room for the expansion of their farms, and of rapacious factors ploughing up graveyards to plant potatoes. My subsequent study of local history makes me suspect that Barabel's narratives were concocted from the legends of several preceding generations, but, like Great Aunt Rachel's sagas, they always had elements of the truth in them. My father was an addict of old folks' tales and, even when he had heard a story countless times before, had the wonderful art of appearing to be engrossed in whatever was being told him while his mind was miles away concentrating on some much more mundane problem of his own. He was the perfect captive audience for Wee Barabel whom he had known from his boyhood visits to Aunt Rachel. And so, from the very first day that we ensconced ourselves in the schoolhouse she would totter down the hill sharp on the dot of eight o'clock, which she regarded as seven o'clock because, like many of the older folk on the hill, she absolutely refused to acknowledge British Summer Time and adhered to what she called 'God's Time'. Her punctuality was nothing short of miraculous because she had never in her life allowed a clock in her house on the grounds that she didn't want to hear her life ticking away. But for once Wee Barabel didn't appear. And all evening my father fidgeted and worried about her, thus totally cancelling out my mother's thinly veiled relief at the prospect of an evening of privacy during which she might pin my father down to discussing matters of fairly pressing importance like, for example, the furnishing of the new house. Long after I had been unceremoniously hustled off to bed I could hear, through the wall, strictures like 'Your son's been at death's door and all you can do is worry about Wee Barabel', and 'If you spent more evenings working on the new house rather than listening to the maunderings of Barabel we might be in a place of our own by winter.' The themes of marital disharmony vary little with successive generations!

Father was very subdued over breakfast, and as soon as it was over he got up from the table and announced that he was going up the hill to see if Barabel was all right. My mother, whose conscience had obviously begun to prick her during the night, agreed that he should. I seized my chance to ask if I might go along to the new house to await his arrival there, and to my slight astonishment my mother agreed – with dire warnings to keep to the side of the road and watch out for cars!

I set off, and to my joy I found myself teaming up with Gillespie, an incomer boy four days younger than myself with whom I had barely made passing acquaintance till then. Gillespie and I were to become partners in many scrapes in the years ahead but, that day, we were still at the stage of warily weighing each other up. He could hardly believe that I had been given permission to explore the new house on my own and we raced each other towards it.

The new house consisted of a concrete foundation out of which sprouted a wooden skeleton of upright beams and criss-crosses of rafter with, at the south end, a stone and mortar stack from which grew a tall cast iron pipe – the chimney that my father had tested the day before. The whole thing looked good and it smelt beautifully of resinous new wood, but I doubt if it would have held our attention for long if it weren't for the fact that, inside, it was an Aladdin's cave of saws, chisels, hammers and nails – all the basic tools of the carpenter's trade which my father would have forbidden me for their safety, and my mother for mine. And there we were, all alone, and with no danger of being interrupted because I knew that once my father reached Barabel's place it would take him a long time to disentangle himself from her yarning while making excuses to avoid partaking of her dubiously hygienic tea. Nobody else was liable to disturb Gillespie and myself. Or so we thought. But, unbeknownst to us, and fortunately for us, there was, plodding towards the village, one of humbler minions of the Board of Agriculture in the shape of the Stallion Man.

The larger and much longer established village next to ours boasted a sizeable stud of plough horses which consisted of a motley assortment of mares and geldings. The latter were not of much use to the former, so the Board had undertaken as one of its duties the provision, once a year, of a stallion to service the mares who conveniently appeared to develop the same desires within the space of the same fortnight. And the Board also provided a little man to service the stallion.

I have never got round to discovering whether the stallion was a highly prized and pedigreed native of Arabia who had disgraced himself with Lord Rosebery or

43

the Aga Khan, or just the bye-blow of some coal haulage company who had escaped the knife. I suspect the former, because he was tall and proud and expected to be waited upon hand and foot and everything else. His attendant wasn't allowed to ride him nor even to place his luggage on his back, and I can recall few more pathetic sights than a five-foot man in an old tweed suit, with a portmanteau in one hand and the bridle of a sixteen-hand stallion in the other, trudging the sweaty Harris miles on a hot summer's day. At least the stallion could look forward to something for which his energies were being conserved. At the end of the day the man would have neither energy nor prospect.

From infancy onwards, we crofter children grew up surrounded by quadrupedal sex and it is a miracle of instinct that we didn't accept quadrupedal modes as the norm instead of having to await enlightenment from *Playboy* and the *Kama Sutra*. We had seen the bull and the ram, the dog and the cat, set about their business purposefully after minimal skirmishing. But our aristocratic stallion – and for all I know this may be an effetism of aristocracy at all levels – had to be helped. After a bit of sniffing and snorting around an impatient mare, the stallion would wait for the man to take him by one of the front fetlocks and encourage him upwards. Only then would the animal languidly release from his body something which, for all the world, resembled the black concertina hose which comes out of the back of a modern tumble-drier, and this the stallion man had to guide into the appropriate channel. It can't have been the most enlightening of professional duties although veterinary surgeons have to do worse, but it didn't deserve the opprobrium which accrued to the poor Stallion Man. He was the object of jibes and innuendous jokes to his face and behind his back, and, to this day there is no greater Gaelic insult to hurl at a toady or someone who performs another's menial jobs than to call him a 'cock boy'. But that year's cock boy was to gain for himself a moment of glory, and a dinner before which, for once, he wasn't made to wash his hands.

Gillespie and I had had a hey-day, sawing and drilling and nailing together pieces of wood into models of our imaginings, and we had begun to tire of the whole thing while we still had ten fingers apiece. Just as we were thinking of trailing off in search of some other adventure I spotted the box of matches which my father had forgetfully left on the new hearth. And his comments about having tested the chimney flashed back to me. It was obvious from the charred remains of shavings at the base of the chimney pipe that they were the very stuff that he had used, and there were still mounds of them around. Between us, it took only a few minutes to make a sizeable heap and, after several broken matches, we had it ablaze. Had we left it at that things mightn't have got out of hand, but our triumph went to our heads when we looked up and saw, spiralling from the chimney top, shapely puffs of creamy white smoke that would have sealed the election of half a hundred Popes. We decided to compound our success by heaping on to the burning shavings all the constructions that we had nailed together during the previous hour, and soon we had a roaring bonfire that would have roasted an ox – and might conceivably have roasted us had the Stallion Man not arrived at the gate as the wooden frame-work of the gable-end began to catch fire.

It must have been the first time that the Stallion Man moved quickly in his life. He whipped the huge felt horse cloth off the horse's back, rushed into the house, threw us out bodily and unceremoniously, and, like a man possessed, began to smother the flames. The situation was under control by the time my father arrived on the scene, gasping for breath and ashen faced, after a burst across the hill from Barabel's such as he had probably not indulged in since he had gone over the top at the Battle of Arras.

'Thank God you're all right', he said, looking at Gillespie and myself. 'And as for you', he went on turning to the

Stallion Man, 'it was Fate that sent you the way.'

The Stallion Man appeared not to hear him.

'This is as tattered as a whore's hole', he grumbled, thrusting his raw, scorched fist through the middle of the singed horse cloth, and I noticed the muscle in my father's jaw twitch as his eyes flicked in the direction of Gillespie and myself. 'The Board's going to have something to say about this!'

He was wrong. By the time he left the schoolhouse, cleaned and salved and with a good meal in him, the stallion's broad back was draped in a folded suit-length of Harris Tweed which had been ordered for Sir Thomas Lipton who was an occasional visitor to Harris on one or other of his yachts. As it turned out, the ripening years wouldn't have allowed Sir Thomas much wear out of the tweed anyway, but when the cock boy came round the island next he was sporting a suit that would have graced a game-keeper while the stallion seemed perfectly happy in a traditional horse cloth with the Government's seal still crisp on it.

I don't know what quiet persuasion my father had used on my mother but, apart from the first flurry of nervous anxiety, she never referred to the near catastrophe again. Father mentioned it once during the evening. While my mother was putting the baby to bed he looked at me for a long time over the bowl of his pipe, which he had a habit of tilting ceiling-wards when he was in quizzical mood, and then said, 'I don't believe in giving rows for things which won't happen again anyway, but I'd give a lot to know what you'll be up to next.' Obviously I was in no position to hazard a guess myself, but before the silence became embarrassing my mother came through from the bedroom having remembered that she hadn't heard what had befallen Wee Barabel who had been tangentially involved in it all.

Apparently the whole problem had been there for my father to see and to solve as soon as he reached her little hovel. On the night before last a couple of the hillside lads

46

– 'the bloods' as they were called – had crept up while she was asleep and stuffed her one and only window with turf. And she had spent thirty-six hours in bed waiting for the dawn, puzzled only by the fact that her bladder was making her reach for the pot more often than usual. It was while he was letting in the light and trying to comfort Barabel for the lost day in her life that father had noticed the smoke and flames rising from the roadside down below.

'Boys!' said my mother, as she was to say so often in the future, 'I'm afraid it's worse they get as they get older.' And that reminded her that it was time for me to be in bed. I was conscious of the fact that she was even more solicitous than usual as she tucked me into bed, whispering so as not to waken the baby.

'You close your eyes and go to sleep now; you've had quite a day of it!' She kissed me and crossed over to close the curtains against the light of the setting sun.

'Look mammy', I said, sitting up and holding up the old woollen bedspread which had come down through a couple of generations, 'this coverlet is as tattered as a whore's hole.'

She jerked as if someone had hit her in the rib-cage. Her mouth opened, but she decided to say nothing. And she walked quickly from the bedroom leaving the curtains half drawn. I lay back on the pillow confirmed in my suspicion that I had found a new phrase worth hoarding for future use.

Chapter Six

My father went through the whole of that portion of his life in which I shared, with a mortal fear of fire. In all the years of my boyhood nothing would persuade him to go to bed before every other member of the family had retired, and when the lean years came and my mother would sometimes have to sit up late into the night spinning, he would sit up with her, reading or just puffing at his pipe. And often, during the night, I remember half wakening as he padded through to the living room to check yet again that the last embers were ashing, even although he had raked and doubled raked them before going to bed in the first place. Heaven knows he was a late bedder at the best of times, but though he fervently maintained a theory that a man's sleeping pattern is governed by the state of the tide at the moment of his birth, I suspect that the tidal influences – in the theory of which, incidentally, I firmly believe – were, in his case, heightened by the more mundane effects of the scorch inflicted on his persona by the efforts of Gillespie and myself.

The near-destruction of the house before it had been built was, paradoxically, responsible for it being completed on schedule when it had been limping along before. My father, swallowing his pride, got up early the next morning and set off to walk the sixteen miles north, whence we had come those many months before, to solicit the help of my mother's cousin, who was a carpenter to trade and a shepherd at heart, and had the good nature that one would expect in one embodying such hallowed characteristics. He jumped at the chance of spending a week in highly prized sheep country and, in a couple of days he arrived with a year-old ewe as a contribution to my father's flock, and a box containing a neatly arrayed outfit of carpentry tools which I was allowed to admire only from afar. Each day he worked from eight o'clock till six – all the while discoursing on sheep through endless mouthfuls of nails – and, in the evenings, he tramped the machair and the moorland sizing up the crofters' sheep and lambs as if he were contemplating buying them. Which is probably how he dreamt. Although he was a fortunate man with a trade, the myth of the freedom of the land was in his essence. He lived in the cheek-by-jowl environment of a harbour village – a town by our standards – and he could only indulge his fancy by grazing a few sheep on the rough hill above Tarbert. To him our green acres must have been the Canaan of his imaginings, and his gift of a young ewe, although generous beyond measure, was also, probably, an unconscious sacrifice to the undefinable 'might-have-been' which puts a slight check in the smile of most of us as we look across our own boundary walls.

Within a week the new house was finished. Its corrugated iron walls gleamed a blue grey; the roof was a bright red, and the windows white; it consisted of two rooms, each twelve feet square with a door leading straight from the living room to the bedroom. There had been some corrugated iron left over, so a small porch had been added at the front to take the bite out of the west winds which would blow square on from the Atlantic. The porch was a luxury, because the grand design was that the house would serve as a home for a year or two till a roomy stone house would be built, subsidized by the Board of Agriculture, and the original building would become the byre. That was the pattern which had been established in places like Skye and the mainland where the crofters had won their land long before us, and that same pattern was now beginning to be seen to establish itself in Harris.

For some reason or other I have no recollection of moving in although the day must have been a very important one in my parents' lives. Vaguely, I remember a hurried slapping of wall-paper, a table and four chairs arriving from somewhere, a tall press into which were unpacked boxes of crockery – some items of which were greeted as half-forgotten wedding presents from Aunt Catherine, from Uncle Alex and the rest. Beside the press and conveniently placed for the door stood an old fashioned wash-hand basin and ewer table which had been adapted to hold two large pails which, as I was to discover very quickly, had to be kept permanently filled with water from the river which ran behind and round the house. The south, gable-end of the room was dominated almost entirely by a massive black iron stove decorated with a stainless steel fluted border round the top edge – an adornment which, I concluded fairly early on, had been put there for the sole purpose of making the black-leading of the monster even more of a Saturday night chore than the ritual polishing of the family boots. Of its time it must have been very advanced in design, and geared for the house-wife working without the advantages of any form of interior plumbing. On top it could keep two pots boiling and four simmering, while the central fire heated a large, efficient oven at one end and a capacious water boiler at the other. Along its front the whole contraption was heavily embossed with its trade name which proclaimed it to be, for some reason best known to the makers, a 'Modern Mistress'. I haven't seen its counterpart for many a year, but I'm reminded of it from time to time when some local Highland newspaper or other carries an advertisement from an antique dealer looking for one. The text can range from the vulgar to the lewd depending on the urgency with which the would-be purchaser attempts to underline his quest, and the state of repair which he is willing to accept.

50

The pride of my father's life was the ancient tall-backed five-seater bench which ran below the window at right angles to the stove, and took up every inch of the front wall right up to the back of the living room door. It was useful in that it sat five or even six people, albeit in circumstances that were conducive neither to comfort nor conversation, and because it could serve as a rather spartan spare bed for visitors who weren't kith or kin enough to treble up with my brother and myself in the second double bed in the bedroom. It looked exactly like what it was – an oaken church pew which, according to my father, had been the family seat of the Clan MacLeod in the ancient Church of St Clement's in Rodel. St Clement's, notable as the only cruciform church in the Outer Hebrides, had last been renovated by Lord Dunmore in 1840, or thereabouts, and I was never able to discover where, or how, the pew had weathered the intervening hunk of century. Its alleged antiquity earned for it, in my father's mind, the sort of mystic reverence that many English people accord to the Coronation Chair of Edward I, and rather fewer to the Coronation Stone at Kingston-upon-Thames. But the more eloquent he waxed about its religious antecedents the less comfortable my more superstitious mother felt with it as a piece of domestic furniture, and she found it hard to summon up enough imagination to make it more acceptable just because it had been hallowed or otherwise by successive generations of her own Chief's bottoms. As time went on, however, and no strange lights, or apparitions or rattlings of ancient bones manifested themselves, I suspect that she began to doubt its authenticity and thus managed to live with it as she lived with so many of my father's more romantic notions.

I suspect that he himself would have queried the suggestion of a romantic streak in his nature and arrogated to himself, rather, a sense of history. But the dividing line between the two can be strangely blurred during times of scrabble for survival such as the early years undoubtedly were for some of the new villagers, and certainly for my parents. I am sure, for example, that my mother, who had come out of a fairly comfortable parental home, must have wished that she had more money with which to furnish the new house instead of having to make do with ecclesiastical discards of questionable aestheticism and unquestionable discomfort, and so, inescapably ecclesiastical as the connections might still be, her optimism must have been kittled by the news of the Manse roup – an event of such rare occurrence nowadays, as then, that it may require a bit of scene setting even for Scottish readers. . . .

Today there still stands, high above the village, a superb Georgian building which is haunted from time to time by such unethereal spirits as Derek Cooper and the man from Egon Ronay searching, in the public interest, for rarefied qualities of bodily and spirituous comfort. It was built, around the middle of the eighteenth century as the residence for the local minister who was, at that time, appointed and retained by the local landlord and was, consequently, divided in his loyalty between his Lord and his master in much the same way as the clerics of the unreformed Church in England have now to balance their allegiance discreetly between the Monarch and the Almighty. The manses were built large so that their incumbents could, in their off-duty times, act as hosts to the hordes of visitors who were then beginning to descend on the Highlands in the slip-stream of Queen Victoria, and whose blood or station entitled them to hospitality one degree lower than that of whichever belted earl happened to be the landowner at the time. With the Disruption, however, the Church in Scotland largely cast off the shackles of patronage, and big manses such as ours were freed from the influence of the estate and left to be the private homes of ministers who – no matter how formidable their virility – could not afford families large enough to fill the honeycombs of bedchambers, any more than they could afford to offer hospitality to the overflow guests from the 'Big House'.

The venerable gentleman who was minister of South

Harris at the time of our arrival there had, late in life, married, most improbably, a French woman many years his junior – which had probably no bearing on the fact that he died very suddenly round about the time that we moved into the new house. And shortly afterwards it was announced that the contents of the manse would be sold off by public roup or auction. In those days it would have been a very intrepid dealer indeed who would have ventured to the Outer Hebrides on the strength of one single domestic auction sale, and my mother must have had a shrewd idea that a few items of suitable furniture would be going at bargain rates – certainly something in the way of small easy chairs to add a modicum of comfort to the tiny area of living room that was left available to her by the pew from St Clements.

It would be ridiculous to pretend that I remember the briefing she gave my father as she rummaged in the trinkets compartment of the big red chest which had been pressed into service as a sitting place at the end of the table. But I do remember that the money with which she emerged was the sum total of what she had set aside for the purchase, in due course, of congoleum which was the very latest in floor covering of the period and considered to be very much more 'in the fashion' than the traditional wax-cloth. Nor do I more than suspect that it was after some considerable heart-searching that she had made up her mind to forgo the coveted congoleum in favour of possibly unrepeatable bargains of furniture. In fact I would probably have forgotten the whole evening long ere this were it not that there was something incongruous, which couldn't fail to imprint itself on my mind, in the picture of my father setting off for the manse with a wheelbarrow and wearing his Sunday suit.

It may have been, of course, my mother who stamped the evening on my mind. It is difficult now to disentangle her subsequent good-humoured recountings of the event from the actuality, but it's highly probable that she spent the long hours of waiting describing to me the arm-chairs

53

which she had remembered seeing on one of her few visits to the servants' quarters of the manse. And methinks there was mention of a rocking chair. And may be she kept me amused by telling me where each item might go, and which of the present items would have to be moved and where. The evening would certainly be long, because anything which savoured of social intercourse – be it sheep fank or prayer meeting – was liable to be protracted in a community in which the population was scattered, and new to each other, and with few excuses for meeting socially in more than ones or twos. It's strange how long a new populace, artificially planted, takes to develop the rhythms of a society; we were too new even for funerals.

There must still have been some lingering daylight when my father returned because long before he reached the gate I could see that, if he had bought anything at all, it was of such small dimensions that it didn't show above the sides of the wheelbarrow. When I drew mother's attention to this she merely shrugged in the resigned way that she was already beginning to adopt and said something to the effect that the prices must have been too high.

But her guess was wrong. And her resignation vanished when my father appeared with a slightly guilty smile on his face and carrying in his arms a bundle of trophies from the roup. It consisted of two ancient dinner plates of the kind that one hangs on the wall with wire and hopes, usually in vain, that some future generation will redeem them for their antique value, and a large bundle of books which included Gibbon's *Decline and Fall of the Roman Empire*, *The Lays of Ancient Rome* by Thomas Babington Macaulay (with whom Great Aunt Rachel claimed acquaintance) and some obscure volumes on the language and literature of the Scottish Highlands. Before he realized that his popularity was not exactly at its zenith he let slip that he had bid for a fiddle which, mercifully for him, he had failed to get. For sure my mother's friendliest remark of that evening was that the house would be the envy of the neighbours when she carpeted the floor with *The Lays of Ancient Rome* with *The Decline and Fall* for underfelt! But the fact remains that one unimpressive-looking volume out of that night's bundle has, by chance more than by design, followed me through the years, and if I were to take it from my book-shelves and sell it now it would cover the house in Wilton carpeting from wall to wall – let alone congoleum. And as for *The Lays of Ancient Rome*, I owed to them more than a little of whatever facility I came to acquire in the English language in my early years.

The congoleum, however, would have made a big difference to my life as well as to my mother's. Even today, when it's usual to have gravel paths or pavings round houses, when there are modern floor coverings and carpets by the acre everywhere, and when there is a whole science of gadgetry for lightening cleaning, keeping a country cottage floor clean can be one of the minor irritants of life. It was more than a minor irritant then.

One of the many things which we never achieved was a path from the main road to the house, and even had we done so, all our outdoor work was concentrated in fields which – whatever the golden memories of childhood may suggest – got their fair share of the rain which falls generously in the Western Isles. Consequently, no matter how diligently one scraped one's boots or bare feet, as the case might be, the 'keeping respectable' of the floor was not only an irritant but a problem. And it was a problem in which I had to share.

For as long as I can remember my mother was determined that if any of her sons should ever find himself 'widowed or worse' (whatever that might mean) he should be able to look after himself and his house, and, from the earliest days that I can remember in a home of our own I had to do my share of the house-work, come what may. In due course the chores were to be extended to include making and mending and cookery – for all of which I have subsequently been grateful – but in the beginning, even before I went to school, the clearly defined areas of my responsibility were the water pails, of which two had to be filled night and morning and four on a Saturday night; the polishing of the range (as the 'Modern Mistress' was called for short); the constant replenishment of the peat bucket from the pile at the end of the house; and the provision of *mealtrach* and fine shell sand for the cleaning of the floor.

I have never had occasion to find out what the English for *mealtrach* is, and it's not worth my while finding out now since I am unlikely ever to have to use the word or the substance again. It is, in fact, the very fine roots of the marram grass which mat loosely together and fringe the under edges of the wind-blown sand cliffs of the sea shore like pubic hair peeping out from an incautious bathing costume. Every Saturday in life, till blessed linoleum came along, I had to forage along the sea cliffs and collect a sackful of *mealtrach* and carry it home, and then, from the same source, ferry innumerable pails of fine white sand. Then, on the Saturday evening, my mother would scrub the wooden floor with carbolic soap, using the *mealtrach* as a scourer, and before the floor was dry she would cover it liberally with sand. Just before bedtime she would brush off the sand, leaving the wooden flooring pristine white for the Sabbath. Woe betide the person who left nature's last call to 'the pee-tub' unanswered till after the sand had been swept!

During the period of settling into the new house I had lost touch with my erstwhile sparring partner, Molly, whose family must have moved out of the schoolhouse and into their new house about the same time as we moved ourselves. It was a friendship that was destined not to last anyway because a couple of years' difference in age is a life-time in a boy and girl relationship at that stage but, as so often happens, they are the childish scrapes into which we got together that have cemented a friendship in life much later on. When we meet now on what was once home territory for us both, and still is for her, the conversation invariably includes reference to some trifling incident that was important of its time, and which the one recollects and the other pretends to remember.

The reverse was the situation with Gillespie. A life-time and, literally, the depth of the world have separated us almost certainly forever, but as we grew up and the village grew up around us we were closer than many brothers. We weren't encouraged to see much of each other for a few weeks after our escapade with the matches, and I suspect that the one mother was, in the nature of things, inclined to blame the other mother's son. But we teamed up again when it turned out that *mealtrach* collection was one of his mandatory duties too, and the companionship made the chore into more of an adventure. And then, as August wore on, a whole new world was opened up to us as we began to accompany our mothers when they went crotal scraping.

Moors can still stir deep hidden, primeval, fears in the most sophisticated of people, and the very adjectives that are most frequently used to describe them, like 'bleak' and 'empty' are evocative of aloneness and remoteness from help should help be required. Our moor was vast, and I never felt afraid on it except once in sudden fog, but our women would never venture far on to it except in couples when they had to, which was only really at crotal gathering time. But they were, of course, the last generation to emerge from the thrall of superstition which is part of the warp and woof of the traditional fabric of primitive country life everywhere before education rips it apart for better or for worse. It was only in my father's boyhood that the various Compulsory Education Acts began to be enforced, but it was to be a long time before reading and its various allied leisure pastimes began to supplant the dark night story sessions about creatures like the 'Water Horse' who could emerge from moorland tarns and, briefly assuming handsome human form, would capture and carry off into the depths unwary young women wandering the moors for some purpose like the collecting of crotal! It takes a long time to expunge deep-rooted traditions from

57

the sub-conscious and, unfortunately, they're the best traditions that tend to go first.

Crotal is a brittle grey lichen that grows slowly on undisturbed rocks and ancient walls. When it is 'ripe' it begins to lift off the parent surface and, at that stage, it becomes what has been for centuries the most popular agent for the dyeing of wool for tweed, and, for the last hundred years or so especially Harris Tweed.

Every colour imaginable could be obtained from a common vegetable source, and the tweeds from particular districts could be fairly accurately identified from the proliferation of plants native to these parts. In our area, which had been the heartland of the Harris Tweed industry when it became formally established as a craft, there was a wealth of colour to be distilled from nature because of the lush growth on machair and on moor. And every girl, up to my mother's generation at least, had to know exactly which colour each plant provided when it was boiled with a fleece. For example crotal itself gave a rich reddish brown; groundsel gave a bitter lemon; rib-wort gave blue; water-lily, black; heather tips, pastel green; willow leaves, soft yellow. And so on. Even the peat soot from the chimney gave a beautiful cinnamon colour. And when each individual ingredient was boiled with the wool the addition to the brew of a handful of sorrel ensured that the colour remained fast forever more. The list of colours and their blendings was endless. But the most popular of them all was crotal, except among sailors who would never wear it because they maintained that crotal always returned to the rocks.

The only implement required for scraping the crotal was an old soup spoon with one side diagonally sliced off so as to leave a sharp tip to reach into crevices; and it was armed with a soup spoon and a sack and a pack of oatmeal scones and milk or whey that Gillespie's mother and mine set off on their expeditions into the moor to build up their stocks of lichen against the late summer, by which time the sheep would be sheared and the fleeces cleaned and ready for dyeing in the aged three-legged pots which were as essential an item of equipment as the pee-tub itself.

Because crotal was such a popular item in the dyeing process the nearer rocks had been scraped clean by successive generations of the old population, and because the lichen took years to regenerate itself our mothers had to press further and further into the moorland to find rocks that hadn't already been denuded. Gillespie and I were howled down for sacrilege when we suggested, as we thought helpfully and logically, that the whole operation could be completed easily and expeditiously in one quick sortie to the old graveyard where the tombstones of the past were coated with enough crisp rich crotal to dye flocks of sheep. Apparently not only the spirits of the long since departed but the Lord in person would wreak vengeance for such desecration.

Moorland air and coastal air are as different as wine and beer, and it's on the same senses that they make their separate impressions. The breeze from the sea attacks the taste buds and the nostrils, wrenching an immediate response. But, even half way up, on the hip of a mountain, the wind has a bouquet that is light and heady at the same time and the sleep that follows a day of it is as smooth as the sleep that follows love.

Nor is the moor silent as people would have one suppose. Unless the spiralling song of a lark is silence, or the purr of a dragonfly, or the rustling of the heather in a breeze that is too light for the face to feel. No, the moor is only *comparatively* silent when there is another noise level with which to compare, and that is why the desultory distinctive scrape of the crotal spoons on the rocks has etched itself on the memory and can be recalled now in the conscious act of remembering.

Our mothers talked little as they worked. Now and again one would call out to the other that she had found 'a good rock' and her claim would be confirmed by the long peeling scratch of her spoon as she eased a blister of lichen

59

off the stone and into her sack, and that would be followed by urgent little tinkles of metal on stone as she dug into the crevices for the more reluctant morsels of crotal. 'Make sure it isn't Goat's Beard!' would come the taunt, referring to another yellowish crust that had no value as a dye and would only be mistaken for crotal by a novice or a half-wit. Ripostes that had long since lost any claim to originality were still good for a giggle when the heart was young and the mind was spare of experience beyond the paramaters of domesticity.

Gillespie and I were invariably enjoined to search for White Heather and not to come back till we had found 'an armful'. It was a dodge to keep us occupied because to every acre of Bell Heather and Common Ling there was rarely more than a modest clump of the white kind and it was as difficult as four-leafed clover to find. But there were other distractions to take over. Occasionally a vacated grouse nest. Now and then a secrecy of blaeberries which had to be plucked as gently as joy if they weren't to burst before surrendering their succulence which was tart and sweet at the same time. And everywhere – some still shoulder high to a boy – the ancient ruins of the generation of ancestors, who, two centuries before, had been the first batch of West Harris people to be evicted and shipped off to Canada but had never arrived on the other side. Of course we didn't know that then, nor would we have understood if we had been told. Even our mothers, who balked at the thought of scraping crotal off the ornamental tombstones in the kirkyard, thought nothing of scraping clean those sadder, lonelier memorials to which history had denied even the dignity of haunting.

If there were ghosts around perhaps they smiled to hear laughter coming back as the women called halt for the 'half sack break' as they called it, because the moment to stop and eat was not dictated by the hour but by the achievement of the first half full sack of crotal. And then the scones and the milk were laid out on the cloth in which they had been wrapped and the four of us would sit down to what

60

the gentry would doubtless have called a picnic. 'The best cook is hunger', according to the Gaelic proverb, although it goes limp in the translation; but the sharp appetite of the moorland has an edge of its own. And, added to it, the glow of importance that hasn't altered or diminished a whit for ever sophisticating generations of boys when mothers sit down and embrace them in talk which is neither lisped nor joked nor forced nor condescending – only warm with love, and generous of time.

But in the last of those crotal outings that I took part in, there kept intruding on my instinct a recurrent and only half understood theme of conversation, plucking at an indefinable and elusive worry. It had all to do with new trousers and new jerseys and that the days were running out and that school was about to begin. Not yet. Not tomorrow. 'But not . . .', snapped Gillespie's mother when he spilt the milk over her ' . . . not before time.'

Chapter Seven

If it is true that only those whom the Gods love die young, then Miss Dalbeith is still around somewhere . . . which is why I have given her a name other than the name by which she was christened or launched or whatever. Not that the name really matters because, whatever I call her, there are at least sixteen people who, if they read this, will know who I'm talking about – sixteen out of the seventeen who were present on the day that school began.

I remember that my father was very edgy and nervous that morning, but at first I put it down to the fact that he was probably ill at ease in his Sunday suit on a week-day. And, even in retrospect, I prefer to think that some secret thought was worrying a man who had spent five years in the trenches other than the idea of meeting Miss Dalbeith.

I myself wasn't all that relaxed. For one thing, my father insisted on holding my hand for the full five hundred yards which separated our new house from the school and I was anxious lest it get round the village that I needed moral support from a man who was six times my age. There was the memory of the veiled threats which had been made of what would happen to me if I didn't temper my transgressions when I went to school. And, above all, I couldn't help remembering how firmly my mother used to check of the men for using certain adjectives when they were discussing the teacher in front of me. These discussions hadn't meant much to me at the time, but fragments of them were niggling at me now that I was on the point of meeting the lady face to face.

It was on the tip of my tongue to suggest to my father that we should turn back home and devote a day of autumn sunshine to painting the outside of our new house. But as I was framing the idea so that it wouldn't sound suspicious in words, the school gate creaked under my father's hand. It was a low, slow skreek . . . as if the gate, which had seen so many boys come and go in its day, was warning me – like a dog baying a warning of approaching doom. The immediate result of the rusty protest was that it brought the head of Miss Dalbeith to the window as the bell brings the waiter in a well oiled hotel. The head stayed there, between a pile of books and a vase of dejected wild flowers, and only the eyes moved behind horn-rimmed spectacles to follow us up to the blistered green door. The picture has been re-lit for me from time to time in recent years, when I have watched television close-ups of weathered female politicians at Party Conferences listening disapprovingly to speakers resisting the re-introduction of capital punishment.

To say that my father abandoned me is just stating the simple truth. He exchanged a few incomprehensible sentences in English with Miss Dalbeith as he handed me over, and, out of the corner of my eye I saw him turn on his heel and walk back to the school gate like a man with an old weight off his mind and a new one on his conscience.

At the age of five, everybody over twenty is ancient to a little boy, and so I can't say whether Miss Dalbeith was really old or not. And it is also why I can't be sure that she isn't alive and fit and well and reading this. But she was certainly an imposing woman – taller than all but one of the men in our village; and she held herself very straight because she believed that posture was the prerequisite of well-being – physical and moral – although, with hindsight, I doubt if temptation ever came her way to incline her from the upright. For my part, I was to suffer much in

63

the months ahead from her disciplines, not least of which was spending endless hours standing in a corner of the schoolroom with a book balanced on my head as she tried to eliminate the slouch with which the Almighty has endowed my particular branch of Clan Donald for generations.

Her spectacles were so heavy that I can remember little about her face except that it was tanned a rich compost brown, and, come to think of it, so must have been the rest of her, because she was forever being stumbled across, sun-bathing in the nude in odd corners of the common grazing land, when the men were out shepherding. But despite the disparagements of the time it was later claimed that our sheep were never so well tended as they were in the summers of Miss Dalbeith.

Like a lot of people I still have a slight horror of walking into a crowded hall, and, for me, I think it started that moment when my father deserted me inside that schoolroom door. Sixteen pairs of eyes seemed to be tearing me apart as if they were trying to recognize a stranger inside the new Harris Tweed suit which my mother had finished making for me just the night before, and when I attempted to twitch a cheery little smile there was no flicker of recognition from the boisterous boys and girls – some of whom I had been playing with yesterday. When I was beginning to wonder what had transformed them all into a crowd of zombies, I was given my first clue. There was a bellow from behind me, followed quickly by a vicious tug of my left ear and I was spun round to stare into the knees of Miss Dalbeith's hand-knitted stockings. I didn't have time to ponder that I had never seen a strange woman's knees before, or that Miss Dalbeith was ahead of the fashion charts, because a scalping tug of my fore-lock and another stream of English incomprehensibility took my head back and my face up to meet her spectacles. What did dawn on me was that Miss Dalbeith and I were going to have some difficulty understanding each other, because, while I had enough Gaelic to last me for the rest of my life, she didn't have a word of Gaelic in her head.

I would willingly have solved the language problem for her by slipping off home – but she was a resourceful woman. She led me by the forelock to the end of a five-seater desk where there was an empty seat beside a girl. She patted the wooden seat first, and then mine. She said 'sit' and pressed me down hard, and so I learnt my first word of English as if I were being groomed for Crufts. From a slot in the front of the desk she extracted a wooden framed slate which she presented to me along with a thin slate pencil and she signalled that I should occupy myself in silence while she proceeded to harangue Primary Five which consisted of one boy called George. I had always envied George his skill in shinning up the telegraph poles which were beginning to sprout in our village. Now I envied him his apparent mastery of the English language.

The schoolroom was square and high and green and yellow. On one wall there was a huge faded parchment map with vast areas of red on it which I learnt in time to be the British Empire. There was a variety of jaded posters, only one of which I remember because of its manifest absurdity. It showed scantily clad, floppily bosomed women up to their knees in water cutting corn, and it didn't take much education to recognize that it was fake. Putting aside the artist's eye for colour completely, I knew that our women would rather die than be seen in that state of *déshabille*, far less cut corn in weather like that. I forget which member of an upper form later informed me loftily that they were Javanese women harvesting rice, but it still seemed to me to be unsound agricultural policy. In one corner of the room there was a round iron object which I jaloused to be a new-fangled stove because of the pipe which led up from it to the ceiling. Beside it was a blackboard on a four-legged easel – at least it had been black once but pale patches were beginning to appear on it like elbows through a jacket, and Miss Dalbeith seemed to spend most of her time scratching words on it for

George to repeat over and over again. Her own desk and high chair stood below a window which never closed winter or summer, and on our side of the room there were ten long desks each of them meant for five pupils; but seven of them had been vacant for many years.

There was a great tedium in not knowing English, so I spent some time scratching surrealistic pictures on my slate till the thing was full. I was wondering what to do about it when the girl beside me leant over confidentially and indicated that I should spit on my sleeve and rub. I did, and, lo and behold, the slate was like new. That was the second useful thing I learnt in school that morning, but I was to pay for it a few weeks later when Miss Dalbeith caught me at it and decided to teach me the word 'hygiene' with a cuff on the ear for every time I got it wrong. She was fanatical for hygiene, and in all the time I knew her, I never saw her use a handkerchief. Instead she ripped a piece from an old copy of *The Glasgow Herald* kept specially for that purpose . . . which she trumpeted into and then ceremonially burnt in the round black stove.

I was in the midst of rubbing out my umpteenth work of art when I became aware that a peculiar silence had fallen on the room, and when I looked around I found that George's English appeared to have deserted him. As the teacher's exhortations became shriller, George's face became redder. But it was total stalemate. And it ended only when an unmistakable word of command brought George shuffling to the front holding out his hand as if in reluctant greeting. For the first time in my life I saw two feet of leather strap being wielded by an enthusiastic and muscular woman. And I thanked God quietly that I had no English to forget.

The way that my first school-teacher could ply that belt would probably have earned her stardom in some deviant areas of today's sophisticated society. For all I know, Miss Dalbeith may have been a lonely disciple of the Comte de Sade, banished to a Hebridean outpost where the only deviations known were from the Ten Commandments which appear to have been carved in the days when men were men and women were women. Certainly there was an ecstatic gleam in her eye on that first morning of school as she leathered George for not knowing whatever it was he was supposed to know. For my own part, I watched the proceedings with a sinking heart, realizing that this was one of the things my mother had so often prophesied would happen to me when school began.

Whether or not it was sheer terror that brought the crisis on, I will never know. But, for the past few minutes I had been becoming aware of an increasing discomfort for which there didn't appear to be any solution in that particular green and yellow room. The uneasiness and the pressure increased with the knowledge that my neighbour was a girl whom I could not possibly consult, and if I couldn't ask Peggy in Gaelic how much less could I possibly ask Miss Dalbeith in the only language which she knew but which I didn't. By the time she noticed, the pool of my embarrassment was rivuletting its way towards her desk, and there was nothing she could do about it except splutter something that I couldn't understand . . . take me by the ear . . . and set me on the road for home. As I was going out through the gate, so much earlier than I had expected, I could hear her quelling the giggling which had been building up in my wake.

To this day I don't know why Miss Dalbeith let slip her first opportunity to use the leather 'Lochgelly' on me for what she must have considered a deplorable lack of self-control, but, fortunately for the tattered remains of my peace of mind the possibility of it didn't occur to me. I was too concerned with what my mother would have to say about the new Harris Tweed trousers that she had so painstakingly stitched for me and had put on me for school that morning for the first time – dry. All in all life seemed pretty bleak as I slunk past the workmen who were making our new road, and my face was hot from their banter about 'the boy who was expelled from school after only two hours of education'. Looking up, I suddenly knew that all would be well; coming down the track into the village was my Grandfather whom I hadn't seen in months, leading my mother's belated dowry on a rope, in the shape of a black short-horn cow. The days of the crowdie and cream were about to start . . . as were the days of the bitter-sweet.

This was 'Big Grandfather' – all six-foot-two of him – who was married to my mother's dumpling little mother. (On the other side of the pedigree, the situation was totally reversed – 'Big Grannie' being married to 'Wee Grandfather' – which probably explains why I've come through life labelled 'Height – medium', a description for which one is only grateful if one is being sought for a crime . . . But be that as it may, it was a good thing for a boy to grow up with two intact generations ahead of him, and to be the first grandson was just fine!) Instead of turning into the new house, I ran straight up the hill to Grandfather and explained my indignity to him – and my predicament. I can't remember what he said but he made it all seem very unimportant as he swung me on to Daisy's broad black back – steaming hot and sweaty from her long walk. 'Look at the boy's new trousers – soaking from that cow's back,' said my mother as I was lifted off at the door. And the old man winked at me, and neither of us had to tell a lie.

Daisy was, as I said, my mother's belated dowry, and I stress the *belated* lest anyone wonder why my mother should be receiving a wedding present on the day that her first son was starting school. In those days, it was the custom for the bride's parents to give their daughter a start in married life by giving her a cow in calf on her wedding day. But that hadn't been possible in my mother's case because, when he came back from the war in 1918 my father had no land.

That was the first visit of 'Big Grandfather's' that I can remember, and I probably remember it because of the way he took things in hand. My mother was the youngest of his daughters, and maybe he resented the fact that she was the first to leave the nest in the same way as Laban was loathe to lose Rachel. Maybe I was just witnessing the age-old jockeying for position between the wife's father and a new son-in-law. Or, on the other hand, it may have been that he quite genuinely believed that my parents were incapable of bringing up children although he lived to see them bring up two more than he had done. Whatever it was, in the early days, he gave every appearance of being in charge, and that suited me very well; the threat of 'just you wait till your grandfather goes away' hung over me lightly, but in the event of any trouble I stuck closely by his side.

In the early autumn days, Daisy would spend her nights outside, tethered to keep her away from our first crop of corn, and my Grandfather felt it his duty to stay on to supervise the building of a byre for her against the coming of winter. Perhaps my father could have built it for himself, but I have a feeling that the old man suspected that he would never get round to it in time, because there runs in the paternal stream of my ancestry an inclination to . . . not necessarily to procrastinate, but to get side-tracked into lotus lanes. My father's obsession was with reading, and it was one that wasn't easily satisfied in a community far removed from libraries, and into which the newspapers were only beginning to percolate by post. The fact that they were a week old didn't matter because in those pre-wireless days topical stories were none the less welcome because they were mature.

Sometimes my father, slightly self-consciously, would lose himself in an aged copy of *Woman's Weekly* or *The People's Friend* which the minister's widow would hand on to my mother for their knitting patterns. But his salvation was Gibbon's *Decline and Fall of the Roman Empire*, which he made a point of reading once a year from the day he bought it, and his tattered copy of Macaulay's *Lays of Ancient Rome* which he read aloud to me till I knew 'How Horatius Kept the Bridge' off by heart before Miss Dalbeith had got me as far as 'The Cat Sat On The Mat', which is precisely what my new cat didn't – because my Great Aunt Rachel had sat on it. But that's another story.

Big Grandfather didn't approve of his son-in-law's literary bent, particularly during the hours of daylight each one of which he thought, like Kipling, should be used to the last second. My father was willing enough to labour and hold posts straight while the old man (who must have been all of fifty-five) architected and ordered and designed. And if anybody went against Grandfather's way of thinking he took an attack of sore feet and hirpled into the house for tea and sympathy till it was agreed that, maybe, his way was correct after all. Whereupon he made spectacular recoveries and hustled on with the job in hand.

It was in the evenings that my father came into his own. Being an inveterate 'reader-out-aloud' he revelled in bringing Grandfather up to date with the news from the least ancient of the newspapers to his hand. And whatever the news was – if it was serious – it always got a mention in Grandfather's prayers when, by virtue of his seniority, he took 'the books' as we called prayers at the end of the day. Not that the old man couldn't read for himself – otherwise he couldn't have coped with the mandatory psalm and chapter from the Bible, but, in the early years that I remember him, he confined his reading to *Cooper's Little Red Book of Sheep Management* and the Bible; he knew both pretty well by heart, which showed in his remarkable ability to open the Bible at a chapter appropriate to the news items which my father had imparted to him. A hurricane in the Pacific would automatically guide him to the Lord quelling the tempest on the Sea of Galilee, while at the news of an earthquake in Peru he would light upon the collapse of the walls of Jericho.

Unlike my father, who must have tested God's hearing to the uttermost, my Grandfather prayed sonorously and aloud, but as my education cumbersomely advanced I began to query the efficacy of praying for the safety of mariners in the aforesaid Pacific hurricane when, by the

70

time the newspapers reached us, their fate must have been decided one way or another anyway. But, on that particular visit, he seemed much concerned for the safety of men who, by their skills, were preparing to face the dangers of the skies. He prayed with such vehemence that I began to wonder on my aching knees if another flood was pending despite the rather ambiguous promise God had given when He put the rainbow in the sky.

It was only recently that curiosity made me try to find out what had so concerned the old man, and I discovered that, while he and my father were building that byre in Harris, away down in England men were putting the finishing touches to the R 101. I wonder if, away up there in the islands, the old man had some prescience of disaster. If he had it wouldn't be for the first or last time.

Chapter Eight

The only thing that marred that first visit of Grandfather's to our new house was the crisis which blew up in school. George had not taken his leathering meekly, and the very next day – my second day in the establishment – he had taken advantage of one of Miss Dalbeith's 'excuse me' absences from the classroom to dash to her desk and with unerring aim had flung her 'Lochgelly' high up through an open hatch in the ceiling and into the cobwebby darkness of the loft. It didn't take her long to discover her loss, and the interrogations which followed were of the type which anticipated by two decades the techniques developed to a finer art in the Third Reich.

By that second day in school I had learnt only two bits of English. One was that 'sit' meant 'sit'. And the other was that on the onset of the faintest feeling of discomfort in my nether regions I had to put up my hand and snap my fingers till I attracted Miss Dalbeith's attention and then say, parrot-wise, 'Please Miss, I want out'. It wasn't much to be going on with, particularly in the situation now developing which was obviously, in due course, going to embroil *me*. I have never been in an identity parade but I suspect that my feelings were like those of an innocent towards the tail end of the line who suspects that an accusatory finger may be pointed at him and that he may be totally unable to prove his innocence.

Miss Dalbeith started with the oldest boy in the school – a fellow who was a mere half-head shorter than herself and built like an ox. He was at a stage of manhood when the mothers in the neighbouring villages locked up their daughters when he did one of his occasional forays on the decrepit bicycle he had built himself out of bits and pieces; but his manhood was patently at a droop as he faced up to Miss Dalbeith's staccato. After an age she dismissed him and ordered him to the far end of the room, to stand on one leg with his back to the wall. The parade to the desk continued and, one after the other, in descending order of age the suspects were harangued and obviously threatened with dire consequences and then duly sent to join the lengthening queue of delinquents standing for all the world like bedraggled storks against the wall. Having seen George dispose of the strap through the opening of the loft I had a fair idea what the to-do was about, and I was impressed with the air of injured innocence with which he faced up to his ordeal before joining the queue at the wall. I myself wasn't unduly perturbed because I felt fairly immune behind my ignorance of English – there was obviously little that I could contribute to the drama on a vocabulary of 'sit' and 'Please Miss I want out'. But I reckoned without the resourcefulness of Miss Dalbeith.

Peggy was my immediate predecessor in the dock, but instead of being sent to the wall at the end of her interrogation she was kept back beside Miss Dalbeith who beckoned to me. As I went out I could sense the tension in the room mounting, and I could feel twelve pairs of eyes boring into my back; there was no doubt that I was being regarded as the weak link at the tail end of the chain of resistance. Miss Dalbeith turned to Peggy and delivered a long sentence.

Peggy turned to me and said in Gaelic, 'She wants to know if you saw anyone stealing her strap and if you don't say "no" the boys will kill you after school. Shake your head.' So I shook my head.

Miss Dalbeith was obviously losing heart and her next question was softer and shorter and, once again, Peggy interpreted as follows: 'You're doing very well. She wants to know if you know it's a sin to tell lies. Nod your head.'

So I nodded my head.

It must have been the blush that rose to my cheek at Peggy's compliment that convinced the teacher of my innocence because she indicated that I should return to my desk in solitude while Peggy took up her one-legged stance at the wall. I felt very warm towards Peggy for the way in which she had softened my ordeal for me. She was, even then, a strikingly beautiful girl with blue eyes and the jet black hair of the Iberian/Celtic race – her appearance, if anything, enhanced by a set of gleaming white, but protruding teeth. A few years later I was to kiss her on a cold and frosty Hebridean beach, and it was an experience which came back to me much later on in manhood when I bit into my first Baked Alaska.

Anyway, that was the second day of school, and also the end of the week because, then, new terms always began on a Thursday. For me, and a couple of other monoglots, a pleasant week-end stretched ahead. Not so for the rest. Having failed to illicit any information about the missing tawse Miss Dalbeith issued one of her standard punishments to the rest of the school. They were to come back on Monday morning with the whole of Psalm 119 learnt off by heart, and with the solemn assurance that each slip of memory would incur one stroke of the belt – the new belt which Miss Delbeith assured us she would have procured by then. For those who are not well up in the Scottish metrical psalms I should, perhaps, explain that 119 is the longest of King David's many compositions and must have been composed during a year when the lambing was poor or affairs of state were not pressing. It is over five hundred lines long, and somewhat lacking in continuity, and the devilishness of the punishment was that it would involve the entire literate section of the community since even the most advanced pupils were not totally fluent in English and would have to seek parental or friendly advice on words like 'statutes' and 'testimonies' and 'precepts'.

Miss Dalbeith, in all fairness, added one codicil – that, in the event of anybody accruing more than six penalties, the balance would be spread out over an appropriate number of days. She was thorough. Very thorough. But she made one mistake. She informed us triumphantly that she personally would contact Calum the Post and arrange for him to bring her a new strap on the Saturday morning and that it would be ready and waiting and locked in her desk come Monday morning.

Calum the Post was one of us, and Miss Dalbeith was a foreigner: she came from somewhere on the wrong side of the Minch and didn't speak Gaelic. Calum knew all the regulations of the Post Office off by heart and by Saturday evening the village knew that the postman had informed Miss Dalbeith that, much as he would like to oblige her, the rules forbade him delivering anything which did not come through the normal Post Office channels bearing a normal Post Office stamp. And so we breathed again, knowing that, between the uncertainty of the mail in those early days and the self-controlled uncertainty of Calum's memory there was little chance of Miss Dalbeith being armed for at least a week. And so it turned out.

Calum the Post, as I've just said, knew all the Post Office rules by heart. He also, doubtless, knew the Ten Commandments, and if he could adjust the laws of Moses then there would seem to be little reason why he couldn't put occasional variants into the laws of the Postmaster General.

Long before the threats of energy crises prompted some enlightened government to dream up the idea of combining the delivery of mail with the transport of passengers in thinly populated rural areas, we had a Mail Bus of our own. But nobody ever heard about it because Calum the Post would have lost his job, and that would have been a bit pointless because the weight of public opinion would have made his successor carry on where he left off anyway. The only difference between now and then was that our Mail Bus was a large red van with a large gold coat of arms painted on its side and the words Royal Mail in black. It was provided by the Government to travel northwards up the west coast of Harris every Tuesday, Thursday and Saturday delivering letters and parcels to the straggle of new croft houses. And on Mondays, Wednesdays and Fridays it travelled south picking up what was optimistically known as Outgoing Mail. For the latter purposes the Post Office also provided red pillar boxes – with GVR embossed on them so heavily that it suggested Royal immortality – into which the villagers were meant to pop their letters for Calum the Post to collect at the precisely stipulated hours on his southward journey. In those halcyon, pre-vandalism days the idea had obviously been proved to work in well organized places like Inverness and Islington, but it was different in Scaristavore.

For several reasons. First of all, those of the villagers who could write didn't have any compelling reason for doing so, except on the rare occasions when they wanted to order goods from the Mail Order Warehouses of the mainland, and when they did write they never had any stamps and it was easier to waylay Calum at the croft gate and hand him a penny ha'penny and the letter. Another reason for writing might have been to ask after the health of one's relatives, but that was a cumbersome way of going about things when one could get news from Calum not only of one's own but of other people's relatives as well. And then, of course, it became quickly obvious to everybody that it was a waste of government money to have a large red van trundling up and down the road with a few letters, a couple of parcels and a lot of empty space when a sack of seed potatoes needed to be transported from one croft to another, or a half-hundredweight of oatmeal had to be brought from a store nine or ten miles away . . . or even when an illicit salmon had to be taken from the vicinity of the landlord's river to a more deserving destination. At times of funeral or festivity the van could take up to a dozen passengers at a time, and while it was illegal for Calum to carry them it would have been even more illegal to charge them . . . and highly impractical for him to consider sticking them with penny ha'penny stamps.

Calum the Post was an immense personality. By law, he was supposed to stop his van at each croft gate if he had mail to deliver – lock the van and walk up to the house with his packages. But such servitude would have been undignified for someone who had probably been a corporal when our men were privates or matelots. And so, instead, he blasted his klaxon horn till somebody went down to the van to collect a letter or hear a bit of news. Only at two houses did he observe the law. At the Manse, and, of course, at the Schoolhouse where Miss Dalbeith would have reported him if he hadn't personally delivered the *Glasgow Herald*s into which she blew her nose.

Calum had a great heart and a good memory, and rarely did he pass a house without something to deliver – if not a letter, an ounce of tobacco or half a pound of baking soda or cream of tartar where these had been omitted from the weekly parcel of groceries. And the villagers, in their turn, dug him out of ditches when he went off the road, and straightened his mud-guards when he went too near a dyke, and they all took a personal pride in the certificate he received for careful driving after he had been twenty-five years on the road. Round about the middle of December Calum would begin to remind people gently that Hogmanay was drawing near, with a forecast that there was going to be 'a shortage' but that he himself might be in a position to help a friend should a bottle or two be required 'at the old price'. He was too honest to suggest that the price was going up, but there was something galvanizing about the phrase 'the old price', even in those days, and within a week his order list would be complete. And then, round about Christmas, he would begin to fall slightly further and further behind with his delivery schedule.

Not because he was bowed down with today's kind of excessive Christmas mail, but because he seemed to take it into his head that he should observe Post Office regulations for a trial period – taking selected houses in turn. He ceased to blow his horn and, instead, would in regulation fashion get out of his van and lock it and walk up to the door carrying under his arm a parcel which had never seen a sorting office. It embarrassed him to have to accept the price of the order, meticulously ticked off in his little red notebook (which, like the van, had GVR on the cover), and it really pained him to have to accept a glass in reward. But he always succumbed graciously, and he always removed the Crown's hat before bending the Crown's law. And so, he worked his way along the route, careful never to supply more than two or three houses on the one day lest his glasses of reward made him falter in the service of King George.

Ah well! He's been up there many years now, has Calum, and I often think that he must smile to himself and give his red-piped blue halo a tilt backwards when he sees his successors in the Mail Bus service punching tickets and accepting money for the things he did for our village for free.

Chapter Nine

I have never been able to discover the formula by which the Board of Agriculture, in far away Edinburgh, selected the eight successful candidates for the new crofts. For sure they were all ex-servicemen, but that was the only thing they had in common, and there must have been scores of disappointed applicants with that particular qualification. In the cities now, there is a tendency to allocate council houses on a 'points' system which would seem to favour couples of proven fertility and infinite patience and, occasionally, discreetly corrupt cousins in high places. But there doesn't seem to have been any obvious code of conduct or misconduct applied to the plantation of our village, and, in two or three cases, crofts had been allocated to bachelors who, for all that anybody knew, might have turned out to have neither the will nor the ability to guarantee the succession.

In the event the Board's judgement turned out to be sound, and, in due course, the bachelors succumbed in turn either to the urgings of their loins or the persuasions of inconvenience. But the man who started off the procession to the altar was not a crofter at all, but a man called James who lived with ageing parents in the old village and who had been known for some time to be courting my father's cousin Mary. Cousinage is a relationship which is carried to extremes in the Hebrides, and Mary was not the daughter of any of my father's uncles or aunts but she was of the same stock as Great Aunt Rachel and that was good enough. James was in the same sort of relationship to Gillespie and it was from the latter that I heard first that there was going to be a pre-wedding party to which everybody in the neighbourhood appeared to be invited except himself and myself, and, of course, my brother and his sister who were too young anyway. Needless to say we both vigorously challenged the manifest unfairness of the whole thing but we were told very firmly that the occasion was 'not suitable' and that was that.

The party began to assume extremely puzzling dimensions in our imaginations when it transpired that it was obviously going to be 'not suitable' for James either, and that he was going to be the 'looker after' (the word 'baby-sitter' had not been invented, far less translated) of the four of us, and that, to facilitate matters, Gillespie and his sister were to spend the night in our house. It was unheard of! People just didn't spend nights in other people's houses unless they were grandfathers or such! As the days wore on and the subject of the party took up more and more of playtime discussion in school, it turned out that Gillespie's information had not been wholly accurate and that, in fact, only the three or four oldest pupils were being invited and then only for the earlier part of the proceedings. That mollified us a little. But not wholly. Our other uninvited contemporaries lived much further away and the party wasn't on their doorsteps. Nor were James and Mary related to them.

At last the evening arrived, and, with it, feverish activity. Daisy was milked early. Gillespie and his sister were delivered to our house and fed. My father got into his navy-blue serge Sunday suit, and mother into a frock which I didn't even know existed. At some stage or other she laid out the two younger ones side by side, cross-wise, in the double bed normally occupied by my brother and myself and, alternately threatening and wheedling, she obtained promises from Gillespie and me that we would obediently climb in beside them as soon as James so decreed. If we were good, she promised, James would let us stay up a little later than usual. Little did she know it but that was the last thing we wanted.

'O Lord,' said my father, 'here comes James taking the width of the road!'

It was an expression I hadn't heard before, but a quick glance through the window soon clarified it. James was a hero of mine for many reasons, but principally because he frequently took me for rides 'cross-bar' on his bicycle of which he was immensely proud and on which he was an expert. Tonight, though, his flickering carbide lamp was pursuing a decidedly erratic course along a road which was so moonlit that a lamp was totally unnecessary in the first place. However, by the time he came through the door he was impeccably sober as only a consciously inebriated man can be.

'You'll be all right, James?' said my father in a half questioning tone obviously meant to reassure himself if nobody else.

'Certainly,' said James.

'You needn't be bothering with the fire,' said my father, carefully closing the doors of the Modern Mistress.

'Not to worry,' said James producing his cigarettes, 'I've got matches.'

My father paled slightly, but my mother took his arm and oxtered him out through the door before he could begin to have third thoughts.

'You'll find milk and sugar and everything in the cupboard, James,' she threw over her shoulder as she closed the door behind her.

'Nothing like milk. Very good for one,' muttered James to nobody in particular as he sat down carefully on the red kist at the end of the table and began to arrange a half bottle of whisky, two packets of Capstan Full Strength and a box of Swan Vestas on the new oilcloth. 'James will look after the boys, won't he, boys?' and as if to underline his best intentions he produced two large bars of Toffee Cow as we called the succulent bars of MacCowan's Highland Toffee which were the vogue at the time and which must surely have been the inspiration for the 'lock-tite' glues against which television adverts were to warn future generations.

'All right then, boys, time for bed!' said James as soon as he heard the gate squeak shut behind my parents.

'My mother said that we could stay up late if we were good and we haven't done anything.'

We wanted to go to bed early, but not yet.

'What your mother said was that you needn't go to sleep early but that doesn't mean to say that you don't have to go to bed.'

Sheer semantics! The phrase my mother had used could, indeed, be twisted to mean what he said, but the plan we had worked out was designed to allow us to keep James company for as long as possible rather than that we retire and risk falling asleep. And we wanted James to be so fed up with our company that he would be glad to see the last of us. Under no circumstances did we want him coming into the bedroom to check on us once we had gone through.

'My mother doesn't let me eat toffee in bed in case I choke.'

Gillespie's ingenuity took my breath away. I knew that toffee was as much of a rarity in his home as it was in my own, and that the chances of there being any left over at bedtime were slim indeed.

'Very well then!' He was getting snappy, which was just fine. 'Get on with your toffees; I'm going out to the end of the house.'

We could tell by the sound of his feet on the one little gravel patch at the door of the porch that he hadn't gone to the end of the house so we got on our knees on the bench and lifted our separate corners of the blind. James was on his way to the roadside gate and, for a moment, we thought that he was going to get on his bicycle and go away.

'No,' said Gillespie. 'His bottle of whisky is still on the table.'

82

James fumbled around his bicycle for a few moments and then lifted a parcel, which had obviously been strapped to his carrier; this he proceeded to lay on the dyke and unwrap. There was enough moonlight for us to see him lift to his mouth a glinting bottle of the type known as a screw-top. We wondered quietly to each other why he hadn't brought it into the house along with his half-bottle of whisky. But whatever his reasons, he was in no hurry to return to us and he continued to take long leisurely pulls till, presumably, the bottle was empty, when he swung it round his head a couple of times and flung it far away on to the machair. He glanced in the direction of the house but obviously didn't notice anything untoward with the blind which we didn't have time to replace. Thus satisfied, he took a second screw-top out of the parcel and rammed it into his breast pocket. He then scrumpled up the paper and jammed it into a niche in the dyke.

When he came back in we were sitting just as he had left us, chewing away at our Toffee Cow. He sat down at the end of the table keeping his arm carefully crooked over the bulge in his jacket.

'Is that a screw-top you've got in your pocket, James?'

He looked taken aback for a moment and then decided to laugh it off.

'Dash me, yes. I'd forgotten about it.' He took it out and put it on the table beside the whisky. 'Aye. Yes. Well you see – I didn't want them to think I might be drinking when I was looking after the two of you. Parents are very old-fashioned you know. I know fine that you two are perfectly able to look after yourselves, and I thought I would just be having a wee drink if I got lonely after you went to bed. That's reasonable enough isn't it?'

Gillespie and I had long since learnt to distrust adults when they were trying to sound reasonable so we said nothing. James lit a cigarette, and there was silence for a while.

'Why aren't you at the party?'

'Och it's just an old custom. The man who's going to get married is never at the *reiteach*.'

'What's a *reiteach*?'

'It's a party that's held a few nights before the wedding just to make sure that everything's all right and people bring presents and things like that. It's an old custom.'

'Is Mary going to have a baby?'

That startled him.

'Who did you hear saying that?'

'Is she going to have a baby?'

'Of course she's not going to have a baby! People don't have babies before they marry.'

'Marsail MacInnes isn't married or anything and she's got twins!'

'That's different! And will you stop pestering me! Where does your mother keep the glasses?'

'She hasn't got glasses.'

'Where does she keep the bloody cups then?'

He strode over to the big cupboard and began to fiddle with the key. As soon as his back was turned I closed the damper on the *Modern Mistress* so that peat smoke began to wisp into the room. James finally got the cupboard open and found a row of tumblers staring him in the face.

'I thought you said—' He broke off as he turned round and saw the smoke by now billowing from the range. 'What the devil have you done now?'

'I'll tell my mother you were swearing and drinking whisky and beer.'

'You'll tell your mother bugger all of the sort or I'll screw your neck for you and I'll never give you a ride on my cross-bar again. Now get into that bed and if I hear one word out of either of you I'll come through and bang your heads together till you're unconscious. Get going!'

He slammed the tumbler on the table and turned his attention to the stove.

'Leave the door open so that we have light to see to take off our clothes.'

'I'll leave the door open till I get this damn stove fixed and then I'm closing it for the night whether you have your clothes off or not!'

We could hear him twiddling the damper as we climbed into bed fully clothed and pulled the bed-cover up to our chins. In a few moments he came through and though we could only see his silhouette against the oil lamp in the living room we could tell by his voice that he was slightly surprised and considerably mollified to find us in bed.

'Good night, fellows', he said. 'You're not such a bad couple after all. I'll tell them how good you were.'

He closed the door. We waited till we heard the clink of a glass and, a moment later, the scrape of a match. We then slipped out of bed, swung open the bedroom window and set off for the party.

The first couple of hundred yards were exciting and then, as we got further and further into the moonlit emptiness I began to feel an inner cold creeping up on me that had nothing to do with the chill of the night. Now and again a puff of cloud would drift across the moon and I could feel myself flinching. I was just on the point of suggesting to Gillespie that it might be wise to forget the whole ploy when he turned to me.

'Are you – are you scared?' he whispered.

'Of course not,' I hissed back. 'Are you?'

'Of course not.'

That clinched it. The last moment for return had been squandered by each of us and now there was nothing for it but to press on.

'Let's run,' Gillespie gasped as we suddenly found ourselves in the shadow of the churchyard wall, and we set off as if every demon therein was on our tails. It felt like hours before we broke out of the shadows with our lungs bursting, and we could only stand and gasp when we finally gained the steely blue moonlight beyond. As we stood and fought for breath neither of us dared look back, and then, one of us spotted the light from Mary's home in the distance and the terror began to ebb away. We set off

85

at a jog trot and didn't pause again till we were a few yards from the door. Even at a distance the noise was deafening. It was a noise we had never heard before: the whole village joined together in the chorus of a raucous Gaelic song. We crept up into the shelter of the wall beside the door.

'How are we going to get in?' I asked Gillespie.

It was a question that had never occurred to either of us, but before we had time to debate it the door swung open and a young man and woman we didn't know slipped out hand in hand and tiptoed off in the direction of the barn on some private errand of their own, leaving the door of the house wide open behind them.

It was a big old-fashioned cottage which had once belonged to a gamekeeper or somebody of that standing, but Mary's old father now occupied it by virtue of being orra-man (ploughman, handyman, shepherd all rolled into one) to the landlord who had clung on to the home farm when the estate had been taken over and divided up. We were standing at the back door which led into a small scullery, past which we could see through another door into a turbulent mass of Sunday-best villagers swaying backwards and forwards between us and a huge white draped table loaded with food of a dozen kinds. We glanced at each other and I don't think we exchanged a word.

We dropped on our hands and knees and crept in through a jungle of legs whose owners, in retrospect, must have lost all feeling in them as we squeezed past. Somebody stood on my fingers and I nearly yelled with pain, but it passed in a flash as I pressed on. We hardly dared breathe as we squatted on the floor directly below the table, shielded, as we thought, by the drapes of the heavy linen cloth. I could just see Gillespie's face dimly in the half light below the table and, presumably, he could see about the same amount of me. We didn't dare speak but, from time to time, we gave each other triumphant little winks and smiles as the spirit of the evening began to percolate through to us. Apart from one cattle sale day and James, I had never seen anybody even remotely tiddly before, but I had heard disparaging conversations about drunkenness and had always understood it to be not a good thing. Here, however, it seemed to be epidemic and far from discouraged. The most used phrase of the evening seemed to be a slurred 'Come on, another wee one won't do you any harm', to which the recurrent response was 'Ach well . . .'

'Peter MacAulay, stand out here and give us a song, will you?'

Angels and ministers of Grace! Peter MacAulay was the prim, white moustachioed precentor, or leader of the praise in Church, and he was reckoned not much good at that. On one occasion, the minister, in deference to some visiting Englishman who had dropped in on a Gaelic service, had persuaded Peter to lead the congregation in the Old Hundredth Metrical Psalm which begins

> All people that on earth do dwell
> Sing to the Lord with cheerful voice . . .

When Peter protested that he didn't know a tune that would fit, he had been persuaded that Robert Burns's 'Banks and Braes of Bonnie Doon' would fit fine. Thus assured, Peter had embarked on the most hallowed of the psalms only to get carried away with himself to produce an excellent opening which went

> All people that on earth do dwell
> How can ye bloom sae fresh and fair . . .

before the minister could tactfully interrupt and take over the duty of precentor himself.

But here now was Peter (having silenced his wife's protestations) in full flight with a Gaelic wedding song which was, in today's terms, 'explicit' in the extreme, bringing half-hearted protests from the women and roars of approbation from the men. It went on for verse after

87

verse, and it was beginning to pall on me because its innuendo (if that isn't too delicate a word) was far above my head, although, as the years went on and the inevitable prurience of adolescence asserted itself, I was able to recall and relish swathes of it long after it had been forgotten by the rest of those present on that night.

Song followed song. Somebody played the bagpipe, and somebody played the trump as the Jew's Harp was called. Now and again Donald John Murray was prevailed on to lay down his drink and pick up his melodeon and the company erupted into dancing which involved frequent lurchings into the table. I was beginning to feel bored and sleepy when I felt the linen table cloth rustling at my ear, and I looked round to find a horny hand which I couldn't possibly identify waggling two slices of sponge cake in my face. I nudged Gillespie and we hesitantly took a slice each and munched – waiting with each bite for our presence to be announced and Nemesis to strike. But no. From then on, from time to time, the table cloth would rustle and the hand would appear – sometimes with a rock cake, sometimes with a leg of chicken, sometimes with a slab of currant cake and, now and again, with a mug of fizzy drink. Just a hand with a gold signet ring which seemed to be held in place on the pinkie by a large brown wart. At first it was a weird sensation to be establishing a relationship with a disembodied hand, but, fairly quickly, inhibition vanished giving way to a certain sense of security.

'Silence!'

I cringed. The voice was my father's. And all my rock cakes and chicken legs and fizzy drinks seemed to solidify cold in my stomach as I thought that he was going to sing. Because I knew that he couldn't.

But no. Instead he assumed to himself a strange and pompous voice which was untypically forceful and, truth to tell, rather pleasantly lubricated.

'My friends', he said, 'the time has now come!'

The time! The time for what? I looked at Gillespie and,

to my horror, found that he was slumped on the floor sound asleep. If the time had come to go home we were in serious trouble because our plan had been to be away and safely in bed before anybody knew that we'd been out of it. But it wasn't that. It became quickly clear that some new ploy was afoot, as my father, by dint of reason and persuasion and hectoring managed to divide the motley throng into two groups in such a way, happily, that I was left a clear, uninterrupted, worm's eye view of the far end of the room where Mary's old father, looking even more venerable than usual with his white goatee beard, neatly trimmed, stood erect and patrician looking, with his roly-poly wife clinging, apple-faced and twinkling, to his arm. I found it in my heart to feel sorry for them if they were going to be made fools of in anything resembling the way that the rest of the company seemed bent on making fools of themselves. But they seemed quite composed and, indeed, Mary's mother, judging by the beam on her twinkly-wrinkly face, was enjoying her glisk of the limelight.

My father, having got the company ordered to his satisfaction, launched into a measured, flowery, speech. On behalf of himself and everybody within and outwith the parish he thanked the old couple for their hospitality, and for 'the use of their roof', as he put it, for one of the best parties he had ever attended. Now, he wondered if they would extend their kindliness and good-will still further and receive a stranger who had arrived unexpectedly at the door.

Mary's father bowed graciously and said that his home had ever been open to the stranger and asked that this one should be brought forward. A man who was, indeed, a stranger to me stepped forward and bowed gravely to Mary's parents. My heart turned over when he held out his hand to the old man and I saw a glint of gold ring on his pinkie. I didn't need to look a second time to ascertain whether or not the ring was being held in place by a wart because gold signet rings just didn't sprout on the pinkies of our crofters. I was convinced that this was going to be the moment of betrayal and was trying to make up my mind whether to waken Gillespie or make a break for it on my own when the stranger began to speak. And if my father had been flowery, this fellow was worse. It turned out that he was a sailor home on leave and though he had been at parties in every corner of the globe this was, by far, the best he had ever enjoyed and he was sorry to be the one to introduce a note of solemnity into the proceedings.

'I am here', he went on, 'representing my good friend James, at whose shoulder I will be standing if and when the day comes that he gets married. James himself cannot be here tonight because he is practising the great art of looking after children, and it is to be hoped that he is learning well in case the day comes when he was to tuck in his own . . .' A great roar of laughter. The stranger appeared to glance at his shoes as he waited for the hilarity to subside but, in fact, he was looking me straight in the eye as I cringed under the table.

Resuming his speech he went on to explain that he had been sent, because of his great experience of boats and the sea, to buy a boat for James! It had to be a good boat – a boat that had not been ill-treated in any way; a boat that could stand a tall mast; a boat that would last well and would not be expensive to maintain . . . It was a long speech, made longer by the gales of laughter that greeted every apparently innocent sentence, and he described a boat that was out of this world.

'And finally', concluded the stranger in his smooth Gaelic, 'it must be known to you that my friend James is a man of great experience with boats (howls of laughter from the company) and a man who knows a good boat when he sees one and will not be taken in by paint and varnish! I am asking, therefore, if you can sell me a boat that is sound from prow to stern (more laughter), one that will stand up to whatever weather comes her way, and will not ever drag her anchor.' The stranger gravely acknowledged the applause and stepped aside.

Mary's father stroked his beard and held a serious whispered conversation with his wife. He then moved slowly forward and took my Great Aunt Rachel by the hand. She was creased with laughter and I noticed that she had put her teeth in for the party. 'Here', said the old man, 'is a boat which has weathered many storms, but she's good for a few years yet. As far as we know she's only ever had one mast (complete uproar) and only her present owner has ever hoisted her sails.' (Pealing laughter again.) 'This boat has been well cared for. She may look weather-beaten but her beam is sound!'

It was some time before the stranger could reply, but when he did it went something like this: 'A fine boat I have no doubt but not suitable for the shallow waters around these parts. Top heavy too unless my eyes deceive me. But, worst of all, old boats have characteristics of their own and they are not always obedient to a new hand on the rudder. No. If you can't do better than that I must look elsewhere.'

My Great Aunt Rachel squeezed herself back into her armchair with her bosom heaving and tears of laughter streaming down her face. I took advantage of the applause to shake Gillespie awake, and clapped my hand over his mouth before he could ask where he was. For the rest of the pantomime he crouched on his hands and knees looking mystified.

Mary's father proceeded to bring forward, one after the other, four or five women from the neighbourhood although, mercifully, not Gillespie's mother or my own. And one after the other the stranger turned them down – sometimes with ribald comment where the candidate was a buxom adolescent; with great graciousness where she was a modest matron. At last he seemed to lose patience and made as if to go, but before he could do so Mary's father took his daughter by the wrist and pulled her, protesting coyly, into the ring.

'Very well,' he said, 'this is my last offer to you. Here is a boat I have always meant to keep for myself. But if your friend James will promise to look after her I might consider letting her go.'

The stranger beamed. He took Mary and spun her round and round, pretending to be running his hands over her but not touching her at all. 'My friend', he said at last, 'this is the very boat for James, and, if I mistake not, perfect for the kind of cargo he has in mind for her . . .' As the laughter began to well up again, my common sense told me that it was time to make our get-away; I tugged a bemused Gillespie by the sleeve and we began to thread our way on hands and knees back through the legs.

Outside, the gibbous moon had worked its way round so that the kirkyard wall no longer cast a shadow, and we sped past it in silence. Gillespie, having missed the first Act, could have had no clue as to plot or denouement: I myself had only a vague feeling that, by a combination of sense and good luck, his friend had done well by James. What I was not to realize till much later was that I had been privileged to witness an old Highland wedding custom that I was never to see again.

We found the bedroom window ajar as we had left it, and after we had climbed out of our clothes, leaving them in a heap in the middle of the floor, we eased open the living-room door. The half bottle was lying empty on the table, the tumbler beside it with half an inch still left in it. The top of the Modern Mistress was littered with ash and cigarette ends. And on St Clement's bench lay James, snoring, satisfied that he had discharged his duties, and blissfully unaware of how close he had come to finding my Great Aunt Rachel standing waiting for him at the altar.

Chapter Ten

On the morning after the *reiteach* my father was not his usual easy-going self, and, from behind the heavy tweed bedspread which he had pulled up to his eyes he sustained an acrimonious interchange with my brother and Gillespie's sister who had been gallumphing through the house since dawn. Not unnaturally they were curious to know why James, fully dressed, was sound asleep in our living room. Was he sick? My father hoped so. Would James be all right in a wee while? My father hoped not.

At last my mother couldn't keep quiet any longer.

'For goodness' sake leave the children alone; they haven't done anything to you. Your own mother's sister warned you last night what you'd be like if you didn't take it easy, but . . .'

'Rachel thinks she's just got to put her hat on and her teeth in and she's God Almighty. In any case I'm not looking for an argument; I'm just telling those children to keep quiet while I get some sleep. Is that too much to ask?'

'They're hungry', I volunteered. And I should have known that any suggestion from me would be inflammatory.

'Go and feed them then seeing you're so smart!'

'The fire's out.'

'Light it then!' He jerked up in bed. 'O God, no! What am I saying? Don't go near the fire or I'll flay the backside off you. Just go back to sleep everybody till it's time to get up in a wee while.'

He stretched out his arm from below the bedcover as he lay back on the pillow and brought the little tin alarm clock up to his face. He looked, and looked again, and in what was virtually one movement rammed the clock back on the cabin trunk by the bedside, flung the bedclothes back, reached for his shirt forgetting he still had it on, and swung his legs to the floor, looking slightly surprised to find that they were still in his long johns.

'It's eleven o'bloody clock and the cow hasn't been milked. What'll the neighbours think? It's Saturday and the postman will be here any minute and we'll be namely from here to Luskentyre.'

'Well I can't get up till you get James roused,' my mother mumbled. 'In any case I doubt if the postman'll be round today; he was still at the *reiteach* when we left and showing no signs of leaving.'

'He'd better be round with my *Weekly Scotsman* even if he's got to get someone to drive him.'

'Pappy, why are you putting on your Sunday trousers if it's Saturday?'

He glared at me and began to reverse out of his navy-blues. 'Since you're so damned clever get out of that bed and get into your own trousers and let the hens out and bring in a pail of water.'

I slid out of bed and Gillespie, who hadn't uttered a word, slipped out after me and, covering his manhood with one hand, began to struggle into his trousers. We wasted no time getting into our things, and though the water pail clanged like a tocsin as I picked it up on my way through the living room, James didn't stir. Out of the corner of my eye I noticed that a burning cigarette had obviously fallen out of his sleeping fingers at some point; a pencil of grey ash lay in a scorch mark on the floor. I had a feeling that James was in for a very rude awakening indeed.

My father needn't have worried about the village. There wasn't a trace of movement anywhere, nor a wisp of smoke from any chimney. But over the caged clucking of our own hens and Daisy's groaning, one could hear the protests of imprisoned animals from north and south. The *reiteach* had obviously paralysed the community at large.

After we had released the hens from their end of the byre and thrown them several handfuls of corn from the sack in the corner, we made our way to the 'well rock'. The word 'well' was the name for any source of drinking water, and the well rock was a large flat rock jutting into the river; whether the water was high or low some of it was channelled through a V-shaped gouge in the rock forming a spout below which one could hold a pail for filling. Usually I could manage three-quarters of the galvanized pail, which was a fair weight even when it was empty, but with Gillespie to help me we were able to fill the pail to its brim and thus, with any luck, save ourselves a second trip for a while. We were walking gingerly out of step, which is the only way to carry a bucket of water without slopping it, when we met James on his way from the house to the river with a towel draped over his shoulders. Save on the coldest of winter days all our less private ablutions were performed in a pool below the level of the well rock and even if a skliff of ice had to be broken from the surface, that was preferable to the chore of carrying pails of water into the house, pouring into a basin, and slopping out again.

'You're up, James!' we chirruped. But it was a fact of which he was oblivious or else was unwilling to concede, because he strode past us without glancing our way.

Miracles had taken place in our short absence. The empty bottle and the glass had disappeared. The floor was spotless apart from the pale brown scorch-mark which was to resist several attacks with *mealtrach* and sand before it finally vanished. There was a bright fire crackling in the grate which was gleaming black again. Not for the last time I marvelled how a woman can in a flash create tidiness out of chaos. Mother was standing with the lid off the kettle waiting for us to arrive, and father was collecting the milking jug and pail in readiness for the job he hated

most in life. He was still unshaven but his old imperturb-
ability had returned.

'Be sure you strip her properly!' my mother said as she
lifted the pail from us. A cow will very quickly go dry if
her udder isn't completely emptied at each milking.

'Do I ever do otherwise?'

'When did you milk her last?'

But the tone of each was bantering, and it was reassur-
ingly clear that life was getting back to normal. Or as
normal as it could be with three extra people for breakfast.

'And to think that the wedding has still to come!' my
father muttered as he went out.

The wedding still to come! I hadn't thought that one
out.

'What does he mean, mother?'

'James's wedding, of course. That was only the *reiteach*
last night . . . the preparation for the wedding. James and
Mary are getting married next Friday.'

'Friday. When we're in school?'

'We're going to see about that. You and Gillespie sit at
the table there with the wee ones, and I'll give you your
brose when the kettle boils. I want you out of the way
quickly so that I can get on with feeding your father and
James.'

There were a whole lot of questions I wanted to ask, but
we were interrupted by James who came back in from the
burn looking slightly fresher but still tight-lipped. My
mother smiled at him and took the towel.

'Sit down on the bench there James. I'll get you a cup of
tea till the breakfast's ready. And don't worry. He didn't
mean what he said. You won't make a lou – er – rotten
husband for Mary, and he knows it fine. If only you hadn't
let that cigarette burn the floor; he's terrified of fire
since . . .' She glanced in my direction and stopped short.

'He sounded to me as if he meant every bloody word of
it – especially the bit about five years in the army doing
me good. It wasn't my fault that I was too young when the

war ended. And I wasn't tupping women in the haystacks when he was in the trenches . . .'

'James! I won't have that language in front of the children. Sit down!'

'Tupping!' said my brother rapping his spoon on the table.

'See what I told you. He'll come out with that when Murdo Mor's in the house.' Murdo Mor was a kirk elder and very pernickety in his language as in his manner. James sat down and guiltily lit a cigarette, taking exaggerated care to put the spent match in the ash pan.

Father came back from the byre in due course, beaming with success and with the milk pail three quarters full. Daisy had obviously been so glad to get rid of her burden that she had refrained from lashing out at the pail at the last moment. He used to claim that she deliberately lulled him into a sense of security by chomping at her cud right up till the moment when the pail was full and then, when he was off his guard, she would either kick the pail over or stick her foot in it. He would never concede that the beast might possibly be getting bored with his amateur slowness.

Gillespie's father arrived to collect his children before breakfast was over, and he sat with a cup of tea reminiscing over the highlights of the *reiteach* and discussing the plans for the day of the wedding. It was his idea, I think, that the minister's widow should be approached to negotiate with Miss Dalbeith in the forlorn hope that the latter might be persuaded to give the school a day off on the day of the wedding – even if it meant having to invite her to the celebrations herself. She wouldn't last long, Gillespie's father thought, without a word of Gaelic in her head.

The idea worked. Miss Dalbeith agreed to close the school for the day – on condition that the pupils put in a full day's attendance on the Saturday. It was a mean and grudging concession in view of the fact that, weary or otherwise, parents would have to be early afoot – overhung or otherwise – to get their offspring to school for ten.

97

She declined her invitation with unwonted grace and, to everybody's surprise, announced that she would like to donate a present to the bride and groom. The surprise was compounded when the present was unveiled to reveal an original oil painting by herself – an impressionistic canvas portraying the hoary old legend of the Viking invasion of the Scarista beach in which the horned Norsemen, armed to the teeth with assegais and double-barrelled shotguns resembled, unmistakably, kenspeckle local worthies – the Black Shepherd, Murdo Mor and our gentle and much revered veteran of Mafeking and Mons.

Inevitably, Gillespie and I both independently let slip that we had been to the *reiteach*, and the reactions of our parents had been exactly the same. We were accused of telling lies and concocting fairy tales from snippets that we had overheard – and that was that. Even had we persisted there was a powerful witness against us in James, who would have sworn in a court of law that we were safe in our beds; so we didn't even have to be on our guard against slips of the tongue any more. In any case the week ahead was full to overflowing. Miss Dalbeith saw to it that the euphoria which was gripping the village did not infect the schoolroom, but in the evenings we were allowed to savour the excitement of the preparations which seemed to involve everybody, whether or not they were related to either Mary or James. I found my every moment taken up with chores even more tedious than usual and whenever I protested I was bribed with promises of being 'allowed to go to the wedding for a while'. It was long afterwards that it dawned on me that even the bribes were hollow: I would have had to be allowed to the party anyway because there wasn't a willing 'looker-after' available within the confines of six parishes!

One of the routines I had always minded least was feeding the hens. Our stock had risen to fourteen and two haughty and argumentative cockerels. The hens and one of the cockerels were White Leghorns, and the odd one out was the newcomer to the fold – a hefty Rhode Island

Red cock with a stride like a Guardsman and a crimson serrated comb which he wore like a royal hat. 'Joshua' was the name I had given him because, presumably, the name had caught my fancy during one of my Grandfather's Bible readings, and the rival Joshua was on the point of demolishing was just plain 'Doodle-doodle'. I was on excellent terms with the white hens, each of whom I knew personally by some name or other, and because I fed them so often they were all friendly with me; some of the older ones would even squat down when they saw me coming and allow me to tuck their heads under their wings and rock them till they went to sleep. They were part of my education too since it was with them that I had learnt to count up to fifteen – and then sixteen – long before Miss Dalbeith had got round to producing her multi-coloured abacus.

And so, on the Wednesday before the wedding, I only had to count twice to know that my brood had mysteriously shrunk to thirteen. Doodle-doodle was gone and so were two senior White Leghorns called Cailleach and Mairon. It was on the cards that Cailleach and Mairon had gone broody and taken themselves off to nest in some patch of bracken whence they might emerge in three weeks – each with a brood of a dozen fluffy chicks in tow. But it wasn't a very satisfactory explanation. It wasn't the right time of the year. And, most certainly, no such urge would overcome Doodle-doodle.

I ranged the croft banging my tin basin and chook-chooking at the top of my voice, but nothing happened and I was on the point of giving up when I heard an answering echo from the direction of the neighbouring croft. It was Gillespie, on the same mission of mercy as myself. It came out that he was three hens light too – or, to be more precise in his case two cockerels and a hen. We gave up after a while and decided that there was nothing for it but to report to our parents and face up to the blame which would, inevitably, be laid at our door. But, on the contrary! My mother showed no concern whatsoever. Nor

99

would she volunteer any theory or explanation. Instead she switched me on to filling those interminable water pails, and after that I was to go and help my father at the byre. She herself was getting ready to go out for the evening, and would I please stop asking questions and do what I was told? And no, I couldn't go with her. And, for the last time, would I take myself off to help my father? And would I kindly take my brother with me from beneath her feet?

My father was behind the byre wrestling with a long bamboo fishing rod to the end of which he was tying a large white pillow case. He was in expansive form unlike my mother who had been unusually keyed up. He was, he explained, making a flag, and if we would just be patient we could help him fix it to the chimney stack when he was finished. And mother? Why, she was at the Hen Wedding and wouldn't be home till late. A Hen Wedding sounded a distinctly peculiar affair considering that the hens seemed, hitherto, to have conducted their marital cavortings without formalities of that order; but he was so engrossed with his flag that it was manifestly pointless to press him for further explanations. In the morning, he assured us, all would be revealed. In the meantime, the dark was fast coming on and would we please carry the ladder down to the end of the house. We did. And we watched, spellbound, as he climbed carefully to the top of the iron chimney stack and, using yard upon yard of coir rope left over from the corn-stacking, strapped the bamboo fishing rod to the chimney. When he was satisfied that it was secure he reversed down and removed the ladder. He stood with his head tilted back and a smile on his face. 'Look at that boys,' he said with pride, 'there won't be another flag like that in the village!' He was right. Just as he spoke a puff of wind blew into the mouth of the cotton pillow case which he had forgotten to stitch closed, and it swelled out into a big white sausage which might have been perhaps more aptly described as a 'wind sock' had there been aeroplanes around at the time. 'No,' he repeated, this time slightly ruefully I thought, 'there won't be one like it in the village right enough!' He reached for his pipe. 'I just hope', he said to himself more than to us, 'I just hope the wind doesn't get up or the chimney will be away!'

But the wind didn't get up, and when I looked out in the morning not only was our flag flying bravely, if slightly obesely, but there were flags flying above or beside every house in the village. Most of them were white pillow-slips like ours, but one or two were pink and, wonder of wonders, above the school there flew a Union Jack.

It was a long day. James and Mary and the best man and Mary's sister had set off for Stornoway in two hired cars. It was an extravagance which would not, normally, have been contemplated, but our own church was vacant and the village hadn't yet organized itself sufficiently to set in motion the complicated machinery for finding and inviting a new minister. It was a blessing in disguise, according to James's best man; by getting married in Stornoway – fifty miles away – they were spared the danger of the minister accepting an invitation to the festivities. 'Clergymen are fine for marriages, but bloody wet blankets at weddings', was the way he put it.

Fifty miles over our rutted roads represented a two-and-a-half-hour journey then, so – allowing for a marriage service with all the Presbyterian trimmings and admonitions and insurances against every possible eventuality of this life and the life to come, and a couple of hours for a meal in a hotel – the earliest that the villagers could expect the newly-weds back for the celebrations was six o'clock. And even at that there was the danger that daylight might be beginning to fade and that people might be deprived of the chance to cheer the bridal car back home. My brother and I were scrubbed and spruced by four o'clock and forbidden to put our noses outside the door till we had our parents' say so. They themselves had just begun to get dressed when one of 'the bloods' came racing to the gate on his bicycle and shouted that the car had been seen coming into Tarbert where the couple had stopped for afternoon tea; this meant it would be arriving in the village in about an hour's time.

By five o'clock every family in the village stood in a finely arrayed knot at its own gate, and everybody, from the youngest toddler to the oldest Granny had a handkerchief or a pillow-case or a coloured scarf to wave – and Grannies and Grandfathers and sundry other relatives had descended on the village from all over the island. My own father's parents – Big Granny and Little Grandfather – had made one of their few trips south, but they had elected to stay with Great Aunt Rachel who had room to spare and, if truth be told, a large feather bed which suited Big Granny better than anything we had to offer. Not for all the tea in China would she have submitted herself to a made-up bed on St Clement's bench.

It was a beautiful evening with a late autumn brittleness in the air. It is a mainland presumption that autumn is a season of mellow browns and golds, with the earth giving back of the warmth it collected in summer. In the treeless islands it is different. For sure, here and there an intrusion of bracken may give a russet blush to a fallow sward, and a patch of ripened corn may reflect a glimpse of Keatsian sun; but the Hebridean autumn is the beginning of winter rather than the end of summer, and the mountains appear to be beginning to age and the sea to feel heavy. And there is a quality of silence as if the Heavens were drawing their breath for the storms. Set against such a background that childhood scene remains imprinted on the mind; and what could only have been a sprinkling of people, a little more colourfully attired than usual, against a vast landscape, has come to assume Lowrian proportions in a sprained memory. But the bagpipe was there, for certain, playing tirelessly and endlessly, and at its sweetest as it always is in the evening distance, whiling away the time as we waited for the car to crest the top of Back of Scarista Hill.

Then – horror! Three gates away I caught sight of

102

Kenneth Macleod squinting along the sights of a double barrelled shotgun!

I knew that Kenneth had been a suitor for Mary's hand, and that he had been alternately teased and consoled by people like my own mother when Mary had plumped for James. And here he was now, obviously out for revenge. I screamed at my father and tugged at his jacket, startling the living daylights out of him. He snatched me up thinking that some sudden hurt had come to me, and then burst out laughing when he heard my garbled fears. He explained that it was Kenneth's allocated duty, as the only owner of a shotgun, to fire a saluting volley over the car — and not at it — to welcome the married couple back; the Royal Navy, he added, did the same sort of thing on the occasion of the King's birthday but, so far, not one salvo had gone near the person of His Majesty. I felt slightly foolish, but relieved withal! In a few moments a shout went up as the car came over the hill, and people began to clap and cheer, and Kenneth began to shoot like a man in the front line.

In the normal course of events the wedding party – unlike the *reiteach* which was always in the bride's home – would have been in the couple's new house but, since James didn't have a croft of his own, he and Mary were going to live with his parents till either he got a croft or else decided to go back to sea. For the time being he was earning a living, like quite a few of the men in the district, working on the new road. It was in his parents' house that the Hen Wedding had been held the previous evening, and it was thither that the whole population of the village was wending its way now – not hurrying, so as to give the host and hostess a chance to spruce themselves up after their long day. A day which, according to all speculation was going to stretch well beyond the statutory twenty-four hours!

We were about the last to arrive and, at first, I thought we were never going to get in. The *reiteach* had been thronged, but this was mobbed with people from all the villages around. Individual invitations as such were

103

unheard of then, and anybody who knew the bride or groom at all just arrived and was welcome; in fact, not to attend a wedding would have been insulting, and even people who were comparative strangers to the families made a point of making a token appearance with a gift. By the time we arrived the room was already steaming hot and throbbing with people and, for a while, it looked as if all I would ever see of the proceedings was yet another forest of legs. But somebody shouted 'Give the little ones a chance!' and we were lifted on to window sills, the sideboard and even broad shoulders.

From my particular vantage point I could see that several tables had been pushed together to form a large T-shape which occupied most of the room, and James and Mary – the one looking as flushed and self-conscious as the other – were already sitting in the middle of what would now be called the 'top table'. Glasses of all shapes and sizes were being handed around, and I was given a tumbler of red fizzy stuff which I had never seen before in my life. I scoffed it off, and the tumbler was promptly replenished. I was half way through that one when I noticed that nobody else was touching his, and I stopped with a guilty start. Murdo Mor, Kirk Elder and all as he was, was climbing on to a chair with a brimming glass of whisky in his hand. He was, as he said himself, 'going to make a speech to the bride and groom', whether people wanted to hear him or not. I didn't hear him, except that I was conscious of the fact that he kept repeating the phrase 'man and wife' and every time he said it people roared approval as if he had invented a sentence of stunning originality. My attention was focused elsewhere.

On the far side of the room I could see a long table, made up of two barn doors laid end to end on top of barrels, its whole length covered with the corpses of several dozen very naked and very cooked hens. It didn't require much imagination to jalouse that, on their backs with their legs raised heavenwards like the rest, there were two White Leghorns called Cailleach and Mairon and a cockerel called Doodle-doodle.

I felt sick.

'Where did all the hens come from?' I hissed to my father.

'Ssh!'

'Who cooked all the hens?' I insisted, not caring whether I was interrupting Murdo Mor or not.

'Your mother and the women, of course! What do you think the Hen Wedding was for last night? Will you shut up now!'

I shut up.

It was the first genuine act of betrayal that I was ever aware of. Conspiring in an act as opprobrious as hame-sucken, my own father or mother, or both, had stolen into the byre while I and the hens were all innocently asleep, and thrown the necks of three of my senior charges and plucked them and gralloched them and boiled them without as much as leaving a tell-tale feather! I felt my gorge rising, and would probably have sicked up my fizzy drink if there hadn't been, at that point, an explosion of applause as Murdo Mor finished speaking, and the room cascaded into a Gaelic song. When it was finished, the first thirty or so guests – the closest relatives – were called to the first sitting while the rest embarked on an orgy of whisky and song.

'Look!' said Gillespie who had sidled over beside me.

I followed his finger, and there, over in a corner balanced on what looked suspiciously like a pee-tub, was the school blackboard. But instead of being covered in the usual hieroglyphics it was loaded with trifles, and jellies and puddings for which I didn't have a name.

'They'll be all gone before they reach us,' said Gillespie.

But we needn't have worried. At the only village wedding which I ever attended, the ones who were best looked after were the very young and the very old.

Poor James and Mary. They sat at the head of that table through seven sittings that I saw, and they were still there, laughing and smiling when I was wakened at four o'clock in the morning to be carried, uncomplainingly home. It was a brilliant silver night, and the moon had fattened out since the *reiteach*. The flags were sleeping against their poles. I could hear the grumbling of the waves on the beach, which one never noticed during the day, and through it, receding in the distance I could hear the chorus of 'Horo my nut-brown maiden' being sung for the umpteenth time.

As I was pushed in between the blankets I had a passing thought that weddings were better things by far than Hogmanays, but, as I slid into peacefulness it never once crossed my mind that my feeling of well-being might be due in no small measure to two large helpings of White Leghorn hen.

Chapter Eleven

Birth, marriage, and death are the syntax of a community. Even in amorphous urban smothers their incidence draws together, sometimes for a rare occasion in a lifetime, people of forgotten bond – be it kinship or friendship or even childhood acquaintance – who have long since ceased to consort habitually, and, for a brief duration they become a community within the anonymity. But the effect of the wedding of James and Mary on us was an enduring, cementing one. Our eight crofter families had been drawn from different airts, and even if, perhaps, some of the men had met or known each other before, their wives had not; and since the village was strung out over three miles, and the women because of infant families were relatively housebound, they had remained distant neighbours and acquaintances without developing close friendships. But the *reiteach*, the Hen Wedding and the wedding itself had changed all that. The whole population had been thrown together in a prolonged proximity of celebration and co-operation, and the foundations of an identifiable community were laid down.

The festivities dragged on for a week, in much the same way as a Scottish Hogmanay tends to prolong itself into the New Year's maturity. And for the same reasons. It wasn't possible for the entire circle of friends and acquaintances to get together on the one night without bringing the economy of the island, such as it was, to a total standstill, to say nothing of letting cattle beasts and bedridden ancestors starve. There was nothing else on the scale of the wedding night itself, but James's parents were forced to keep open house for days, and a stocked larder and a supply of whisky against the arrival of friends and relations with gifts and thirsts.

The brand new couple went off to Glasgow for a week's honeymoon the day after their wedding, and as far as I could make out they just rose straight from the wedding table after the fourteenth or fifteenth sitting, changed into fresh clothes, and set off by yet another hired car to catch the *Lochmor* – our thrice-weekly ferry-boat to the mainland – at Rodel. That created a small stir. There were the inevitable derisory comments among the young men about James's lack of initiative, and how they would have gone about matters had they been in the bridegroom's place: they certainly wouldn't have spent the night sitting upright at the head of a table; it wouldn't have been the Minch they'd have been bouncing on next morning; and it wouldn't have been the *Lochmor* they'd have been aboard. From the fact that my mother kept 'tut-tutting' and shushing them up I guessed that some of their remarks were worth remembering for later understanding. The older folk thought a honeymoon an alien idea, to say nothing of an expensive one, and Great Aunt Rachel was heard to declare that the morning after her wedding she had been up to milk the minister's cow at seven o'clock as usual. Despite her undoubtedly strong personality and her forthright views, Great Aunt Rachel firmly believed that a woman's place was in the home, and one step behind her husband. She always addressed her husband as 'Man', in public at least, and he always addressed her as 'Woman', and if she had lived to see the dawn of the feminist movement the only thing she'd have thrown away would have been Germaine Greer.

We younger ones were brought firmly down to earth by having to go to school on Saturday – the morning after the wedding. Miss Dalbeith rattled her way through the attendance register as usual and every single name that was called responded with the usual 'Present, Miss', one of the first

108

English phrases hammered into every new recruit. One quick look round would have been enough to inform her whether anybody was missing or not, but that was her way of it. And in the event of somebody not being present, the person sitting next to him or her was expected to jump up and say 'Absent, Miss'. It may have been her way of ensuring that we learnt at least three English words. And we did. Because she went through the process first thing every morning and, again, first thing after the dinner break. God help the person who was declared 'Absent, Miss' at two o'clock; it was inconceivable that anybody should be overcome by ill health in the middle of the day.

We didn't do too much work that day – either because she regretted having to be on duty herself on a Saturday when she could have been indulging in her winter pastime of hillwalking, or, more likely, because her blackboard was still in James's father's house presumably not yet cleared of the remains of jellies and trifles. The morning passed wearily; the mid-morning break felt much longer than usual even though we all had tit-bits of information to exchange about the wedding, and the two oldest boys entertained us with some salacious bits of information anent what brides and grooms got up to once the festivities were over. It was that morning that I heard for the first time of a most mysterious piece of apparel called a 'French Leather', and, a year or two later it became, for reasons which I cannot for the life of me disentangle, confused with the word 'chamois'. In the mind. Not, fortunately, in any remote reality.

An uncomfortable shuffling of feet began to develop in the classroom as our stomachs, in the absence of anything resembling a clock or a watch, told us that it must be one o'clock and time for lunch. But nobody dared raise the question with Miss Dalbeith, and she, certainly, would not deign to inform us of her intentions. It felt like an eternity till she announced that it was now two o'clock, and that she would call the afternoon register and dismiss the school. She had made her point. She had observed the letter of the law and registered the two attendances that the School

Board expected of her, and should her books be examined by some officious minion of the Department of Education at some future date, they would show, in all truthfulness, that the 'scholars' of Scarista School had clocked in ten times that week! As far as we were concerned, the best of the weekend still lay ahead and she had forgotten to give us any homework. Even now I cannot credit her with the possibility that she might have refrained from doing so out of any spirit of goodwill.

There is nothing stranger than the things which stick in one's mind except the things which escape it. It is not, perhaps, surprising that I remember the wedding in vivid detail because it was, by any standards, a momentous landmark not only in my own small life but in the early life of the new village. Nor is it surprising that I remember Miss Dalbeith in such detail that if I were to meet her on Carter's Bar or in Wheeler's in Old Compton Street – which Heaven forfend – I would recognize her immediately and tremble. But curiously I cannot remember the first Christmas in the village, perhaps because it wasn't celebrated or accepted as a Presbyterian festival, nor, even more curiously, can I remember the first New Year, which was. I cannot remember ever going to Sunday School although I have, in front of me, an elaborate certificate signed by the minister's French widow crediting me not only with 'Regular attendance' but also with 'Good conduct', signed Adèle Kerr. I do, however, remember the day of Wee Barabel's funeral although I don't suppose there are many others who do, for the poor soul just slipped away in a ripeness of years that even she could not enumerate.

In addition to my Sunday School Certificate, I have also in my possession a silver medal and a copy of the *Concise Oxford Dictionary*, engraved and inscribed respectively, to testify that I had seven consecutive years of perfect attendance at school up to the time that I graduated, at the age of thirteen, to the delinquencies of what was then honourably called Junior Secondary School. I set out recently to discover why, if I was such a little masochist, I didn't have *eight* years of perfect attendance which would have been the maximum possible in Primary School. It wasn't difficult to check because I have also, by means which matter not, the official Record of the 229 pupils who attended our particular brand of Public School from the day it opened on the 24th of July, 1893, till the day it closed forever, sixty years later, in 1953. And I discovered that all my defections took place in the reign of Miss Dalbeith, which proves that my masochism wasn't so devout after all. The last of these must have been at the end of winter or in very early spring because there was snow on the ground and I had acquired enough English to know what was going on.

I shouldn't have gone to school at all. I had wakened up with a miserable chesty cold, and my mother wanted me to stay in bed with a wadding of red flannelette soaked in Sloane's Liniment which was the panacea of the age – probably because it was heavily advertised in the *Christian Herald* under the photograph of a venerably bearded gentleman who could be taken to represent Mr Sloane or the Lord, depending on one's imagination and credulity. But I would have none of it, because I knew from my own experience, and that of others, that if I missed a couple of days of school Miss Dalbeith would leather me on two counts – firstly for being absent at all, and secondly for daring to contract a cold in flagrant breach of her credo that gaping windows and draughts of snell Atlantic air were antidotal to everything from sneezles to measles. To be absent for a month was acceptable, because it might presage the onset of T.B. which was still the scourge of our society, and, in any case, a prolonged absence necessitated a certificate from the doctor or the nurse and not even Miss Dalbeith would fly in the face of one of those.

With hindsight and the mellowing of the years it is becoming more possible to concede that much of Miss Dalbeith's preoccupation with fresh air and hygiene may have stemmed from a deep-rooted fear. Our people had come to accept tuberculosis (or consumption as it was more commonly called) as one of the awesome hazards of life in much

111

the same way, I suppose, as people in parts of India or Africa accepted leprosy as endemic or even maledictory. To end up in the sanatorium' was a terrible threat to hang over one person out of every three, but that was only a statistical rationalization of the situation. In the reality it was worse. When tuberculosis struck a family, living in the smoky, clammy, confines of an airless thatched house, it wasn't just the one member it claimed – over the years it could creep its insidious way through the family, picking off its victims in completely unpredictable order. It was a fearsome social blight, and the efforts to combat it were pathetic. In some areas of the island, a patient fortunate enough to be released from the sanatorium after treatment was often lodged in a shack away from the rest of the family and was condemned to spend years, if not the rest of his life, in virtual isolation. By the same token, families with an afflicted member would find their homes shunned by neighbours fearful of infection. Nobody could have foreseen then that, even within the lifetimes of those already middle-aged, the whole plague was to be eradicated from the British scene almost overnight. And only those of us who remember the magnificently orchestrated campaign of 1952 can appreciate the miracle of the erasure of the most dreaded definition of the word 'consumption'.

Our village was almost free of the disease by sheer virtue of the fact that most of the houses were new and, consequently, built to much higher standards of hygiene, even though interior plumbing was mostly not considered necessary; they were, after all, only meant to be temporary. But the shadow still hung over us, and it must have been even more menacing for somebody like Miss Dalbeith whose education would have made her more conscious of its danger; besides she was, manifestly, a fitness fanatic anyway. Probably the very idea of being cooped up for eight hours a day in the same room as thirteen potential carriers of disease was enough to give her nightmares, and would explain why, whenever she found the slightest excuse, she conducted classes out-doors. Hebridean weather didn't always abet her and, for her own sake presumably rather than for ours, she didn't usually take us out on days as inclement as that day of Wee Barabel's funeral. But that day, out we were sent – with instructions to wipe the seats dry of snow before we sat down!

I don't know how long we had been outside before my father, muffled to his chin, came trudging along the road on his way to the cemetery. I can see him still – stopping dead in his tracks at the playground wall with disbelief writ large over what one could see of his face. 'Miss Dalbeith!' he called, with an unusual edge to his voice, and without a trace of 'please' or 'excuse me'. We couldn't hear what he said to her when she went over to the wall but, whatever it was, she seemed to take it in amiable part; and she was still smiling as she came back to us and began to give one or other of the pupils some instructions till my father had turned the corner on the way to the churchyard. She turned to me then and the ice in her voice was as chill as the snow on the ground.

'Your father says you shouldn't be outside in the cold. Come inside and I'll give you something to warm you up!'

I understood the words, although I didn't appreciate what she meant. But the oldest boy present did. And, doubtless fortified by the knowledge that he was due to leave school forever at the end of term, he stood up and began to remonstrate on my behalf. Unfortunately, for him and for me, he suffered from an affliction which the late Patrick Campbell has since made respectable on television, and before he could get out the 'P-p-p-please . . .' of 'Please Miss . . .', he was ordered inside too.

I got four of the belt, and he got six of what was known as 'cross hands'. The latter was a method in which the back of one upward-facing hand was supported on the palm of the other, with the right and left being alternated on each command of 'Change over', so that the recipient of the punishment received the maximum amount of pain from the impact of leather on flesh, and the donor achieved the max-

113

imum satisfaction. We were then ordered back outside with the assurance Nobody will tell me how to run my school!'

Since in our neck of the woods anything remotely connected with the mills of God ground more slowly than elsewhere, it must have been quite a while before the men returned from the burial ground. This time they were in a group. Six of them had fought the Kaiser, and one had fought Kruger as well. And even those who hadn't fought at all had heard of the Geneva Convention. They all stopped at the playground wall and leant over it in a line, looking for all the world like an unarmed firing squad; and it was obvious to the least bilingual of us that Miss Dalbeith was not being treated to Hebridean banalities about the weather. The long and the short of it was that she dismissed school for the day, and went inside and marked us all *absent*.

Our house was, at that time, the nearest occupied house of the new village to the school, and the men all solemnly turned into our gateway and into the house where my mother had already laid out the customary spread of scones and oatcakes and crowdie and cream, knowing that some of those who had furthest to walk would call in on their way home from the funeral. But she couldn't possibly have expected the whole crowd. It must have been clear to her that there was something afoot and, using my cold as a pretext, she bundled me off to bed where I promptly propped myself up with my ear against the partition. The discussion was, as I had suspected it would be, about Miss Dalbeith, and I revelled in the sentiments expressed with liberal sprinklings of words that had been invented at Vimy Ridge or Mons or Wipers (as it was called) in flagrant disobedience of the third commandment that the Lord had given to Moses on Mount Sinai.

But soon the voices began to blur, coming back to me only now and again as if from a great distance and in a great confusion. And I slipped into an oblivion out of which I didn't emerge till my mother's gentle coaxing brought me back to a hazy consciousness sometime during the next morning. Apparently the nurse had been called during the night and had diagnosed measles, and I was told that the landlord had kindly arranged to lend his car and his chauffeur so that I could be evacuated north to my grandfather's in the hope that my brother and sundry others would not be contaminated. It didn't cross my mind to wonder how the landlord, who, except for a few weeks of the shooting season, spent all of his time in his native Huddersfield, could have been made privy to my incapacity, far less why he should have responded so helpfully and so uncharacteristically. It didn't matter. It was thrilling to be going for a ride in his car with his chauffeur – a local man who would have been popular anyway even if he hadn't made free with his master's car in the service of the community from the time that the latter boarded the ferry to the mainland till he came back again.

I didn't have measles. I had scarlet fever followed by various complications which resulted in a long, long stay with my grandparents. And by the time I returned to the village and to school – glory be! – Miss Dalbeith had disappeared. She had been, in the jargon of the Civil Service, *transferred* to a certain remote island in the Inner Hebrides which is now – and I make no comment – a Nature Reserve. In her place had come the woman with whom I was to achieve my seven years of 'perfect attendance'. She had a tawse – oh yes, that was, till very recently, part of the impedimenta of the Scottish school teacher – but she used it sparingly and wisely, and the leather was soft. Which was why one of the wits who read English magazines dubbed it her chastity belt.

I wish I could remember more about the circumstances surrounding the arrival of the new teacher whose name is still revered by all who sat under her, but, at the same time, the village took another step forward in its development.

'The Duchess' opened a shop.

'The Duchess' was Molly's mother who had shared the schoolhouse with us during the year of the dandelions. It was only recently that I discovered that she had, somewhat tortuously, inherited the nickname either because her father had been in the service of a duke, or else, according to other sources, his father had been rather ruthless in the acquisition of land during some of the earlier land troubles. I had always thought that the name was a result of that certain air of imperiousness which, seemingly, one has to assume when one becomes head of a precarious trading enterprise, be it the British Steel Corporation or the village shop. And certainly, if the Duchess hadn't already had a slight 'cut-above-the-rest kind of mien, she would have had to acquire it on being thrust into a situation of charging her neighbours money for things like bread and tea which she had been in the custom of serving them free at her own fireside. And to survive in business at all, she had to learn where to draw the line in the matter of 'tick' in a community which had to depend, to a certain extent, on credit facilities in between the sale of one tweed and another on the doubtful markets of the early thirties, or between the equally unpredictable incomes from the sales of heifers or tups. She was also quickly forced to learn that she must handle the business alone and unaided; her husband, the Boer War veteran, had one of the biggest hearts I've ever come across in any man, and, given an hour unsupervised, he would have given away the entire contents of the shop for free.

I remember the Duchess with affection for many reasons, but for two in particular. It became one of my more pleasant chores to walk, or run, the two miles to her shop for messages (a much nicer word than the English 'shopping') and occasionally I would be rewarded with a halfpenny or a penny for myself. On a 'halfpenny day' I would invest in Toffee Cow which had that picture of the Highland cow on the wrapper – so named I suspect because it enshrined the sweetness of temperament and the toughness of character of that famous breed of cattle. Apart from the odd occasion, like the night of James's *reiteach*, I hadn't had great experience of Toffee Cow but, with my own halfpennies, I began to develop an inordinate taste for it. It was difficult to get one's teeth into a hunk of it, and, once in, it was even more difficult to separate upper and lower jaws with the result that one could only surrender to a delicious period of succulent lock-jaw. That was a good thing when the value of a sweet was judged by its lasting quality.

Recently I came across what used to be a halfpenny bar of Toffee Cow in my local tobacco shop and, grudgingly, I invested eight pence in it for old times' sake. But, alas and alack, teeth ain't what they used to be, and I decided not to bite too hard on an old memory!

On a 'penny day' the option was much more sophisticated. The Duchess did a good line in square, creamy, toffees which she sold at a dozen for a penny, and although financial stringency ensured that they could never do my teeth or my waistline much harm, they certainly damaged my arithmetic because I grew up to believe that a dozen was thirteen.

'To him that hath shall be given', is one of the truisms of Holy Writ, and, by virtue of having the only shop, the Duchess was, in due course, allocated the sub-post-office, and, by virtue of having the sub-post-office she was later still given the Telephone Exchange of which she herself was the sole operator. It wasn't a very onerous duty because there was only one other telephone in the village in those days, and that was the one in the landlord's house which had to be routed through the Duchess. Had she happened to be curious, she could have kept check on all the movements of the landlord and his family when they were in residence, and kept the village informed on whether he or his gamekeeper was liable to be in the vicinity of the salmon river on a given night. I was too young to take an interest in the catching of salmon then, but I enjoyed the taste of it fine . . .

It was with the Duchess that I listened on a telephone for the first time. I was in the shop when the bell tinkled and she 'shushed' me and gently picked up the receiver. She listened for a few moments and then thrust the instrument into my hand with signals not to make a noise. The tinny, English conversation didn't mean very much to me because, although I had mastered the first principles of the language, I found a Huddersfield accent hard to understand. But it was fascinating listening to the metallic disembodied voices. When the conversation was over I signalled to her and she replaced the telephone on its hook, assuring me that the speakers were just engineers testing the line and that there was no law against listening to them. Later I was to wonder how, in those pre-liberation days, one of the engineers came to be a female, just as, at the time, I wondered what kind of new English word 'dahling' was.

The Duchess was a very well-informed person, probably because she also retailed the first newspapers to come directly to the village. For the first while we had been dependent for such newspapers as we saw on those sent second-hand by friends, or on the *Weekly Scotsman* which my father got from Edinburgh by post. But now we were getting into the mainstream and, via the Duchess, we were getting the daily papers in pairs two days after publication. Our ex-servicemen were avid readers of them because there were rumblings of wars in places like Russia and Japan and Spain. And we, of the younger generation, tottering into literacy, were becoming members of the army of the followers of Rupert Bear. Yes! Lord Beaverbrook was seeking to further his fortunes in Scaristavore. But he reckoned without the Duchess.

The *Daily Express* expansion plans were very simple, and based on a system of 'sale or return'. But, to save the cumbersome business of parcellage and postage it was sufficient for the retailer to cut out the serial number on the front page of the unsold copies of the paper, and send the serial clippings back to Glasgow once a week, and be credited with X numbers of papers unsold. The rules said 'unsold', not 'unread', and the villagers, co-operative by nature, each took a copy of the *Daily Express* and, in due course, returned the serial number to the shop. The only person who could not be expected to co-operate was the minister's widow whose allegiance to one Lord inhibited her from defrauding another. Fleet Street must have rated our village low on the literacy charts. But it wasn't so. And it was becoming less so as the new teacher got into her stride.

I am sometimes asked why a village which started off with such promise and such optimism should have failed to burgeon and thrive and grow as it should have done. And I have to answer that one reason was the new teacher, Miss Martin. She commanded a deep loyalty, and, in the raggle-taggle clutch of 'scholars', devoid of morale, left behind by her predecessor, she instilled an extraordinary team spirit. Without realizing the consequences, she infused in all of us, to some degree or other, a passion for education, and education meant advancement, and advancement meant going away. That decreed that virtually all of the new generation, the ones who should have been the second growth of the village, left not only the village but the island. It wasn't, of course, an isolated instance of the problem, but it was acute in its microcosm in our little patch of the Highlands.

Miss Martin was a very devout woman, belonging to what is often thought of as one of the narrower and more fundamental sects of the Presbyterian Church. She was a good woman, which is sometimes a better thing to be than overly devout, but she was not above bending the rules, and bending them in such a way that those who made and administered the rules never even suspected. One of the first of her Herculean labours was to convince the Authorities in Inverness that she could raise the new village school out of the doldrums in which Miss Dalbeith had left it. And here, she was ably abetted by the Duchess and her telephone.

As soon as Inverness decided to send one of His Majesty's Inspectors of Schools on a 'surprise' tour of his constituency, a note would reach our teacher telling her that he had boarded a certain train, and by the time he had reached Kyle of Lochalsh to cross the Minch Miss Martin had been briefed on every school that he had visited, and on the questions he had asked in each one of them. The result was that, by the time he reached us, we were being prompted *not* to give the right answer before the Inspector had finished asking a question, lest we give the show away, and,

119

here and there, ever so discreetly, a wrong answer would be planted lest we should all appear to be pedigree Mensa. Thus, rapidly, our teacher put herself into a position of strength whereby she could obtain from H.Q., without query, everything extra that she needed in the way of educational aids and equipment before settling down to the serious business of training us for the County Bursary Examinations which, by the age of eleven or twelve, would be our passports to our futures. And her God must have forgiven her her little manipulations of destiny, as He must also have forgiven the Duchess for any 'accidental taps' of the phone.

I have beside me a copy of an entry made by an Inspector in the School Log after one such 'surprise' visit. It reads thus:

Not only are the students in this school extremely versed in the three R's as we call them nowadays, but they have answered all my questions with self-confidence and a rare sense of humour. I may, perhaps, indulge myself to the extent of quoting one example of this humour, since it is a quality hitherto unassociated with this particular school. When I asked one boy a question which I intended as a jest – i.e. 'What is better than one plate of porridge?' he hesitated for a moment only, and then replied with a beguiling twinkle, 'Two plates of porridge, sir.' I have given the school a half day's holiday.

I was to get to know that Inspector well in later years when he was a venerable and highly honoured member of the Education Establishment. I hadn't seen that report of his then. Even if I had, I wouldn't perhaps have spoilt things by confessing to him that my hesitation was due to stark terror at his sudden switch from the scheduled questioning, and that the twinkle, as he called it, was relief when the teacher, standing behind him, held up two of her fingers behind his head!

Chapter Twelve

Time as it is lived doesn't slide into neat compartments, least of all in the long memory. The diarist or the historian or the biographer may be forced to define his parameters and affix his tags of time and date, and by doing so achieve an accuracy which is a different thing altogether from the truth, just as the photographer, freezing his bit of landscape, can only hope to capture a view while letting the scenery escape. And so, even if I were of a mind to do so, I could not hope to catalogue the building of the village stone by stone, because it wasn't of stones alone that it was built, but of moments, of moods, of happenings that were sometimes long and sometimes short and frequently overlapping; most indefinably of all, it was built on tears and laughter.

The sudden death of Gillespie's young sister is only remembered because of a grown man sobbing as he came to the door in the night looking for a thing called help, which he couldn't define, and which couldn't, with all the warm will in the world, be given him except in tears and platitudes. I won't even recognize her if I meet her in a Great Beyond, and yet it had been a glimpse of her naked body while we were playing one day that had first flashed into my consciousness the difference between boys and girls, and dispelled forever the puzzlement of procreation without destroying the mystery. It would be senseless to put a date or time on such a legacy. But her death was a stitch in the tapestry of our community because her father, who had been the singer of the village, never sang a Gaelic song again.

But nothing else stopped. The clover still ripened before the corn, and the autumns still followed the summers. The years were just the times we lived in, and it is successive generations that have called them 'The Thirties' and given them labels like 'hungry' and 'angry' and the rest of it. We who lived in them hadn't learnt not to be optimistic. But slowly, and behind the rest of the country, the Depression was beginning to reach out to us. Two or three of the crofters had been able to take advantage of the Government's 'Grant and Loan' scheme, and move out of their temporary shacks into grand new stone houses with two spacious rooms downstairs, and two bedrooms and a closet upstairs and, wonder of wonders, a bathroom where, as one old man put it, he was 'expected to do inside the house things for which God had provided secluded corners in the fresh air'. Suddenly, however, the 'Grant and Loan' scheme was frozen, and only one bachelor crofter was able to continue with the building of his 'white house', as the new agricultural cottages were called, and it was a mystery to people how he was able to carry on when he couldn't possibly have had any more financial resources than the rest.

The *Daily Express* was full of stories of riots and marches in Glasgow, and pictures of people queueing up at soup kitchens in cities throughout the land. But it all seemed very remote and far away, and no more immediate to us than the potted history that was beginning to be fed to us in school. The disasters of strangers are always remote, even today when television and radio bring Bangladesh and Kampuchea into our living rooms, and as children we were only vaguely aware that there was a certain sombre quality creeping into the conversations and attitudes of our parents and friends.

We were all right. By now, Daisy's first calf which, in the homely and meaningless little tradition, had been given to me and left to me to name, was now in calf herself. Unlike her mother who was pure black, she was almost white with black patches, and, with great originality, I had christened her Spotty. I have never been able to puzzle out why our domestic animals were always given English names. The village was full of Rosies, and Pansies and Slippers and nobody seemed to find anything incongruous in a red, broad-shouldered Highland stirk, with a menacing mane flopping over his beady eyes, being called Brasso after a popular metal polish. Our own menagerie consisted of Daisy and Spotty, and a Rosy who was Spotty's half-sister; the sheepdog Fanny had been sired by Grandfather's Pharaoh; the Persian cat which came after Great Aunt Rachel's victim was called Tiger; the bottle-fed lamb, which grew into a hefty ewe and haunted the doorstep for years in search of tid-bits even when she had lambs of her own at foot, was called Betsy. Poor Betsy! She slipped on the ice and broke her leg one winter, and we ate her without a qualm.

I can only assume that the yen for English names for the beasts was merely because people revelled in the freedom of being able to call them what they chose, instead of being hamstrung by the immutable tradition which decreed that children had to be named, in strict rotation, after relatives from alternating sides of the parenthood even where, as often happened, that resulted in there being three Donalds in the one family, or two Johns, or a Mary Kate, a Mary Effie, and a Mary Jean. It was a tradition which led to absurd situations in cases where, for example, a John, called 'Big John' by virtue of being the first born, turned out to be a five foot nonentity, while his younger brother, Little John, grew into a six-footer with shoulders like a bull.

Anyway, the accouchement of Spotty was awaited with great excitement, because this was going to be the first calf that we could rear for sale. I remember it well, because I was allowed to sit up into the early morning to await her delivery. Being a first calf, one couldn't be certain how the mother would react, and, in any case, an extra pair of hands would come in useful to hold the lantern and help clean the little newcomer and lift him into the straw-lined cage that had been prepared for him. There was also the fact that I had slim hands and was already expert in turning lambs threatening a breech delivery. Although such a feat would be beyond my strength in the case of a calf so positioned, I could, at the very least, help ease his head through without damage to the mother's vulva if he happened to be one of those awkward ones with stumps of horns developed in the womb or had the umbilical cord wrapped round his neck. Crofter boys had to learn how to deal with such exigencies in those days when we had no access to vets.

I always felt very important on the rare occasions when, for some reason or other, I was allowed to sit up late alone with father. They were few and far between. Sometimes it was when a storm was blowing and he would keep watch in case a haystack threatened to blow away; occasionally if there was a serious illness in the village he would delay going to bed lest somebody come for assistance; once or twice a year it was to await a new calf. He was at his relaxed best then and always spoke to me as if I were an adult. He would explain an item from the newspaper, or he would discuss some aspect of village life; but, sooner or later, the subject would turn to my future, and, without undue hectoring or admonition, he would enlarge on the benefits of education and point out the many advantages I had over himself when he was my age and schooling was regarded as a frill on the edge of living. That he was well educated himself was thanks to his mother's influence (she had inherited a reverence for education from the clerics) and, later, as a result of his voracious reading. He always hinted that journalism would be a good career, and I suspect that that was what he would have liked to have done himself.

The only subject that he would not ever be drawn on was the one that I wanted most to hear about. The war. Neither with me nor with anybody else would he ever discuss it, and it was from others that I gleaned that he had been a sniper. He would never allow even a shot-gun in the house, and although he allowed me to borrow a neighbour's when

I grew older, he wouldn't let me take it into the house nor would he handle it himself. 'Your father had nine lives if ever a man had,' an old comrade of his once said to me, but he wouldn't enlarge on what he meant. And so that was all I ever got to know about that area of his life which most stirred my curiosity as an adventure loving boy.

Sometime before dawn, Spotty calved. The birth was straightforward and uncomplicated, but I'll never forget the look of bewildered disbelief on my father's face as he stared down at the limp and lifeless form lying in its gelatinous film. 'It's dead,' he said softly, automatically reaching for his pipe. 'God, that's all we needed.'

The deadly seriousness of his tone registered with me, but I didn't feel like querying it. I was too busy gritting back the tears as I automatically scraped some of the mucous off the calf's nose and held it out to Spotty to lick. I had been taught that a cow wouldn't let her milk flow until she had been allowed at least a token licking of her calf.

'Let's leave him on the dung heap till morning', my father said flatly, 'and make sure the dog doesn't get out.'

He sealed off the cord, and we carried the little black body out of the byre on the sack that we had laid over the gutter to receive him. We didn't speak again as we went into the house. Father paused to check on the fire before he blew out the lamp, and we went through to the bedroom and undressed in the dark. As I slipped in beside my brother I heard my mother stirring and whispering 'Male or female?'

'Male,' he replied, not bothering to lower his voice. 'Still-born.'

'Oh, no!' Again the extreme concern in the voice was noticeable, but I buried my head in the pillow and sobbed myself to sleep. I had come across stillborn lambs by the dozen. I had killed rabbits. I had drowned pups and kittens. But there was something new and awful about a big, sinewy, dead calf.

'John! Finlay! One of you! Come here quick! Both of you! Quick!'

125

I was still half asleep as I collided with my father in the bedroom door.

'What the hell's the matter?'

My father rarely used an expletive, but I think he thought my mother had had a seizure or been attacked by one of the cows as he looked at her leaning, gasping, against the doorpost with her hair uncoiled over her shoulders and the empty milk pail in her hand.

'The c-calf!' She spluttered. 'He's at the end of the house!'

By the grace of God there were no neighbours around as my father and I padded into the muddy, bitter morning in our shirt tails. Not that it mattered. If one were to believe the song that Gillespie's mother composed later, the whole village was out and beheld us in unmentionable detail. Gaelic poetic humour is capable of ribaldry that, in English, would be deemed coarse beyond measure!

What mattered at the time was that, there, standing splay-legged, wide-eyed and shivering, was an angular black calf, looking bemused as if he had come from another world. Which, come to think of it, he probably had.

He had been no trouble to carry out to the dung heap a few hours earlier, but now, active and gangling and slippery, it was all that the three of us could do to get him back to the byre and into his cage. Whatever psychological effect his experiences may have had on him, his lungs were unimpaired, and, in no time at all, he had his mother and the other two cows bellowing in response. They raised a sympathetic echo which spread from byre to byre till the township sounded like a festival of bassoons.

'Hurry back to the house before anybody sees you. I'll give him some of his mother's milk and he'll be fine.' My mother had recovered her composure, and was now trying to control her smile, knowing full well that a man in his shirt tails is spare of a sense of humour at the best of times, even more so when he's up to his naked ankles in the muck on the floor of a byre. I knew better than to say anything as I sat waiting for my father to finish with the basin so that I could wash my own feet.

It was early evening before he made any reference to the subject. Mother had just come in from her third milking of Spotty and we were all sitting round the table having a supper of beestings.

'I'll have the naming of this calf', he said, looking at me with the tell-tale muscle in his jaw twitching.

'What?' I asked.

'Lazarus.'

And so it came to pass that Spotty's first born was Lazarus. And if I hadn't remembered Lazarus just now, I would have forgotten what a treat 'beestings' was in the relative monotony of our diet; it is a delicacy fast going out of existence, like crowdie and cream itself, as the domestic cow disappears, and the impersonal vans with their crates of milk slip through the villages, furtively, in the mornings.

The second and third batches of milk that come from a cow after calving are the best for beestings. The first milking is syrupy thick and yellow and it was always fed to the calf to get his digestive system going. And there was, usually, just enough to feed the calf. But, by the second milking, the cow was giving far more than the calf could cope with, and the milk still had a strong thickish quality which continued into the third or even the fourth day. This was beestings. And when the milk, at that stage, was heated, it turned into something resembling granular curds and whey, but with a far stronger flavour. It was claimed to be very nourishing, and a plate of it was a meal in itself.

It was only for one season that we had three cows, because they proved to be more than we could house, and harvest for, and more than my mother could milk. Had there been any co-operative type planning of our agriculture, things could have been so organized that a croft like ours could have been the milk supplier for the township, while others might have concentrated on the specialities for which they were best fitted, be that the production of vegetables, or cattle feed, or wool or mutton. On the face of it there is no reason why Harris mutton should not be as highly prized and marketable a commodity as Harris Tweed. But the crofter was, by his very nature an individualist, and though, in times of trouble or of need he would share out his last handful of meal or his last bag of potatoes, his philosophy was one of self-sufficiency and independence. A philosophy, however, is rarely a substitute for a policy.

Two cows were judged to be the manageable ideal for a family. One could be kept farrow for a year to supply milk in the winter while the other was in calf, then their roles alternated. A cow like Daisy, who was a superb milker in her prime, could produce four gallons of milk a day when the machair grazing was at its most lush in summer. And the variety of food forms into which that milk could be converted was almost endless. First there was, of course, the milk itself for drinking. The balance was set out in large flat basins to yield enough cream to keep the family in fresh butter for immediate use, leaving pounds over each week for salting for winter. Once the cream had been removed, gallons of thick, sour milk were left over each week, and the sour milk, when it was stood on a warm fire, converted into crowdie (or cottage cheese as it's now called) which floated to the surface of tangy, refreshing whey – the ideal drink for hot days of peat-cutting or hay-making. Some crowdie was used fresh, while the bulk of it was salted and put into heavy presses lined with muslin, where it matured into kebbucks of cheddar which would store indefinitely. But the greatest delicacy of them all was the crumbly crowdie mixed with fresh cream which, piled high on a fresh oatcake spread with fresh butter combined into a flavour with an inbuilt memory. Crowdie and cream! The bitter and the sweet blending as they so often do, in an experience for which there isn't one single word that I know of, whether relishing the dream or the reality.

We didn't dream for long, or else we dreamt too much. The revival of Lazarus was not a portent of good days ahead, romantic as the notion could be made to seem if truth didn't dictate otherwise. Although I didn't know it at the time, my father's distress, echoed in my mother's whispered 'Oh, no!' at the news of the stillborn calf was not just the normal reaction of the farmer or crofter to the loss of an item of stock. We were to lose many beasts over the years and I was to hear their losses bemoaned, but no response of my parents was to impinge so sharply on my subconscious as that one. Much later I was to understand why. Before he was born, the calf had been earmarked for sale as a stirk, and he represented the next year's rent. Without realizing it, we were moving further and further into a money economy, and we were doing so at a time when that economy was in desperate recession in the rest of the world.

Unbeknownst to us, things that had been luxuries, like Glasgow bread, tinned meats, bacon, jams, and countless other things that I can't even isolate now because they're such mundane items on every shopping list, were, suddenly, no longer luxuries but necessities. Our main source of hard cash had always been the tweeds that my mother spun and which (till such time as we got our own loom) were woven for her for free by my grandfather on father's side who was a handloom weaver by trade. Our sheep-stock hadn't built up sufficiently for us to be able to sell many lambs without depleting the source of our wool for tweeds. The circle was closing into a vicious one.

Slowly the mainland markets for tweeds dried up as the textile industry throughout the country ran into difficulty, and we were forced back on the local merchants who – sometimes ruthlessly and sometimes because they were in trouble themselves – exploited the situation by buying at rock bottom prices and, gradually, by not buying at all except on a barter system whereby they would take a tweed at a nominal price of half-a-crown (twelve and a half pence) a yard, and refund its value in groceries over a period of weeks. If the merchant could hold out till times improved he was bound to make a killing because he was trading in in wholesale terms, and selling at full retail profit. It was inevitable that human greed – the quality as hackneyed as the phrase – would evince itself, and some merchants soon became notorious for 'having a broad thumb'. They were the ones who would go to the length of counting their own thumb in with the yardstick when they were measuring a tweed for purchase, and the web of tweed which a woman had measured as forty-five yards on her own kitchen table, could well be forty-three on the merchant's counter. Having been lucky enough to get a lift to the shop in Calum the Post's van, she would be unlikely to face up to the prospect of humping the tweed back home on her back even though those two yards represented the loss of a goodly part of a week's necessities.

Steadily, matters got worse. There was a limit to the amount of tweed that even the best intentioned merchant could afford or risk to stock-pile, and the women, since it was they who were in the front line when it came to shopping, were increasingly forced to plead for 'tick' against the day when 'things would get better' as they surely must. That was where poverty ended, and humiliation began. In a society where credit and overdrafts are an accepted and even applauded way of life, and where, sometimes, the bigger the debt the greater the credibility, it is hard to imagine the degradation of a woman with a hole in her shoe begging for a quarter pound of tea and a pound of sugar 'till next week', as if the world was going to change in seven days.

Worst of all was the dread of 'going on the parish'. It was an old phrase for a current phenomenon. Times have changed in that respect too, and the phrase 'social security' isn't even a euphemism – it's an honourable description of an entitlement, and it is, by and large, anonymous. But, in a small community which had started off with high hopes and pride, 'going on the parish' was all the more degrading because the arbiter of need was, invariably, someone who had once been a youthful equal in courtship or in play.

Charity came on Thursday. That was the day on which Calum the Post stopped at practically every door in the village and dispensed buff envelopes containing Money Orders which he invariably cashed on the spot. There were various official phrases that Calum was unable to understand, and 'Not negotiable' and 'Payee only' were two of

130

them. I have no idea how far the dole – the blanket term for meagre state hand-outs – went. But, at the very least, it must have covered essentials like paraffin and oatmeal and the salt herring which was the keystone of our diet and which we had to buy because we couldn't fish our Atlantic shore, having nowhere remotely safe enough for anchorage.

There was, of course, no danger that we would starve. Our poverty was relative to standards which were new to our parents' generation, and it was acute only relative to their aspirations. During the winter that I went to school for several weeks on end wearing sand-shoes with no soles to them except bits of dried rabbit skin which my father had to replace every second morning, I still had a bowl of oatmeal brose for breakfast every morning, potatoes and salt herring for lunch every day and eggs in some form or other every night. And, usually, a salt mutton meal on a Sunday. It was only once that I remember hearing a strange, intermittent noise and looking up to find that it was the sound of my mother's tears sizzling on the top of the stove as she tried to manufacture some kind of oatmeal patties from the only ingredients she had in the house. I suppose I only remember it because it was dramatically unusual, and because the memory appealed to the sense of the dramatic in myself in later years.

Lazarus represented the nadir of our fortunes. When he was sold (as a yearling) at the annual cattle sale – a sale which was by then reduced to a symbolic sham – he fetched less than a pound, because any more would have made it uneconomical for a buyer to ship him to the mainland. It was that year too that we killed Daisy. She had been a mature cow when we got her, and we could no longer afford to feed her when there was no market for her progeny, and there were two other younger cows to maintain a milk supply. We needed meat, and we could deplete the sheep-stock no further. One or two of the other crofters had already killed their older cattle, and having salted as much meat as was prudent or possible had divided the remainder throughout the village. We did the same with Daisy, and my last memory of her is of yards of her intestines, cleaned and salted and inflated and hung to mature in the peat smoke till such time as they could be made into mealy puddings. Daisy had not only launched us on our way, she had kept us going when the way got rough, and, long after the boards had begun to show through the cheap bedroom linoleum, we had a warm cowskin rug under our feet on winter mornings.

Times of depression and recession are alleged to breed crime and prejudice, and, in urbanized communities where the pressures of proximity can throw disparities of standards into bitter relief, it may well be that the patterns of order and mutual respect can be disturbed and normally containable grievances fomented. But, in a small rural community wherein there is no real spectrum of 'haves' and 'have nots' hard times can cement relationships and strengthen foundations, and the Polonius dictum on borrowing and lending gets stood on its head. Putting aside the rapacity of a few merchants – which was forgiven as an understandable human failing anyway – only two incidents occurred that were sufficiently different from the humdrum norm to stamp themselves on the boyhood memory.

I mentioned earlier that the taking of rabbits was forbidden to us, and yet the reader must have guessed that my father couldn't very well have lined my sand-shoes with rabbit skins without inflicting a certain amount or grievous bodily harm on the original wearers of the skins. In truth, the landlord's prohibition was more honoured in the breach than in the observance, and by none more so than our cat Tiger who, true to his name, was a killer of the first order. He could take a buck rabbit twice his own size without effort, and without leaving a mark on him. But he didn't have any great flair for skinning and jointing, and the result was that, on any given morning, the first person to open the front door was liable to find four or five rabbits, still warm, laid out side by side on the front step, with Tiger patiently waiting for somebody to do the bloody work of gralloching them and feeding him the tid-bits of liver and lights. If the Reverend Dr George Macleod could see the hand of the Lord in shipwrecks of timber landing on the beach when he was rebuilding Iona Abbey, I don't see why we shouldn't see the finger of God in the claws of Tiger. But, be that as it may, we took little convincing that Tiger's ancestors must have more than justified the veneration in which they were held in the Middle East in ancient times when he began to supplement his free-will offering of rabbits with plump sea-trout. It was on a Sunday morning that my father first opened the door to find five sizeable sea-trout laid out neatly on the step, with the cat looking even more pleased with himself than usual. Some of the neighbours with whom we shared our bounty pretended not to be as surprised or puzzled as we were, and one or two who were, in most things, more worldly-wise than the rest, were able to confirm that cats were not as scared of the water as popular belief would have one accept, and they could even cite cases of cats that had been seen to hook fish out of rock pools. Nobody however could explain why Tiger should always go fishing on a Saturday night.

When news began to get round that the landlord was accusing his tenants of thieving, people just smiled and assumed that he was referring to the occasional salmon that disappeared from under his gamekeeper's nose, or the even more occasional stag that vanished from his hill. But the smiles hardened when he was heard to be accusing the locals of gaining entry to his game larder and removing the Saturday catches of his guests and himself. 'Clever buggers,' he said to my father whom he trusted, 'but stupid for all that! Beats me why they clean out the sea-trout and leave fourteen-pounders of salmon untouched!' My father could hardly explain that even a muscular cat would find it hard to get a fourteen-pound salmon through an eight-inch airing shaft. But he took extra care to see that Tiger didn't get locked in the house on a Saturday night from then on, and the neighbours accepted any slurs on their honesty with a shrug and a quizzical smile.

The second episode was a different matter altogether and, even now as I write, I cannot help hoping that the man at the heart of it is still around to read this. When the inevitable day came that even the kindliest merchant could no longer take tweeds on spec, people continued, helplessly, to search for outlets for the only marketable commodity they had. Long since, the miserable, drenching, salty scrabbling for whelks among the seashore rocks had ceased to offer its meagre reward; it now cost more to send a bag of whelks to Billingsgate than one could hope to get from its sale. But, from time to time, a rumour would reach us that a woman in some other village had managed to sell a tweed to some shop or firm in Edinburgh or Birmingham or somewhere and, immediately, there would be a slight surge of optimism and that particular shop or firm would be deluged with two-inch square samples (or patterns as they were called) of tweeds from all over Harris. Sometimes the shops replied saying 'no'. Sometimes they didn't even acknowledge the letter. Very, very rarely there would come an offer to buy – usually at a mean price; but no matter how poor the price, it still represented hard cash and as such was worth more than the barter value in the local shops. Such sales were few and far between, but they kept hope alive.

Then, one week, there appeared in the local paper an advertisement *asking* for tweeds, and offering two-and-six-pence a yard for self coloured tweeds and two-and-eleven-pence a yard for checks. Samples were to be sent to a Mr Brooks in Manchester. It was incredible! Somebody was actually asking for samples. And the price was good. A wave of hope went through the township; neighbours called in the house to ask if mother had heard about the advertise-ment. My father remarked, rather guardedly, that things were 'maybe beginning to look up'.

My mother had two or three tweeds of different lengths stacked under a dustsheet in the bedroom, including one of which she was inordinately proud – a fifty-yard web of black and white dog-tooth or shepherd's check, hand-spun throughout from some fine wool which she had selected from the few Cross Cheviot fleeces that we had. A shop-keeper who was vaguely related to her had, rather reluc-tantly, agreed to buy it, but when she went to see him he was only too delighted to be released from his side of the bargain.

'Another letter for Brooks, eh?' said Calum the Post when I intercepted him with an envelope containing the standard two inches square of sample next morning. That told its own story. Calum probably had a letter from every house in the village, each single one carrying a fragment of a family's hope under its flap.

Mr Brooks was not only a selective dealer, but a courteous one into the bargain. By return post he replied to every single letter – alas, not always placing an order but, at least, regretting his lack of interest in this particular piece of tweed or that, and returning the sample with the hope that he might be in a position to do business at some future date. As far as one could make out, as the women met to commiserate or congratulate, he placed firm orders for about half the tweeds that had been put on offer, and it was clear that he had a distinct preference for fairly bold patterns and checks. He went out of his way to be complimentary about my mother's 'shepherd's check' and the tone of his letter implied that this was no casual dabbler in the market; a couple of phrases suggested that not only did he appreciate the subtle differences in quality of certain wools, weaves and finishes, but also that he was acutely aware of the flaccid state of the market at the time. There was a heady air of high spirits in the house that night. My father had been a grocer's assistant for a short time in his youth, and he always prided himself on his talent for parcelling; that evening he excelled himself as my mother teased him for creating a work of art that Mr Brooks would duly rip apart without even noticing. But he joked back that the real art of salesmanship was in the presentation of the product; his neat packaging might impress the Macdonald name on the Brooks memory more than the quality of the tweed, and when the time came for a repeat order Mr Brooks would call for 'the address of the man who makes the artistic parcels in Harris'. Long before bedtime the tweed was packaged as if it were destined for Sotheby's of London instead of Brooks of Manchester, and in the morning it was taken on its way by Calum the Post, although by no stretch of the imagination could fifty yards of Harris Tweed be deemed to fall within the weight restrictions of the Royal Mail. 'The van's down on its springs with tweeds,' said Calum; 'it's just as well it's by sea and rail they're going, or the Post Office would be charging a fortune in stamps.'

Two weeks passed. And then three. Courteous letters went off to Mr Brooks. Then angry ones. But there was no reply. People unsophisticated in the complexities of trade didn't know how to proceed, and in the end they turned to the one man with whom most of them had had least dealing – the Bank Manager. There was little he could do, but it was enough. No such man as our Mr Brooks had a bank account anywhere in Manchester, nor was there any record of his existence. The address to which the tweeds had been sent was a temporary 'convenience address' and the premises had been closed and shuttered for a fortnight. And that was the end of the story. There was no point in starting any complicated proceedings for the sake of a few hundred yards of tweed of little or no current market value. Nothing had been lost except long days and evenings of effort. And a few days of hope.

I have no idea how those incidents were juxtaposed, or why they even found a compartment in the long memory which is so short on worthier counts. Probably just because the incidents extend naturally into stories. There is no story in a parcel of groceries from an aunt . . . nor in a dollar in an envelope from an uncle faring not much better in America . . . nor in a visit from the Duchess, just dropping in to rest her feet, and the finding of a quarter pound of tea on St Clement's bench after her departure . . These were just stitches in the tapestry of the years of the Crowdie and Cream, and the touches that put the sweet in the bitter sweet.

Chapter Thirteen

Just when it seemed that the village had settled down to its final format – in as much as a community ever has a final format – its whole character was suddenly changed by the removal of the old hillside population. It was as if the old host rose were removed once the new graft had taken hold. It meant that the school roll dropped by four to the thirteen at which it was to remain static for the next five years or so. The four who left were to drop out of my ken forever as they were melded into a new school in a new village seven miles north of us.

From the earliest Clan MacLeod days, the rich tack or estate of Luskentyre had been run on the lines of a sporting estate with a large Home Farm, and occupied, consequently, by a wealthy absentee tenant landlord who required only a small number of retainers to keep the place ticking over in between salmon runs. For some reason Luskentyre had failed to find a buyer when Harris had been sold off in bits and pieces after the death of Lord Leverhulme in 1925, and the estate had remained the property of Leverhulme's trustees but leased to the wealthy Venables family from Kent. The Department of Agriculture made every effort to get the Leverhulme trustees to subdivide the land and rent it out as crofts in the same way as our landlord had been compelled to do, but trustees and tenant alike remained obdurate. At last the Department invoked its powers of compulsory purchase and threw Venables out lock, stock and barrel, refusing to leave him any land whatsoever. They left him only the fishing rights and the Big House which he abandoned and allowed to go to rack and ruin.

Luskentyre was probably a better agricultural proposition than our area, but the farming side of the estate had been allowed to deteriorate in favour of sport, so that by the time the Department of Agriculture acquired it, it was virtually over-run by rabbits. The new superiors estimated that it could be made to carry eighty cattle and five hundred sheep, and, on that basis, they divided it into ten crofts of which the Black Shepherd and his fellow cottars were given one each. Thus, at last, they got their long-awaited reward for their raiding, their imprisonment and their patience, but a lot of the colour went out of our fragile society when they left.

In some ways they got a better deal than we did, because they were the direct tenants of the Department of Agriculture, with no other landlord in between. While we had the umbrella of the Department and its guarantees for the security of our tenure, we still had an immediate private Landlord who had been allowed to retain a sizeable farm for himself and a certain superiority over us. For example, he regarded rabbits, which were the plague of our early existence, as Game, and, instead of taking steps to suppress them, he introduced a strain of black Dutch rabbit to strengthen the breed and make them better sport. Even when they scourged our crops we were not, officially, allowed to trap or shoot or snare them. It was a nice challenge for growing boys!

I reckon that, in the early thirties, we were lapping a full decade behind even the most faintly urbanized areas of the mainland in terms of the most rudimentary social amenities, although by no means so in terms of attitudes of quality of life. The town of Stornoway still didn't have a communal electricity supply, and we hadn't even graduated to the vapourized Tilly lamp whose crisp white light was soon to replace the mellower glow of the double-wick paraffin lamp; the Tilly may have been easier on the

138

reading eye, but its spartan brass and chrome lines never developed into an art form to touch the ornate, fluted, outlines of tinted glass and lacquered pedestals that gave character to the Victorian oil lamp. It was by the light of one of them that I graduated slowly and painfully from the drudgery of the Home Reader to the peripatetic adventures of Rupert Bear in a world which was strangely real, and the world of Dixon Hawke which was not. In London, the British Broadcasting Corporation was taking over the development of television from the Baird Company long before the first wireless set reached our village, and the nearest we had to 'provided' entertainment was my father's square oak box of a gramophone with a large green horn, with a picture of a dog of indeterminate pedigree listening to a square oak gramophone with a large green horn, on which there was a picture of a dog of indeterminate pedigree listening. . . .

The selection of records was limited to a dozen or so Gaelic singers, who were famous in their time, giving renditions of simple folk-songs in ornate, stylized Victorian settings, and two or three Harry Lauder pieces. Sometimes, of a still evening, my father would open the window and push the horn out through it in the hope that it would entice one or two of the younger neighbours to come in. And sometimes they would. And the evening would develop into a story-telling session during which my mother would sit spinning late into the night, leaving the spinning wheel only to replenish the tea-pot. My brother and I would sit quietly listening, careful not to draw attention to ourselves, but, sooner or later we were hustled off the bed. It didn't matter much. We just sat hunched in bed with our ears to the partition, hoping to hear things that we weren't supposed to hear, till sleep overcame us. But such evenings were few and far between. There weren't many visitors to go round, and it was a special occasion when somebody from one of the neighbouring villages decided to make a pilgrimage on his bicycle and drop in unannounced. There was a time when we could have depended on James to arrive fairly frequently, but, shortly after his marriage, he decided that he couldn't make ends meet just by working on his father's croft, and he went back to sea. Instead of being sorry to see him go, people were pleased for him and spoke about how fortunate he was to know a skipper who was able to offer him a berth in 'these difficult times'.

The recession of the thirties did not seem, materially, to affect the education system as much as national crises do now. Certainly not as far as our village was concerned. It may be that the new teacher had acquired so much muscle with the Education Authority that the members of its various committees, who were then, as now, chosen for their spare time rather than their talents, were unable to gainsay her merest request. Or it may be that wise men with abaci, having computed that the population of the world had reached two billion, were confident that a spill-over of the international trend would be evidenced in Scaristavore sooner or later, and that the current stability of the population owed more to good luck than to continence. For whatever reason, there was a sudden descent on the school of joiners and slaters and plumbers, and, without any apparent disruption of the curriculum, we found the building being transformed around us.

It soon became obvious that however little else they had in common, Miss Martin and Miss Dalbeith shared a passion for hygiene. But where the old teacher had been content with punishing us for not sharing her enthusiasm, the new one was determined that we should accept as an article of faith that cleanliness was next to Godliness, and when the green and yellow walls were repainted in the same colours, of which Inverness County Council obviously had limitless supplies, she had a framed motto to that effect hung up in place of the semi-nude harvesters of rice. To ensure that we had the facilities with which to practise the new faith, the dim passage-way that led from the front door to the schoolroom, and had hitherto been furnished only with variously elevated cloakroom pegs, was now brightly lit by a brand new window, and fitted out with wash-hand basins with brass taps that gushed running water. The 'wee houses' at the back, which had been used as lumber dumps for as long as anybody could remember, were cleared and equipped with chemical toilets that tainted the air with a smell less acceptable by far than that which it was supposed to combat. The phrase 'Please miss, I want out' was amended to 'Please miss, may I go to the toilet?' and the idea was that, having been, one then underlined one's mission for the whole school by ostentatiously running cascades of water over one's hands in the cloakroom. The theory was fine, but the end result was that we just refused to ask out, and when the intervals were called the boys made a mad dash to vault over the playground wall and line up against the back of it in the time-honoured fashion. For the girls it must have been excruciatingly embarrassing. They tried to adopt the genteel fashion, but after a few of them had looked up from the crouch to find two sets of grubby male fingers hooked over the top of the door, and two pairs of boggling eyes staring down through the gap below the lintel, they abandoned all pretence of sophistication and reverted to slinking off to the sand dunes, now much more self-consciously and conspicuously than before.

The major transformation – which also had its hygienic associations – came with the disappearance of the five-seater desks. They vanished without warning in the course of one weekend, taking with them whole genealogies in the form of hundreds of initials that had been surreptitiously carved on them by successive generations since 1892. They were replaced by smart two-seater desks, graded in size, each with a locker under a hinged lid. They had no slots in the top. The old germ-laden slates, which had been scratched on and spat on by our predecessors and ourselves, disappeared forever, and the word 'jotter' was added to our growing vocabulary. It was a treacherous, betraying thing, the jotter. No longer could a quick lick and a slick with the finger eliminate a mistake when one glimpsed the correct answer on a neighbour's slate; with the jotter one had to go through the whole tell-tale gamut of stroking out, which was frowned on anyway, or else hope to procure a rubber without drawing too much attention to one's purpose. The abolition of the slate at least lessened the wear and tear on the jersey sleeve, releasing it briefly, for its secondary purpose. One of the very first jotter pages that I ever laboriously filled was 'I must not wipe my nose on my sleeve', only to have to do it all over again. But at least I never forgot again how to spell sleeve!

Gillespie and I shared one of the new two-seater desks, and I suppose it afforded us our first little sensation of relative privacy. We fixed an imaginary line down the middle of the locker, and we came to an agreement that each would housekeep his own side of the line and respect any bits of private property that one or the other might want to store away from the prying eyes and fingers of the family at home. We also devised a system whereby two quick nudges of the bare knee led to a simultaneous lifting of the lid of the desk for a quick conference on a matter of spelling or addition; if we were caught out later with the same mistake we could swear in all honesty that we had not been 'copying', which meant, literally, looking at the other's book and was not deemed to embrace whispered consultations.

I haven't seen Gillespie these many years. Of the thirteen of us whom I have always regarded as being 'the school' because that number remained for the longest time static, Gillespie is the one who has wandered furthest afield. And, although as boys we often swore lifelong friendship as boys do, we have never met or corresponded since we had our one and only evening on the beer just about the time that we both became men. So I've never been able to ask him whether he remembers the sensation that he nearly caused . . . the time-bomb laugh that he planted . . . or whatever it is you call it when you commit a solecism which, only long years later, explodes on the consciousness of yourself and others.

There is an old Gaelic proverb which says that 'rivalry turns a township's best furrow', and it means, I suppose, that no ploughman wants to be seen to be worse at his craft than his neighbour. And rivalry, rather than any goadings or threats, was the means favoured by Miss Martin to spur us on towards an education. Nowadays, in the general frenzy to level life down rather than up, it is not considered good educational policy to create stars, lest the fellow at the tail of the class, be he lout or laggard, develops one of the fashionable complexes of which, it seems, more are being discovered every day. Occasionally our sense of competition was fanned by the promise of some small reward or other; usually it was enough to bask in the approval of the teacher. She may not have been outstandingly successful in her efforts to turn us into well groomed and manicured little ladies and gentlemen fit to grace a garden party, but she was, slowly and steadily, wearing down the contempt for education which had been inculcated in us by her predecessor. We graduated gently from the interminable cats sitting on their mats to simple stories of adventure, and, almost without realizing it, a working knowledge of the English language was creeping up on us, and, with it, a patent need for more and more vocabulary.

The child in an English-speaking community absorbs his vocabulary in the everyday business of living, but even during the briefest of school intervals we reverted immediately to Gaelic, and, from the moment that the school gate closed behind us at four o'clock we didn't hear a word of English spoken unless such parents as were bilingual themselves wanted to converse about something private or otherwise unsuitable for young ears. Under the circumstances, it was astonishing that, by the time we left the village school at the ages of eleven or twelve to go in search of further education, we were reasonably fluent in what was, in every way, a foreign language. One of the teacher's most innovative ploys to widen our vocabulary was what she called 'The Word Game'. It sounded as if it was meant to be fun, and, in a way, it was. The idea was that we should go home each evening and, by any means we chose, find one new word, and come to school next morning knowing exactly what the word meant, able to spell it, and prepared to deliver at least one long sentence involving the word in such a way as to render its meaning clear to the rest of the school. At the end of each morning session the school, or such members of it as were old enough to understand words of more than three letters, would adjudicate and vote on the quality of the words, and the winner would get a red star stuck inside the cover of his or her jotter. At the end of term, a prize would be awarded to the person with the greatest number of stars.

Gillespie and I became great rivals in the Word Game. His father had a lexicon with some pages missing, and mine had a much thumbed, fat, and elderly edition of *Chambers Twentieth Century Dictionary* which he was sometimes driven to read when there was no newspaper and he felt too tired to make yet another sortie into Gibbon's *Decline and Fall*. I don't know what kind of technique Gillespie used, but I discovered fairly quickly that there was a surpassing rich goldmine of highly unusual and exotic words among the Xs, Ys and Zs, and I became expert at regaling the school with dissertations on Vertigo and Xylophone and Yapok. Come to think of it, I'm probably one of the few people around who knows what a yapok is, unless some contemporary in Scarista Public School remembers the difficulty I had in convincing Miss Martin that if yapok were rendered inadmissible just because the animal didn't abound in Harris, then, by that token, elephant and camel would have to be disallowed too. She conceded the point with some reluctance, but indicated that she, personally, would be inclined to cast her vote in future for words that might, conceivably, crop up in the occasional conversation in some part of the British Isles. Looking back on it, the whole project was fraught with danger, and the miracle of it was that the teacher didn't get her come-uppance long before that fateful morning.

Living next door as we did, Gillespie and I invariably walked to school together, and, if we hadn't picked up any family secrets to divulge to each other, the conversation would come round to the Word Game which was always the first item on the agenda after Prayers. There was no point in being secretive with each other. We would never dream of stealing each other's words. There was no need to: there were no points to be scored since each person had to define and talk about his own word anyway. On that particular morning I was rather pleased with the word I had found, and, without prompting, informed Gillespie rather pompously that it was a sure-fire winner. It was, in fact, 'Uxorious', and it meant (and presumably still means) 'excessively fond of one's wife'. His reaction was predictable.

'How many letters?'

'Eight,' I was able to tell him, at the same time secretly wishing that I had plumbed the dictionary a little further, since eight was pretty average for a good word, and Gillespie and I had frequently scored ten in our own private needle contests, despite the fact that the teacher went to constant trouble to stress that the usefulness of a word was not always commensurate with its length. I couldn't decide whether or not I had scored a hit. Gillespie went silent, and for the life of me I couldn't make up my mind whether it was his smug or his sulky expression that he was wearing.

'What's your word?' I asked.

'I won't tell you. It's better than yours!'

'Did your father not know one?' I knew that would sting.

'I didn't ask my father. We've got a dictionary too as you know fine'.

We walked for a while in silence.

'I won't tell you the word but I'll tell you what it means.

145

It's a big kind of piano that they play in churches in the town when they're singing. My father says he saw one in Portsmouth when he was in the navy. So there's such a thing, see?'

That was good enough for me, and I wished that I had consulted my own father who had a vast vocabulary of big words culled from Gibbon and Lord Macaulay. But it was too late now, and by the time we reached school I was convinced that Gillespie must have a word of inordinate length which would knock the teacher for six. Only part of my conviction was to be realized!

School always began with Morning Prayers. Not the token nod in the direction of the Almighty which seems, for the most part, to pass for Morning Prayers now, but a full dress service starting with the Lord's Prayer which we were taught to lisp from the first day that we entered school. The fact that for the first two years at least it didn't mean anything, taught as it was in English, didn't seem to matter; the assumption was, presumably, that He to whom it was being addressed knew it off by heart of old. At a lower level, of course, the constant repetition was excellent practice in the pronunciation of English. But even now it seems strange to me that it was long after I was reasonably fluent in English that I memorized the prayer in Gaelic. Come to think of it, I suppose I was being conditioned to assume that God was a native English-speaker like most of those we were taught to regard as our superiors, just as hordes of people the world over were being taught that the God for whom they were being asked to forsake their own was white and unquestionably pro-British.

The Lord's Prayer was followed by Bible reading and study, and the accent was very heavily on the Old Testament. For a long time I was firmly convinced that the genesis had taken place in Harris, and that Ararat was probably the highest peak of the mountain range separating us from Lewis. A mile or so from the village there was a stretch of marsh land which flooded completely at times of heavy rain, leaving only tall bull-rushes rearing above the water. Here, surely, Pharaoh's daughter, washing herself in the river (as we did ourselves when the weather was reasonable), stumbled across the baby Moses in a wicker basket such as my Grandfather made out of willow to carry home his peat. Sometimes, now, I wonder what city children, brought up in their brick and mortar jungles relate to when they read about the miracles of creation.

Such was the concentration on the Old Testament that we could effortlessly have transferred our allegiance to the Jewish faith. But whatever good our studies of the Pentateuch did our souls, they certainly improved our English, even if, for the first few years our conversation may have had a quaint 'hast and didst' quality about it. Moreover (there I go!) those early books of the Bible provided a rare source of blood and thunder adventure for youngsters who didn't, at that stage, have access to libraries, far less bookshops. Of course, the teacher's attempts to slip over some of the more explicit chapters of Leviticus were guaranteed to send us rushing to them at the earliest clandestine moment, and since they frequently involved recourse to the dictionary I suppose they must have made contributions to our education – liguistic and otherwise.

I will skip over the torture of the Shorter Catechism, admirable though it may be as the good man's Highway Code. It was the third item in the daily Order of Service which ended, pleasantly and mercifully, with a metric psalm. Forty-five minutes or so the Religion period lasted each morning. And then it was 'Bibles away. And on with the Word Game!' I would be dipping into the realms of fiction if I were to pretend to remember which words were trundled out by the various participants that morning. But, by simple dint of checking on the fading school photograph on my desk, I can calculate that five words were produced and defined and spelt and en-sentenced before it came to Gillespie's turn. And he was second from the last immediately before me.

147

'Right then, Gillespie', said the teacher, 'stand up and let's hear your word.'

Gillespie shot me a quick 'wait-till-you-hear-this' kind of look and stood up. I braced myself for some multi-syllabled semanteme which would make my 'uxorious' sound like an infant's burble and totally demolish my hopes of a red star.

'Pennies,' said Gillespie as crisply as his thick Highland accent would allow.

I couldn't believe my ears. Gillespie knew as well as I did that plurals weren't allowed, and when the teacher had made the rule, she had seized her chance to explain to us what a 'plural' was. Her brow puckered.

'You know I only allow one, Gillespie', she said.

'It is one, Miss, it's not "pennies" money.' Gillespie was almost pert in his self-confidence.

'Well, it's new to me then, Gillespie,' she said, and later she must have thanked the Lord that there were no irreverent adults present to hear her. 'Tell the class what it means.'

'It's an organ, Miss,' said Gillespie.

There is such a thing as total innocence.

'Spell it.'

'P-E-N-I-S,' enunciated Gillespie triumphantly, and I breathed with relief as I counted only five letters.

Underneath the calm exterior which she normally presented in front of the school, the teacher was a very nervous person. The sudden appearance of a stranger at the door would bring a flush of red to her neck, and under any sustained emotion the red flush would suffuse her face. It was something of which, I am sure with hindsight, she was deeply conscious. That day her blush could not be appropriately described as red. The exact word for it was vermilion, the very word with which I had unhappily lost a round of the Word Game a few days earlier because I had accidentally put two 'l's' in it! She looked at the class, rustled some papers on her desk, glanced at her watch, and went through the whole classic gamut of reaction of

148

somebody striving to regain composure. 'Thank you, Gillespie', she said. 'Dear me, I'm afraid we've taken longer than usual. That's all we've time for today.' And she called the morning interval without as much as asking Gillespie for his sentence.

Needless to say, the interval was devoted to a lengthy discussion of the incident. Nobody could quite understand what had gone wrong although it was plain that something had gone drastically amiss. And then, one of the older boys had a flash of inspiration.

'It was all your fault,' he said, rounding on Gillespie. 'You shouldn't have used that word. You know fine the teacher belongs to the Free Presbyterian Church and they think it's a sin to use an organ with the psalms!' And that was that.

It was also the end of the Word Game. And, in all those years, neither in writing nor in conversation have I found a chance to use the word 'uxorious' till now.

Chapter Fourteen

For some weeks after the fire curtain had come down on the drama of the Word Game, our vocabularies were left to expand themselves along the more orthodox guide rails laid down in *The Royal Crown Reader*, published for the English speaking schools of the Kingdom, if not the Empire, by Thomas Nelson and Sons, Ltd., of London, Edinburgh, New York, Toronto and Paris.

The Royal School Series (that was the umbrella title) consisted of two Infant Readers and six Junior School Readers, all uniformly bound in sedate dark blue covers sporting a large crown motif to remind us, presumably, that, away in the outmost Hebrides, we were still the fortunate denizens of the great power whose domains were splurged in red across the full width of the schoolroom map. The series, unamended as far as I know, served generations of 'scholars', and I have often wondered if, in faraway corners of those red splodges, future perpetrators of insurrection were having their cultures ironed out of them by means of flat banalities in, albeit, immaculate grammar. The imagination jibs at the thought of, say, Mr Robert Mugabe being made to stand up in front of his class and read aloud such gems of poetry as

> Thinks pussy, 'The ball
> That I see in the hall,
> Is the best ball of all
> That ever I saw.'

> My kittens I'll call
> From the garden wall,
> And we'll toss the nice ball
> From paw to paw.'

or, one class further on

> Dicky bird, Dicky bird whither away?
> Why do you fly when I wish you to stay?
> I never would harm you, if you would come
> And sing me a song while you perch on my thumb.

And yet, why not? Our native culture was as remote from that of the hub of empire as were the separate cultures of Messrs Mugabe and Nkomo, and the grand plan was to smoothe them all out to an acceptable uniformity.

Our teacher was a staunch upholder of the 'system' as a result of her own indoctrination; and it was not her instinct but her training and the policies of government at all levels, that made her labour to hone and polish us so that we could take our places in a society other than our own. 'If you don't do your sums . . . If you don't learn your spelling . . . If you don't practise your reading . . . you'll never get away from here.' Those were the exhortations of school and home, and nobody ever paused to think that, particularly in those days of the hungry thirties, *here* was a damn good place to be. With hindsight it is almost incredible that, all over the Highlands, men who had fought to establish their right to the land and to create new communities such as ours, were subscribing to a system which would ensure that their sons would seek out lives and livelihoods elsewhere.

But our schoolmistress – while having to work within the constraints of a dubious philosophy – was too good a teacher to accept that she could stimulate our fluency in English, far less share the undoubted love that she had for the language herself, by strict adherence to text books alone. The Word Game had been successful while it lasted, and she must have put some considerable thought into finding for it a successor that would be relatively free of pitfalls. She came up with the idea of 'Conversation'. A fairly obvious idea, admittedly, since it was with the avowed purpose of being able to converse in it that we were learning English in the first place. It was also, she explained, something in which all thirteen members of the school could participate, given an accepted principle of handicap whereby the most junior members could get away with 'I have a black dog', while the more sophisticated citizens would be expected to enlarge on the working qualities or other attributes of their dogs, black or otherwise.

We were hers to command, and those who might not be prepared to strive to please were scared to offend. And so, for the next day or two she was regaled with sagas about the village dogs which ranged from the anthropomorphic to the downright untruthful. When some exasperated soul was stung into a protestation of 'Please Miss, Jimmy MacLean is telling lies', it gave her a chance to attempt to delineate the subtle distinctions between falsehood and fiction which is not as simple as it may seem in a basically fundamentalist society. However, when it came to 'There were three dogs on top of our dog last night and my father was throwing pails of water over them', it was manifestly time for her to steer Conversation into broader channels lest she find herself foundering in the treacherous waters of farmyard sex. Already one or two of the older pupils were beginning to revel in the manipulation of the word 'bitch' without fear of reprimand. And, slowly, she began to win. Conversation became a free-ranging half hour of diverse sentences and paragraphs on divers subjects. Till, subtly, the whole village began to become involved.

In no time at all no domestic secret was safe unless parents remembered to warn their offspring not to divulge it under pain of dire punishment. Even then, from time to time, subjects were aired in Conversation which would not normally be the subject of public discussion. For parents it must have been like living under a permanent cloud of censorship, and the end-result was an unexpected and unprecedented involvement of parents in the education of their children, and the least bed-time whisper of 'I haven't got a conversation for tomorrow' was enough to send them on a frenetic search for a subject that could be guaranteed to be innocuous. On occasion mothers and fathers found it more prudent to frame and rehearse sentences themselves, though by so doing they were laying their own syntax and grammar on the line for dissection in class on the morrow. But that was safer than having their private worlds unveiled, and I have always fancied that Conversation, to some extent or other, led to an upgrading of the English of the entire community, since lapses in the King's English could not be overlooked just on the strength of a plea of 'Please Miss, that's how my father says it.'

My own father, having had a minor difficulty with the rent publicly aired, got round the problem very neatly by ordaining that each of my Conversations must start with the words 'I read in the newspaper . . .', thus, by his way of it, killing two birds with the one stone – relieving himself of the responsibility of providing me with a topic, and ensuring at the same time that, to some extent, I actually read a newspaper. I didn't always remember to do so, of course, and frequently had to fall back on my imagination, with the result that Lord Beaverbrook would have been astounded had he heard some of the news items that were being attributed to his journalists. But at least the family's private affairs were safeguarded since even I couldn't dress them up sufficiently to make them attributable to the *Daily Express*.

But not every pupil was as effectively muzzled as I was, and domestic gossip still featured prominently in the morning news sessions. And just as I was prepared to improvise on the news from Fleet Street so other members of the school, desperately scrabbling for copy, were tempted to embellish and concoct according to their individual abilities. More than once families were set at each others' throats over deeds and sentiments which were attributed to them though never, in fact, committed or expressed. Sitting safely on the sidelines I usually derived some schadenfreude satisfaction from the fracas which developed out of somebody

153

else's indiscretion; but it never occurred to me that I might, one day, be the victim of a minor apocalypse myself.

I had delivered myself of my own pronouncement on current affairs – concocted or real I can't remember – and it was the turn of the Primary Six girl sitting behind me to shuffle to her feet. 'My mother was saying to my father last night that Mrs Macdonald is going to have a baby and she's hoping that it's going to be a girl.'

I only half heard, and it was not until I noticed the teacher's eyes flicking in my direction that I felt a lump like a hunk of cold suet pudding forming in the area of my solar plexus, and some fragment of my mind catapulted into action. There were three Mrs Macdonalds in the village! Which? Two of them had had babies in the last few weeks and I knew enough about the facts of reproduction to know that they were unlikely to be producing more in the immediate future. And that left only my mother! No quartz digital display at the Olympics could have flipped to the correct conclusion more quickly. I felt a boiling flush flood to my face and then recede giving place to cold, and then the veins on my forehead swelling in anger.

'Peggy's telling lies,' I blurted out, forgetting to preface the accusation with the customary 'Please Miss'.

'No Miss, I'm not,' said Peggy triumphantly, revelling in the fact that she had scored a palpable hit.

'Sit down!' thundered Miss Martin. And when she used that tone she was obeyed.

'It will be very nice – having a wee sister,' she said to me. There was something about the way she spoke that suggested that the news was not wholly surprising to her.

'No it won't, Miss,' I muttered, becoming aware that Gillespie was smirking with satisfaction, patently smug with revenge for the way I had ragged him when his mother had done the same to him.

'That's enough,' said the voice from the teacher's desk. 'Take out your jotters and Primary Five get on with the arithmetic that we didn't finish yesterday. Primary Six, come

154

out here with your homework compositions. And the rest of you carry on learning your poetry till I'm ready for you.'

The rest of the morning, including the eleven-thirty break is forgotten. At lunchtime I raced off home, hotly pursued by my brother who had had the news translated for him since his own English was still shaky. We burst into the house and demanded the truth from my mother in tones so rude that all we got in reply was a torrent of admonition about bad manners and an unmistakably sincere assurance that one more outburst like that and our trousers – and mine in particular – would be taken down. Dinner, as we called lunch, was eaten in silence. It was perfectly obvious that my mother had been caught completely off guard; that she was angry that the embargo she had put on her news had been broken.

It took me a long time to forgive my mother, and, for truth, I can't imagine why. Perhaps it was disappointment that she hadn't let me in on the secret herself. Perhaps it was selfishness because I had become used to our cosy menage of four and subconsciously felt my status and security challenged. Whatever the reasons, I went through the winter suffering from lapses of sullenness for which I sometimes got upbraided and sometimes punished. I had no idea when the event was due and no interest in its outcome.

Looking back, it has always been a delicate puzzlement to me how a community like ours – a community of virile ex-servicemen and red-blooded women remote from the sophistications of Barbers' and Apothecaries' shops – managed to regulate the expansion of its population in those days when Town and Country weren't planned, far less families. Certainly not every mother was so meticulously scheduled as my own, it will be remembered, who had managed to produce her first two sons at the same hour of the morning on the Fourth of July and three years apart. But, for sure, our village grew in an orderly and subtly pre-ordained way which would have delighted Mrs Indira Gandhi and puzzled the Pope.

Maybe Calum the Post had a hand in the organization of

155

things – I will never know – but he certainly had timeous intimation of every 'happy event', for the simple reason that he was our lifeline with the Manchester Emporia which supplied us with such clothing as was beyond the scope of the local handloom weavers. I have never been able to fathom why Manchester secured a virtual monopoly of our textile imports when there were drapery and napery stores in places like Stornoway and Inverness and Glasgow. But, certainly, Manchester was – and may well still be – the trading centre for the firms of J. D. Williams and Oxendale who had a hallowed place in our cotton and linen liturgy, with a Welsh firm called Pryce Jones coming a poor but honourable third like the Holy Ghost in the average prayer. Their filing systems must have been astonishingly organized; I have known of a note being sent to one of them which read as follows: 'Dear Sir (not Sirs mark you), Please send me C.O.D. a dress like the one you sent Mrs MacLean for her sister's wedding – only blue and one size larger.' And the order was satisfactorily fulfilled.

Oxendale and J. D., as J. D. Williams was popularly known, were far from regarded as totally impersonal. The letters to them frequently ended 'Hoping you are keeping well. We are all fine here despite the cold weather,' or words to that effect. Such informality did not betoken naivete; it exemplifies the breakdown which can take place in the mores of business formality in the course of a long and honourable association – the sort of burgeoning of trust which reached one of its finest flowerings in the relationship that developed between Miss Helene Hanff and Frank Doel of 84 Charing Cross Road. If Miss Hanff could keep the staff of a bookshop supplied with goodies from across the Atlantic, why should not one old lady from our parts send Oxendale a dozen eggs during the years of wartime rationing with a note saying 'Please don't tell J. D. in case he thinks you're my favourite, but the hens aren't laying well just now and I remember how kind you were with the hat when my husband was in hospital.' But the war was light years away when our village was pursuing its peaceful expansion.

Calum the Post enjoyed trust of a different kind. He was a local man with local friends and relatives, but he wore the King's uniform, and he had taken the King's oath which was more specific about the contents of His Majesty's mail than it was about the contents of His Majesty's van. It didn't matter, therefore, that he could probably unerringly identify what lay inside every 'plain sealed wrapper', or that he knew the exact cost of every layette and every wedding gown (they usually came in the reverse order) by virtue of the fact that all mail shopping was conducted C.O.D. But even if infant wardrobes were already to hand from previous occasions, Calum would still be privy to every impending accouchement almost as soon as the father was because it was he, after all, who, personally, conveyed every advance warning note to the District Nurse; it was a bit pointless to stamp it and have it going through the hands of the sorting office when he lived a few paces from the Nurse's cottage anyway.

It was one of Calum's standing jokes that he was a grade higher in the Civil Service than the Nurse, because he did *first* deliveries while she only did second; the point of his joke being that the nurse was rarely in attendance on primiparous occasions – they being the province of Granny, who had personal experience from bed to Z, while a spinster nurse's knowledge was assumed to be theoretical. When my own Grandmother was in her seventies I heard someone mention to her that a certain elderly doctor had a splendid record in maternity, and that he had lost only two babies in his whole career. To which the old lady replied that she had delivered more first babies than she could remember, and had lost none.

By the time that I became aware that the people of our village were busy multiplying themselves, as the Bible had it, Marks 2 and 3 were rolling off the production lines, and their introduction to the cold world was being entrusted to the Nurse who, in addition to her midwifely duties, also attended to most of the other ailments of the parish. The doctor lived in a world apart. He was regarded

157

as belonging to the 'upper crust' society which included the landlord, the factor, the banker and one or two others who spoke English and caught salmon with rods.

The doctor's life in the Highlands and Islands has changed dramatically since the days about which I'm writing. Today it is considered highly desirable for the doctor to be a Gaelic speaker even though the vast majority of his patients is likely to be totally and fluently bilingual. He has the same status as his predecessor even though he doesn't necessarily set out to seek it. If his flock is scattered, he will, nevertheless, attend cases personally and be welcome, and, more than likely, he will pick up a dozen eggs or a bag of potatoes for his pains in addition to a generous mileage allowance for his car. If he is really fluent in Gaelic and inventive of vocabulary he can probably carve out a lucrative little niche for himself with the local radio station pontificating on the latest controversies anent abortion and the pill. Thanks to the traditions established by those same predecessors, however, he is less likely than his city counterpart to be hauled out of his sleep at the frivolous beck of headache or backache or wind. And no matter how remote his patch by city standards, in the event of emergency beyond his own resources he is only a helicopter flip away from one of several of the best teaching hospitals in the country. But in the year of my mother's third skirmish with maternity our temporary ambassador of Hippocrates was one of the most colourful in a long and motley line.

Dr MacBeth was generally accepted to be mad. But I think that was because of a slight misinterpretation of the word 'locum'. Or it may have been because he wore the kilt. Or, again, it may have been because of the brangle he got himself into over the birth of Murdo Mor's first and only child.

Now the wearing of the kilt was a legal offence for only a short while after the Battle of Culloden, and it is, in fact, a very practical garment at the right time and in the right place. Even the Prince of Wales wears it as a gesture to his Scottish ancestry whenever he ventures north of the Caledonian Canal. But it is not, as some people in the Home

158

Counties seem to think, the daily wear of the crofters and lobster fishermen of the Outer Hebrides, and when genteel tourists from England wear it on their occasional forays north it does not help them to blend into the local community which is, presumably, their heart's desire; it tends rather to signal them out as hitch-hikers or Americans or worse. Except, of course, for the Prince of Wales who is kenspeckle from television and is, among other things, the Lord of the Isles.

There are certain things that the kilt does not go with, and two of them are half-moon spectacles and wellington boots. So, by sporting all three while riding a lady's push-bike, Dr MacBeth was not only flying in the face of convention then, but he would be flying in its face even now.

In the normal course of events Dr MacBeth could have come and gone without our ever seeing him because he was based in Obbe some six miles to the south, and we would have had to make do with the gossip about his eccentricities which, in all consciousness, was rife enough. But then came confirmation that the wife of Murdo Mor – the much respected pillar of an older community to the north of us – was on the point of having a child. Rumour to that effect had been flying around for some time, but nobody had taken it seriously because Murdo's wife was a matronly forty-four and had survived twenty years of matrimony without succumbing to matrimony's eternal hazard. Although Murdo was called 'Mor' which means 'big', he was in fact a small, tubby man who had been some kind of commercial traveller or salesman on the mainland for most of his life before returning to his native village with, allegedly, a comfortable bank balance, and a slightly staccato self-confidence which earmarked him for the chairmanship of any small committees that might happen to be set up. Disbelief at his impending fatherhood had quickly given way to inevitable ribaldry, but that had, in turn, died down rapidly when it became known that his wife was suffering the problems that can be attendant on first pregnancies in middle age. Emotionally, the villages rallied round the couple as

159

communities do everywhere under such circumstances, and Murdo's own conduct gained him much sympathy and support as he went quietly about his croft work and, dutifully, every Sunday paid his morning and evening visits to the little exclusive fundamentalist kirk of which he was an elder in another township. If people prayed for him, as I'm sure they did, then in all probability they redoubled their efforts when they began to see Dr MacBeth trundling on his bike to visit the expectant mother twice a week.

At last the great day came. Murdo had graciously refused all but the minimum of help from the township women who, under the circumstances, were even more willing than usual to give of their time and effort. He argued that the extra work in the house helped to keep his mind off his worry. And all the women who called on him came away full of admiration for the way in which he had made preparation for what could be the happiest or the saddest day of his life. House, bed, layette . . . everything was in apple-pie order, and, on the evening before the due day he had killed and dressed a big, fat Rhode Island Red rooster so that there would be a nourishing meal ready for his wife after her ordeal. What seemed to impress the ladies more than anything else was that he had remembered to lay in rice and onions for the chicken soup, and, in universal wifely fashion, they made comparisons from which their own husbands emerged very poorly indeed.

In the event all went well, and Dr MacBeth, with the nurse in attendance, delivered Murdo's wife of a lusty baby boy.

Over the weeks, thanks to Murdo Mor's faithful reportage, Dr MacBeth's reputation had taken a turn for the better. Apparently he had not only been diligent in his attendance – which the village had witnessed for itself – but, by the bedside, he had been courteous and comforting and exuding medical expertise. On the day itself, according to the two local women who were present, the doctor had been completely self-assured and had made light of everybody's fears. He had twinkled at them over his half-moon

160

spectacles, making little jokes and coaxing them to teach him a word or two of Gaelic. He had turned Murdo a further shade of pale by asking him what the Gaelic was for 'twins'. And after it was all over and he had washed his hands, he had been positively expansive over a couple of very large whiskies. But the bubble burst when he was on the doorstep saying his farewells. He was bending down to put on his goloshes when Murdo sidled up to him and, apologizing for getting back to business again, said, 'Doctor – when do you think I can let her have a bit of the cock?'

The doctor shot upright – in the words of one of the women 'leaving his chin where it was'. But when he got control of it again it was to give Murdo a short sharp tongue-lashing of which the most wounding phrase to an elder of the kirk was 'disgusting old man'. The two women, who had only a modest command of basic English, couldn't for the lives of them see what was so dramatically wrong with offering an invalid chicken. The young nurse, who had been trained in a Glasgow hospital, did understand but she couldn't find words to intervene quickly enough without letting her own modesty slip. Before anybody could do anything Dr MacBeth was on his bicycle and away, leaving his Gladstone bag behind in his fluster. And the drowsy new mother in the bed wondered vaguely why everybody denied flatly that there had been a bit of a hullabaloo as the doctor departed.

The baby must have arrived at the beginning of a school long weekend because only a Primary Two bothered to announce 'Doctor MacBeth gave Murdo Mor's wife a baby.' Somebody at the back sniggered but the teacher, blushing only slightly, in her wisdom let it pass.

Chapter Fifteen

The story of Murdo Mor and the doctor went round the four townships like wildfire. The young bloods revelled in it, but, for once, they couldn't improve on it. Some of the older men, who knew only Gaelic, had to have it explained to them, and they marvelled that a great language like English could be so imprecise that one word could mean two such entirely different things. Some people were furious with doctor for even entertaining the thought that Murdo Mor could contemplate asking such an indelicate question; others thought it only poetic justice that he should have his pomposity pricked at last: he had always been only too ready to bamboozle people at Grazing Committee meetings by introducing English technical phrases into the proceedings. And, needless to say, somebody made a song which I was never allowed to hear. . . .

Unbeknownst to us, our own family was scheduled for a meeting with Dr MacBeth which had nothing to do with my mother's impending confinement, of which no mention had ever been made in the house since it had been so unceremoniously announced in Conversation. Out of the blue Calum the Post brought us the news – verbally needless to say – that Big Grandfather was going to descend on us the very next day 'for a week or two'. A week or two! My parents were completely nonplussed. For the life of them they couldn't understand why the old man, who usually timed his visits to supervise the spring work or the harvest, should decide to visit us in bleak winter. Perhaps my father was apprehensive lest his father-in-law, who was very solicitous of his younger daughter's well-being, was going to keelhaul him for putting her in the family way at a time when our circumstances were at a low ebb. Which the self-same father-in-law was quite capable of doing.

But no. The old man had come all the way to Scarista for the express purpose of consulting Dr MacBeth whom he had heard to be 'very good with feet'. Big Grandfather's feet, which had troubled him for as long as I could remember, and which he had ruthlessly exploited for sympathy, were getting steadily worse, and he was now driven to hirpling around on a walking stick. Matters had finally come to a head when he had found himself unfit to take part in the autumn round-up of the sheep on the hill, and when somebody had mentioned Dr MacBeth's hitherto unsuspected talent in pedicure he had clutched like the drowning man . . .

It was obvious that the story of Murdo Mor had not reached Grandfather, and my father, who had been sympathetic to the doctor although he had enjoyed the joke, was certainly not going to embark on stories even remotely concerned with pregnancy and birth to a father-in-law who had not yet indicated pleasure or otherwise at the prospect of being made a grandfather for the third time. Quite apart from that, the old man might have had to have the *double-entendre* explained to him, and that could have been laborious and slightly indelicate. In his youth the old man had sailed as a deck hand on rich men's yachts, and he had acquired a good working knowledge when the mood came over him, of conversational English which he was inclined to flourish by slinging into a Gaelic conversation phrases which could sometimes be slightly off-beat like 'When in Rome, do as the Roumanians do', nobody would ever dream of correcting him.

'It's a great Christmas present your mother's going to be giving you then,' he said as he lifted my brother and myself, one on to each knee.

'What?' I asked innocently.

'A wee sister.'

I could feel the blood rushing to my face.

'I don't want a wee sister! I don't want anything!'

'So I hear,' he said, 'but you're looking at it the wrong way all together. Think how handy she'll be for washing the dishes and fetching the water pails! You'll be having a life of Reilly of it once she's grown up a bit.'

Before I could formulate a response to what I would normally have regarded as commendable chauvinism he turned to my father and said, 'This'll be making you get on with collecting stones for building a new house, or else putting another room on to this one.'

My father was so relieved by the old man's attitude that he decided to ignore the barbed reference to the fact that we still hadn't graduated to a stone house. Instead he came out with a remark which was news to me and completely distracted my attention from the sore subject of the new baby.

'I'm putting an extension on to this house, right enough, but it's for a loom I'm putting it on.'

'A loom!' Grandfather spluttered. 'A loom! The place is a forest of looms, and not a tweed selling anywhere. You must be out of your senses, man. You should be getting on with rearing beasts for the market; people are always going to be looking for meat and that's where they'll first start putting their money when things improve. If things improve. Most of the time I think it'll take a war to get things moving again. But tweeds! Pish!'

This was an old argument. For some reason which I've never been able to discover, Grandfather despised the weaver's trade, and he made no secret of it even though he knew that it was the profession of my grandfather on the other side. The news that we were going to get a loom of our own was exciting, and my brother and I slipped away to discuss it, leaving them to argue till such time as my mother decided to intervene and silence them.

Dr MacBeth arrived next morning. He listened to my

164

Grandfather's tale of woe about his feet, turning to my father now and again for clarification when Grandfather's idioms became too outlandish, and then he got down to the business of examining them. Now and again the old man winced as the doctor pressed and probed at his heels and his soles, and once in a while he let out a yelp of pain. The examination didn't take long. The doctor stood up.

'You're in a bad way right enough,' he said 'you should have been seen to long ago.'

The old man looked at my father triumphantly. At last he was being taken seriously.

'Do you know the shore here?'

The old man looked slightly taken aback, but he nodded.

'The rocky part? The skerries?'

The old man nodded again.

'Do you know the very first little bay you come to when you leave the sandy beach?'

By now Grandfather appeared to be willing to nod in response to anything, although it was beginning to look as if he wasn't really taking everything in. But he took the next bit in all right.

'I want you to go down there twice a day at dead low tide, and paddle for a quarter of an hour each time. A *full* quarter of an hour,' the doctor said emphatically. And then he added, rather unnecessarily one would have thought, 'In your bare feet.'

The doctor picked up his Gladstone bag which he had never opened.

'Make sure he does it,' he said to my father as he turned to go away.

'Don't worry, I'll make sure Doctor!' The enthusiasm in my father's voice caused the old man to glare, but he said never a word during the whole time that my father was walking the doctor down to the gate. He just sat with his hands on his knees staring down at his bare feet, and when Tiger came up to sniff at his toes he kicked him to the far side of the room.

'What the devil kind of a doctor is that?' he exploded when my father returned.

'He's a very brilliant man. He was in Africa for five years before he came here, he was telling me!'

'The damn sea's warm in Africa! If he thinks I'm going to make a fool of myself going paddling at my age in the middle of winter, he's—'

'Oh, you're going all right. I promised the doctor you'd do exactly as he said, and he's coming back to see you two weeks from today.'

My mother spoke for the first time. 'Are you sure he won't catch his death of cold, John?'

'Not at all. He'll have his coat and his scarf and his cap on. It'll do him a world of good. Just you wait and see.'

I had rarely heard my father so enthusiastic, and the more eloquently he waxed the more difficulty he had in keeping the smile in his eyes out of his voice. I felt sorry for the old man. I knew the exact spot that the doctor had mentioned. It had a bottoming of smooth round stones the size of a man's fist, and they were so slippery and coggly that I could barely keep my feet on them. I also knew that even in high summer the sea was icy cold at full ebb.

The voice from St Clement's bench was getting plaintive.

'One of the low tides is bound to be in pitch dark at this time of the year.'

'Pitch dark! There's a moon you could read *Cooper's Wee Red Book* by.' My father had to turn his back, and even my mother's frown was giving way to a twinkle. 'And, in any case, there's a good double-wick lantern in the byre.'

I don't know how much the doctor had enlarged on his treatment to my father when they were alone outside, but it became obvious that – funny though he might find it – father was going to make Grandfather follow the instructions to the letter. And he did. And in all fairness to him he accompanied the old man on every one of his extraordinary excursions. And within four or five days Grandfather was beginning to admit that his feet were getting

166

better. By the time Dr MacBeth re-appeared in a fortnight's time, his patient was like a man who had been given a new lease of life. He went off home with a pair of arch supports which the doctor instructed him to wear inside his shoes for a further fortnight and then throw away.

The old man never had any trouble with his feet again, and by the time the spring sheep round-up came he was on the hill with the rest. There may be more sophisticated cures for fallen arches now, but I doubt if any are more effective than the bizarre treatment doled out by a doctor who was shrewd enough to know that there was enough of a hint of witch medicine in his treatment to appeal to the hint of primitive belief in a big strong man. And it wasn't just Grandfather's feet that Dr MacBeth cured. He healed his own reputation at the same time. He didn't stay with us for long, but when he left, the money that subscribed towards his presentation was far in excess of that which the length of his service would normally have merited, and considerably in excess of what our people, in those days, could really afford.

I wonder where he came from, and where he went to – that lonely, kilted man? What was he seeking that sent him to such extremes of geography as Africa and our Atlantic village? He gave of his talent, but nothing else of himself. Never a hint of a family, or a background, or an ambition. And yet he gave us something undefinable, and something that perhaps we needed more than we knew – a glisk of colour when the world was grey, and something to talk about when conversation was growing in on itself and doubts were beginning to creep into our hopes as our hopes were beginning to fade. There were a few like that who came, usually in search of our quaintnesses so that they could write us up in books, till we began to feel that, perhaps, it might be as well to live up to the image of exotica that they so desperately sought. And in the pleasing of them we were creating the myths about ourselves that we are only now beginning to resent – forgetting that we were accessories to the forging of them.

Even had Dr MacBeth stayed on for another month or two I doubt whether my mother would have called on his services when her time came. First babies are heralded with fanfares of interest ranging from guesses at the sex to countings of the months since the wedding. Second babies are regarded as inevitable. Third ones are usually mistakes or else a frantic re-cutting of the pack in the hope of a change of suit. After two boys, the chances were that mother's third effort would result in a girl since she and father both came from mixed families, but even that prospect wasn't novel enough to tempt my grandmother south in mid-winter since her other daughter was also on the point of providing her with another grandchild nearer home. It was obviously felt that everything could be safely left in the capable hands of a new and highly regarded District Nurse who had come to us from a neighbouring island and, consequently, was a Gaelic speaker for good measure.

Not that I knew anything about what was going on. In fact I must have been singularly unobservant because I didn't attach any particular significance to the more frequent comings and goings by the neighbouring women, or even to the fact that Calum the Post brought a couple of parcels that mysteriously disappeared without their contents being divulged. I was only vaguely puzzled by a day of frenetic activity when my mother set about washing and scrubbing every inch of the house and every stick of furniture with hot water and carbolic soap. I lost track of the number of times that I was sent to the river for buckets of water, and to the end of the house for pails of peat, while my father wandered about aimlessly, filling and re-filling his pipe and being suspiciously solicitous towards us all. And all the while my mother turned mattresses, renewed blankets, and even heaved St Clement's bench away from the wall unaided in search of lurking spiders or offending dust. It was only when my father announced that he was going to milk Rosy and Spotty – the job he hated most around the croft – that I began to suspect that something highly unusual was afoot. And when he went and borrowed a neighbour's bicycle, which I had never even suspected that he could ride, I knew exactly what the unusual occurrence was going to be. It was a Saturday evening, and there was no Calum the Post to take a message to the nurse.

As it turned out, the whole event was an anti-climax. My brother and I were put to bed together on an improvised shake-down on St Clement's bench, and when I whispered to him what was going to happen we decided that we would keep watch into the night. Which we did, nudging each other into wakefulness long after the lamp had been extinguished and my father and mother gone through to the bedroom. But to no avail. It was well into Sunday morning when the clatter of the kettle on the stove jerked me back into wakefulness, and there was my mother preparing breakfast with her girth, which I had noticed for the first time yesterday, undiminished. She smiled at me. 'Sleepy-heads,' she said. 'There could have been a dozen babies arriving here during the night, and you wouldn't even have known.' It was the first direct reference she had ever made to her pregnancy and, suddenly, I felt much more reconciled to the event.

'Is it really going to be a girl, mother?'

'Even if I knew I wouldn't tell you. There are some things that are better to come as a surprise. But, in any case, nobody knows. You don't know what a lamb's going to be till it arrives, do you? And,' she went on gently, 'it's not going to make any difference to you anyway. You're always going to be the eldest.'

There was an irrefutable and reassuring logic about that which I didn't bother to try to analyse. My Grandfather's remarks about a girl 'being useful for going to the well' came back to me, and suddenly I found myself not worrying at the prospect of a new arrival after all, and even half hoping it might be a girl.

But it wasn't. And when he arrived, he arrived stealthily in the night. By Monday, although we were still relegated to the shake-down on St Clement's bench, my brother had

169

given up the attempt to keep vigil, and we were beginning to enjoy the experience of sleeping in the living room because it meant that we couldn't be put to bed till there was no chance of any casual visitor dropping in, and father and mother were, themselves, ready to go through to bed. So, for a moment, I was puzzled when I woke to the clatter of the kettle on the Tuesday morning and found a strange woman standing over the stove making tea. Even if I hadn't seen her before, I would have known from her crisp overall that she was the District Nurse.

'Good morning, young men,' she said breezily in the foreign accent of the island of Uist. 'If you don't hurry up and get your clothes on you won't have time to have a look at your new brother before you go to school. Do you want me to help you into your trousers?'

'No!' I blurted out in horror, not knowing which emotion was uppermost – the idea of a strange woman seeing my nakedness or disappointment at the thought that the newcomer wasn't a wee sister after all. I pulled the bedclothes over my head.

'All right,' she laughed. 'I'm taking a cup of tea through to your mother. I'll give you five minutes to get washed and dressed.' I peeped over the top of the blanket to make sure that she'd gone, shook my brother awake, and we dressed more quickly than we had ever done in our lives before.

I knew that Calum the Post had come to the house with a bottle of whisky and two bottles of port at the end of the previous week, because I'd been there when my father had opened the parcel and given him a dram. But I hadn't realized that he would be the last male visitor we would see for the ten days of my mother's purdah, because, for that time, any man who chanced to come to the house, even unwittingly, would be accused of having a *bial-bangaid* – a birthday mouth – which was the phrase for a man who came to a house on such an occasion in the hope of getting a free dram. No such inhibition applied to the women who had already begun to flock to the house

170

as we got home from school after our baptism of tauntings and teasings. They were intent on making short shrift of the port as they rattled merrily through the housework and the preparation of meals for our mother and father and ourselves. The whisky was left strictly alone, except for a token sip that my father would take every time he poured a glass of port, which he did so often that Calum had to be contacted to replenish supplies before two days were out. It was a fiesta almost on the scale of the Hen Wedding for the women-folk who, in all conscience, found few enough occasions for celebration in those lean times. As for my brother and myself, we were never so over-indulged in our lives, and my mother would have had fits if she had realized the diet of home-baked cakes, and pancakes and scones to which we were being treated. But she was oblivious to what was going on in the living room, and seemed content to remain propped up in bed, looking rested and pretty with her pink new baby almost permanently at her breast. Once or twice, when we crept in to see her, I felt the old qualms of jealousy returning, but she always went out of her way to be affectionate and friendly and make us feel that our importance was un diminished.

In a few days the excitement, inevitably, started to ebb as the women-folk began to ease off and return to the routines of their own homes now that all was clearly going to be well. But it was still going to be some days before mother would be allowed to get up, far less be allowed to tackle the domestic chores, and it must have been a vast relief to my father when Sarah, a second or third cousin of mine, arrived at the door with a suitcase and the news that her mother had sent her to keep house for us till such time as Auntie Kate, as she called her, was well and truly on her feet again. No less relieved was the last of the neighbour women to leave. 'Ah well, that's it till the next time,' she said to my father, who looked embarrassed and tut-tutted. 'You'll be tired of a houseful of women. But you'll be having no shortage of young men around now that Sarah's here.'

For some reason I found myself resenting the prediction although I didn't understand the implication. 'Wee Sarah' as she was called because she had the same name as her mother, had always been a very special friend of mine. We had played together since I was a toddler in the North-lands. It had been to her I had run in tears when my father had drowned the kitten in that peaty pool, and my mother had failed to comfort me, that day now so long ago. Un-beknownst to anybody Sarah and I had taken a long wire and tried to hook the kitten back out without success.

She had been a regular visitor during long week-ends and holiday times while we were staying with Great Aunt Rachel and in the schoolhouse and, more frequently, since we had moved into what I still thought of as the new house. Without anybody noticing she had slipped into teenage and left school, and now here she was, a chubby little girl still in all our eyes, but brought up to be a competent housekeeper by a notoriously house-proud mother. She could even milk a cow, and that gave her extra special prestige in the eyes of my father who had secretly confessed to me that he was worried that the milk supply was going down, and that the cows would be well-nigh dry by the time my mother was up and about. But I wasn't to let on in case mother started worrying and attempted to get out of bed too soon. I understood his fears full well, and knew that it would be serious for us if we began to run short of milk in winter; as it was, Rosy was farrow and giving very little milk; and Spotty was very temperamental and didn't respond well to father's milking. That night in the byre, as I held the lantern for her, I told Sarah about my father's worries, but she tossed her head and laughed.

'It's easy to work a cow back up if you know how', she said. And it wasn't difficult to see what she meant. Unlike my father she was a two-handed milker, and though her hands were barely large enough to grasp the swollen teats, she had the true milker's rhythmic pull, and the two jets of milk alternated into the foaming pail as if they were one continuous stream; it required only a glimpse of the cow's face as she stood contentedly chewing her cud to realize that Spotty knew that she was in no danger of sudden sharp tug or nick and was prepared to let her milk flow accordingly.

Father was delighted to be able to relax over his newspaper again. And I, of course, was revelling in my continued late nights. My brother had been moved back to the bedroom where he would share the second bed with my father, and Sarah and I were put on St Clement's bench which had been widened with a row of inward-facing chairs lined beside it. The evenings went by in almost unbroken silence once my brother went to bed. Sarah had brought with her a pile of some of the comics which were beginning to find their way to the islands then – the *Beano*, and *Dandy*, the *Hotspur* and the *Wizard* – and though some of them were weeks old they were new to me, and exciting beyond description. Sarah, who had read them all several times, would help me get the serial cartoon strips and adventure stories into sequence, and we would sit, without word or sound except for the turning pages, till father finally folded away his *Daily Express* and got up to put the cat out. It was only when the bar of light showing above the bedroom door was extinguished that Sarah and I would begin to talk. She had an endless supply of stories about the boys and girls I had known, and now barely remembered, in the Northlands. Being older she was also privileged to hear some of the adult gossip, and the company of teenagers older than herself had provided her with a fund of the kind of story that parents fondly imagine only boys exchange; my father would have been more than a little astonished if he had heard some of the jokes that his innocent son was being taught to appreciate. Invariably, however, it was father's hoarse 'Shut up you two and go to sleep' that finally drew the entertainment to a close.

All too soon, the night came that was to be Sarah's last. Mother had been getting up for longer and longer each day, and she had announced that she was now ready to take charge. It was like the end of a holiday. And I knew in my heart that once mother was in full charge, there would be a period of tough discipline till she got the household moving in its normal, workaday rhythm again. For a long time after father's demand for silence I lay awake feeling slightly sad; already the first pangs of loneliness were beginning to creep in on me because I knew that by the time I came home from school next day Sarah would be gone. But tiredness was beginning to take over, and I was just dropping over the edge of the dark when I became aware of Sarah's breathing beside me. I snapped back. At first I thought she was crying and I vaguely wondered what had upset her.

'What's wrong?'

There was no reply.

'Are you all right?'

Still there was no reply, and I realized that what had brought me back to wakefulness was the heavy breathing of someone who sounded as if she had been running. Which was a ridiculous fancy. She must be dreaming.

'Are you asleep, Sarah?'

Then, so lightly that at first I thought I was imagining it, I felt her fingers touch my naked thigh. It was nothing. Just a brushing, light, passing touch that had probably happened accidentally a score of times before, except that this time something from an unknown area of instinct told me it was no accident but a signal that I understood but didn't know how to obey. I felt my chest tensing and, incongruously, something inside me going cold at the same time as a radiating heat enveloped me from the young body beside me – a body that seemed to have changed suddenly; although it wasn't touching mine, I was aware that it was full and mature in a way that I had never noticed. Then a dryness of the mouth, and something that savoured of fear. Slowly the lightly caressing

174

fingers moved upwards till they reached that part of me that nobody's fingers had ever touched before except my mother's in a clinical and altogether different way which had left no memory. And now that part of me, without my control or command, sprang into the firm grip of someone who could never again be just a childhood friend.

'Come on', she whispered. 'You know what to do.'

I couldn't move.

'Come on, I'll show you.' And I felt myself being pulled over on my side.

'No', I managed to croak hoarsely.

'What are you afraid of? Come on, it's our last chance!' and she began to kiss me on the lips.

Then something snapped.

'Leave me alone. I don't like you now!' The words came out before I could stop them and without my meaning them.

There was a sudden stillness, and an ebbing of warmth like a door opening on snow. And anger that was like a whiplash as she turned her back.

'Coward. Rotten little baby. You're not even a boy, far less a man.'

The palpable silence of a woman scorned. I lay for a time of which I have no measure, with my whole being urging me to turn to her and beg her to start where she had left off. But my tongue wouldn't say what I wanted, and my hands didn't know where to go. Sometime before morning I fell asleep, and when I woke I imagined I had been dreaming till I looked up and saw Sarah bent over the stove, her face flushed and her eyes avoiding mine. Before I could think of anything to say the bedroom door opened and my father came through. He opened his mouth to say something, and then stopped himself and looked quickly from one to the other.

'All right, Sarah,' he said briskly, 'you go and milk the cows and I'll get the boys ready for school.'

It was a long day. Since the arrival of the baby my brother and I had got into the habit of taking a sandwich to school and having 'a piece lunch' with the boys and girls who came from the far end of the township. We were doing that today, mercifully for the last time, since mother would from now on be back in command. When I got back home at four o'clock, Sarah was gone, and there was nothing left from her visit except a pile of comics on St Clement's bench. I flung my bundle of books down beside them without looking to right or to left or saying hello, and turned, and went back out.

I remember walking slowly up the path which my father had worn beside the river as he went up and down the hill each day for a sack of peat. It was the only path that led anywhere, and yet, without the purpose of the peat in mind, didn't lead anywhere at all. I had reached the boundary wall of the croft when I heard my mother's voice sharply calling me back home to fill the water pails. I turned, automatically, to obey, and I could see the village with its outline already dimmed grey in the early winter dusk, and, for a moment, I fancied that it had changed. Of course it hadn't. A village can't change overnight. But a boy can.

BOOK TWO
CROTAL AND WHITE

To Les Robinson,
who started it all

Chapter One

I have very few certificates to prove that I ever achieved anything, and the lack of them may be, in itself, certification of the real truth! But I have one which I treasure, although I have no recollection of ever deserving or winning it. It is headed *CHURCH OF SCOTLAND Sunday School* and goes on to say *Awarded to Finlay Macdonald for Regular Attendance and Good Conduct. (Signed) Adèle Kerr. Manse. Scarista.* Like that famous portrait of Dorian Gray the certificate has retained its pristine freshness while the years have etched their lines on the face and soul and conscience of its possessor! I remember well the night on which it should have been presented to me, and why it wasn't. . . .

Today the great big manse to which it refers still stands like a Manor House overlooking what remains of the village that my father and seven other ex-servicemen of the First World War carved out of South Harris half a century ago. It was built two hundred and fifty years ago when a huge population were in thrall to landlords of doubtful social morality, men who held the land as if by divine right and as a means of creating wealth for themselves and their descendants. The 'people' were the tools for the extraction of the wealth and, in the nineteenth century in particular, those people lived in conditions which were described by one traveller as being 'in many ways inferior to those of the American negro slaves'. Certainly they were colder, because the main source of landlord wealth in the early 1800s was the collection of seaweed, or kelp, for drying and burning into a powder which was a rich and valuable source of soda and iodine and many

I

other by-products. The landlords made fortunes, which many of them squandered on high living in London and other European capitals; the workers were paid pennies and lived in crowded squalor on the Atlantic shores. It is an old story, of which the memory may have lingered on too long.

In those days the minister was paid by the landlord and supplied with a palatial manse, which accommodated not only his own large family but also provided 'overflow' lodgings for the landlord's occasional summer guests. Inevitably, in time, the minister tended to become the laird's man rather than the Lord's man and put his own and his patron's worldly well-being before the needs of his flock. When the kelp industry collapsed and failed in the face of competition from imported chemicals the population of the Western Highlands became unemployed and unemployable and unwanted. Many of them starved. Thousands were shipped overseas in a pogrom which was, of its time, as ruthless as the Nazi solution of the Jewish 'problem'. The first huge batch of people evicted from the Southlands of Harris disappeared without trace. Their ship may have sunk, along with many others, somewhere in the Atlantic. Or it is just possible that they may have reached the maritime provinces of Canada. There were at least two more waves of eviction after that one, because the soft land of South Harris was highly desirable for successive generations of sheep farmers who did not require a large population to further their own selfish interests as the 'kelp lords' had done. Our huge manse and the church which stood beside it were monuments to those older times, but by the time our village was established we could barely muster a congregation of 30 in a church which had been built for four hundred.

The manse itself has long since been vacated in favour of a modern smaller building more suited to the modest aspirations and the greater continence of today's clergymen, but the old Georgian building still stands, surveying, as it has always done, some three thousand acres of the most beautiful country in Britain – lush meadowland, mountains that are forbidding or inviting according to the seasons and their moods, and an infinity of shell-white sand pounded by the combed breakers of an ocean whose other shore is Canada where live and

2

prosper, perhaps, the descendants of that lost generation I spoke of.

They call it *Scarista House* now but it will always be 'the manse' to me. Its reputation grows year by year as a temple of good living, and on its altar, exotically disguised, are sacrificed the fishes and the molluscs which we regarded as the food of poverty but which, in a new age, attract the gourmet scribes who steal in anonymously to decide which of their gold and silver accolades they will bestow.

I have visited *Scarista House* only once in this new phase of its existence, and met for the first time the enterprising couple who have brought about its transformation. We talked of the old days that I remembered and the new future that they are creating. I was curious to know what memories of the past they had unearthed during their careful rehabi-litation of the old building, what mementoes of those generations of successive pastors of varying personality and ability and divinity? A riding crop in the old stables, perhaps? A faded Victorian portrait in a cellar? A dusty tome in an attic?

'Nothing!' they said. With a curiosity as natural as my own they had scoured the old building from foundations to rafters expecting to find some clue to the character, good or bad, of one or other of their scores of predecessors, but it was as if God had decided to wipe the slate clean and leave no shred of evidence of the worldly frailties of his departed servants. Only the kitchen garden had yielded anything at all, and that was mystery rather than clue. When they had attempted to dig it over in order to add their own home-grown vegetables to their prestigious menus they found they couldn't sink a spade without a clink, as every upturned sod revealed a long-concealed bottle. Bottles upon bottles. And their lack of variety was monotonous in the extreme, even if puzzling in no small measure. The ones that hadn't once upon a time contained champagne, had contained that well known laxative known as *California Syrup of Figs*. Champagne and syrup of figs! An unlikely cocktail. Perhaps the old Scottish metrical psalm makes the only possible comment:

3

The troubles that afflict the just
In numbers many be. . . .

As I left the old manse and walked slowly down the path to
the new road – for which the foundations were being laid when
I was a boy in the new village – I smiled to myself at the
incongruity of champagne bottles hidden in the garden of a
Harris church house. Champagne! Of all things it was
probably the least known in our village. And then out of the
shadowy recesses of my memory came the name on my Sunday
School Certificate. Adèle! It certainly was not one of the
village's most common names. Involuntarily I glanced over
my shoulder back to the big house lest through a casement
window I might glimpse once more her friendly shade.

Mrs Kerr was the young widow of the old minister who had
died shortly after we had started making the village in the new
world of the Southlands. There is nothing unusual about an
old minister leaving a young widow, but what set Mrs Kerr
apart was that she was French. Or to be precise she was a
Channel Islander with a pedigree as French as Fifi; and how
she found herself in the remoteness of the Outer Hebrides as
a very young housekeeper to a Hebridean minister of advanced
middle age I shall never know. Legend has it that my Great
Aunt Rachel, who was employed in the manse at the time, saw
the minister and the housekeeper leave the manse one morning,
not to return till late evening. 'Rachel,' the minister is alleged
to have said when they got back, 'I should like you to call
Adèle "Mrs Kerr" from now on.' 'That,' said Aunt Rachel,
'is much more seemly.' And that was that.

Mrs Kerr must have been a very lonely woman in the years
of her widowhood. There was always a social barrier between
any incumbent of the manse and the local people, and it may
well have been exaggerated in our community by the fact that
our men were all ex-servicemen, some of whom had spent long
years in France during the First World War and, in their
occasionally expansive moments, were inclined to make sly
little references to nights on the town when they weren't in the
trenches. There was little about Mrs Kerr to suggest Mont-
martre or the Café de Paris, but, nevertheless, the village

4

women were inclined to look at her askance. Perhaps it was loneliness that made her, in a manner of speaking, *adopt* the school; and Miss Martin, our schoolmistress (ever receptive to anything that might help widen our horizons), was only too willing to give the lady from the manse the run of the classroom for the last couple of hours of some Friday afternoons. At that time I was just beginning to feel modestly confident in the very elementary stages of the English language, and it came as a shock when it was brought home to me by Mrs Kerr that there was a third language in the world, and maybe even more beyond!

It was Mrs Kerr also who introduced us to the festival of Christmas. Up till then Christmas had just been a date on the calendar, and our seasonal festivities had been confined to the two New Years – the newfangled one on the thirty-first day of December and the old one, celebrated by my Great Aunt Rachel's generation according to the Julian calendar on the twelfth of January. It was around the middle of November, if I remember rightly, that Mrs Kerr announced to us that Christmas was going to be on the twenty-fifth of December that year and that, to prove it, there was going to be a party in the manse.

The 13 of us who comprised the school glanced at each other uncomfortably and shuffled our winter boots on the floor – the nearest that the Hebridean school child of those days could ever get to enthusiasm or applause. Some discreet whispering reassured the more monoglot infants that 'a party was a good thing', and for the rest of the afternoon a general feeling of goodwill pervaded the green and yellow classroom. Only the teacher looked slightly flushed and apprehensive. Obviously the idea was new to her too and, in retrospect, as a member of the fundamentalist Free Presbyterian Church she must have had grave doubts about the propriety of celebrating a festival with slightly Papist overtones in the manse of a not-so-fundamentalist Church of Scotland. But Mrs Kerr was a magnanimous patron of the school in so many ways that a rejection of her plan would have been hurtful. In any case the teacher's reservations were slightly assuaged when Mrs Kerr added that the Sunday School Certificates would be handed

5

out at the end of the proceedings; that must have seemed slightly like 'grace after meat' and from then on she entered into the scheme with enthusiasm.

At the end of the day we were each given a note to take home to our parents; notes which shattered the general bonhomie when they were read, as all such notes were read and assessed, at a conventicle convened below the red road-bridge on the way home. The notes stated baldly that a Christmas Treat would be held in the manse on the evening of 24 December and that all pupils would be kept in school for an extra hour each evening until then in order to prepare items for the party. One further cryptic sentence exhorted parents to assist children with any extra homework which might be involved. Homework! Big Hugh MacGregor, who would be leaving school come summer with barely enough education to be a carter, snorted and declared that if anybody farted in class the teacher would make it an excuse to give us a homework essay on flatulence. The boys laughed uproariously and the girls blushed, but the enthusiasm went out of us. Our only hope was that our parents might find some reason for objection – perhaps the one or two with the same severe attitudes to religion as the teacher – but it seemed a faint possibility; as far as most of the villagers were concerned, their respect for anything savouring of education was as profound as the teacher's own; part of her success was that she had so much of their backing. It was silently that we dropped off in our ones and twos at our respective gates.

At times of peat-cutting or of harvest our fathers and mothers might possibly have made some vague protest against the extra school hour on the grounds that it would be depriving them of extra hands to labour on the croft. But not in November.

November was a dead month in the village, and the nights were long. The brittle crispness of the autumn had vanished, and the school was already being disbanded at three o'clock because it was getting too dark to read. The winds were beginning to haunt the north and the west, and the gales would sometimes be salt from the sea. People didn't go out much at night, unless they had to, because, although we didn't know it, middle age – which came earlier then than now – was

6

already creeping in on men who had married later than usual because they had lost the five most precious years of their lives in the war. The few, from the original population of the village, who were old enough for courting had nobody to court unless they went far afield, and – even if their loins were aching enough to tempt them face the blustery dark – experience had taught them that the soggy ground of winter made even the traditional nooks and crannies untempting for romance. And so all things conspired to cocoon people in their homes with their peat fires and their oil lamps. There was no radio as yet, and – unless a man was an avid reader like my father who would be beginning his annual foray into Gibbon's *Decline and Fall* . . . – they had little to do unless there was a tweed being prepared and the woman of the house needed help breaking up or 'teasing' the fleeces which she had dyed in the autumn, mixing the red-brown gobbets of coloured wool with tufts of untreated white in the exact proportions to give the shade of crotal and white which the water mill in the Northlands would blend and refine and return ready for spinning. That was the only part of the tweed-making process in which a man could help unless he was a weaver, which my father wasn't as yet. As boys, my brother and I could only be called on for occasional help because the mixing of the wool was crucial to the final blend.

As we approached the door I had little hope that either of our parents would raise any objection to the extra hour in school. On the contrary, I suspected that, like all the other parents of the village, they would welcome an extra hour of peace and quiet in the house, and greet any additional homework as something to keep us occupied during the winter nights. Mother had just lit the double-wick oil lamp as I got in and she was standing waiting for the glass funnel to warm before turning up the flame. I handed the teacher's note to father and he read it out aloud when the light went up.

'A Christmas Treat! Well, well, things are looking up for you young ones. Didn't I tell you some good would come out of going to Sunday School, and you grousing your heads off every Sunday afternoon. I wish somebody would organize a Christmas Treat for parents!'

My mother had been going to start setting the table for the evening meal once she'd got the lamp going to her satisfaction but she had stopped to listen.

'That'll be Mrs Kerr's idea,' she said. 'But she's forgetting something. How are you going to see what you're doing in school for an extra hour in the afternoon at this time of the year? You're already being allowed home early because of the dark.'

'Ach, you'd be surprised what French women can do in the dark.'

My mother slammed a dish on the table.

'And there'll be no shortage of fathers to go and meet the children when they get out!'

I noticed my father hiding a smile as he put his pipe in his mouth, but I didn't try to puzzle out what the interchange was about – as I usually did if I thought it was something I wasn't supposed to understand. All that concerned me was that my mother had almost certainly hit on something that Mrs Kerr and Miss Martin had overlooked, and that we might escape the extra hour of school after all. But the prospect wasn't totally pleasing. The idea of a party had been beginning to appeal to me – if a party was something like the wedding I'd been at, as, something suggested to me, it might well turn out to be.

We had all underestimated the resourcefulness of the two ladies in question. When Calum the Post came round with his red van on Saturday morning he knew all about the Christmas Treat.

'What a carry on,' I heard him saying to my father. 'I've got an order from the manse that will empty every shop in the Southlands of candles. She's the one who usually grumbles about the Royal Mail being used for free, but there's no word of that when she wants something herself. "Six dozen candles," says she. "And be sure you don't forget them!" The bloody schoolhouse is going to look like a lighthouse – if she doesn't set it on fire! Which wouldn't surprise me – her with her fancy French customs. Christmas in Paris is one thing; Christmas in Harris is something different altogether. It's bad enough the way things are going for me with all the extra mail that's beginning to flood in every year!'

8

Calum was still grumbling as he crunched the red van into gear. It wasn't like him. He happily carried bags of potatoes and sacks of raw tweed for the crofters without letting it worry his official conscience that not a penny was going into the coffers of the Post Office, but he hated being taken advantage of by anybody in the higher realms of society – as the inhabitants of the manse were deemed to be. However, even in those days, it was difficult to get out of the tentacles of the black economy once one succumbed to it, even for the most charitable of purposes, and Calum would doubtless come to terms with his qualms once he convinced himself, as he would, that he was really acting for the good of the children of the community. And once he remembered that the manse and the landlord's house were the only two establishments on his beat that crossed his palm with silver at Hogmanay instead of giving him a dram.

On Monday afternoon the candles were lit for the first time, as they were to be lit for each school afternoon for the forthcoming weeks. And we all conceded that they created a nice atmosphere in the classroom and gave it a character that was more pleasant than usual by far. As my mother had predicted, the fathers of the village didn't find it in the slightest burdensome to organize themselves into small posses to escort us home through the dark, although not for the reasons that she'd been hinting at. In a small country community the simplest little events became *occasions* when time otherwise tended to hang heavy, and for men without a pub, or any other social convenience to lighten the long hours, even meeting together at the schoolhouse for a brief yarn was a break from the darg.

Right through what remained of that long November and the December which followed we did an hour's overtime each school day and burnt up candles like a cathedral. And time and again, as new ideas came to the rejuvenated Mrs Kerr, hours of preparation were jettisoned and we set off on new tacks. The whole thing wasn't without its interests and excitements, for we were forever being introduced to concepts that were new to us. Carols, for example. Up till then our adventures into singing had been confined to the psalms of

9

that David whom we had hitherto regarded as a poetical shepherd but who now turned out to have acquired a Royal City, and a few selected and highly improbable English songs from the prescribed text-book which had been subtly compiled to give us the impression that our own native culture and language had nothing of merit to offer us. Carols were something new altogether. They seemed to be trying to hide matters of mundanity in dresses of divinity and, for that very reason I suppose, Mrs Kerr and Miss Martin had to do some diplomatic horse-trading before they could agree on seasonal music that was acceptable to their divergent credos and mores. And there was also the matter of finding material that was suitable for the 12 ill-assorted voices of those who could sing – and me.

One that finally seemed to be mutually acceptable was *Good King Wenceslas*, presumably because he was an earthly king who didn't attempt to usurp the throne of the One higher up; because he was good; and because he had obvious leanings towards the new creed of socialism which was just beginning to filter across the Minch. At first I joined in the rehearsals with enthusiasm, which – when it came to singing – was always the last thing that anybody wanted from me, but the two ladies, on various pretexts, kept toning me down and down till at last I was reduced to a mere miming of the words and I lost interest. Instead, I passed the time for myself by attempting to unravel the meaning – if such there was – and the only way that I could get at the kernel of the meaning was by translating the whole thing laboriously into Gaelic for myself.

Good King Wenceslas looked out – that was simple and straightforward, even if there was no Gaelic for *Wenceslas*; the English did have some strange names after all. *On the feast of Stephen* was slightly more complicated, since the nearest approximation to a feast that I could envisage was Sunday dinner of salt mutton and potatoes or boiled chicken or rabbit . . . and splendid though they might be, those things didn't merit songs in our small part of the universe. But the whole thing lost its last claim to credibility on *When a poor man came in sight gathering winter fuel*. The nearest thing I knew to 'a poor man' was old Hector MacGeachan, who lived with his aged sister in a thatched black house on the moor's edge, and the only reason why I imagined him to be poor was because I'd heard people referring to him as 'poor old Hector', which I had thought was because he lived in a black house and not in a corrugated iron house like ours or one of the smart white stone and lime croft houses to which most of the villagers had by now graduated. I was to learn later that the reason why people called him 'poor old Hector' was because he had to live under the same roof as his virago of a sister, and when she died in unlikely circumstances in a ripeness of years I myself was destined to play an unlikely part in securing for old Hector a few final years of peace. But that's another story! Meantime I knew that whatever Hector's other faults might be, he was meticulous in his husbandry and he was always the first person in the village to have his winter peat-stack neatly secured at the end of his cottage. The idea of him plowtering through the moors looking for peat 'when the frost was cruel' was just too absurd for words, and so I abandoned my quest for a great truth in one of the world's best loved Christmas songs. I decided that if I was to indulge in fiction I would have fiction of my own choosing and so, while the others carolled and re-carolled, I resorted to surreptitiously reading my much-thumbed copy of *The Adventures of Dixon Hawke*. If the teacher noticed, she made sure she concealed her relief at being able to concentrate on her more promising choristers. I still can't sing *Good King Wenceslas* but I've still got a soft spot for him from those long years ago.

The first few weeks of preparation for the *Tret* (the word had now become accepted as a Gaelic one) were among the most contented of my school years. As the days wore on the need to conceal my detachment became less; every now and then I would look up and mime a few lines of whatever musical offering was being prepared for sacrifice and then I would return to whichever latest volume of *Dixon Hawke* I had been able to borrow. But then the teacher's enthusiasm took her by the scruff of the neck. One day, during normal school hours, she explained to us very carefully that Mrs Kerr came from another country (which we knew) and that that country had a National Anthem in the same way as our own country had a National Anthem (which we did not know) and that, as a big surprise for Mrs Kerr, we were secretly going to learn her native anthem and spring it on her at the end of the party.

I have had cause to reflect in the intervening years that poor Mrs Kerr had to conceal more than one emotion in the wake of that particular surprise, not least of which was that she had to accept having an alien nationality thrust upon her. We resumed friendship on an adult basis long years later and I learnt that though her maiden name had been Couvée, and though she had a French accent, she regarded herself as British as the Union Jack, and when the time came she chose to go back to her native Channel Islands to die. Perhaps if our 'surprise' had not been so well concealed she might have seized an early opportunity to correct the popular misconception as to her antecedents; but after that Christmas party she could no longer issue a disclaimer without causing embarrassment, and once she was enticed into bowing her head to the *Marseillaise* in public she was too late.

The shock of having discovered that there was a third language was equalled only by that of now finding myself in the situation of having to pronounce it. And there will always be for me a personal private agony in the words

Allons enfants de la patrie
Le jour de gloire est arrivé . . .

and all the rest of them. I was used to the idea of being unable to *sing* the words in a manner satisfying to anybody else, but being unable to *say* them was a totally new experience.

On the blackboard the words looked frightening enough but, at least, I could read them according to the laws of straight English. When it came to pronouncing them to the teacher's satisfaction, it was a different matter, because – to the surprise of all of us – it turned out that not only did she have a knowledge of the French language but a great love for it as well, and we went through painful hours while she tried to contort our vocal chords to produce noises for which nature had never intended them. We had only just mastered the art of toning down our rolling Hebridean rs to the more genteel requirements of English; now we were being pressed to reproduce a smoother type of r altogether from some vague bit at the backs of our palates, and our native nasal 'honk' sounds which were deemed unsuitable for English were now very much in demand in French. The only gratifying thing from my point of view was that, in the general cacophony, my alleged tunelessness passed without comment and my confidence in my own vocal ability began to be restored. We must have rehearsed that blessed chunk of the *Marseillaise* many hundreds of times, while up in the old manse, indulging in a sip of champagne for all I know, Mrs Kerr was blissfully unaware of the surprise being prepared for her. And, down in the schoolhouse, the schoolteacher was equally blissfully oblivious to the fact that the surprise was going to be greater than she expected.

Chapter Two

I N compiling a story in the genre for which the distinguished Antipodean invented the description 'unreliable
memoirs' I am keenly aware that many readers who
know the Hebrides as natives of a younger generation, or as
dedicated tourists visiting the islands under today's sophisticated conditions of transport or accommodation, may feel that
I am writing of a place conjured out of a free-ranging
imagination. But not so. While the tongue can't on occasion
help but wander into the cheek, while memory can play false
to details which are more the responsibility of the historian
anyway, and while discretion – but much more frequently
affection – makes me portray characters who have exchanged
their own foibles with those of others, this is the new village
substantially as it was at the time of the Christmas Treat.

Of the eight crofts which had been allocated to our ex-
servicemen after the war, four had already had their modern
stone-walled, slate-roofed, spacious houses built upon them
with grants and loans from the Board of Agriculture, which,
after many years of tentative effort, now seemed set to make
small-farming in the shape of crofting into a viable way of life.
Three crofts, including my father's, still had their original
wood and corrugated iron temporary shacks on them; the one
which had nothing at all on it belonged to a bachelor who
wasn't in the same hurry to establish a solid base. So long
as a man worked his land, no government pressure could be
brought upon him in terms of when he had to build or what
he had to build by way of family accommodation. In addition
to the eight formal crofts, there were still a few landless cottars

who lived on in their thatched black houses or had followed the lead of the incomers and put up what tended to be called shacks but were, in fact, small cosy homes lacking only in interior plumbing – which was not, after all, given very high priority even in Hebridean houses with more pretensions to grandeur than we had. What our community did have was a heart, unlike some more sophisticated mainland communities today, in the sense that we had, from the beginning, there awaiting us, a school, a church, and of course the old manse. And there it all was in a countryside of especial magic – a magic which is, in no way, the sentimental imagining of a nostalgic heart.

We looked poor to some of the travel writers who were beginning to seek us out with probing cameras and pens oozing purple prose; some of them made capital out of what they called our poverty because they didn't understand that poorness of amenity and lack of cash only represent poverty relative to the beholder's norms. Of course we looked poor to somebody from Mayfair in London or Morningside in Edinburgh. And we looked poor to socially conscious left wing observers like Louis MacNeice who wrote in *I crossed the Minch* about 'a row of poor shacks on the road to Leverburgh'. He was talking about us who were happy and contented – so far. What we did lack was pastime; because we were a new community, without time yet to build up a tradition, we didn't have the in-built traditional community recreations that had matured in old established Hebridean village societies whose folksong and lore were, even then, being archived; and, of course, the day of imported mechanical or pre-packed entertainment hadn't arrived. That was why simple occasions like the Christmas Treat assumed big proportions, and why little jokes got big laughs.

The *Tret* was, very nearly, not a laughing matter! It must have been loneliness, or the desire to be seen to be stretching out the hand of friendship, that prompted Mrs Kerr to invite every adult in the village to the last hour of the party. It was a wrong decision on every count!

The attitude of Western Islanders towards incomers into their communities can be ambivalent at the best of times, particularly if the incomer belongs to – or worse still, pretends to belong to – that strange upper category known as 'The County'! In recent years the attitude has begun to change, and 'the white settler' – as he has come to be called – is inclined to be judged on his merits and on his contribution to his adoptive community. But in those pre-war years, which were the years of my childhood, the islanders were regrettably prone to believe that God had allotted everybody a station in life and that the station of the English-speaking incomer was several rungs up the ladder of social order. There were two principal reasons for that. One was that the incomer (invariably able to buy and sustain a property for himself) was by sheer security and possession surer of himself – even in cases where he had not already had that self-assurance and 'apartness' instilled into him by his heredity or a public school education. We, on the other hand, were beginning to be aware of our lack of material possessions; and those grim generations of eviction and political repression had, unbelievably, left in us a lingering impulse to touch our foreheads to a 'bonnet laird'; there was even a trace of it still in our eight men – even in the ones who had come through Ypres and Mons and Arras, the Dardanelles and the rest.

Some incomers, and Mrs Kerr was one of them, tried hard to integrate into the community, and thought that to be like the people and *of* the people all they had to do was to acquire a smattering of Gaelic, or – at the very least – a Highland accent such as was being purveyed in the city music halls and on gramophone records by people like Harry Lauder. Mrs Kerr had found Gaelic to be quite beyond her, and – endowed as she was already with a French accent – she found it well-nigh impossible to superimpose a 'braw bricht moonlicht nicht' veneer on top of it; so she settled for pre-fixing every sentence with 'Ach well' and pronouncing 'just' *ch*ust. Life must have been very complicated for her because, when her own natural accent made her tend to refer to the more important points of the compass as *Norse* and *Souse*, our people thought that she was mimicking our English accents and they bridled! But, in truth, everybody liked her and felt sorry for her for having been left widowed and alone, and the majority thought that the invitation of the adults to the tail end of the Christmas Treat was a warm-hearted thought.

There were, of course, dissenters. Some people from 'the old village' and some from the neighbouring small township who were still loyal to the tenets of the Free Church or the Free Presbyterian Church disapproved of anything savouring of frivolity being conducted in a church manse – even if it was a Church of Scotland manse and, as such, smacking of Gomorrah. And the inclusion of the more mature citizens caused varying degrees of uneasiness in other quarters too. Our own incomer parents, while normally relishing anything suggestive of entertainment during a sullen winter, couldn't summon up much enthusiasm for dressing up in Sunday best for an occasion which threatened to be 'dry' in every sense of the word. The younger members of the school who had become more and more excited at the prospect of a beanfeast away from parental supervision, now found themselves with their enthusiasm dampening at the prospect of being supervised and drilled and criticized by proud parents. The 'big boys', as my buddies and I were now beginning to regard ourselves, with the pricklings of manhood beginning to make themselves felt, had been prepared to put up with the more formal aspects of the *Tret* for the sake of some surreptitious slap and tickle and the possibility of shuffling belly to belly with the meagre selection of female flesh available. Now suddenly we could see the whole thing disintegrating into a bib and tucker affair of *Grand Old Dukes of York* and interminable gatherings of *Nuts in May* such as we'd had to suffer at an occasional school soirée.

But there was no escape. As mid-December drew near, my mother's preoccupation with the *Tret* became obsessive; somehow or other the party had assumed new dimensions since she had confirmed that she could get somebody to keep an eye on the baby and allow her to have a rare evening out herself. Whatever occasional opportunities the menfolk might have had for getting away from the fireside during the winter, the womenfolk were, apart from the Sunday evening church service, almost totally housebound. Now, not only was she going out but she was going to go in the company of her offspring and they mustn't be allowed to disgrace her in public.

17

It didn't take her long to realize that there was nothing in the red trunk which served as a clothes store that was even remotely suitable for the elegant occasion that the *Tret* was threatening to become. It was a situation which didn't require much investigation since my total array of clothes consisted of two well-patched pairs of home-made Harris Tweed trousers and a couple of woollen ganzies from J. D. Williams or Oxendale. It was decided that I must have a suit. Not just a suit that would do me for the party but one which would see me through to summer when, as usual, I would be going to the Northlands to spend the entire school holiday with my grandparents – both lots of whom still lived there. The qualification about size was an unwelcome one because it meant that the suit was going to be large.

Fortunate people with overdrafts and access to a range of town shops may not see anything serious or complicated in the provision of a suit for a boy, but in a community where copper coins were counted, a junior suit was, invariably and of necessity, a matter of home construction. On the face of it the material should present no problem. Since the great Depression had begun to creep in on us – its grimy tentacles reaching out across the Minch from the cities and searching us out even in our remote corner – the Harris Tweed trade had collapsed, and yards upon yards of beautiful tweed that had been spun with toil and woven with high hope were now stacked unsold in every corner of the house, as symbolic of the times as the rusting hulks on Clydeside. My father had not aspired to a loom of his own yet so the unsold tweeds didn't just represent a stoppage of income; they stood for frozen investment, since he had had to pay the weaver out of the last of his meagre savings. But the store of tweeds couldn't be plundered at will to make a random suit for a seasonal party. The tweeds were of more or less standard lengths, and bits couldn't just be snipped off the ends of them; so my suit would obviously be selected from whatever range of offcuts remained, and the tweeds themselves carefully rolled back in their winding sheets till the economy resurrected and trade picked up again. In the end it turned out that very little was available. All the bits that I considered appropriate and attractive were either too small for the purpose in hand – 'might do for a pair of shorts later' – or else too big and 'might sell to a tourist for a sports jacket in summer'! I could see it coming. I could scarcely avoid it. Two and a half yards of garish experimentation which was the remainder of a suit length that had been specially commissioned by a half-cracked Tory politician who had been round canvassing votes for his hapless protégé in the 1935 General Election. I remembered that my father had said his taste in tweed was in the same place as his taste in politics – because I'd got into trouble for using the same phrase later – and I also remembered how his parsimony had been condemned when he had cut back his order from a suit length to a jacket length when the election had, predictably, avalanched in the wrong direction. And now here I was listening to the virtues of the rejected plus-fours being extolled to me! A large crotal-brown and blue double overcheck on a cream background. Fine for cushion covers or putting below the saddle of a horse, I protested vehemently. But not, please God, a suit. It was useless. I couldn't have a piece off the end of a crotal and white blend, or the herring-bone, or the dog-tooth . . . they would sell when things got better, and I might be able to get a bought suit out of one of the catalogues with some of the money from them. The arguments were still flying backwards and forwards as the huge pattern for an outsize suit was being traced on a sheet of brown paper on the table, and when the big scissors began to snip I knew that all was lost. But I couldn't foresee that worse was to come.

Two or three nights later somebody noticed that my hair was too long. There was nothing unusual about that and I didn't even suspect anything out of the ordinary when my brother sniggered. My mother was by way of being the village barber. A keen eye, an artistic touch, and a reputation for letting the scissors cut rather than pluck had established her prestige even with 'the bloods', our red-corpuscled hobblede-hoys who would come to her for a 'trum' before setting off in search of adventure in the neighbouring villages. I never minded a haircut from my mother; but I looked for a place to hide when she announced that the suit was her contribution to the *Tret*, and that the rest was up to my father. My father!

Whose only claim to experience in that direction was that he sheared forty blackfaced sheep every July.

It would be pointless to attempt to describe the result 'for somebody who didn't know the face below it. In the years since then various outlandish styles have come, have been welcomed or derided, and have gone. *Brando, Tony Curtis, Crew Cut, Punk* . . . they've all had their day, but mine fell somewhere between the one known now as *Skinhead* and the one known once upon a time as a *D.A.*

There is something irrevocable about a botched haircut. The word spoken in haste is heard only by a few and may be forgotten; the deed done in the dark may be forgiven; but the haircut lingers on for an eternity, reproachfully, like a tarnished halo for the world to comment on. And after that haircut had mercifully outgrown itself it was still to live on in the folklore for months while I was referred to as 'an convick' which is, approximately, the Gaelic pronunciation of the soubriquet for certain residents of Dartmoor and Peterhead. It was with very little self-confidence that there set out for the manse on that evening of 24 December a very large suit containing a very bald me.

The *Tret*, although it had been 'billed' for the manse, was actually convened in a vast outhouse which had been a dairy in the days when ministers kept cows and milkmaids. But it didn't look like a dairy any more. The windows had been beautifully draped with curtains from the manse drawing-room and even the walls were heavily festooned with gaily coloured travelling rugs and bedspreads with Celtic designs. At one end of the room a great peat fire was burning in the ingle round which, presumably, the minister's farm workers had congregated in winters of yore at times when the place wasn't being used as a dairy. A huge trelliswork had been erected from which hung streamers and gold and silver baubles that twinkled in the lamplight, and presents in parcels. The proceedings began with our rendering of *Good King Wenceslas*, which drew a hearty burst of applause from Mrs Kerr and her maid, and we were warned that we would have to do it again when the grown-ups arrived. Then there was dancing to a large cabinet gramophone into which Mrs Kerr kept feeding records. *The Grand Old Duke* marched up hill and down dale, bodies whirled and hooched slightly self-consciously in approximations of *Eightsome Reels,* and then *One Steps* and other close ones of which I had dreamt for nights but from which I now crouched sullenly in my corner in my suit. I could see my friends surreptitiously rubbing themselves up against Meg and Peggy and the other girl whom I can only remember by her shape, although every time she slouched past me I was stirringly aware of that indefinable smell of girl of which I'd been becoming more insistently conscious ever since Wee Sarah had kindled a spark that hadn't been strong enough to catch flame, that night that seemed so long ago. I hadn't seen Wee Sarah ever since and I didn't really want to; I knew that the moment had come before its time, but that sooner or later it would repeat itself with someone else even if I had to give opportunity a nudge.

After a sticky tea, small presents were handed out from the trellis which, I was to understand later, symbolized a Christmas tree in our treeless land; the wee ones needed no encouragement to demonstrate their enthusiasm for their toys, but the big ones had to be encouraged out of the side of her mouth by the teacher to simulate excitement as the torn wrappers revealed worthy books like *Coral Island,* the illustrated child's version of *Pilgrim's Progress* and *Milestones On My Way* – all of which carried little labels declaring that they had been donated by a worthy body called 'The Band of Hope' (for whose best known charity there was precious little demand in our bit of the kingdom in those days). I was one of the fortunate ones, landing a copy of *Coral Island,* and I was to derive a lot of pleasure from R. M. Ballantyne's little classic once I realized that his characters weren't all the goody-goodies that the lurid wrapper suggested. Despite myself my spirits were rising, and they soared when I saw everybody being presented with a false face amidst much hilarity. I stuck mine on and immediately felt that upsurge of self-assurance which character actors get from the layering of their make-up. But it was short-lived. I was beginning to chassé my way through the throng with my ardour rising and Meg firmly in my sights when the voice of my bosom crony and habitual partner in crime, Gillespie,

21

piped in my ear, 'How's an convick?' and my enthusiasm chilled as I realized that the only bit of me I had concealed was the only bit that I didn't mind being seen.

Mrs Kerr clapped her hands for silence, and when she got it she announced that our Sunday School Certificates would be handed out when our parents arrived – as they should be doing in about half an hour's time – but would we all now please form a ring for *The Farmer Wants a Wife*? O God! There is no more emasculating charade for a self-conscious pubescent than that particular game, nor anything more designed to hold him up to ridicule if his particular weaknesses lie in the spheres of dancing and singing. I prayed that I would be the wretched bone and, thereby, be the last to be hauled into the centre of the ring – even if I knew that my friends would spare not an ounce of their energy when it came to thumping my new suit. But my whole instinct screamed at me that I would draw the short straw and be the farmer, stuck there in the middle of the ring for the eternity of the dance looking like somebody who hadn't even been dreamt of then – the scarecrow from Judy Garland's *Wizard of Oz*. My instinct was right. Miss Martin had obviously noticed that I had been keeping a low profile for most of the evening and she must have dreamt up some charitable reason of her own for my unwonted reticence. 'Finlay will be the farmer!' she shouted. 'In you go, convick,' hissed Gillespie as a dozen hands pushed me into the centre and somebody struck up the inane recitative as they all began to twirl round me. I was grateful that my mask at least hid the red blood that was puffing my face, and concealed the fact that I wasn't joining in the singing. Whatever other enthusiasms I had been nurturing were banished emphatically, as I shuffled from leg to leg in imitation of a solo Highland dancer and the fearsome hairiness of Harris Tweed especially designed for leathery deer-stalkers and hillwalkers began to take its chafing toll of my thighs and every other part of me that it could reach. In a fit of defiance I seized on a toothless little mite from the Lower Infants when the moment came for the farmer to choose a wife, and I didn't give a hoot for the shouts of derision from my own classmates with whom I'd been exchanging boasts for weeks. The little girl, who had shed her mask somewhere, looked up at me in gummy adoration and I think I loved her for the innocence which blinded her to my tonsure and my tweed. The game was grinding to its inexorable climax as the door opened and the village began to shuffle in.

We had been swopping apprehensions in school from the day we heard that the adults were to be invited but, contrary to our worst fears, the night burst into life when they arrived. I suspect that they had been girding themselves for a grim evening, and the result was that they put all their efforts into preventing it from going that way; either that, or the false faces with which they were issued by Mrs Kerr and Miss Martin – with much giggling and coy little asides to the men – gave them the kind of self-confidence that mine failed so signally to give me. Mrs Kerr began to dole out lemonade to all and sundry and people tipped back their false faces like visors to drink; the men proclaimed hearty toasts and drained their glasses as if they contained champagne – which, come to think of it, they may have done! Music erupted as our hostess fed a more adult record into the cabinet gramophone and the celebrations took off. Men who couldn't, danced with their own and their neighbours' wives; those who reckoned they could, queued up to partner Mrs Kerr – presumably deluded into thinking that their wives could be persuaded to believe that they were duty dancing, or else that they couldn't be recognized behind their papier-maché alter egos. The only person who didn't dance was old Hector MacGeachan who had screwed up his courage and decided that his sister could harangue or ail in solitude to her heart's content; Hector had been given an express personal invitation by Mrs Kerr, and he was given a seat of honour at the fire. And it was Mrs Kerr in person who stuck a bearded false face on him during a pause between dances and, giggling a lot as she was doing that night, dug into his pocket and produced his old pipe and stuck it into his mouth. 'There you are, Mr MacGeachan,' she said. 'You light up and enjoy yourself. . .' but before she could say anything else another father grabbed her by the waist and whirled her away into an old-fashioned waltz or something equally intimate.

Old Hector may or may not have wanted to smoke, but he

was one of those whose forefathers had suffered from the landlord purge and he himself was descended from three generations of ghillies. It was in his blood, therefore, to do whatever he was bidden to do by anybody whom he considered to be his superior, and some people used to claim unkindly that he would take an order from a tinker's donkey if it was in English. It wasn't true. Old Hector was a kindly man who would suffer hurt himself rather than hurt anybody else, but I doubt if he held the centre of any stage till that night . . . or till the last few years of which he hadn't yet as much as dreamt. Anyway he began to part the long white whiskers on the false face so that he could better manoeuvre his pipe into his mouth, and he began to feel through his pockets for the old page of newspaper which he always carried with him for spills. He found it just as the dance ended and as the teacher, indiscreetly showing a knee, climbed on to a chair and called for silence. 'Ladies and gentlemen,' she said in her best classroom voice. 'Before we all get carried away with ourselves we must express our thanks to Mrs Kerr for her great kindness, and I think the children and I can best do so in a little surprise that we have prepared for her!' I knew that the moment had come for the dreaded *Allons enfants de la . . .*

But it wasn't just Mrs Kerr who was in for a surprise!

Unnoticed by anybody, Hector MacGeachan had lit a large spill of newspaper and, in the process of negotiating it towards his pipe, he had set the beard of his false face on fire. Not badly, but on fire. Without wishing to disturb anybody, and with great presence of mind, he had removed his false face (probably acting more quickly than he had done since he had gaffed his last salmon many years before) and had flung it into a corner where, unhappily, it had set fire to one of the damask curtains that had been commandeered from the manse drawing-room. Smoke was eddying round the room when Mrs Kerr noticed it and shouted 'Fire!' – without waiting to establish whether or not this was the surprise that the teacher had in store for her.

The effect of that word is universally dramatic, but probably never anywhere more so than in a room crowded with mothers frantically searching for their own offspring in a melée looking devilishly the same. There were only two calm females in the room and, for once in her life, one of them was my own mother. She had no problem identifying me, and we could see that my father already had my younger brother by the hand. And there was the devout old Widow Montgomery who had always maintained that no good would come of celebrating a Romish festival. As the room emptied she sat on in her chair, rocking backwards and forwards, and chanting 'For behold the Lord will come with fire to render His anger with fury, and His rebuke with flames. . . .'

Somehow we all found ourselves on the lawn whither Mrs Kerr and a couple of men had carried the burning curtain and stamped it out. Our hostess hadn't for an instant panicked but she now stood looking slightly forlorn and bemused, wondering perhaps what she could do with one damask curtain. My father took me by the shoulder and began to lead me away, but the voice of the teacher rang out and stopped us. 'Children!' she shouted, 'All's well that ends well. But though we've had an exciting evening we mustn't forget our surprise for Mrs Kerr!' And she signalled us to group around her while our hostess stood looking as if she'd had enough surprise to last her a lifetime. But when the teacher shouted 'One. Two. Three . . .' and we struck up the *Marseillaise* she stood very still and tried to look patriotic. The rest of the company shuffled and looked questioningly at each other – except for eight men who didn't hesitate before standing stiffly to attention.

A few hasty 'good nights' were mumbled, and as we made our ways quietly down the path to the new village road a delicate flutter of snow began to come down, as if somebody with a sense of humour was throwing a handful of confetti, or giving Mrs Kerr a gentle reminder about the Sunday School Certificates.

Chapter Three

B Y morning a thin coverlet of snow had draped itself over the village. Not the kind of snow which sends mainland boys rollicking into campaigns of snow fights and their seniors flapping up mountainsides risking coronaries in order to come slithering down again on skis at further risk to life and limb. We rarely got that kind of heavy fall because of being on the Atlantic's edge, and – although it could be cold – it was a damp kind of cold that we were accustomed to; the sort of cold on which rheumatism and chestiness thrived till the Hebrides took their gigantic leap forward into the realms of central heating in the last twenty or thirty years and creature comfort ceased to be regarded as a weakness of the flesh or the spirit. I have often wondered how dramatically the life of my own island of Harris would have been changed if the new village of my boyhood had been able to sustain its original momentum, if a world depression hadn't slowed up a hinterland which is always slower to recover, and if the amenities of which we kept hearing and reading had been available to us on our own home territory instead of beckoning us far afield like a tawdry grail. Perhaps the population of the island wouldn't have dropped by a third – as it has done in my lifetime – and perhaps I would have been there rather than here writing about it. But, for the boy getting up late on that winter's morning, the world held only the future and the great beauty of the snow.

I stood in my shirt-tails at the window looking out on it, conscious of its beauty without revelling in it, because the country boy grows up to accept nature as part of his due inheritance just as the country man grows not to notice it till it turns against him. I loved the rocky Northlands in which I'd been born and brought up for a few years – and to which I went back from time to time – but, because the Southlands had come as a surprise to me when I first glimpsed them, as we topped the Back of Scarista Hill on that first day when the village became ours, the meld of beach and sea and mountain never lost its magic for me, nor its ability to surprise. Here it was now, yet again different. The machair that had been warm with daisies in the summer was now bleached white with the rime of the snow and I was thinking to myself that that was what the Holy Land must have been like, judging by the few Christmas cards that I had seen, despite the fact that my reading in school seemed to suggest a climate that made snow unlikely. I had long since given up asking the teacher questions about the discrepancies between her gospel teachings in the morning and her geography teaching in the afternoon.

'You'd better put your trousers on if you're thinking of going out,' my father said as he came in from the byre with the milkpails. 'Your brother's out there with a snowman as big as himself!'

'Of course I'll put my trousers on,' I said with as much asperity as I could risk. 'I'm not going out yet!' I wondered why he had taken to doing the morning milking; if we hadn't already got a fairly new baby I might have suspected that my mother was succumbing to the fresh epidemic of maternity which was sweeping the village. But no. The idea was ridiculous.

'And don't forget to put something on your head before you go out.'

I bit my lip hard and stared straight out of the window. I hadn't spoken to him ever since he had given me the haircut two nights ago. I had been very skilful about it. I had been disarmingly obedient and had performed any little chores demanded of me with no demur; I had kept my looks from being insolent; I had been utterly charming to my mother. But I had studiously avoided addressing one single remark to my father or reacting to any comments of his; I knew that he knew, and I knew that he knew why. And now I had fallen for a sucker punch because my mind had been wandering idly over the more pleasant aspects of last night's party (which really boiled down to the fire) and the compelling beauty of the snow. I didn't have to turn round because I could tell from the way he was whistling tunelessly that he was stifling a smile. My father and I had developed a marvellous relationship which puberty, paradoxically, was strengthening rather than abrasing. He had an extraordinary love of books and a sensitive feeling for poetry, both of which he was unobtrusively instilling in me and which, in turn, resulted in the bond which was undoubtedly there – although there was precious little evidence of it that morning. In fact, a further resentment – which I had almost let slip – was at the fact that he had collared *Coral Island* as soon as we got home from the *Tret* and I hadn't seen it since. Now certainly was not the time to ask him about it, so I turned on my heel, dashed past him into the bedroom, pulled on my trousers and ganzie, and ran out to join my brother at his snowman. My brother was getting to the stage where he could provide good companionship when Gillespie wasn't around, but he didn't have Gillespie's sophistication nor the supply of dirty stories and vocabulary that Gillespie was forever gleaning from older cousins of his. Not the least of the failings of the educational system of the time was that my brothers and I had, perforce, to leave home at an early age for our higher education – and so we were men before we became friends.

It was Donald who noticed Calum the Post's van coming into the village. There had been doubt whether there would be a Post at all since it was Christmas Day, but no holidays were mandatory as far as Calum was concerned and the general consensus had been that he wouldn't miss out on the pre-Hogmanay hospitality which was now beginning to seep through, and that he would choose to take a day in lieu at peat-cutting or sheep-shearing time. There he was now, staggering up to the manse, laden with parcels.

'I wonder if he'll have a parcel for us?' My brother was an optimist, and I told him so. The most we could hope for in the way of Christmas correspondence was a Greetings Card or two from some mainland cousins of my father or mother. The increasing burden of Christmas mail which Calum had begun to grumble about in the early thirties had receded, although we as children didn't attach any significance to it; but what *was* increasing, peculiarly enough, was the volume of advertising mail as the entrepreneurs of the cities began to discover our existence. Charles Atlas was offering to build Hebridean muscles; compilers of encyclopaedias were volunteering to fortify our minds; Glaxo were eager to build bonnie babies, happily unaware that all they were building in Harris was a repertoire of ribald jokes. Whenever I found an advertisement with a postage pre-paid coupon I sent it off, just for the fun of having Calum stop at the roadside gate with a letter addressed to me personally, and all the older boys and girls in school did the same.

One or two of them got into serious trouble with their parents when they went on to commit themselves to courses offered by sundry body-builders for sums greater than one would expect to pay a contractor for a modest house, but they always got extricated by the teacher – who had a great talent for writing to the vendors letters which made their actions sound criminal. She sometimes ended up with token little gifts from them for sparing them from legal action which she had had no intention of instigating and in which they would, in any case, have been proved totally innocent if slightly imbecilic for being taken in by semi-literate Gaelic-speaking boys and girls in the Western Isles. I am sure that only as a final resort some city executive would glance at a map and look away in hasty horror on discovering that he had been spending his company's resources on specks of islands in the Atlantic where the natives probably wore marram skirts.

One triumphant advertiser was a Mr Alexander Kennedy of Glasgow. Mr Kennedy, in the late twenties or early thirties, had gone into the laundry and dyeworks business, for which he found a lucrative and expanding demand in Glasgow. But not content with that he decided to push his frontiers nation-wide and right out into the Outer Hebrides where professional laundry did not come high on the list of priorities. Mr Kennedy was obviously perfectly well aware of that, and his campaign was directed at the future. He formed the *Castlebank Children's Circle*, with its headquarters at (and the address is indelibly imprinted on my mind from all those years ago) *Castlebank Dyeworks, Anniesland, Glasgow*. For no membership fee, except the signed promise to be a loyal member, a youngster enrolled in the CCC and got a certificate of membership and a beautiful enamelled badge of a knight in black armour on a black horse in front of a turreted castle. I have no idea now what the significance was; I am reasonably sure that suits of armour and horses and castles did not come within the scope of Mr Kennedy's laundering and dyeing facilities. Every child in our school became an accredited member of the *Castlebank Children's Circle*, and in exchange we became eligible to compete in painting competitions, essays, and puzzles of all descriptions for which there were reasonably generous little prizes. The activities of the club were so varied and involved such a wide range of general knowledge that even the brightest of us had to involve the assistance of parents and school to an extent that could well have justified an honorary senior club membership with an appropriate enamel badge to match. All of us involved in the ever increasing ordeals of tests and examinations in school probably owed more than a few marks to Mr Kennedy; we certainly owed him a great deal of our general knowledge, and had he been alive today he would probably have qualified for a grant from the Arts Council. Or the Arts Council might have received a grant from him. By the time I came to live in the city, and moved into realms where dry cleaning and laundering were normal routines of life, it would have been as instinctive for an otter to pass by a salmon as for me to bypass one of the innumerable Castlebank laundries. I regret not one penny of mine that went to swell into millions the take-over value of his business a few years ago; my only regret was that I never met him, although he and I lived only a mile or two apart in the city for many years. He might have smiled to be told that his was the only Christmas card that Calum the Post had for my brother and myself that day, that year long ago, and that it brightened life for a whole family.

Calum was in an evil temper as Donald and I joined my father at the red van. I automatically assumed that the purple language sizzling the frosty Christmas air was directed at one of his usual targets – the Bolsheviks, Hitler or Franco. 'Mark my words, we're heading for a war,' he used to thunder at my father. 'And you and I'll be in it. We're the very kind they'll want – men with experience. If my mother was alive I'd ask her to her face if I was born in a bloody uniform; I've never been out of one anyway. . . .'

But the warmongers were not the objects of his venom that day; it was 'that bloody woman', who turned out to be Mrs Kerr. 'I'd hoped to be home early today; the wife's roasting a cockerel seeing it's Christmas, or supposed to be anyway, and there's hardly any mail. Now I've got to stop at every damn house in the place to deliver *these*, just because I was fool enough to take a glass of piss-tasting sherry and a sixpence before I realized what she was up to.' With that he thrust into my hand, past my father, the two envelopes containing Alexander Kennedy's Christmas cards and a large square piece of ornate pasteboard showing a picture of what I took to be a couple of crofters labouring on a Hebridean croft, or they might be a couple of Galileans labouring in a Galilean vineyard. In either case it is still my certificate to prove that I attended a Sunday School regularly and with good conduct, although – struggle as I may with my memory – I haven't the faintest recollection of ever having attended Sunday School in my life.

'My, my, Calum was on the bow today,' my father said when he finally joined us in the house where my mother was admiring the Castlebank Christmas cards and setting them out on the brass fringed mantelpiece above the stove, in between ornate tea caddies on which King George V and Queen Mary were celebrating their silver jubilee, Edward VIII was celebrating nothing in particular, and King George VI had pride of place because he had been crowned along with an honest Scottish woman with a good Highland name. Divers reminders of the great moments of human glory and tragedy and dignity, events that had set the world by the ears and passed us by with scant notice in our once hopeful new world, now encapsulated on a simple little shelf edged with sixpence worth of brass. 'I think it must have been the sherry that did for poor Calum. If Mrs Kerr had given him a good

31

dram of whisky it would have been all right, don't you think Finlay?'

'I don't know,' I replied.

'But for sure he wouldn't have delivered the Christmas cards if Mrs Kerr hadn't given him the certificates to hand round. She must have forgotten to hand them out last night in the stramash!' I noticed the twinkle in his eye, and remembered that I wasn't talking to him. But it was too late; he had got the better of me again. There was an unmistakable smell of fruit dumpling coming from a pot on the fire, and my common sense told me that it would be churlish to keep up my resentment when mother was obviously trying to mount some little token celebration of the day.

'Big fellow, what about coming up the hill with me? I'll have to go for a bag of peat with Sunday coming up tomorrow. In the excitement of getting ready for that party I forgot to bring home an extra bag and, in any case, I wasn't to foresee that it was going to snow today. Perhaps you could manage a half bag yourself, eh?'

The reference to the hill and the snow in the same breath would have sounded inconsequential to a stranger, but I guessed what he meant and I felt a little flattered to be considered in the role that he had cast for me. He had a wholesome respect for the hills, and although Bleaval was by no means the cruellest of our mountains it was a fairly steep climb up the riverside track to the shoulder where our best peatbanks lay. It was just a foot-wide path which he had worn out himself over the years, taking advantage of rabbit and sheep tracks where he could. Every second day in life he had climbed up, filled a hundredweight sack of peat, and – tying it round his shoulders with a twist of coir rope – had trudged back down with it again. Once one learnt how to pack the sack so that sharp edges of peat didn't dig into the spine, and once one had got the knack of placing the fulcrum and distributing the weight it wasn't as burdensome as it sounds; but it was bad enough, and for the life of me I have never been able to figure out why he had never invested in a horse or a pony which would have lightened the work on the croft in a hundred different ways. I can only imagine that it was because he was a Northman and wasn't used to horses. One of the most exasperating things about the crofters of our place and that generation was that they were reluctant to adapt to even the most tested of labour-saving tactics. Those who did were the ones who survived. The reason my father wanted me with him on the hill that day was that he knew that, higher up the hill, the conditions would be worse and that a simple slip and a twisted ankle could land a man alone with a heavy load on his back in trouble, and lead to endless trouble for others. He was practising the preaching that pleasure hill-walkers ignore so often, and so often to their cost.

We walked slowly up the hill together, pausing now and then to look back down over the village from which the peat smoke was rising as straight as a pencil from each house. 'It's going to be a fine day tomorrow. Frosty perhaps, but fine. There's no surer sign than the smoke rising straight up. It's the same idea as a barometer, you know. . .' and on he went feeding me knowledge in the guise of chit-chat. And then he got on to his favourite topic of the old stone ruins more clearly visible than usual with the light snow on the winter heather. 'They're not all eviction houses you know. Some of these were summer houses built here when the place consisted of a few large farms; in the summer the milking cows used to graze on the hills without coming back down to the machair at all, and instead of calling them home for milking in the evening as our women do because they've only got a couple of cows each to deal with, the milkmaids used to come out and spend weeks on the moors in these huts, making the milk into butter and crowdie and pressing the crowdie into cheese. Then from time to time the men would come out and carry the salted butter and the cheese home and store it for the winter. Good stones, these. We might find a way of getting some of them down to the croft when we come to building the new house.'

My interest brightened.

'The new house? When are we going to start?' I'd begun to become conscious of our cramped living quarters; I relished the freedom of my grandfather's grand two storey house in the Northlands; and I was getting envious of those of my school-friends whose fathers had already moved into their 'white houses'.

He took his time to answer. 'O I don't know. Maybe we'll begin collecting stones soon.' A strange distant look came into his eyes whenever he mentioned the business of collecting stones for the new house. 'The country's in a bad way just now and money's scarce for grants and loans. But I don't know why you're bothering anyway. You'll be sitting your bursary next year and you'll be getting away from here. Another three years and Donald will be going away. And in no time it'll be Alex's turn. . . .'

'The baby? It'll be ten years before he's sitting the bursary! And, in any case, we'll be coming back.'

'Aye, maybe. You never know how things go. There was a time when I never thought I'd be coming back here, when I was working in Glasgow. But the war changed that. And the way things are looking there'll be another war before all that long.'

He changed the conversation.

I didn't notice it of course, but the relentless conditioning of the mind was going on, perhaps subconsciously on his own part. Phrases like 'you'll be getting away from here' and 'I never thought I'd be coming back here' passed unnoticed over my immediate understanding, but he had mentioned the bursary again and that reminded me that the bursary examination was, indeed, not so very far away. It had been drummed into me as the first great hurdle of my life, and by now I had accepted that one of those coveted County Council awards was the only key to success and prosperity. In my own mind I had decided that I must win.

When we reached the peat stack he packed a fairly full bag of peat for me, and taught me how to sit down on the edge of the raised bank and get the sack balanced on my shoulders. 'Don't tie the rope,' he said as he put it round the bag and gave me the loose ends to grip. 'Just hold the ends tightly, and that way you'll automatically let it go if you stumble and you'll come to no harm. We don't want you strangling yourself before your hair grows.' That way the subject of the haircut passed smoothly into the realms of humour, and, indeed, I

34

found that the full bag of peat carefully balanced was a much easier heft than a half full bag gripped over a shoulder by its neck and swinging round my buttocks.

'What about you and me going to church tomorrow? It might be a nice idea seeing it's the day after Christmas.'

He must have taken my silence, as I concentrated on the footpath, for demur.

'You wouldn't have to wear your suit,' he added. 'Your old trousers and ganzie would do fine.'

So the whole matter was settled without my having much say in it, nor yet being made to feel pressurized in any way. By the time we got home, the old closeness was back, and the little house, warm in the lamplight, had about it a great feeling of what I was in later years to come to know as Christmas. After we'd eaten as much currant dumpling as we could stow away we all sat quietly round the stove. Resignedly, I went back to *Dixon Hawke* – which I was beginning to know off by heart – while my brother thumbed through the picture book that he'd been given at the *Tret*, and my father puffed contentedly at his pipe, having dug *Coral Island* out of a corner where I'd never thought of looking. My mother knitted and smiled contentedly as she looked round her brood.

Church next forenoon was bleak and cold. Ancient stone takes a lot of warming up at the best of times, but our huge church had little warmth to retain from the bodies of the 30 people who sat in its cavernous emptiness once a week for an hour and a half. Having no minister of our own, our less urgent spiritual needs, including the Sunday morning service, were attended to by the man whose designation was 'missionary' – a title dating back to the middle of the eighteenth century when, indeed, missionaries had been sent to help 'civilize' the Highlands after Culloden in much the same way, and with much the same motive, as missionaries were despatched to darkest Africa and other anonymous fringes of the Empire. The Highland ones were safe from the danger of being eaten, but, in all other respects the early ones must have felt their purpose to be the same – to lead His people out of darkness to the feet of a stern and unforgiving God, who would, in His own good time, forgive them their sins and their rebelliousness against the Establishment. By our time, of course, the role of the missionary had changed although his title had not. He was now really a lay preacher, an ex-shepherd or fisherman who had seen the Light and felt confident enough to lead others through the gloom. They had good precedents in fishermen and shepherds and, as in former days, the system threw up some very powerful men; preachers who could, by sheer oratory and belief launch religious revivals which swept the land. Others had an undoubted sufficiency of holiness, and a doubtful sufficiency of grammar.

Having deposited our penny and halfpenny respectively in the wooden plate at the door, father and I made our echoey way down the flagged aisle to our seat. Although the whole congregation could have crowded for warmth into two seats at the very most, the code of the family pew was strictly observed and our pew (the eighteenth down on the right if I remember rightly) was the one which had been occupied by the Clerics, my father's ancestors on his mother's side, for the best part of two hundred years. By taking his place there when he came to the new village he was, in his own romantic heart, picking up the threads of the traditions of a lineage of which he was very proud. There were two beautiful oak pulpits, one above the other, at the altar end of the church, and when there was a fully qualified minister in charge of the service he occupied the top pulpit and the precentor, who led the singing, occupied the lower one. No mere missionary, however, would dare occupy the top pulpit; his humility didn't allow him climb so near to God as the man entitled to the round collar, and so the precentor was demoted to ground level while the missionary took the lower pulpit. That day the precentor (one of the crofters from the village next to óurs) was already in his place, but the missionary hadn't arrived and nobody was quite sure who he was going to be. After ten minutes or so of throat-clearing and feet-shuffling we heard him coming heavily down the aisle, with the slow solemn tread of the presbyterian who thinks he is carrying the Almighty on his shoulders instead of the other way round, and as he passed the end of the pew I heard my father mutter below his breath a heart-wrung 'O God, no!' I knew that things were not promising.

36

The service started and followed its usual pattern – the style still followed in most Western Island churches – with the audience sitting to sing and standing to pray. My father couldn't sing and I know not what he prayed, but whatever it was he had plenty of time to do it; even my young legs were aching by the time we got sitting down. At least I enjoyed the singing, because it was the easiest of all types in my reckoning; the precentor 'gave out' each line of psalm and the congregation chanted it with him when he repeated it, with the few who could claim good voices grace-noting the musical lines. There are few more moving experiences than being in among a large Gaelic congregation singing in the traditional manner with soul and feeling. It is more than moving; it is unforgettable in the depths of one's being. There is a discernible gap between that and the paean achieved by 30 self-conscious souls in a miniature cathedral, frozen to the marrow and bored to extinction.

I knew that my father was impatient for the sermon to start and, when at long last the missionary got round to it, father's head went down on his folded hands on the narrow ledge in front of him with a sigh of relief. He always did it. And he had always assured me that it was because he had to shut out the view from the spacious windows because his mind wandered. He hadn't expected me to believe him, so he didn't regard it as lying. Today was different. I had just got nicely engrossed in trying to decipher some initials carved on the pew in front of me when I heard a distinct and satisfied-sounding snore. For a horrified second I fancied that the preacher had broken the rhythm of his monotony and was going to address a remark directly to my father but, to my relief, he carried on. I kicked my father sharply in the region of the ankle and he sat up with a start. He looked balefully at me, collected his wits, confirmed for himself that the situation was as bad as he had feared, and put his head back down on his hands. In a few minutes he was snoring again. I kicked him again, and again he went through the exact same range of reactions, except that his glare at me was even more explicit. But it didn't matter; I couldn't bear the thought of a public rebuke from the pulpit – which was not at all an unheard of occurrence – and a missionary of insecure self-importance was more likely to indulge his authority than an experienced minister. But it was a blessing in disguise. My preoccupation with my father passed the time for me, and I developed a refined technique of being able to kick him on the deep exhalation which I had come to recognize as the precursor to the snore. Mercifully the sermon drew to its close, the last prayer was said, and the last psalm sung with me happily unaware that it was virtually the end of my dream of myself as a vocalist of potential that people were merely being slow to appreciate.

Normally the end of the church service was followed by a long and leisurely exchange of news and views in which the visiting preacher would often take part, bringing reports of goings-on in other parts of the island. Most usually of late the conversation was on political lines and on the more and more familiar themes of Bolshevism and Fascism and all the *-isms* for which there appeared to be no Gaelic. That day the colloquium was much shorter, because people were frankly worrying about burnt dinners. One sentence reached me, as I stood on the fringe of the group, and it stirred some considerable alarm in me. George MacLellan, who was a staunch Liberal and inordinately proud of it, said something like 'We're having our own Bolshevik here if what they tell me is true. . .' and the rest of what he said was lost on me as people hurried to get away before the preacher emerged.

'What's a Bolshevik?' I asked as we walked down hill.

'A Bolshevik. O, a kind of revolutionary. . .' he broke off and shook me good humouredly by the shoulder. 'That reminds me; that was a very dangerous thing you did in church today. You should never give a man a fright when he's sleeping. . . .' And there followed a long and colourful story of the French Revolution. Apparently when the bloodshed was at its height, a lady with Royalist sympathies, terrified for her life, went to church with her maid. Even in the midst of her distress, weariness overcame the lady as she tried to concentrate on the preacher, and she fell asleep and had a fearful dream that she was being made to kneel beneath the guillotine. Just as the blade was about to descend, her maid, horrified, noticed that her mistress was asleep and, in order to waken

38

her, tapped her smartly on the back of the neck with her fan. Whereupon the poor woman, taking the tap of the fan to be the blade of the guillotine, fell down dead. The story was very dramatically told and lasted all the way home. It was guaranteed to ensure that I would never waken him in church again, but at the same time I had received a preliminary little lesson about the French Revolution so that when I did, years later, come up against Robespierre and company they didn't come as complete strangers to me.

'But what's a Bolshevik revolutionary person coming to this village for?' I asked as we reached the gate.

'O that? What Geordie MacLellan was talking about? I'm not sure, but I think she's going to bring about one of the biggest revolutions of all; she's going to teach you to sing!'

She? A Bolshevik? A revolutionary? Going to teach me to sing? It didn't make sense, and it was obvious that he didn't know any more. It was also obvious that I was going to have to wait for the school holidays to pass before I would find out.

Chapter Four

WE could be very cruel. The Gaelic word for 'feet' is 'casan', and so we called the new music teacher 'Miss Casan' because we reckoned that she had three feet. She didn't, of course! The poor woman had a deformity which looked like a tiny foot protruding from one shin bone, and because her name was Bassin and rhymed neatly with 'casan' she was landed with an allonym which was as unworthy as it was unkind. In later years Ethel Bassin was to become a good friend of mine, and the more I got to know her the more I admired her courage and her musicianship and her tenacity. Of the last quality there is no greater proof than that it took her five years to accept that she couldn't teach me to sing. From the beginning she was intrigued and, indeed, bemused by the phenomenon of somebody who could produce each note in the scale with alarming confidence, but could not *re*produce them in any required or pre-ordained order, which – after all – is the most basic requirement in the aspiring singer's art.

Music has been a torment for me all my adult life, and an ungenerous Divinity has ruled that it should be my lot to live out my time in an environment ringing with musicians. One eminent one is my dearest friend, generous in every respect save one; when the jokes have all been told and the night is wearing thin he will invariably try to rekindle the merriment by recalling some aged anecdote involving me and my infirmity (as he manifestly regards it), whereupon the company erupts into interest which varies from incredulity to demands that I demonstrate my incapacity as if I were a circus freak. But such occasions are, at least, normally private. The much greater punishment is to have been born into a nation hell-bent on singing "Auld Lang Syne" once after meals and twice before bedtime, and it pains me to remember the number of excellent, well-oiled top table dinners that have been ruined for me by having to attempt to stand at the end between two enthusiastic dinner jackets, miming with feigned feeling the words

And there's a hand my trusty fiere
And gie's a hand o' thine!

while long tablefuls of ears seem to be straining to catch my every syllable. But for Miss Bassin they might be getting more entertainment than they bargained for!

By the time Miss Bassin had arrived, as the first of a new breed of invading itinerant teachers of the fine arts, our village school had settled down into a cosy community of 13 – a figure at which it seemed to remain static for two or three years with new raw recruits arriving from time to time to replace the slightly less raw 'seniors' who moved on to the realms of higher education or else moved out at the age of fourteen to take their places in the society of the village where they would, invariably, stay only till such time as they got a chance to get away to some mainland job. A *chance* to get away! For all her good points – and they were many – Miss Martin could not get away from the intellectual malaise of her generation; to 'get away' was synonymous with success; to stay and build on the promising foundations of a new village was failure. But at least she did ensure that everybody who went through her school in her time had a grounding in general knowledge far beyond the formal bounds of the official curriculum. She taught the boys to cook and sew. She taught the girls the rudiments of gardening. She taught us all to follow world events in the newspapers and, later, on the radio. And she taught everybody to sing – except me!

From tenderest infancy I was convinced that the art of singing was a simple matter of striking a high falsetto and rendering a lyric *con amore* and *fortissimo*, and nobody had ever informed me to the contrary. The only instruction I had ever received at home was 'to be quiet'. When the teacher first

41

produced a modulator and a tuning fork I found the whole business of rattling through from one 'doh' to another singularly boring, and I was glad when I was left to my own devices while she concentrated on select pupils like Gillespie, who seemed to be having difficulties with 'fah', 'me', and 'ray', short simple words though they were.

I came into my own – to my own satisfaction at least – when we moved on to actual songs, even although the choice was not often very inspiring. As with everything else, music was taught in English and the repertoire – presumably dictated by the same central authority that supplied the one and only book – ranged from "The Lass of Richmond Hill" to "I'll go no more a-roving". The young child learning a song or a poem will, inevitably, seek to relate its content with a place or a situation within the sphere of his own knowledge and, at the best of times, that can create its own problems; but the problems are compounded for the child dabbling in a language which is not his own. As far as we were concerned, Richmond Hill, wherever it was, must surely correspond to one of the tall heather-clad mountains surrounding the village on three sides, and a lass attempting to live on one of them even on a May day morn must have needed her head examined. And why, having painstakingly learnt that 'ruin' was pronounced 'ruin', were we now expected to pronounce it 'roo-aye-in' just because it was set to music? Truly the ways of English song were strange, and it was probably just as well that it was only during the last week of term or on the eve of a mid-term break that it was inflicted on us at all. That is, till Miss Bassin stumped onto the scene.

If the teacher knew of the impending visit she certainly did not inform us, and the first we knew of it was when the door burst open and an amply proportioned lady of incredible volubility demanded that two boys go out to her hire car and bring in her piano. We had seen a piano in the manse, and the idea of a car big enough to contain one was as incongruous as the notion of two boys being able to carry it. There was a rush for the door but it was quickly checked by the newcomer whose very tone was enough to warn us that here was somebody whom it would be foolhardy to contradict. 'Two, I said. It's not the car I want brought in!' And the two boys nearest the door slunk out, to reappear a few minutes later with something that looked for all the world like a miniature coffin, which she ordered to be laid across two desks while a third boy was detailed to place a chair in front of it. After a few minutes of conversation with the teacher the latter, looking rather relieved, left the room and headed for her own living quarters, presumably to prepare tea, leaving us to the mercies of Miss Bassin who, we were informed, would be teaching us music for an hour every Thursday afternoon for the foreseeable future. Teaching us! This was putting music on a new plane. Up till now music had been supposed to be fun even if it provided little in the way of laughs.

The newcomer sat down to her box-of-tricks and, when she opened it, there sure enough was a row of black and white ivories with the black ones arranged in twos and threes just like the black ones on the black and yellow keyboard in the manse. And as if to prove the pedigree of her kist the lady brushed off a couple of arpeggios before turning to us and demanding to know the extent of our repertoire. It didn't take long to recite. "The Lass of Richmond Hill", "I'll go no more a-roving", "A rose-bud by my early walk", "Marching through Georgia" and, as the list petered out an infant voice lisped "In and out the dirty blue-bells", causing a ripple of laughter which subsided under the steely gaze through the pebble glasses. For what I was later to learn must have been one of the few times in her life, Miss Ethel Bassin was speechless.

'What . . .' she said, 'what about Gaelic songs?'

'What *about* Gaelic songs?' said our silence.

'What Gaelic songs have you been learning?' she said slowly, thinking that her first question hadn't got through to us.

Silence.

'What about. . .?' And she proceeded to accompany herself in a rendering of "The Eriskay Lovelilt" in passable if slightly fractured Gaelic.

No, we hadn't heard it. No, we didn't learn Gaelic songs.

That, she assured us, would be remedied. But, first of all, she must establish our various capabilities. And she began to tinkle out little runs of notes which we were all invited to reproduce as 'la-la-la-tum-tetee-tum-tetaa' or noises to that effect. When it came to my turn I obliged with zest, and for the second time that afternoon speech forsook Miss Bassin.

'Once again!' she said after a disbelieving pause. And once again I thought I repeated what I thought I heard. Her lips pursed slightly but the gaze through the plate glass spectacles was more puzzled than unkind. She hit one note at one end of the keyboard and then one at the other end.

'Can you hear any difference?'

Of course I could hear a difference between a *ding* and a *dong* and I told her so. She muttered something to the effect that that was some small consolation, but she suggested that I might like to sit in one of the seats at the far end of the classroom till the end of the lesson and, perhaps, read a book till she was ready to give me some undivided attention. It was mortifying, but there was nothing else for it but to sit in solitary silence while the rest of my friends received their first lesson in their own native music from someone who turned out, on later acquaintance, to be a White Russian.

At the end of the lesson, and for several weeks thereafter, I was afforded varying periods of what was elegantly described as 'private tuition' after the rest of the school had gone home, but even the indomitable Ethel Bassin had to confess defeat. She assured me, rather hesitatingly, that there wasn't much wrong with my ear. By which she meant, I suspect, that I could hear. She was to return to the fray in later years, but for the duration of her weekly visits thereafter I was dismissed to my small corner with a book, to the possible benefit of my English and the undoubted detriment of my ego.

For a couple of weeks I was able to cajole or bribe my young brother into keeping quiet about my ostracism, and questions about my musical prowess were side-stepped with relative ease. It was only when Miss Bassin began to dish out homework that it became impossible to maintain what was a pretence rather than a deception.

'Why don't you ask your brother to help you?' said my mother, having finally grasped that her younger son's query anent crochets was to do with music and not with knitting. As luck would have it diplomatic relations between him and me were strained for some reason or other.

'He can't help me. Miss Casan says he's just a stookie at music; he's not allowed . . .'

'Miss *who*?' My father erupted from behind his *Daily Express*. 'Don't let me ever hear you making fun of a human failing or I'll take your trousers down and you won't be able to sit for a week!'

I seized on a chance to change the subject, making a mental note to get equal with my brother later.

'Why is it wrong to call her Miss Casan when you yourself call Duncan MacLennan "Deaf Duncan" and you call Mary Stewart "Lame Mary" because she limps and you call . . .'

'Will you keep quiet! Nobody asked you for your opinion!'

It was an old scenario, and one that is enacted between fathers and adolescent sons the world over. For most of the time we were very close friends and he rather welcomed it when I challenged his views in a genuine quest for knowledge, but when he suspected that I was being deliberately provocative he was liable to flare into a momentary rage. And doubly liable if he suspected that he wasn't on very secure ground.

'Those are our own people,' he said. 'It's different with somebody who comes among us as a stranger – and a lady at that.'

I was going to challenge the validity of his argument when my mother stepped in.

'Stop arguing with your father! And what's this about you being told you're a stookie at singing?'

'She never said . . .'

But my young brother was exultant at my humiliation and the whole story came tumbling out, with a graphic description of my exclusion from the nest of singing birds, and it was all I could do to prove that I hadn't practised a deliberate deception by not having admitted to it earlier. My mother was mortified beyond all normal reason. I don't know whether she had cherished a secret notion of a budding Caruso in the family or whether she expected her first born to excel in everything remotely connected with school and education. But there was no denying her disappointment, and her upbraiding had the effect of bringing my father round to my support.

'Well, if the boy can't sing, he can't sing,' he said. 'It's not as if he can't get through life without it.'

'So long as he keeps quiet on Sunday!' she said.

Sunday! I'd forgotten about that. Sunday was going to be the day of the christening, and already there was an undertow of excitement in the village, as there always was in anticipation of anything which savoured of a social event – be it cattle sale or wedding. We had a family stake in this particular event because the infant to be christened was the little girl who had been born to James and my cousin Mary nine months and a few days after their wedding (the exactitude of the period had been checked and double checked by the women of the village with much counting of fingers, and had caused them to concede that there might be some efficacy in a mainland honeymoon after all). At the time, the idea of a honeymoon away from the island had been slightly sneered at as 'swank' and Great Aunt Rachel had been heard to declare that the morning after her wedding she had been up at dawn to milk the minister's cows at seven o'clock as usual, and that 'the young folk of nowadays couldn't even survive their first bedding without a convalescence'.

Just as the wedding of James and Mary had been the first wedding in the new village, so the christening of Jane was to be the first christening. Jane was not the first child to be born in the village – not by any means – but, at that time, the Presbyterian Church in Scotland was emerging from one of its many upheavals and our parish hadn't decided whether it was going to go out on a limb of fundamentalism or going to return to the arms of the 'Big Church' as the mother 'Church of Scotland' was called. Consequently our local pulpit was untenanted for a long period and our more urgent spiritual needs were attended to by divines from here, there, and everywhere. Christening, for some reason or other, didn't seem to rate high on the calendar of priorities and, during the years of ecumenical uncertainty, the new arrivals were being stockpiled, unchristened, like automobile chassis awaiting engines during a period of strike.

46

James and Mary couldn't afford to join the queue. He had gone off to the Merchant Navy shortly after his marriage and it was by sheer good luck that the end of his first voyage coincided with the birth of his first child. Nowadays, seamen are flown home from the ends of the earth by Concorde if Granny develops a verucca but, in those days, it was a man's bad luck if a crisis of any kind hit his family when he happened to be on the wrong side of the world. For all anybody knew, James's next trip might last for a couple of years and so it was decided to get the christening over during his three weeks of leave. At the root of it also, I suspect, was the islander's traditional and lingering distrust of the sea and the feeling that the end of the next voyage must not be taken for granted. Anyway, it was decided that a minister from a neighbouring parish should be enlisted to perform the ceremony on the afternoon of the last Sunday of James's leave, and – since it hadn't been decided which hallowed path of sectarianism our congregation was going to follow – the christening was going to be celebrated in the house.

James and Mary had set the community by the ears when they let it be known that the infant was going to be called Jane. There wasn't anything wrong with the name as such. It wasn't unknown; it appeared, respectably, in the newspapers from time to time. But it wasn't a family name; it wasn't even a village name. For generations past our people had called their first-born after the wife's mother or the husband's father (depending, naturally enough, on whether the child was female or male!) and from then on succeeding infants were given family names from alternating sides of the pedigree – moving into the realms of uncles and aunts only after the four grandparents had been commemorated. The system hiccuped slightly from time to time: for example if three girls arrived in succession then the third one was destined to go through life burdened with an adaptation of a Grandfather's name and, even now, when exotic names like Samantha and Clarinda are beginning to creep into the occasional lineage, it isn't unusual to encounter a wisp of a Hebridean girl bowed under an uncompromising name like Hectorina or Martinetta – signalling that the girl is the third of three females and that, lurking somewhere, there was a grandfather craving a whiff of immortality. Perhaps it wasn't even the name of Jane that caused the mild stushie in the village, but the reason for it which was, quite simply, that James had once sailed as a deckhand on a ship called *The Lady Jane*. Somebody with a tongue that could 'clip cloots', as they say, was quick to point out to Mary that she was fortunate her own father hadn't been given to fancy notions because he had sailed for years on a yacht called *The Yamahurra*!

But if the advent of the christening caused a stir in the village it caused dismay in the school when the teacher announced that the last hour of Friday afternoon (an hour normally regarded as a leisure period) would be devoted to the *Shorter Catechism*, and, in particular to Questions 94 and 95 which we had not yet reached in the course of our normal morning sessions of religious instruction. Questions 94 and 95 were (and are) respectively *What is baptism?* and *To whom is baptism to be administered?* And the answers are very complicated indeed. Question 95, in particular, takes a typically Presbyterian approach by responding in the negative: *Baptism is* not *to be administered to any that are out of the visible church, till they profess their faith in Christ and their obedience to him; but the infants of such as are members of the visible church are to be baptized.* We were instructed to get our parents to help us over the weekend, and to come back to school on Monday with our responses word perfect.

I spent the Friday night crouched over the little book of many words, going on the principle that it was better to get the grind over on the Friday night and leave the rest of the weekend free for play. My father was more exhausted than I was by the time the night was over, because to him fell the task of trying to explain all the obscure references in the texts, and though he was as bilingual as any father in the village he was hard put to it to find simple Gaelic interpretations of phrases like *doth signify and seal our ingrafting into Christ* and *members of the visible church.* When I pressed him for an example of an *in*visible church he remembered that he had the byre to secure for the night, and he left me with an assurance which was now becoming monotonous – 'that I would understand it all when

48

I grew up'. And so I abandoned any attempt at understanding and got down to the business of mugging the whole thing up word by word, feeling like a budding Rembrandt being made to paint by numbers. By Monday morning, like all my fellow sufferers, I was parrot perfect, and the teacher was mighty pleased.

Although no further reference had been made to the subject, my mother had obviously spent ten days agonizing over the revelation that I wasn't opera fodder, and, on the Saturday night while she was putting the finishing touches to a less garish pair of trousers that she had made for me she mentioned with studied casualness that there would be singing at the christening – two psalms, she thought.

'O good! Will they be ones I know?'

She winced, and agreed rather sorrowfully that they might be. 'But,' she said, 'you're not to sing.'

'Why not? Anybody can sing psalms; you just sing the line after the precentor. It's easy.'

'That's not the point. I want you to promise me that you'll keep quiet.'

Some instinct told me that this was a situation that could be exploited, and so I said nothing.

'Do you promise?'

'I don't know.'

For once in her life she resorted to bribery.

'Look here. I'll give you thruppence if you manage to keep quiet for the whole of the service. I'll give it to you on Monday morning, and you can spend it any way you like. Will you promise now?'

Of course I promised. Thruppence was a vast sum of money in my youthful world – enough to buy six bars of Toffee Cow in the Duchess's shop. I went to bed thinking that it was a strange thing – to be offered payment for *not* doing something.

Next day I felt very important indeed as I walked down the road with my parents. I was the only child in the village allowed to the christening; the others had had to be content with the little party which Mary and James had given on the Saturday afternoon – a new fangled idea which didn't meet with approval among the older folk because it smacked of mixing revelry with religion – but I was a relative of the new baby's and, besides, I was now what was termed 'a big boy'. Nevertheless, with the exception of the baby I was by far the youngest person present, and as we went through the door my mother seized a chance to pull me aside and reiterate her instructions on behaviour. . . . I was not to talk except when I was spoken to, and even then I was to give replies and *not* opinions; I was not to laugh at anything whether I thought it funny or not; and, above all, I was to observe strictly my contract not to sing. The last inhibition was the only one that irked me even though I stood to gain thruppence; whatever Miss Bassin might feel about my talents in the realms of secular singing I still felt it in my bones that I had a contribution to make to the psalms.

Everybody was there. All the relatives from Great Aunt Rachel downwards – seated stiffly on straight-backed chairs in a semi-circle round the room. The formal seating arrangement would have inhibited conversation even on a weekday, and the long silences were broken only by Aunt Rachel's normally timid husband who kept on sighing 'Aye, aye' to himself and rubbing the bald bit on the top of his head. James looked as if he had been starched into his navy blue serge suit; he looked flushed and uncomfortable, and every now and then he kept glancing furtively at a booklet which he kept slipping out of his breast pocket and which bore a strong resemblance to an aged copy of the *Shorter Catechism*. The only thing that broke the monotony for me was the discovery that when I slid up or down on my chair my new trousers remained where they were, like a snail's shell remaining still while its tenant slips in and out of it. I had a splendid game to myself, trying to calculate how far I could move without alerting the trousers, and I became so engrossed that I didn't even notice the big stern-looking minister entering the room. He, alone, looked totally at ease and, if anything, was tending towards the irreverent with his reference to the state of the crops and the peat and other worldly things. I came to the conclusion that, being on more intimate terms with the Lord than the rest of us, he had special dispensation to talk about such things on the Sabbath. However, he didn't waste much time on small talk and, after a few minutes, he asked Mary and James to step forward. They did so, with Jane by now sound asleep in her father's arms, blissfully unaware that he was trembling so much that it looked as if, at any moment, he would drop her.

There was a prayer and a reading from the Bible and then Murdo Mor precented a psalm in the singing of which everybody joined except me. It was one I knew well, and the temptation was sore, but I kept my lips tightly closed and thought of thruppence. The minister then intoned a little homily on the responsibilities of parenthood and, during each of several pauses, Mary nodded and James mumbled something as if on cue. When that was over, James was asked to hand the baby over to Mary and, from a certain stiffening on the part of the audience, I guessed that something important was going to happen. I got the shock of my life when the minister produced a copy of the *Shorter Catechism* and began to fire questions at a demoralized looking James.

What is the chief end of man?

James told him.

What rule hath God given to direct us how we may glorify and enjoy him?

James knew that one too. But as the inquisitor moved relentlessly on, picking questions at random, little beads of sweat began to break out on the upper lip of the man whom I had once heard boast that he had been drunk in every pub from Southampton to Singapore. However, he managed to navigate the treacherous waters of *the estate of sin and misery*; he steered his way round *effectual calling*; and he coped manfully with a random selection of the ten commandments. In short, in my opinion James was doing remarkably well for a man who had been away from school for a handful of years; but as the pages were turned relentlessly over it was becoming clear that he was becoming less and less sure of himself, and I began to suspect that his revision had become less thorough as he had waded through the first fourscore questions. He managed to convey that *faith in Jesus Christ* was indeed a saving grace; he gave a reasonable version of what *repentance unto life* ought to be; and then he fell at the water jump. 'Question Number 94,' said the minister, '*What is baptism?*' '*Baptism*' mumbled James '*is a sacrament . . .*' and the minister nodded agreement. '*Wherein the washing with water in the name of the Father and the Son and the Holy Ghost . . .*'. And having got over the water and the Trinity, James ran out of steam. There was a deathly, long silence which became harder and harder to bear. And then, as if from a distance, I hear my own voice, totally outwith my control, confidently, if squeakily, proclaiming '*. . . doth signify and seal our ingrafting into Christ, and partaking of the benefits of the covenant of grace, and our engagement to be the Lord's.*' I heard the voice finishing and I had time to notice that the minister was wide-eyed and open-mouthed, before by mother, crimson in the face, took me by the shoulder and led me from the room.

I recall nothing of her upbraiding. It was all lost on me when I realized that my thruppence was being forfeited. 'But I didn't sing!' I protested.

'You did worse,' she said. 'You made a fool of James and an even bigger fool of me!'

I suppose I did, in a kind of a way. But I don't think it mattered very much. Jane was duly christened, and now has children of her own who have both been perfunctorily splashed with dubious looking water purporting to have come from the River Jordan. Their father had to answer no questions from the *Shorter Catechism*. Nobody even raised an eyebrow when she called them 'Marigold' and 'Frederick Stephen'. And for sure these were never village names.

James called in to say Goodbye before he returned to sea, and he made soothing noises when my mother apologized for the embarrassment I had caused at the christening. 'Not at all,' he said. 'I would never have remembered that bloody covenant of grace bit if it hadn't been for our friend here, and that old codger of a minister might never have finished baptizing Jane.' I warmed at being referred to by James as 'his friend', and as I turned over his shilling in my pocket I thought that maybe it wasn't such a bad thing to be lacking in the gift of song.

Chapter Five

I grew up believing that Parliament was a nice, cosy, committee of gentlemen of faintly divergent beliefs who didn't really need a job but were glad of an extra £8 a week in those hard times. The impression of a friendly coterie was probably fostered by the fact that all the parliaments of my childhood were coalitions, and that my father (who maintained all his life that the ideal system of government for Britain was a Labour administration with a strong Tory opposition) voted socialist himself but at General Election times acted as the local agent for the Liberal candidate – because 'the poor man needed somebody to put up his posters for him and organize his meetings'. When it came to polling day he organized a Liberal car to take the allegedly infirm Liberal voters to the polling station five miles away in Leverburgh; Murdo Mor, who was a dedicated committee man with English every bit as good as my father's, laid on a car for the halt and the maim of the Labour party, and the Landlord, who had a car of his own, took the rest whom he assumed to be Tories. Since the community was reasonably young and fit the problem was always to find one aged member to sit in the front of each car to provide moral justification for its journey; but since it was generally conceded that our total votes were split evenly three ways it would have been as well for everybody to stay at home, by doing which they would have cancelled each other's votes out just as effectively. But Leverburgh was a stone's throw from the only hotel in the Southlands and opportunities for a day out were few and far between. The only elections which were really deemed to matter were the local County Council ones and, tragically for the fibre of the community, the choice there was between a selection of English-speaking incomers from the 'big houses' and a few ministers of the church with a genuine social conscience. The most hopeful development in the Western Isles in recent years, unknown then, is that local men of calibre have begun to take the reins of local administration into their own hands.

But there was increasing evidence that government at some level or other was beginning to take an interest in us. Once the new village had begun to take form and most of the new houses had been put up, the 'men from the ministries' had begun to tire of their tours of supervision and we were left to our own devices for a while. But then, when it was already almost too late, a new breed of official began to appear on the scene and hold meetings in the schoolhouse. Men and women with grittier mainland accents, well-worn suits and broken fingernails, who gave lantern-slide lectures on animal husbandry, land tillage and drainage, the use of fertilizers, milk and egg production and all the rest of it. Of these the 'Hen Wife' was far and away the most popular. She was young and attractive, with an infectious giggle, and men of all ages who had hitherto regarded hens as the curse of the cornfields began to accompany their wives to listen to lectures and see slides of Red Wynadottes and White Leghorns and Rhode Island Reds. I remember my mother being demurely flattered for being singled out as 'the woman who starves her hens in summer so that she can feed them up and get the eggs in winter'. It was a superb example of a woman with personality and charm being able to fire a sceptical audience with enthusiasm for a new expertise.

Already the old Highland malaise of 'what was good enough for my father and grandfather is good enough for me' was beginning to undermine the confidence of the community. Had those people come around at the beginning, when enthusiasm was high and before the world recession had begun to gnaw at us, the attitudes of mind might have been differently channelled and the future of the village differently moulded. There was a certain amount of sarcasm when a man from Barra was sent to teach weaving (what made a Barra man think he could teach Harris Tweed weaving in the island that had given the cloth its name?) but it was Peter Haggerty who planted in my father's mind the seeds of the idea of getting a loom of his own, and that loom was going to save us in the years ahead.

The agricultural experts had the most difficult time of it. Not only were they trying to change the established methods of ages, but they were too late. The man who addressed a packed schoolhouse and entertained us with his stories about the adventures of the potato on its travels from Peru to Europe in the sixteenth century was talking patent sense when he warned the crofters that their potato strains were running out, and that they must buy in some of the new seed being developed, but he was talking to men who couldn't now afford to invest in new seed potatoes: when he went away all that they remembered of his lecture was that the initial European resistance to the newfangled potato from South America had only been over-come when word got around that it was an aphrodisiac, and that it was the Empress Josephine's addiction to it which brought the great Napoleon to his knees with his heartfelt plea of 'Not tonight, Josephine!' That was good for a bawdy local joke or two, as the men opened up the last of the pits where the potatoes had been buried against the cold of winter and began to sift through the meagre remains of last year's crop for plant-ing. 'Lay your seed potatoes out in a cool dark place for a few weeks till they're sprouting,' the man from the College of Agri-culture had said. Fine theory, and fine for prosperous farmers with potatoes to spare. Our men would go cannily through their traditional *Kerr's Pinks* carefully cutting out the best 'eyes' from each potato for planting, keeping the rest of the tuber for the family pot. In normal times these left-over bits would be used as feed for the cattle, but these weren't normal times. Still, winter is long and spring is late in the islands, and the men of learning helped to pass the time.

Because spring was short it was hectic. The sea-wrack which the winter gales had left in long black smelly swathes on the beach had to be collected before the spring tides and the east winds cleaned it away again. Even the youngest members of the family were regimented to collect the stinking wrack into piles on the foreshore while the tide was out, and fathers and mothers crammed it into willow creels and carried it on their backs the half mile across the common grazing land to the crofts on the upper side of the road ready for spreading on the fields with manure from the byre to fertilize the land that was to be put under crops. It was back-breaking work, cold and wet and miserable, and I suppose not unlike the dreaded kelp collecting of such hated history. But we were doing it for our own benefit if not profit, and in time we would reap its harvest. Yet we knew we were working for a bare existence and, in the mind of the boy like myself, it was a further spur; a reminder that somewhere else there lay an easier life than this. Our parents told us so, our teacher told us so, and our books told us so; and all of them combined to convince us that the key to that better life was in books and learning. Had the authorities which had finally capitulated to the demands of the crofters for land of their own been whole hearted in their commitment, they would have sent their men from the colleges earlier to guide us, and they would have equipped us with even the rudiments of the mechanization which had already transformed the lives of small farmers on the mainland. We had been beguiled into a Garden of Eden without fruit trees, and without the means and the knowledge to make the fruit trees grow.

And yet spring was good. It brought alive again the camaraderie that had been dormant during the winter. When the peat-cutting started the families combined together to climb the hill and cut each others' peat banks in turn. The men who had ploughs and horses would turn the fields for those who hadn't. My own favourite was the big gentle quite-spoken man with the hole in his cheek, where a bullet had entered when he was 'going over the top' at Arras and had come out through his neck leaving him short of one tooth. When they found him he had enough blood left in him to keep him alive, and they were able to keep him so to see the rest of the war through. Like my own father and the others he never spoke about it, and I thought it was a big dimple till another boy told me what it really was. The best day of spring was the day on which he would arrive with his half Clydesdale horse and his plough and come in and tease my mother for a cup of tea till the rest of the village assembled.

My father and mother and I would have the field all spread

and ready with cow manure and seaweed a few days before, and we would be up early to lay out half a dozen bags of potato eyes at each end of the field, and as many buckets and basins as we could muster. In dribs and drabs the other crofters would arrive, some bringing their own hessian aprons made from old sacks, and a few of the women would come with covered baskets full of pancakes and oatcakes and home-made scones; one or two who had good yielding cows would arrive gingerly carrying pails of whey because, if the day was hot, the potato planting could be thirsty work and sore on the back into the bargain. The two or three venerable old women from the old township would trundle slowly along with their knitting; they were too old to help and nobody would expect them to; their presence was like a blessing, a routine which they had observed year in year out, and in their inmost ears they would probably be hearing the distant echo of the laughter which had been their own in days long past. I could see father's eyes glancing down the road and, though he never said anything, I knew that he was waiting for Great Aunt Rachel to arrive and that he would find some excuse to delay the proceedings till she did so. Not that excuses were hard to find. It took a long time to slice ropes of black twist tobacco with stubby cutty-knives, rub it between rough palms till the consistency was just right, scrape pipes and stuff them just tightly enough and no more, and then get them going and capped against the breeze. At last all would be ready. An experienced man would take the big black horse by the head and lead him in a straight line first up one side of the field and then down the other as the man with the hole in his cheek held the plough down, cutting the outer furrows which would mark the extent of our potato field for that year. After that the horse would follow the furrows on his own with only an occasional twitch on a rein to guide him as the ploughshare turned over the foot-wide sods with surgical precision. When the first gash was laid open several men with farmyard graips switched manure into it, and the rest, along with some of the women, followed – placing potato eyes at precise 18-inch intervals. Slowly, behind them, Great Aunt Rachel would walk with a mug of fresh water gently sprinkling each newly planted eye; nobody would pay any attention to her; nobody would speak;

the horse would be held still at the top end of the far-side furrow till she reached the end of the first one, whereupon she would straighten up and walk smartly down to the house shouting to my mother to bring the teapot to the boil. One or two of the men would smile to each other, and the man on the plough would crack his reins and the planting would get under way in earnest with its usual ribaldry and badinage and good humour. By some miracle of precision which I could never fathom there were never more than half a dozen potato eyes left over when the two ever widening sets of furrows met in the middle, and these were given to the horse while he was being unyoked.

It never occurred to me to ask anybody why Aunt Rachel performed her little ritual; there was something about the silence that hung over the field that discouraged curiosity. In any case the country boy grows up to accept traditional ritual as a matter of routine, and to probe that little ceremony would have been like asking my father what he said in his silent prayers when he 'took the Books' before bedtime. It was only a few years ago, when I was reading *Dr Salaman's History and Social Influence of the Potato*, that I read how – after the devastating Irish potato famine of 1845 – the Catholic priests in Ireland adopted the practice of sprinkling the newly-planted potatoes with Holy Water to bless the crop and ward off such tragedy again. In the Highlands, in that same year, we'd had our own potato famine of proportionately tragic dimensions; by then Great Aunt Rachel's forebears were already established as Clerics in the Presbyterian Church up on the hill, but in the Celtic countries rituals have had a habit of surviving in the folk tradition long after religious schisms and bigotry have obfuscated their original significance.

The potato planters sat down to a huge high tea when their day's work was over, swopping yarns and discussing the township's business. Never, as the starry-eyed writers of Hebridean romances would have one believe, quaffing drams and singing the night away into morning. I would fidget on the fringe of the gathering hopefully, till the man with the hole in his cheek would look up with a twinkle in his eye and say, 'I think the horse will be dry now, Finlay; would you like to do me a favour and take him home?' A favour! And the responsibility of it!

Time and the pretensions of sophistication have blunted many memories, but never the thrill of clinging on to the slippery bare back of a hefty plough horse pretending to be riding him like a cowboy from a story book while in reality the great beast was carefully picking his way home just as he would have done anyway. The man with the hole in his cheek had an understanding of boys surpassing that of anybody I ever knew, and in all our conversations he never spoke to me as if I were a year younger than himself. He never had a son of his own, but the last time I saw him he was surrounded with grandchildren and one of them was named after himself. Apart from the fact that he offered me a dram he spoke with me exactly as he did on the days of the potato planting.

It was shortly after the potato planting and the peat cutting were over that the first of our seasonal visitors arrived. The Black Man we called him; not in any pejorative sense, but because that's what he was. As yet we didn't have a name for him because he was a bird of passage, and he wasn't the same man every year. He was an Indian (the great sub-continent hadn't divided then) and it was one of the great mysteries how he and his fellows made their ways from wherever they came from across the Minch, and a greater mystery still how they expected to make their journey pay. But, shortly after the first cuckoo, the Black Man would appear with his heavy case strapped on to the carrier of his bicycle and knock politely on the door. Nobody ever turned anybody away so he was always invited in and offered a cup of tea which he always attempted to refuse. Visitors to the Outer Hebrides are subject to no hazards or dangers out of the ordinary save one. And that is tea. The seasoned traveller like myself, going back to my own native island, would be expected to cope with most of the traditional exigencies; but I have never found the art of dodging 'the wee cup of tea', which is anything but what it says. When the English say 'a cup of tea' they mean that; when the Hebridean hostess uses the same phrase it embodies at the very least two home-baked scones, two oatcakes with cheese and two pancakes! In the first house it is invariably welcome; in the second it is acceptable; in the third it is impossible, and equally impossible to avoid without giving offence. I have been driven to missing out visits to some of the homes of my best friends for fear of being killed with kindness, but I know not how Indian pedlars of those days survived when the acceptance of hospitality must have seemed a prerequisite if there was to be hope of a sale. But a sale there invariably was!

The procedure was always the same.

The housewife would say coyly and with patent sincerity, 'Now, it's very nice seeing you and I hope you will call back whenever you're passing this way, but I don't want you to be wasting your time opening your case. I don't really need anything today.'

'O no. Plenty time – just show you!'

'O, I know. Perhaps the next time you're passing.' Then, confidentially, 'To tell you the truth, times are very hard just now and I can't afford anything. You see, tweeds aren't selling just now and we just haven't got any money to spare.'

'Money very short everywhere. Very bad in Lewis. But fortunately it cost nothing to look.'

By now the case would be open, and the garment on top would be a dress of shimmering beauty and of total impracticability, but before the victim could say that, the Black Man would say it himself, 'This is no good. Too expensive. This is for the town, and a lady in Stornoway will buy it. But you feel.'

That was innocent enough, and honest. And irresistible. But there is something that happens to a woman when she feels a good quality material, that is like the break-down of the enzyme in the liver of the alcoholic. Layer after layer of garments of surpassing beauty (and rarity in a part of the world which then lived out of catalogues) would be folded neatly back on the flat lid of the case, with invitations to admire and feel but positive abjurations not to buy. In fact there was always a gentle undertone of suggestion that an offer to buy would be embarrassing because it would have to be turned down. And then a blouse would be flicked over rapidly without even an invitation to touch it. 'No good. Too like the one Mrs MacLaren bought.'

'Wait a minute. Let me have a look. Did Mrs MacLaren buy one of those?' (Strange, that. Mrs MacLaren hadn't sold a tweed in months either, and Charlie hadn't even sold a stirk at the last cattle sale.)

'No good for you. Too expensive. Right colour for Mrs MacLaren but wrong colour for you.'

It was probably the 'too expensive' suggestion that was the first twitch of the bait.

'It's very nice though. Can I have a look at it, please?'

'Sure. But not right. Mrs MacLaren more – er – more . . .' and the hands would indicate girth, while the tone bespoke reluctant delicacy.

'Stouter?'

'Yes. English not good. Mrs MacLaren more stouter.'

Two hits! Two palpable hits! Not only was this a man with good powers of observation, but here was a poor soul with poor English far from home.

The rest was easy. A blouse. A pair of knickers. Two pairs of pure silk stockings for the price of one pair, (The Trades Descriptions Act hadn't even been dreamt of) and, of course, it would indeed be sound policy to buy a light-weight semmit for the man of the house now that the warm weather was coming along. There would be just enough money in the shottle of the red kist, and the semmit would be produced first at the first appropriate time – maybe tonight, maybe tomorrow, but at the right time!

In truth, in our house the sale would be made even more easily if father happened to be in, because any visitor from across the Minch, far less from overseas, was a joy to him. The chance to exchange views with a stranger, the chance to hear news from foreign parts, the chance to open even a peep-hole on the outer world was bliss for him. For a gently extrovert man to feel that he was closed off forever in a small community, earning a livelihood in a manner for which for the greater part he had no heart, must have been a sorer trial than he admitted even to himself. Certainly he was shortly to take a step that would bring fresh interest into his life and build up an unexpected circle of friends, but he wasn't to know that then.

I don't know why the Black Man was accepted in the island without any of the appalling reactions that have met his kith and kin in more sophisticated communities. Or perhaps the answer lay in that very lack of sophistication. It may be that the man who lives close to the soil is more concerned with values deeper than the colour of skin. Perhaps we saw in him somebody who was struggling hard to survive as we were struggling ourselves. Certainly each one who came left behind him the sort of reputation that made his successor next year welcome, and, in due course, when one of them decided to settle in the community and marry into it, he was accepted and given a place of honour. But that was Ali, whom the older men called Alick as if he were one of themselves. It wasn't Ali who was alleged to have brought about the death of Hector MacGeachan's sharp-tongued sister; it was the man who sold Mrs MacLaren the blouse.

He earned every penny he pocketed, that man. Not only did he trundle our indifferent road of those days on his rackety old bicycle calling at every roadside house; he would get off his bike, prop it against the roadside fence and trudge up the winding footpaths to the remotest houses on the hillside, and he made his sales in the unpromising looking black houses as unerringly as he did in the croft house or the manse. It was just unfortunate that the young man he met on his way up the hill was one of the most popular rapscallions of the place, a lad in his late teens with a taste for the beer and an eye for the girls, but with a sense of humour that made him one of the most popular characters in the five villages, and would make a saint forgive him for sin. The story of the encounter was his own, told many times with a smile that was tinged with conscience.

'Ah, Mohammed. . .' he said.

'Excuse me my name not Mohammed. My name . . .'

'It doesn't matter; you're the man I'm looking for. See that house up there. That's Hector MacGeachan's house, and his sister wants to see you. She's out at the peat-bank just now but she'll be back home in a few minutes. The door's open and you're to go in and wait for her. She's desperate to see you; there's something she wants to buy for a wedding.'

The poor Black Man wasn't to know that there wasn't a wedding on the horizon in the whole island, and the idea of somebody actually so desperate to make a purchase that he mightn't even have to suffer yet another cup of tea must have been something beyond his wildest idea of success. And so –

thanking the cheerful messenger – he hoisted his case on his shoulder and climbed the steep track to Hector's house.

Now the description 'black house' doesn't mean very much to people who didn't know the pre-war islands, and to people in the Home Counties the totally appropriate alternative description of 'thatched cottage' conjures up a wholly inappropriate picture of a highly desirable, highly listed, National Trust type cottage with Norfolk reeds at the end of a Somerset lane. A 'black house' in the Hebridean sense (and Hector's was one of the last remaining ones in our parts) had a dry-stone wall about two feet thick, a roof of heather thatch, a floor consisting of the God's earth trampled solid by many generations, and a peat fire in the middle of the floor, with the smoke (or most of it) escaping through a hole in the roof – a hole which could not, of course, be directly above the fire or else the rain coming through would put the fire out. The window was deeply recessed and small. And all those qualities made for a house which could be very warm and comfortable but so dark that it earned to the full its description of 'black house'.

The Black Man would be no stranger to them. Up till the war they were still quite common in the Western Isles, before the islanders took the biggest leap forward in their history to the stone and lime 'white house' as the new type of building was, naturally, called for its very contrast.

The Black Man went into Hector's house and felt his way to a stool by the fire and sat and waited.

His informant hadn't been totally misleading. Hector's sister was indeed at the peat-bank, and about the time that the Black Man went into her house she was on her way back home with a small sack of peat which would keep her going till Old Hector got back from whichever house he was gossiping in, and, doubtless, she was framing the words with which to salute him when he got home. The poor woman flung down her sack, according to herself, and, gasping for breath from her exertions went into the house.

'Hello Miss MacGeachan,' said the voice.

Hector's sister nearly jumped out of her skin at the unexpected greeting. When she recovered sufficiently to peer into the darkness all she could see was a set of gleaming white teeth and a very large pair of disembodied white eyes staring at her from a height of three feet above the floor and she collapsed in a dead faint. So – nearly – did the Black Man. And the good Lord only knows what dire imaginings of punishment he dragged from his mental transposition of similar circumstances to whichever primitive part of the Raj he came from. He did what any man of any colour would be tempted to do. He picked up his case and ran for his bicycle.

When Hector MacGeachan got home, unaware that the Black Man had been in the country, far less of the circumstances, he fell over his virago sister, speechless for once, and prostrate on the floor. In falling he thrust out his hand to stop himself and put it right into the centre of the smouldering peat fire. It was his yell of pain as much as his collapse on top of her that brought her round out of her faint and, on Hector's own wistful admission later, her tonguing put the pain out of his hand for an hour. But it also brought out a forgotten spark of his manhood. He was prepared to accept much maligning for the sake of peace, but he was not going to accept the responsibility for two non-existent large white eyes and a set of smiling teeth in the dark. He was as superstitious as the next man, but that particular phenomenon didn't fit into any of the accepted catalogues of superstitions or premonitions. His sister was either hallucinating or lying, and he told her so in a voice that carried to the nearest house – which wasn't exactly next door.

Nobody ever heard where the Black Man whose name wasn't Mohammed disappeared to, but he was never seen in Harris again. Hector's sister survived for a week to harangue him and to stravaig the village telling her story, and a week was long enough for the village to be able to absolve everybody from guilt when she took a stroke and died.

'Poor woman,' they said. 'With that temper of hers it's a miracle that she didn't burst a blood vessel long since.'

Chapter Six

THERE is an old Gaelic proverb which says that 'no man ever saw his own tree plantation grow.' I'm sure that like most proverbs it has its equivalent in every language under the sun since all it's saying in effect is that subtle change and development are going on around us all the time, so gently that we don't notice them. I'm not sure that – in any language – the proverb is valid any more, because accelerating technology can change an area of our environment overnight; and as environments change so habits and modes of life change, and 'tradition' which we used to think of as the mellowing harvest of sown experiences, is now giving way to that thing known as 'a phase'. Distance and inaccessibility, and – above all – that stretch of ocean known as the Minch, allowed the Outer Hebrides to cling on to their old ways, good and bad, their language, and the depth of their religious belief, long after the power-houses of the cities had tended to send their waves of uniformity out over all but the remotest corners of the mainland. It's a generalization of course, because even cities cling on to their own enclaves of style and custom, and everybody knows that the great sprawl we call London is, basically, a huge collection of villages; but, in most of the everyday conducts of life, less and less separates the man in John O' Groats from the man at Land's End. The man in Barra watches the same *Coronation Street* as the man in Bermondsey; they watch the same politicians arguing the same points; and, inevitably, exposure to the same banalities and the same philosophies will produce common attitudes to most things.

The Minch has ceased to be a great dividing barrier between mainland Scotland and the Western Isles except in so far as the cost of crossing it puts a huge economic burden on the islanders. If it ceased to be an economic barrier and became a cultural one instead, then there might be a greater hope that the islands could survive to appreciate their own language, and the traditions which a language, more than anything else, encapsulates. But the airwaves and the airways don't acknowledge the sea as a hindrance, and both those have served to accelerate change in the islands more than anything else; the former because they overwhelm viewers and listeners with a beguiling and glossy alien culture; the latter because they have removed the mystique of time and distance for the very people who go in search of it. It is nice and convenient to have coffee at Heathrow and lunch in Harris, but one hasn't explored anything on the way. The airwaves had already begun to search us out by the time Hector MacGeachan lost his sister; the airways found us on the day they buried her.

There is no ultimate difference between the cold fact of death in Glasgow now and death in our village almost half a century ago, but there is a mighty big difference in the ceremonial attending it. When I go to a funeral in the city now I put my black tie in my pocket and wrap it round my neck in the crematorium car park, and I'll be taking it off again before the ashes have barely had time to cool, and hastening to vacate a parking space for a car in the next waiting cortège. When Maggie MacGeachan died, work in the village stopped for the three days of her lying, and for three nights men and women took it in turn to go and sit in 'the house of watching', a quiet, sober, and solemn version of what the Irish call a wake. There was none of the Irish festivity that playwrights have found so much inspiration from; just quiet talking about matters of life and, occasionally, a prayer from a man whose nearness to eternity gave him sufficient confidence and authority to pray. But during the three days there was much work to be done. Food had to be provided for those who came to pay their respects, and it turned out that Maggie (as people took to calling her now that her back was turned forever) had many relatives in the Eastlands who had found the distance too long

66

to visit her while she was alive; the old women who, wise in the ways of birth and death, had to wash and lay her out; the men who had to go to the joiner three villages away and tell him to bring down the boards which he always had seasoning in the rafters of his workshop against the day that would require a coffin. Not that Old Hector's sister would require many boards; what there was of her in life was mostly tongue they used to say, but of course she had good points too, they were now remembering. When the morning of the day came, the joiner would deliver the coffin in good time along with a handful of screwnails.

Many island schools would close for the day, or at least for the afternoon of a funeral, but our school was only a quarter of a mile from the cemetery which served most of the island and if we closed for every funeral dozens of attendance days would be lost. So a respectful compromise was reached. The school closed for the whole day if a funeral concerned the immediate family of one of the 'scholars' as we were called, but if it didn't we merely stood in silence for a few minutes as a cortège passed the school; or, if it came from the opposite direction, we observed the silence for a token while during the period when the teacher adjudged that the graveyard service was being conducted. The latter ordinance would, in the normal course of events, have been observed for the Mac-Geachan funeral, but events did not turn out to be normal.

Ours was a one-teacher school, and, therefore, it was impossible for her to organize any form of segregated school activity, so 'drill' – or physical training – was tailored to exercises that the boys and girls could perform together without embarrassment to the latter. Gardening and cookery provided no problem at all; the boys took cookery along with the girls, and the girls were introduced to the skills of gardening along with the boys. The funeral was due to take place on a gardening afternoon – a fact which I could not possibly have remembered if the day hadn't turned out to be momentous; but not only do I remember what we were doing, I remember that it was an exceptionally beautiful afternoon. Gardening was very good fun. I have never been able to understand why the crofters were so indifferent to the possibilities of a vegetable plot unless it was because the depredations of the rabbits took the heart out of them. Certainly in our minute little school patch of light sandy soil we could grow vegetables of all ordinary variety – lettuce, turnip, beetroot and so on – and we were each able to take at least a token sample home from time to time. We did, on second thoughts, have the advantage of a plot surrounded by a high stone wall, to which the only access was through the school – and it would have been a fairly courageous rabbit who negotiated that.

We were all bent over our individual areas of horticulture, with the teacher sitting relaxed with a magazine which, we were lead to believe although it was never expressly stated, contained gardening notes. The fact that the cover proclaimed that it contained a revealing article about the present life and whereabouts of the Duke and Duchess of Windsor one week, and promised full coverage of the Royal State Visit of King George VI and Queen Elizabeth to Edinburgh next week, was probably coincidence. We weren't worrying anyway. Gardening was interesting, and we were allowed to talk quietly to each other while we were getting on with our work. And then we heard a car approaching and we straightened up of one accord.

'Never mind the car. Get on with your work or I'll take you all inside and give you sums!'

We knew perfectly well she didn't mean it, just as we knew she'd be having a sly look herself when the car came nearer – because one could glean a lot of contemporary social history from the purposeful to-ings and fro-ings of cars in those days.

'It will be a car for the funeral,' I whispered to Jamie MacInnes who was weeding the row beside me. 'I heard my mother saying that Hector MacGeachan had relatives in Tarbert.'

'Shut up,' he hissed. 'I think she's forgotten about the funeral, and if she remembers she'll take us inside to stand up!'

I couldn't quite see the logic of going inside in order to stand up for the mandatory minutes of silence, when the people most closely involved would be performing their obsequies by the graveside in the open air. I didn't argue with him because

Jamie was a bright lad and he could read the teacher's mind better than any of us. But there was one thing he didn't jalouse, just like the rest of us; and that was that this was no approaching car. As the droning noise kept getting nearer there was no suggestion of the noise of tyres on gravel, and suddenly somebody yelled, 'It's an aeroplane!' and even the teacher sprang to her feet.

Aeroplanes weren't totally new to us. On very rare occasions we had heard them overhead, and had even seen the odd one like a dot in the sky in the distance. But never one as low as this. It was coming over the Back of Scarista Hill, a grey bi-plane moving incredibly slowly – it seemed to us as we stared open-mouthed at it – and it kept losing height as it approached, till by the time it was overhead we could read the letters printed on its side, and, as he passed, the pilot waving to us.

'It's going to crash!' somebody shouted.

'Nonsense!' the teacher yelled, 'Didn't you see the pilot waving; he wouldn't be doing that if he was going to crash, would he?' And then, after a pause, and without the slightest attempt to keep the excitement out of her voice, 'But it's going to land on the sands, that's what! Listen to me. You can all run down to see it, but then come straight back here and tell me all about it. Remember now, straight back. Off you go!'

We went like 13 greyhounds out of their traps, racing down the machair land and the rolling dunes that lay between us and the flat tidal sands of Northton. We were to realize later that our own expansive beach was too soft and yielding for an aeroplane to land on, whereas the sands of Northton are as hard as a blaes tennis court – when the tide is out and they're baked in the sun. I don't suppose the two miles of machair between Scarista and Northton have ever been covered in faster time, and, sure enough – when we arrived – there, like a grotesque double-winged fulmar, the grey aeroplane was resting on the sands with its propeller idling to a stop and the pilot climbing down out of his cockpit. As we arrived we were aware of people converging on the scene from every direction, from Northton village, from Kintulavig further down the road, from our own village, and down from the moor's edge – looking like people from another world – an incongruous knot of people in black with the men wearing black ties.

When the excitement had begun to die down, one of the older girls passed word round that the teacher was expecting us back, and she pointed out that it had been good of her to let us free. 'Remember Miss Dalbeith?' she said. 'She'd have locked us indoors and not let us even *see* the aeroplane!'

'The aeroplane wouldn't have come if that bitch was here!' one of the boys muttered as we headed back for school. Those of us who remembered Miss Dalbeith were, mercifully, getting fewer; the generations were rolling on.

'I bet you she'll give us an essay about the aeroplane,' Jamie said as we jogged along.

'No,' I said. 'That would just be giving herself work correcting them.'

'Like buggery,' Gillespie puffed. 'She'll give us a composition and then not bother reading it. Anything to keep us in the house in the evening.'

In fact, quite perceptibly, our noses were being eased more and more towards the grindstone. There was a definite firming of work and of purpose, and we all knew that it was because the bursary examinations were drawing near. The generation immediately ahead of the three of us would, in fact, be sitting the County examinations and having their futures decided in a few weeks' time, and then next year it would be our turn. When we got back to school, it turned out that Jamie and Gillespie were half right and that I was totally wrong. The schoolroom looked as dark as a winter's evening after the sunshine on the white sands, and as dull as a moorland cavern. From where I sat I couldn't see the teacher's face as she stood silhouetted against the window questioning us on what we had done and what we had seen, nor could I get a word in edgeways for the girls and the infants blattering on and on – the girls about the pilot and the infants about the aeroplane. At last she called a halt to the hubbub.

'Now listen all of you,' she said at last, and Gillespie nudged me hard in the ribs. 'I've been thinking while you've been away. You've had a marvellous experience, and by the time you're grown up you'll be travelling in aeroplanes as people now travel in buses. I want the two top classes (we'll let the young ones off this time) . . . I want the two top classes to go home and write a one page composition – just one page – describing exactly what happened today, what you saw and what you thought about it. Remember now – not just a description of the aeroplane but a description of the whole scene – and then tomorrow I'll pick the best bits out of all the essays and I'll send the story off to the *Daily Record*. Who knows? One of you might work on a newspaper one day, and you'll look back on this as your starting point. Right. Here are your papers, and off you go!' As we filed past her she handed the members of the two oldest classes foolscap pages with our individual names already written across the top.

'I told you so,' somebody muttered as we went through the school gate. But nobody really condemned the idea. The *Daily Record* (a Kemsley paper) was then challenging the monopoly of Beaverbrook's *Express*, and cartoon strips like *Lauder, Willis and Lorne* (founded on the three leading Scottish Music Hall figures of the time) and *Bringing up Father* were attacking the empire of *Rupert Bear*, but I doubt if either Press Baron was filling his coffers appreciably in Scaristavore. Newspapers were not peaking much circulation in our village although the occasional ones that we saw were fat, and beginning to breathe optimism.

'She forgot the Lord's Prayer,' somebody said when we were well clear of the school. And, sure enough, for the only time that I could remember the teacher had forgotten to close the day in the usual way.

'Shut up or she'll call us back if she hears you.'

My father still hadn't returned from the funeral when we got home, and my mother was not in the best of form as she scrubbed the flabby ware potatoes for our evening meal.

'I've never heard the like of it,' she said. 'People rushing away from a funeral to go risking their necks in an aeroplane.'

'There hasn't been an aeroplane before!' My brother had begun to practise the art of retort, and he hadn't yet learnt when it was wiser to keep quiet. My mother wasn't a deeply religious woman in any of the fashionable fanatical moulds, but she had a wholesome respect, not untinged with superstition where matters of death were concerned.

'You keep quiet and bring in two pails of water from the burn.'

'I can't carry two pails.'

'You can carry one pail at a time, and if they're not full to brim when I look at them you'll get the fetter-rope across your calves!'

She really was in a bad mood, and I didn't even chance a smirk in my brother's disgruntled direction. The fetter rope was the short rope that she used to tie round the cows' hind legs when she was milking, and it always hung on a nail beside the mantelpiece, not because she was sadistically keen on wielding it – although it was a favourite grudge of hers that she was always being cast in the role of dispenser of punishment; the fetter rope was there so that she would know exactly where to lay hands on it at milking times. But it was a deterrent, in those days before the word had assumed any more awful significance.

My father came in whistling cheerfully just as the salt herring were coming to the boil, pulling off his black tie as he came through the door.

'Dinner's ready!'

'God look down on you woman, you don't expect me to sit down to potatoes and herring in my Sunday suit, although I confess I'm starving.'

'You didn't have any qualms about going chasing off after an aeroplane in your Sunday suit and your funeral tie, from what I hear. A judgment will come on you people for your behaviour today. Mrs MacRae was in here and she'd been watching the whole thing from the Back of Scarista Hill. She said that you looked for all world like a stream of black cockroaches making for a dead sheep's carcase. It was easy to see that it was the missionary and not the minister conducting the funeral service, Mrs MacRae was saying, or he wouldn't have tolerated the gang of you rushing off to an aeroplane before poor Maggie MacGeachan's soul had been laid to rest. Mrs MacRae was horrified, and I'm not surprised!'

'If God sends an aeroplane for Hetty MacRae's soul the way he did for Maggie's *I'll* be the one who's surprised!'

'John!'

My father also knew when to shut up, but gave us a broad wink as he went through to the other room to change. . . .

Our report was published in the *Daily Record* the following Saturday – a distillation, as Miss Martin had promised, of all the best efforts submitted to her the next day. Alas, it contained not one single word that I had contributed; I had gone off on a very oblique new angle (inspired by stories of the use of aircraft in the Great War) about aeroplanes with machine guns some day threatening Northton Sands. I searched out the story just a few days ago with some considerable help from the Mitchell Library in Glasgow, and I can do no better than quote it verbatim – in the certain knowledge that the *Daily Record* will not mind after all this time. It was headed:

FIRST AEROPLANE IN HARRIS

With a whirr of sand rising from its landing place and settling in its wake, an aeroplane made a landing in Harris, on the golden Northton sands. Soon nothing was to be heard but the patter of little feet and big feet, racing cyclists, hooting cars, all forgetful of speed limits, making for that unique object, the first aeroplane to land in Harris. What a scene of animation and what a babel of voices! Countless questions were showered on the patient pilot who imparted the required information, allowed the spectators to examine the machine and offered them a short and free trip in the air.

With a full complement of local people from Scarista and Northton, the 'plane rose gracefully, sped across the sands rising higher and higher and in ever widening circles, thrilling the passengers and causing the panic-struck cattle and horses to scatter hither and thither.

The islands of Taransay, St Kilda, Shellay, Pabbay, Bernera, Killegray, Ensay were seen in rapid succession ere the delighted and grateful passengers were disembarked on the sands.

A third landing was effected on a neighbouring meadow, which is evidently an ideal landing place.

The initials are MM. But I remember that the gist of the story was Jamie MacInnes's, already displaying the beginnings of a talent which, alas, the scourge of the Hebrides at the time did not allow to flower. One phrase, though, was certainly inserted by the schoolteacher who'd been to college on the mainland: to this day 'speed limits' are unheard of in the Western Isles – except for one in Stornoway, whose introduction had as its one result, according to one Lewisman, that 'the Harris bus had to accelerate'.

As I thumbed through that old *Daily Record* I stumbled across bits and pieces that blew ashes off the embers of memory. Some anniversary of the days of Savoy Hill was being celebrated by the BBC, although the wireless had not yet reached our village. Not quite. But it and the aeroplane came in the year that Maggie MacGeachan died, and between them they heralded the beginning of the great levelling out which is now accelerating around us, and bringing Heathrow ever nearer to Harris, and Bermondsey to Barra.

Chapter Seven

THAT summer was supposed to be my last holiday in the Northlands anyway, and as things turned out it was just as well that everybody had become conditioned to the idea. It saved my Big Grandfather the embarrassment of having to declare me *persona non grata*, thus hurting the feelings of his younger and favourite daughter; and it saved giving the neighbours a chance to detect a rift in the family lute. From the time that we had left the Northlands and settled in the new village in the south, I had travelled north every summer and spent the long school summer holidays with Big Grandfather – a near neighbour of Wee Grandfather, my father's father. Thus I was encouraged to maintain the strong family bonds which were so treasured in the Hebrides, and which were more difficult to maintain in the case of ourselves once we had uprooted ourselves to become strangers in a strange land. I suspect that, family feeling altogether apart, my mother was keen that I should have some fragmentary roots in the Northlands because, much as she liked the freedom of her own home in an undeniably beautiful setting, she missed the community closeness in which she had been brought up – a closeness which was really the product of overcrowding, and part of the very reason why it had become necessary for our people to move and follow their star to the good land and the wide open spaces of the south. But the open spaces can be daunting to the person not born to them, and the unease my mother suffered from was not so very different from that affecting overcrowded city dwellers finding themselves transplanted to planners' paradises. And, as far as I was concerned, not only did I have an indefinable soul link with the Northlands – much as I loved the freedom of the machair – but I was experiencing the holiday syndrome of the country boy coming to town.

The Northlands had a town in the shape of Tarbert with 13 shops, a pier which bustled thrice a week when the ship came in, a harbour which swarmed with fishing boats in those days, and a surpassingly beautiful anchorage which was speckled white in summer with rich men's yachts. And the country had an awesome beauty of its own; a land of great grey slabs of Lewisian gneiss dominating the heather, sprinkled with trout lochs that sparkled in the evening sun like unexpected diamante on a cloak of hodden grey. There was freedom too; the kind of freedom that grandparents lavished on their young guests before grandads became golfers and grandmothers took to bingo and cocktail bars. There was another freedom for me in the shape of a big house with an upstairs and a room to myself; a room with coom ceilings and a skylight which I could open on the morning to watch the Scalpay fishing boats chugging in leisurely through the yachts with their choruses of seagulls that seemed to be attached to them like wind-blown veils. And there was new company; a host of cousins above all else, including one of my own name who was a year or two older than me and wiser than me in the ways of the adolescent world. He was the only person who was dearer to my heart than Gillespie, because he knew a thing or two, and what he didn't know he invented. He taught me to smoke and when the day of reckoning came it was he who paid the price much much too soon.

Sixteen miles of a remove doesn't sound like much of an adventure for a holiday, but the miles are as long as the state of the road. The first little bus that attempted to establish a weekly connection between north and south was a 7 seater which took an hour to do the journey, and the men had to get out and push it up the steeper hills. The next bus was bigger and posher and it must have had its origins in some greater part of the mainland, perhaps the city, because it had a notice saying 'Spitting forbidden' – which was good for a laugh among men who smoked black twist and bogey roll. The concession to run the first thrice-weekly service was won by the man with the 'new' bus or, rather, *accepted* by him because everybody was sure it would never pay, and nobody could decide who was dafter – the man, who had saved up five pounds of his own money, or the banker who had lent him another five to pay for the bus. But the man had a personality that would have taken him to the top in any walk of life. His boast was that he had attended school for only two days and for them only because his grey-bearded grandfather had sat in the classroom with him to make sure he didn't run away. He hid an extraordinary shrewdness behind a beguiling eccentricity and the people who laughed at him were the people who loved him most. Many years later, when the bus with the 'Spitting forbidden' sign had multiplied into a large fleet – which, on the mainland, would have been a target for take-over – I teased him about his wealth and, over a dram, asked him what he reckoned he would have achieved if he had stayed in school and acquired an education. He replied with beguiling simplicity, 'I'll tell you that, boy; I'd be a bloody schoolmaster.' But that was long after the days of the last holiday, far less the first!

Invariably I set off for the Northlands the day after school closed for the summer holidays at the beginning of July, and without fail I landed at Big Grandfather's the week before summer Communion. I always arrived with money in my pocket because the man with the bus had a very bad memory when it came to accepting fares from little boys, and he would swear that he had been paid at the beginning of the trip. By the time Communion was over I was rich beyond measure.

Communion means to the city man a holy ritual at a morning service, three or four times a year if he's a Scottish Presbyterian; oftener if he belongs to one of the other faiths. But Communion in the Hebrides was a festival in those days. It began with us on Thursday, which was a Fast Day, although it was marked only by the cessation of all activity and the closing of all shops rather than by the ancient act of starving. People would assemble from the far corners of the islands, starting to arrive on the Wednesday evening having walked sometimes 20 miles. They would arrive in their hundreds and find accommodation with friends in the village in which the ceremony was due to be held, and from the Thursday to the Monday they would attend two church services a day and a series of evening prayer meetings as well, before the more devout of them moved on to a similar festival in another village or maybe another island. It was a moving and sometimes overwhelming experience to be caught up in the tension and occasional hysteria which could develop; it was an unforgettable new experience for me, since our own parish didn't have a resident minister at the time and consequently the ritual of twice-yearly communion had gone into abeyance. It was a strange beginning to the holiday, having to be on best behaviour for five days of continuous worship, and I got the full brunt of it in Big Grandfather's house because, although he wasn't an especially devout man himself, he had plenty of accommodation to offer and he was very hospitable.

For the days of Communion time I had to surrender my little attic room and sleep in whichever corner was available, because, with anything up to 20 guests in the house, bedspace was at a premium. But it was worth it. Each guest who arrived was, by virtue of being of Christian spirit, also disposed to be of Christian charity and every handshake for a little boy was accompanied by a surreptitious sixpence or a shilling – or even a half-crown, if the visitor happened to be a comfortable merchant haunted by the thought of that camel and the eye of the needle. In early years I still had money left to take back home with me at the end of the holiday, but when my cousin had taught me to smoke I found my donations weighing less heavily on my pocket.

And as I got older I became less amenable to the disciplines of Communion time and instead of allowing myself to be led by the hand to endless church services I found ways of slipping off unnoticed and spending the day trout fishing with the other Finlay. All of this was part of the rebelliousness of puberty which, strangely enough, led to more tension between Big Grandfather and myself than, as is more traditionally the case, between my father and myself. The difficulties were exacerbated by the fact that it was undoubtedly from Big Grandfather that my mother had developed her nervousness and the imagination to conjure up the possibilities of danger in connection with the most ordinary of boyish ploys. My grandfather, of course, had the added responsibility of looking after somebody else's child and he would never have forgiven himself if some mishap had befallen me while I was in his charge for what must have felt to him sometimes as seven very long weeks. He saw danger everywhere. On the shore cliffs below the house, in the tarns on the moor where my cousin and I used to wander, in the deep river pools where we fished brown trout, and even in the tinker camps which sprang up along the road which led between the houses of my two grandfathers.

The tinkers certainly looked a fearful lot. Big black avised men who got drunk even on Communion Saturdays and who fought with each other, and would have fought even with the visiting ministers if they had crossed their paths. Their women were large-boned and black-eyed, and they could be whining and suppliant when they chose or aggressive and foul-mouthed if they were crossed. They made their living out of selling odds and ends of ironmongery, mending pots and pans and making tin milk pails. They were extremely proud and tribal and regarded themselves as descendants of the broken clans who had not been cowed by the harsh Hanoverian repressions which followed Culloden, and rather despised the rest of us because we had succumbed to the soft life and good manners. Their marriages and their funerals were conducted according to age-old secret customs of their own, and they married not only within their own tribes but within their own sects, which had their individually defined traditions and taboos. God help the ordinary man who, in a drunken moment, made a pass at a tinker lassie; he was liable to end up in a ditch with every bone in his body broken and no trace or evidence of who did it. But nobody ever got so drunk as to try. I passed their encampments day in day out, and all I ever got was grunted Gaelic greeting in an accent that was different from our own. Tinkers, like Holy Communion attenders, had special standards for youngsters, and I could never understand Big Grandfather's hatred of them.

It was with my cousin that I got to know the Northlands like the palm of my hand. He knew every trout loch, and he had an instinct which told him unerringly when it was safe to go on a landlord's privately stocked loch in search of Loch Leven trout – instead of the pink-fleshed brown trout of the mountain streams. Our only equipment was a willow rod with a simple line and hook on it, but he could thread a worm so that it looked as live and juicy and wriggly as when he yanked it out from beneath its cowpat or its stone. And if he didn't have a line and hook it didn't bother him unduly. He could see a trout below a stone where I could see nothing but slippery pebbles and peaty mud; and he could slide up to the bank on his belly without causing the ground to tremor, and tickle the trout till it opened its gills with pleasure so that he could slip his finger in and howk it on to the heather with one flashing movement of his forearm. I could never master the art. 'It's just like a girl,' he would say as he lay back flushed with success beside a big brown trout flapping on the heather. 'You just keep stroking in the right places till the right moment comes and she opens up for you, and once you get your finger in there the rest's just a matter of moving in on your advantage. And man, oh man . . .' He was a Lothario by his way of it, with a power of description that set my head and my belly on fire just listening to him.

During those later summer holidays we became like blood brothers and he used to look forward to the day when I would win my bursary, as he was sure I would do, and come to Tarbert School. What ploys we would have then! What fun there was in Tarbert village on a winter's night, which, of course, I had never experienced – nor would ever have been allowed to, at that age, by Grandfather. The temptations to work hard to win the bursary were fast becoming stronger than mere scholastic ambitions, and I began to see Junior Secondary School as a brave new era even although I would, perforce, be a lodger in Big Grandfather's house. That had always been understood from the beginning. The £11 of bursary which I hoped to win would barely cover the better clothes that I would require for Tarbert School and a minimal contribution to my grandmother for my keep. Without that bursary I would never graduate to Tarbert, and the more I talked to my cousin the more alluring Tarbert sounded. Yes, this would have to be my last holiday; the next time I came it would be to stay, and the return to the village between terms would be the holiday then.

My cousin, with no malice aforethought, helped considerably towards making that last holiday short.

'Have you got the usual load of holy Willies and praying Marys in your Big Grandfather's?' he asked on Communion Saturday.

'Yes.'

'And are you sleeping in the cubby-hole as usual with two Lewis crones in your own bed?'

That was a sore point, and he knew it. I treasured more than anything else the privacy of that little attic room with the coom ceilings and the skylights.

'Well Sandy Malcolm was telling me a trick that he heard at the salmon fishing in Perthshire, and it'll get you the laugh of your life – and I'll bet you two pounds to your Communion takings that they won't be back next year!'

He knew that my little gifts from the Communion visitors had amounted to just under two pounds, which was a small fortune, and he knew that I knew he didn't have two *shillings*; but that was just his way of being emphatic, and he would have given me his last penny, far less take a halfpenny from me. He proceeded to detail the joke that Sandy Malcolm had brought back from the Tay fishings, and by the time he was finished I was sobbing with laughter.

'It can't fail man. And there's no way you can be caught unless you play daft. I'd give my last fag to be there to see it; make sure you remember every word that's said so that you can tell me.' He sent me off with two Woodbines to smoke on the way home. 'Keep your eye open for the new maid in the doctor's house,' he whispered as I was going away. 'She's from Skye with red hair and tits like turnips, and the Tarbert boys say she's game. Have a look round church tomorrow.'

I set off into the night with that irritating tingle in my lower belly again, and the tin he had given me tucked carefully below my ganzie. 'Red hair and tits like turnips.' There wouldn't be many to fit that description in church on Communion Sunday. It was dark by the time I was nearing the tinkers' encampment, and I could hear it long before I came in sight of it round the Devil's Elbow as the hairpin bend in the road was called. When I did see it, it was like a battlefield such as one was to become used to, in years to come, in second-rate cowboy and Indian movies. The tinkers had obviously had a high old night in the pub in Tarbert while the rest of the community were attending the Saturday evening prayer meeting. And the tinkers could afford a night out; they made money out of their domestic tin-smithing, they still sold their pots and pans and milk pails, they lived off the country, they probably collected dole money by forging signatures on the red-printed application forms; and, of course, they stole. Now there was a bloody fight in progress. It appeared to be between two families because men and women were involved, twisting and weaving in among the sailcloth tents backlit by the huge peat fires which had been freely fuelled from the township peat stacks. I stopped transfixed. The women were the archetypal witches of my story books as they clawed at their opponents with their talons or pulled a female enemy to the ground by her hair and then smashed a bare foot into her belly; the men were using their fists by and large, but one, older than the rest, was laying about him with a club of some sort and I could swear that here and there I saw a knife flashing. The screaming must have carried to the villages but, of course, nobody would pay any attention; it was something they were used to on occasional Saturday nights during the summer. The language was lurid. I thought I had heard most of the colourful words in the Gaelic vocabulary by that stage, but it was obvious that my education had been sadly monitored. I stood transported, soaking up words and phrases that would dazzle Gillespie when I got back home at the end of the holiday.

I felt the scalp rising from my head when hands gripped me out of the dark.

'And where do you think you're going, cove?'

I was pinioned between two wicked-looking youths a head taller than myself; one of them with two missing teeth where their absence was most noticeable, and the other with a scar running from below his greasy long hair to his jawbone.

'H-h-home,' I managed to stutter.

'And since when did you set up home here?' The other thought the joke was uproariously funny.

'I don't mean that.' My mouth was dry and I could hardly get the words out. 'I live with my grandfather in the big house down at the shore. He's a big man,' I added lamely, a statement whose only possible virtue in the circumstances was that it happened to be true.

'Oh, he's a big man is he?' I writhed at my voice being mimicked and the Harris genteelity of it being held up to ridicule by this ruffian. 'Well you tell your Granda that we've got big men here too if he wants to come and visit us. But on second thoughts you better not. In fact you better not even mention that you passed this place tonight because if we hear that you've said a word about what you saw here tonight we'll boot your arse so hard that you'll go sailing over your Granda's big house right out into the middle of the bay. Got it, cove?' And to prove that he meant business he put his foot against my backside and sent me flying. I picked myself up, and not even Tam o'Shanter's mare would have caught up with me as I raced for Big Grandfather's house. I stopped outside the door, waiting for my heart to steady, and I winced when I felt a stabbing pain under my ganzie. And then, relief! It was the tin my cousin had given me; it was still safely there and I must have hurt my rib on it when the tinker boy sent me flying. From inside the house there came the sound of hymn singing. That was a good thing. It meant that Big Grandfather wouldn't be able to say anything to me in front of his worshipping guests; tomorrow was the biggest Sunday of the year, and by Monday his wrath at my late homecoming would have died down.

I slipped into the house and crept upstairs to my own attic bedroom which, as my cousin had guessed, had been commandeered for the duration of the Communion by the two holy old women he had described as 'the two Lewis crones'. I got down on my knees beside the bed and found the handle of the china chamber-pot, the one with the red and yellow roses painted on it. It was empty, as I knew it would be, because Granny was a meticulous housekeeper. But to make sure it was bone dry I gave it a thorough wipe with an old shirt of Grandfather's left there for polishing shoes. I then tipped into the pot the contents of the tin of *Andrew's Effervescent Liver Salts* that my cousin had given me, and went downstairs to join the worshippers, hiding the empty tin in the cubby-hole on my way past. My grandfather looked at me over the gold rims of his spectacles, but there was nothing he could say without interrupting the spiritual voyage of 'The Ark of the Covenant', which was the hymn being sung with shut-eyed fervour by the dozen or so visitors. The Saturday evening domestic prayer meeting was a fringe event of the great Communion festival itself. It was a relaxed affair at which lay hymns were sung instead of the psalms (the equivalents of "The Old Rugged Cross" or "Morning Has Broken", which would not find a place in any formal Gaelic presbyterian service). I would have enjoyed myself fine once upon a time, but my enthusiasm for singing had been diminished since Miss Bassin had put the seal of officialdom on my incompetence in that direction. Saturday night was an unwind; a relax before the great day of Communion Sunday itself, most of which would be devoted to long services and spartan celebration of the Last Supper. The hymn singing finished in time for copious cups of tea to be served before one last prayer was said, so that everybody could be in bed by midnight.

I must have caught the last half hour of the service and it was only the thought of tea that kept me awake after my day on the moor and the excitement of the journey home. I watched the two holy old women of my bedchamber savouring cup after cup of Granny's strong brew, smiling to myself, but as soon as the last prayer was over I slipped off to my cubby-hole lest Big Grandfather be reminded to corner me and challenge me with my lateness.

I lay on my makeshift truckle-bed listening to the men slipping out to the end of the house 'to see what kind of night it was'; Grandfather had not yet installed the bathroom which, a few months later, would take over the cubby-hole in which I now lay. I knew that the women would be lifting their skirts behind the peat-stack at the other end of the house, and I hoped that the two holy women had drunk enough tea to make

84

their bladders trouble them a second time before morning. One by one people came back into the house and, with whispered 'Good nights', they slipped off to their crowded quarters throughout the house. I knew that my grandparents had surrendered the two double box-beds in their own bedroom and would be having yet another cramped night on the couch in the living room. The peace of what was by now the Sabbath morning descended on the house, and only an occasional snore from somewhere disturbed the tranquillity, and the rare miaou of a seabird haunting the moonlit ebb at the foot of the croft.

I was on the point of falling asleep when I heard the bed in the room above my cubby-hole creak, and a mumbling voice as one of the two occupants presumably apologized to her neighbour for disturbing her. I heard a gentle clink as the rose painted chamber-pot was pulled from under the bed, an audible sigh and a moment of silence. And then all hell broke out. The old woman upstairs screamed and called on the Almighty. Her companion shouted at her, startled, enquiring what was wrong. 'The Devil's work!' she yelled. 'A judgment on me!'

'More like a case for the doctor!' shouted her friend.

Then cries for help, and all over the house doors began to open. With my glee stifling me, but keeping my face straight, I went out to the lobby where Big Grandfather was standing with a lit candle in his hand, and from all over the house sleepy-eyed men of God were appearing in their shirt-tails looking like Old Testament prophets hearing the earth shake around Jericho. Modesty was thrown to the winds as everybody crowded upstairs, flannel nightgowns mingling with shirt-tails. Being smaller I managed to squeeze up beside the banister just as the frothy trickle from the attic bedroom reached across the linoleum of the landing and began to trickle downstairs round bare old feet. People crowded into the little bedroom ignoring the modesty of the one standing in the middle of the floor, oblivious to the fact that she still had her nightdress gripped round her knees like a tentative Blackpool wader, and to the one in bed with the bedclothes hugged to her chin. All eyes were on the rose painted peepot which was foaming like

85

a cauldron out of *Macbeth*. Then, as the froth died away, the tumult turned to puzzlement and sympathy, while the victim protested that she had been feeling in perfect health and that such a thing had never happened to her before. Yet one or two looked at her askance as they made their ways back to their disturbed slumbers, and Big Grandfather looked askance at me.

Matters of earthly import weren't discussed on the morning of Communion Sunday no matter how out of the ordinary they might be. People were up early to await their turns for hot water for their ablutions, and to allow each other elbow room for climbing into their Sunday bests. The women helped Grandmother prepare breakfast and, by half past eleven we were all setting off to church in our twos and threes so as to arrive there for eleven o'clock, God's time. The church did not acknowledge British Summer Time which was an unwarranted tampering with God's long-standing subdivisions of the day.

The church was crammed to capacity, as always on Communion Sunday, and heavy with the atmosphere of sanctity spiked with the sharp smell of mothballs. Four ministers, including the local one, were in charge of proceedings, flanked by a cohort of elders which included distinguished men from other parishes. In the Hebrides, and in much of the Highlands still, only a small minority actually participate in the celebration of Communion – men and women who are deemed by their peers worthy to partake of the sacrament, and, more importantly, who deem themselves worthy, something which struck me then and has always struck me since as being paradoxical in view of the humility which is supposed to be one of the keystones of the Christian ethic. The vast majority, attending all the services over the five days with devotion and sincerity, take their places in the wings on Sunday hoping, presumably, that when the Great Day comes the final arbiter will be less selective. The service was, as usual in those days, four hours long as some patriarchs prayed and others testified. I sat, wedged between my grandparents, hearing a sentence here and there, scanning the church furtively for a glimpse of red hair in the vicinity of the doctor's pew, puzzled that my cousin – usually so wise in the ways of the world – should have

86

forgotten that one of the female prerequisites for church attendance was a very large concealing hat!

It was, as always, a long and wearing day. We just had time to walk back home for the very special lunch of Communion Sunday before returning to church again for the evening service. It was a day on which no work whatsoever was done – even less than that permitted on a normal Sunday. In fact I think that the milking of the cow and the feeding of the hens (such as remained of them after the four days of banqueting) were the only two deeds that qualified for exemption under 'the seventh day rule' as *works of necessity and mercy*. Needless to say, modesty – as much as the patent inadmissibility of such a subject for Communion day conversation – precluded any reference to the events of the night before, and by Monday it was forgotten in the rush of preparation for departure after the Monday morning service. Forgotten by all except my grandmother, who took one second to put two and two together when she discovered an empty tin of *Andrew's Effervescent Liver Salts* in the cubby-hole as she strove wearily to restore the house to normality when the last visitor had left. It was probably my imagination that made me think that some of the pious visitors had a stern look in their eyes as they bid me goodbye and wished God's blessing on me in tones which suggested that I needed not only His blessing but His mercy; and it was probably that same overactive imagination which conjured a twinkle in the eyes of those whom one would normally be tempted to believe walked closest to God.

But there was no twinkle in Big Grandfather's eye. 'There was a time,' he said, 'when I used to look forward to your coming here on holiday; but I've spent the last two or three years wondering what the Devil was going to find for you to do next. This house has always enjoyed a reputation as a house of hospitality; its name will now go far and wide as a place where holy old women can't sleep in safety and Heaven knows how that story will get twisted in the telling.' He said a lot more than that, and the business of having had to moderate his language for five days meant that his vocabulary was supercharged. He refrained from packing me off home, but forbade me to leave the confines of the croft for a full week,

'Nor must that skinnymalink of a cousin of yours come near you! If you were my own son instead of my daughter's I would have your trousers down and your backside as red as a boiled lobster!' His own son, one of the heroes of my boyhood, was at that precise moment somewhere off Newport Island, America, aboard *Endeavour II* which was preparing to challenge for the Americas Cup.

Chapter Eight

'RUN down and bring me up a pail of oysters from the shore,' my grandmother would sometimes say. She could read and write English rather laboriously but not, apparently, enough to know whether there was an 'r' in the month. I think she had been to Glasgow once to visit a sister in the Highland enclave of Govan, but she would have confined her explorations to a few well-known landmarks like Wilson's Zoo, the Botanical Gardens and Sauchiehall Street; she wouldn't have been to any posh restaurants and so she wouldn't see anything wrong in boiling oysters till they opened, then rolling them in oatmeal and frying them to eat with potatoes.

Or her eagle eye would spot a huge skate left behind on the Yellow Reef by the tide, stranded by its own weight of eggs in their leathery pouches. 'Quick before the seagulls get at it, and take something to wrap round its tail in case it gives you a nasty hurt!' It was always a race with the seagulls but I never lost because the seagulls had long since learnt that a stranded skate could give a very vicious swipe with its spikey tail. Sometimes it took all my strength to drag the brute all the way up from the shingle shore (the Northlands had no beaches like those of home) but once I got it up to the house it was guarantee of a good meal for several days. Unlike most fish the skate is better left hanging for a day or two. There were all sorts of crude legends about skate because the female ones had some remarkable human resemblances anatomically; fishermen wouldn't eat skate before going off on long fishing trips because they were supposed to be very aphrodisiac. Perhaps the fishermen were right. . . .

The Northlands didn't suffer as much from the Depression as we did, just as the Southlands suffered little in comparison with the cities of the mainland. The Northlands, for one thing, were surrounded by rich seas fit for fishing, while our Atlantic coast was wind-lashed at the best of times and we couldn't very easily manage boats. But apart from that the people of the Northlands had evolved their own survival methods over generations, and they were more self-sufficient than we had yet had time to become. Although they had moved into a money economy just as we had done, they had graduated to it around a market centre with a hotel and offices and shops which generated an essential minimum of jobs, and even the wages of one girl working as a waitress in the hotel or as a clerkess in an office could make a colossal difference to a family with even a tiny patch of land such as they had and exploited to the full in the Northlands; the shops would buy eggs from people like my grandmother to sell to people in the administrative ranks in Tarbert while my mother, in the south, couldn't sell eggs because everybody around had hens of their own. In short the Northlands were reaping the benefits of a minuscule mixed economy with their aged traditional modes of life being underpinned by the money beginning to turn over in an adapting society. There were other factors too, and ways in which the overcrowded conditions which had sent us south were working in favour of the generation that had stayed behind: instead of being able to get land as we had done, many of the other younger ex-servicemen, or those who had been just too young to go to war, were driven to seek work in the cities; and now, with the country's economic upturn beginning to be felt more quickly in the cities than in the islands, those people in the cities or in the merchant navy were able to send cash home to their old parents. We who had appeared to be the fortunate ones were now beginning to feel that fate had dealt us a yarborough.

Big Grandfather was a man of his word, and when he said that I was to be confined to the croft for a week I knew that there would be no remission. But he was also a man of extremely soft heart especially where I, his first-born grandson, was concerned. So, unobtrusively, he went out of his way to make the period of my detention as easy as possible. He involved me in countless pleasant little jobs round the croft, like tarring the roof of a shed, fishing for cuddies off the Yellow Reef when he deemed the tide to be safe, searching the croft morning and night for lambs that might be getting into trouble for one reason or another. It is a fact, common to city and to croft, that work which is a bore and a chore for parents is a pastime when they're being performed for somebody else. And Big Grandfather could be excellent company; he had been in the militia in peacetime, and he had sailed for years as a young crewman on rich men's yachts, so he had fascinating yarns to tell. He had always followed Britain's efforts to recapture the Americas Cup and he knew all about the efforts made by people like Sir Thomas Lipton with his *Shamrocks*; and now here was his own son involved in the most hopeful attempt yet, an attempt to be made by T. M. Sopwith with *Endeavour II*, on which he had spent close on two hundred thousand pounds. Sopwith had strong ties with the Northlands; his yachts *Vita* and *Philante* had been regular visitors to the anchorage below my grandfather's croft, and both of them had been skippered by a Harrisman from next door. So there was plenty to talk about.

On the Monday when my detention order expired I was allowed to take the road over to Wee Grandfather's house where my cousin was waiting to greet me with joy. In no time we were out on the hill, and as we lay in a shady little hollow smoking and rigging our fishing rods I regaled him with all that had happened. He took the success of the chamber-pot episode as personal triumph for himself, as well he might since he had instigated it and provided the machinery for it, and he began to rack his brains for some means of trying it out himself. It wasn't easy because their house was much smaller than Big Grandfather's and the visitors they had tended to be relatives who used 'the outside' before going to bed. He was a bit disparaging about my failure to dispose of the evidence. 'You're a bitch of a fool,' he said, using one of the best swear phrases in the vernacular.

91

'You're not all that clever yourself, asking me to look out for a red-headed pusher in church when you might have remembered that every woman in church would be wearing a hat!'

'Hell,' he said. 'I never thought of that. So you didn't see her eh? Well I can tell you something, boy. I've seen her in Tarbert outside the doctor's house, and she's a beauty. A Skye woman. They don't make them like that in Harris. She's about as tall as I am and as slim as a rake except that she's got headlamps like a bus. And she's easy! I'm telling you. Jocky Kerr and Calum Marion have both had a go, and I'm telling you I'm going to find an excuse to get into Tarbert as soon as I find out when she's got her evening off. Just for once I wish school was open. . . . I'm cut off here with no proper excuse to go to the village. . . .' He waxed eloquent for ages, and certainly if even half of what he claimed to have heard was true the doctor's Skye maidservant was 'a bombshell'.

That conversation changed the atmosphere of the whole day. We ate the food that we had brought with us and began fishing till our stomachs told us it was time to go home. I had been given permission to stay and have my tea in Wee Grandfather's and the only condition laid down was that I should be back in Big Grandfather's by eleven o'clock without fail. In view of the diplomatic situation prevailing there I thought the terms quite reasonable and I was determined to be back on schedule.

Big Grandfather, as I have said elsewhere, was married to dumpy little 'Wee Granny', and 'Big Granny' (who was Great Aunt Rachel's sister and built on the same scale) was married to 'Wee Grandfather'. A more disparate set of grandparents one could not find short of carefully arranged marriage contracts between Lilliput and Brobdingnag. But each of the four was an individual personality of considerable consequence. 'Wee Grandfather' (from whom my father took his equanimity I'm sure) was one of the gentlest characters I have ever met, and where Big Grandfather was respected in the community, Wee Grandfather was loved. He was a weaver to trade, and a story-teller of rare quality. He spoke only Gaelic and I've never forgotten the shock I got when I asked him one day – long before the day I'm talking

92

about – o tell me what the caption was to one of the pictures in Arthur Mee's *Children Encyclopaedia*, which my cousin and his sister had got from somewhere and which I coveted beyond all else. 'Ah, my darling,' he said. 'I can't read.' Up till then I had taken it for granted that all adults could read English. But anything he lost through his inability to read he made up for fully with his gift of narrative. And like my father, he was never loth to lay down what he was doing and embark on a story. And so, after the evening meal, the hours flew by and, with a start, I realized that I would have to move pretty smartly if I was to reach my Big Grandfather's by quarter to eleven which, my cousin had slyly suggested, would be a good tactical move on the first day of my new-found freedom.

I set off. The evening light was fading and giving way to a brilliant full moon as I jogged along the road. This was another aspect of the moorlands which flanked the road all the way. Big rocks cast shadows and gave contour to the view; the burns actually tinkled over the shingle; the mountains formed a tall dark ring like the walls of an amphitheatre except for one break in the east through which one could see the Minch like a sheet of undisturbed mercury stretching all the way to the mountains of Skye. In the way that they always do, the mountains seemed to be trapping the moonlight so that I felt as if I were moving through a pool out of which I'd emerge at the other side. Any such poetic thoughts were banished when I realized that I was almost at the tinker encampment and I moved on to the heather verge by the roadside and slowed down so that I made less noise. I shuddered inwardly at the memory of the fellow with the lank greasy hair and the scar running down his cheekbone; if ever there was a candidate for the gallows he was one. But all was quiet. I could see lamp or candlelight coming from each of the tents and, in an occasional one where the flap was open, I could make out a glowing fire with dark figures round it. But the murmur of voices was peaceful, and if I didn't know better from experience I could have made myself believe that I was seeing a colony of the eccentric English tourists who occasionally came to our island to spend summer weeks under canvas in the most outlandish places. But I did know better, and I was glad when the encampment was safely behind me and the voices had disappeared. I resumed my leisurely jogging and, without meeting a living soul, I covered the remaining mile and reached the gate at the top of the path to my grandfather's house. I turned down to the gate and stopped. I couldn't believe my eyes. There, exactly as my cousin had described her, was the willowy red-head with her headlamps, as he had called them, resting on the top bar of the gate as she gazed moodily out across the Minch. I felt the saliva thickening in my mouth. She obviously hadn't heard me, and with my heart thumping in a highly erratic rhythm I muttered 'Excuse me' in English and leant forward to open the gate.

She turned towards me smoothly, without a hint of surprise or hurry and the red of her hair caught the moonlight. She smiled a white provocative smile.

'Excuse me!' she said. 'And since when did Harris boys start speaking English?'

'I didn't know you spoke Gaelic,' I mumbled, feeling myself caught wrong-footed.

'As good as your own,' she said quietly as she stepped aside.

I unhasped the gate and was half-way through it when she spoke again.

'Do you not have much time for girls then, or is it that you like plumper chickens?'

My tongue felt as if it was trapped in syrup, and the tightness in my solar plexus was spreading rapidly to my groin.

'I think you're fine,' I said.

I wished I'd read more of my mother's magazines.

'Are you not going to ask me in then?'

'Ask you in! I live with my grandparents and they'll be going to bed.'

'There are beds and beds,' she whispered coming up so close to me that I could smell a gentle heathery aroma off her hair. 'The bracken's nice and dry on the hillside down there, and there's a place you can't see from the road.'

'I can't be long,' I managed to stutter, 'they'll be waiting for me.' It sounded not only inept but cowardly as well.

'It won't take long,' she said in the same whisper, slipping her arm through mine and, with what I'd taken to be her

94

shyness now completely gone, she led me confidently off the path and down the side of the hill. We didn't speak another word till we reached the bracken hollow that she'd spoken of, and I was glad to arrive because I was beginning to find walking more difficult. When we reached it I stood like an idiot wondering if the laws of etiquette which dictated that one always waited till a lady sat down also decreed that the lady lay down first. She solved the problem for me by flinging herself down and dragging me down after her.

She had lips that scorched and a tongue that darted like an elusive minnow. They were no longer headlamps that rubbed up against me but tantalizing, large, soft breasts that asked to be hurt and yet stopped one short before the point where hurting would have been sin. She was in an ecstasy that I had never known existed, and I was in pain as she rubbed herself closer till I could feel one nipple hard against my chest with the other one like a marble in my hand. She pulled her face away for an instant. Her eyes were closed and her breath was hot on my cheek. 'Downstairs,' she almost spat out. 'Stop wasting time.' I needed no second bidding and all the fantasies of adolescence leapt into a sure experience. My hand slid up and I didn't even notice that she was wearing nothing below her rough tweed skirt; all I felt was a wave of overwhelming giddiness as my fingers found a mound that felt like rough marram grass and the gateway to ecstasy in the middle of it. Her hand had feverishly ripped open the buttons on my trousers and reached inside, when I felt my whole being explode from the waist downwards and a collapse of dignity and everything else. She froze and whipped her hand away as if she had put her hand in a rabbit hole and found a weasel.

'You son-of-a-bitch,' she said. 'You've buggered it!' She wiped her hand on my trousers and jumped to her feet. 'Couldn't you have waited? Or have you never been in before? Or are you one of the ones who's so shit scared there's a bastard at the end of every screw they're happy to spend their lives playing fingers with girls and playing girls with their fingers?'

Not only did she speak Gaelic but she spoke it very fluently and I couldn't even look at her with my face bursting hot with

95

shame and indignity. She was towering above me straightening her clothing, I could sense, and then she came out with the ugliest laugh I'd ever heard; a shrill, harsh laugh that surely couldn't belong to the doctor's maid my cousin had described. It had a shiver of cruelty in it. 'Wait till I tell the boys about the limp-cocked gomeril I found myself tonight!' and she was off over the hill like a hare.

I lay for a few minutes feeling that I was going to vomit, and then I picked myself up and tidied myself as best I could with tufts of bracken and made my way down to the house. My grandfather was on the other side of the door as I opened it.

'Good fellow,' he said. 'You're not so much behind your promised time. I was just going to take a walk up the path to meet you.'

My grandmother was standing at the table with a glass of milk and a plate of oatcakes. She looked at me.

'What's happened to you? Your trousers are wet and your knees are dirty. Did you fall?'

'No,' I said testily. And I felt like adding, 'I tried to but I didn't manage.'

I went to bed fully expecting to lie awake for ages, but I barely managed to pull the bedclothes over my hot face, and, in a few minutes it seemed, Big Grandfather was calling me down to breakfast. The tetchy tone of his voice suggested that it wasn't his first shout.

They had finished breakfast when I got down, and he had obviously 'said the Books'. He always showed a neat economy of time, combining the grace after breakfast with the first prayer of morning worship. He was pulling his second Wellington boot on in order to go milking when a rap came on the door. He craned round to look through the window. 'These damn tinkers,' he said. 'What are they after at this hour of the morning?'

I looked and froze with my porridge spoon half-way to my face. Standing at the door was a big ugly tinker, and with him two people who were presumably his son and daughter; a wicked-looking boy with greasy hair and a scar down the side of his face, and a tall willowy girl with red hair who could never, in the light of day, be mistaken for a maid to the doctor!

'Would you like to buy a new tin for your milking, man of the house?' I heard the familiar silky voice asking my grandfather as he opened the door. Only now it had the well-known tinker whine.

Keeping my back to the window I slid silently and swiftly into the scullery where I stood quaking, remembering stories of the occasional tipsy lad who had wakened up in a ditch, beaten to a pulp because he had made a pass in a drunken moment at a sexy tinker lass. I felt that the big tinker and his son with the scar would not debate any fine issues about who started what. There and then I knew that even if Grandfather did ask me to stay on for the rest of my holiday, the Northlands would not be the place for me to be for the rest of that summer.

Big Grandfather could resist tinker wiles more successfully than I had managed the night before; the tinkers soon left. But I kept close to the croft till Wednesday, and took the bus south on the pretext that I was going to start revising for my bursary which would be coming up next May.

Everybody was very impressed and I got a name for being a swot all of a sudden. My father asked me if it was the Communion which had give me a thirst for knowledge instead of the thirst for righteousness which it was supposed to give. I didn't deign to reply to him, but he was obviously a puzzled man. For my part I kept close to the house except when there was a valid excuse to go up the hill to lift or stack peat, although it was getting near the end of the peat season by then. But even when I appeared most engrossed with my books I always had a weather eye open in case a tinker caravan appeared over the Back of Scarista Hill.

For the only time in my life I was glad when school resumed, and even gladder when the autumn was over and winter came early that year.

Chapter Nine

BIG Grandfather had a licence to kill. His contracts were almost all for the Northlands, and for the village of Tarbert in particular, and he was inordinately proud of his steel-barrelled gun, which he kept wrapped in lightly greased flannelette in a mahogany box in a corner of the big oak chest in his bedroom. At least that's where he kept it, safely locked away, when I went north to spend my summer holidays with him; but that was probably because he had never got over the shock of the time that I had banged off the old rusty shot-gun at my grandmother when she was too slow to respond to my demand of 'Hands up!' either because she was sleepy after her Sunday lunch or was unfamiliar with the terminology of Dixon Hawke.

My father had an aversion to guns for a different reason. He had spent four years behind one as a sniper in the First World War and although he would never be drawn in the very slightest on any of his experiences till the day he died, he would never handle a gun or allow one into the house except, very reluctantly, when the days of the Home Guard arrived and all our men were issued with .303 rifles which they kept in their respective attics and produced only for periodic official 'man-oeuvres' in the sand dunes or rather less official forays into the deer forest. My father eschewed the latter even more studiously than he attempted to avoid the former because, whatever happened in 'no man's land' those many years ago, he had a deep-rooted and unshakeable aversion to taking life. And when it was necessary to do so he sent for the old man – my grandfather who was, of course, his father-in-law.

That September Big Grandfather didn't come.

I remember it was September because we used to call September 'the month of shoes'. Nothing in our young lives equalled the thrill of the May morning when we discarded our heavy footwear and savoured the first tingle of the unawakened dew except, conversely, the excitement of that brittle September day when our thick stockings and winter boots went on again. By now the May feeling had worn off. Gone was the memory of the first gingerly crossing of the gravel road, the helter-skelter rush across the common grazing land trying to get the blood to course, the flick of the daisies' heads clipping off between soft pink toes, the agonizing pain of a hidden stone going straight from naked sole to heart. By midsummer we could paddle the stoniest bedded stream without a tentative feel for the smoothest surfaces and walk a shingle beach as confidently as shod horses treading turf; and so, through August and the beginning of the hay mow and right up to the return to school, we continued to develop pads that were more like hooves and would be insurance against corns and kindred ailments in the more sophisticated years to come. But come the resumption of classes, with the inevitable curtailment of freedom, and a subtle softening began. And come September, the barefoot freedom began to pall.

The first twinges of frost come early to the Western Isles even though they rarely develop into the deep penetrating hardness of the mainland freeze. Like the sharp little pricklings of myriad needles they come, as the sea begins to get heavy and the heather begins to lose its bloom and the only patches of colour are the cornfields like golden tufts on an ageing counterpane. In those days it was the scythe that laid the corn, and as we got home from school we would cringe inwardly at the sight of the long swathes awaiting us. No time for play. Straight to the cornfield. And the backbreaking monotony of an armful of corn being picked up, its cut ends patted with the palm of the hand to a uniformity, nine or ten stalks whipped out of the parent sheaf and knotted round its middle as tightly as the belt on a blossoming girl. On and on and on it went, with the back getting sorer and stubble underfoot beginning to feel like a carpet of thorns. The autumns had been fun once upon a time, with father keeping up a deliberately inane barrage of banter to spur us on. But father had been becoming very morose of late.

By the time the harvesting had won the race against the frost, and the corn had been stooked and stacked in turn, all 26 young feet in the school were beginning to go through the annual ritual of 'the month of shoes'. The twitches and the wiggles would start during the rhythmic rendering of the Lord's Prayer as the glow generated by the run to school began to wear off. Those of us in the middle class were always the ones to give the first sign; the big fellows wouldn't deign admit to feeling the cold before us and nor would the wee ones dare brave our contempt. But as the days went on the toe-twitching would spread through the whole class-room and extend beyond the '. . . forever, Amen' through the whole long Bible lesson and into the period known as 'Conversation' when we flexed our accumulating knowledge of the English language. Then, as the twitchings developed into the rasping of 26 soles being rubbed stealthily on the wooden floor, the observant onlooker would notice the beginnings of a fraternization of castes at the mid-morning interval, and would realize that 'the month of shoes' was approaching its climacteric. The fraternizing never went beyond the bounds of one theme. Questions would be casually asked and information would be laconically volunteered as to whether Calum the Post had brought a 'C.O.D.', for every boot or shoe worn in our village came from a certain Northampton emporium which had the foresight to distribute foot-charts on which feet were outlined to guarantee accuracy of size when we came to 'walk the Barratt way'.

By the end of September, every home in the village would have received its 'C.O.D.' and on the first Monday in October the school gate would begin to clang earlier than usual. A full quarter of an hour before the whistle blew for line-up a knot of stiff-legged self-conscious males would be assembled in one corner of the playground comparing notes. First to be settled was the question of price. Our parents must have had unlimited resources and the emporium concerned must have made astounding profits because, invariably, the claims put forward would have made even today's city prices seem modest. After price came quality. Here no false bragging could escape challenge. The superiority of boots was judged by the size of the steel plates on toes and heels and the numbers of clusters of three 'tackets' in the soles. The stiffness of the toe-caps was good for a few points, as was the height of the heels and the flexibility of the soles; but armour plating was what mattered most, and that couldn't be put to its final test till night came and it could be adjudged – well away from the ken of parents – who could kick up most sparks from a flat rock or the surface of the road.

That had been the pattern for the few years that I had accumulated, but then came the September when no 'C.O.D.' arrived.

I don't know how the news was broken to me or how I received it. The poverty of the 1930s had crept in on us so subtly that the child, at least, didn't notice it any more than he noticed himself getting taller or his hair grow. The barefoot summer had seemed no different from the rest. The new potatoes had been picked and relished along with the last of the yellowing salt herring from the bottom of the barrel that had seen us through the winter and the spring. Spotty had had a calf which was still with us because it had failed to find a market, and she and Rosie had kept us in a plentiful supply of milk and butter. Once or twice I had noticed that my mother had sent me to the new grocery van which had started doing a weekly round with a pencilled note instead of the usual pound note or the handful of silver, and the driver had grunted and put the note on a nail on top of a pile of others and handed me a single loaf (a 'half loaf' as he called it, instead of a 'quarter', which was – paradoxically – two loaves stuck together), a quarter pound of tea and two pounds of sugar. A boy wasn't to know that that was the maximum to which 'tick' could now be extended, or that mother couldn't summon up the courage to face the grocer herself despite the fact that (or maybe because) they had been schoolmates in their youth. Poverty is different from being broke; poverty doesn't permit of a hope for the future, just as – in retrospect it rarely produces songs, except from those who have only read about it in the history books or have had it interpreted for them in the cause of a political ideology. The person suffering from poverty has merely fallen from a standard of living to which the generations before him have aspired.

In the middle thirties, we in the Hebrides were fortunate – although we didn't see it then – that we hadn't been caught up in the rampaging progress which had been accelerating through the western world since the middle of the nineteenth century, and 'white loaf civilization' was still new enough to us for us to be able to reach back to a way of living which still survived in the older memories. A bowl of oatmeal brose with fresh milk was ample breakfast for a working man; mussels from the sea rocks, boiled till they opened and then rolled in oatmeal and fried would probably be extolled by today's dieticians; dulse seaweed eaten raw might not keep a man alive forever but it probably contained nutrients such as sophisticated health shops now build fortunes on; carrageen seaweed boiled in milk occasionally features in expensive leather-bound menus. All these things were dredged out of the folk memory, but I can understand why people like my parents, who had set out with high hopes to create a new and prosperous life in a new community, felt that the clock was going back for them and that the dawn of their dreamt future was slipping back into dark.

It was Gillespie's mother who had introduced us to sand-eels. The generations of my people who had sojourned in the Northlands before returning to the Atlantic shore and the white beaches had forgotten those long silvery denizens of the wet sand of the ebb. 'When you see the seagulls walking on the sand at the wave mouth, that's the surest sign of a shoal,' she said, and thrusting a rusty serrated sickle into my mother's hand she led us down to the sandy bar left exposed by the low tide. Flexing herself into a crouched position like a hovering wicket keeper, she plunged her sickle into the sand in front of her and drew it steadily towards her with her left hand cupped ahead of it. Nothing happened for the first pull or two but she kept advancing slowly, always slicing into the virgin sand on which we hadn't stepped. And then, suddenly, she jerked the sickle and clenched her left hand round a fistful of wet sand which contained a nine-inch-long eel of shimmering silver and as thick as her thumb. 'There you are,' she laughed triumphantly. 'I told you they were here; they're always here when the seagulls walk on the sand!' Patiently she instructed mother and Gillespie and myself in the art of sand-eel catching, but it was long ago and if I were to claim that I caught one on that first day I'd probably be succumbing to the fisherman's best known failing. But she filled a pail; enough for a good meal for each family. Once she drew her hand away and didn't seize the fish, leaving it to flounder on the surface of the sand instead of flashing back down into it in a blink as the sand-eel did. 'You've got to watch that fellow,' she said, pointing to a thick stubby fish with three vicious-looking spikes in his back. 'That's a *stangarram*; his sting can swell your arm to the shoulder, and he's even been known to kill. But it's not often you come across one, and you'll get to know the heavy feel of him on the sickle.' Sand-eels rolled in flour and fried, linger on the memory's tastebuds as few other things do; I think I'd prefer not to taste one now in case the memory is playing tricks again, but Gillespie and I became reasonably expert at catching them, and pailfulls of them went a long way towards helping us over the lean years. But sand-eels disappear in autumn to wherever sand-eels go.

I accepted that 'the month of shoes' was not going to bring me a pair of new boots that year, and that the sandshoes from spring were going to have to be revived for a month or two. I accepted with bad grace, dreading the humiliation of being different. But there was no 'month of shoes' for any of us. One or two of the boys whose fathers were employed by the Estate may have had new boots but, if so, they must have been well rehearsed not to boast about them. The fire in the school was lit earlier than the statutory 10 October, and if the weather was bad we were encouraged to spend our playtimes grouped round it. It's a peculiarly inconsequential detail to remember – the business of spending playtimes round a schoolroom fire – but there's a reason for the memory which was important of its time. One of the sacrifices some families had to make was the regular copy of the *Daily Express*, but one boy's father had been able to keep his daily paper coming and Farquhar brought the cuttings of Rupert Bear to school each morning, and it was easier to pass them from hand to hand round the fire than in a windy corner of the playground!

The pegs that anchor memories can be as flimsy as the well-thumbed cuttings of the adventures of Rupert Bear, or the noise that made me sit up and take notice from where I sat crouched in the dusk on the corner of St Clement's bench – the long wooden settle which had come from the ancient church at Rodel when it was being refurbished. Tea, as we called the evening meal, was late. Father had gone for paraffin and the lamp couldn't be lit till he returned. Mother was bent over a frying pan, obviously in a bad mood because she had barely spoken since I'd come in from school. I sat sulkily, unable to go out to play because it was too cold; unable to read because it was too dark. And then I became aware of a steady 'phut' and hiss noise which had a regular monotony to it, but which I couldn't identify. Instinctively I looked at the window to see if it was rain on the corrugated iron – which I would have known it wasn't if I'd stopped to think. In any case the noise was coming from the direction of the stove, and when I peered closely I froze. Mother was listlessly turning over some kind of small oatmeal bannocks in the frying pan, staring silently in front of her, and every now and again a tear rolled down her cheek and sizzled on the hot surface of the stove. I couldn't say anything; I didn't have the words or the way. But suddenly all sorts of fragments of hitherto meaningless overheard conversations fell into place for me; I knew that she was crying because she had nothing in the house to cook except those handfuls of oatmeal, and instead of hunger I was overcome by an ungovernable embarrassment and wished to God that my father would come home.

'Well, we'll have light at least,' he said as he came in and took the lamp out to the porch for filling. 'I don't know what I feed a big boy for when I've got to go traipsing a mile to the shop for paraffin.' He sounded cheery, whistling quietly to himself as he filled the lamp, and I knew why; he had met one or two of the villagers and had some conversation with them. Just that. Several times recently I'd heard him complaining of lack of company, and the fact that we rarely had visitors those days. Nobody had. People cease to be sociable when there's little to be sociable about and no hospitality to offer except the kind that would be most welcome.

'That's a bit better!' My mother had whipped the corner of her apron away from her eyes when she saw the light coming into the room, but he noticed and his stride checked momentarily before he continued his walk to the table with the lamp. He turned the two wicks up slowly so as not to crack the glass funnel, and as he turned round his hand went automatically to his pocket for his pipe which I knew would be empty unless somebody had given him a 'cut' of tobacco while he was out. He stood looking at my mother for a few moments and the strained little smile couldn't make its way to his eyes.

'So that's it, is it? It's come to this. Well, that settles it. I'm going to kill Betsy tonight. I was going to send for the old man tomorrow, but I'm not going to watch you going through this any longer. I don't like doing it, but that's that!'

Betsy! I was too stunned to speak, and past the age of crying. Betsy was the pet sheep I had helped to bottle feed the year I'd first gone to school; she had lost her own mother, and, having been brought up on the bottle she had never taken to going to the moor or the machair grazing with the other sheep, choosing instead to hang around the croft and steal hay from the stackyard in winter. Her last two lambs had been stillborn, and with the tweed market in the doldrums even her fleece wasn't of any practical use. Deep down I had known for long enough that her days were numbered, but I had always assumed that father would try to sell her, or, at the very worst, that Big Grandfather would arrive with the mahogany box containing his gun, the humane killer which some new-fangled law had made it compulsory for him to have in his capacity as part-time butcher to the Tarbert shop. But here was father going to do the job himself, although I knew he hated it. And I knew who would be called on to stir for him.

'Poor Betsy,' my mother said, looking relieved nevertheless. 'I'll be sorry to see her go. But there's nothing for it; there isn't another scrap in the house. You'll manage?'

I wondered at the concern in her voice; at that time I hadn't realized the depth of my father's aversion to killing.

'Of course!' he said gruffly. 'The big fellow here will give me

105

a hand,' he added, looking at me. 'But we'll leave it till the young one's in bed.' I didn't know where my brother was – he was probably in the bedroom playing with the baby – but I was secretly glad for him that he wasn't around. By morning, when the deed would be over, he would view the carcase quite dispassionately and probably ask if he could have the horns to play with, or forget it as quickly as I had forgotten the killing of the hens for Mary's wedding feast. Such was the pragmatism of the country boy of those days. And may be still.

My brother created the usual fuss about being sent to bed before me, but at last he was tucked in and – despite inevitable protests about not being sleepy – he was dead to the world in minutes. Patently trying to conceal his reluctance, my father lit the storm lantern and prepared to go to the byre. 'Give me a few minutes and you follow on with the pail and the spirtle,' he muttered to me as he went out. My mother emptied one of the white enamel pails that was normally used for drinking water, dried it, put a handful of salt in the bottom of it, and handed it to me along with long-handled wooden stirring spoon. By the time I reached the byre father had Betsy trussed on a wooden trestle with her head hanging over the end of it to expose her neck, and he was giving his pocket knife a final rub on the whet stone.

I had often helped Big Grandfather slaughtering sheep for the Tarbert shop, but that was a much more impersonal affair. His gun was styled exactly like a pistol except that there was a gap between the barrel and the loading breech so that it couldn't be fired till the end of the barrel was placed against the back of the victim's head, between the horns, and pressed till the gap closed; the instant the gap was closed the trigger was pressed and the animal was dead before it was bled. But this was different. Betsy winced slightly as father slashed the jugular vein but, thereafter, she seemed to feel no pain as she lay watching me as I stirred the blood flowing into the enamel pail to get the salt through it and keep the blood from congealing so that it could be used for black puddings; it was only as the pail neared its fill and the pulsing flow slowed to its final trickle that she must, for one split second, have felt life leaving her; she gave one frightened little grunt and it was all over. The rest was routine – the skinning and the gutting; the separation of the liver which would be tomorrow's meal; the final cutting off of the head, which would be hung for a couple of days before being singed and made into sheep's head broth. Not one scrap would be wasted. Next day mother would empty and scrub the stomachs and the intestines in the river and stuff them for a variety of puddings – black, oatmeal, and flour and currant. Even the skin, with the wool still short from the summer shearing, would be cured and dried to serve as a bedroom rug for a while.

Betsy, jointed and salted in a pickle strong enough to float an egg would have seen us through a bit of the winter, but it was when we were hauling up the carcase by its hind legs to hang it from the byre rafter that I noticed a pile of rusting gin traps lying in a corner. My father and I hadn't exchanged a word till then.

'Why don't we trap rabbits?' I asked. 'Other people do.'

'Ach, I don't know. I was thinking about it; that's why I got the traps. But I'm not much of a hand at it; I wasn't used to it.'

Sure enough there weren't many rabbits in the Northlands from which we'd come, and the ones that were there were wiry little things that lived in scraggy burrows in among the rocks where it was difficult to get at them. But the rich machair lands of the new village were alive with rabbits – big strong fat ones, living off the lush meadowland and the crofters' crops. The landlord, at some point, had imported a large batch of black Dutch rabbits to strengthen the breed, and – although the black strain could now only be detected in a darker than usual tinge of the fur – the machair rabbits were as big as hares and one of them was a full meal for a family of five. We weren't supposed to kill them even when they pillaged the corn or the cabbage patch because they were classed as 'game', but our cat, Tiger, wasn't well versed in the laws of crofting tenure and in the spring and summer we were likely to find as many as half a dozen unblemished dead rabbits lying neatly laid out on the doorstep some mornings. Tiger was a great hunter but a fastidious eater and he preferred to have his catch gralloched for him, provided he was rewarded for his labours with what he considered the delicacies – the livers and the hearts! So although they were technically forbidden to us, we were no strangers to rabbit stew during the good weather when the bucks and the bigger young ones were good eating, although the does were out of season. There are few more delicious dishes than jointed rabbit rolled in flour, fried in butter to a deep brown and then simmered with onion and carrot. And rabbit soup thickened with cornflour and seasoned with water-cress and dulse is gourmet fare. But, unfortunately, Tiger was a fine weather hunter, and in the winter his expeditions were confined to the stackyard where his catches were more to his taste than ours. Poor Tiger! There was no way of salving his wounded feelings by explaining that there was a subtle difference, in the realms of human gastronomy, between a plump rabbit and a fat rat.

'Can I go trapping?' I asked my father.

'You'd take the fingers off yourself.' He was only half listening as he mopped up the strains of blood and the wisps of wool.

'No, I wouldn't. I know how to do it. Look!' And I sprang a gin trap with my heel, latched the right hand jaw, fine set it, and lowered the left jaw.

'Look at that. A fly couldn't walk over that!'

'You're right at that.' He looked at me quizzically. 'So that's how the gin traps were always lying scattered about. You've been practising, eh? Well you better not tell your mother till you've brought your first rabbits home, or she'll be imagining you without an arm, far less a hand! And don't get caught or you'll get me evicted for poaching!'

'How can *you* be evicted if *I'm* the one doing the poaching?'

'Oh, stop arguing for God's sake and take that pail of blood into the house!'

Of course he wouldn't be evicted for poaching a rabbit, but it was better not to cross the landlord unnecessarily. I wasn't to know that it was the killing of the sheep that had put my father's nerves on edge.

'Father's in a bad mood again!' I said to my mother as I handed her the pail.

'Ach, poor man, he hasn't had a smoke for two days. But the dole will be here tomorrow and you can over to the shop and buy him an ounce. Many a man would complain more than he does. Wash your hands and get to bed now; you'll be even more like a ghost than usual in the morning.'

She filled a basin from the brass tap on the Modern Mistress stove and I scrubbed my hands with white Sunlight soap till they were red and raw, but they were still smelling of blood and tallow as I climbed in beside my brother.

'We're going trapping tomorrow!' I said in a loud whisper, but he was away in the depths beyond dreams. I lay awake for a long time planning which warrens to start with, and scheming how to outwit the rabbits when they would start coming out of their burrows at dusk and at dawn. Life was good again; there would be a good feed tomorrow and there was adventure on the horizon. The memory of Betsy's last gurgle makes me squeamish now, but I fell asleep that night without giving my erstwhile pet lamb a second thought.

Chapter Ten

I T would be foolish to pretend to remember that I spent that autumn night dreaming of the assault that was about to begin on the rabbit population of the sand dunes, and daft to pretend to know whether or not they huddled in their families, deep in their sandy burrows, shivering from premonitions of impending doom. What I do know is that they gained an unexpected reprieve. I was wakened at cold first light by a great hubbub. The baby was ill and in danger of dying, according to my mother. The baby was sick but in no danger of dying, according to my father – who was, nevertheless, in an unusual state of panic padding backwards and forwards between the living room and the bedroom with basins of water and towels. The 'baby' was a muscular two-year-old by then, but he still slept with my mother and father in the big double bed which was at right angles to the equally big double bed shared by my other brother and myself. I had resented the belated arrival ferociously, and doubly resented the fact that, during the summer months and the sunny days of play, I was forever being lumbered with him when I would rather have been roaming the beach or the lower reaches of the moor with Gillespie.

From somewhere or other a contraption called a go-chair had appeared – probably a secondhand gift from some cousin of my mother's who had abandoned child-bearing – and if the day was bland at all (indeed if it was the kind of day that Gillespie and I would class as ideal for a ploy) then, as sure as the turning of the tide, I would be detailed to take the baby with me and 'be sure not to wander far out of sight of the house'. It was enough to lose any twelve-year-old his dignity, and it would certainly have been enough to lose me my best friend if he had been someone of lesser loyalty. But Gillespie was not only loyal but resourceful as well. He it was who discovered that with the baby out of it the go-chair would fold flat like a toboggan on four wheels, and that, lying flat, face downwards on it, we could career down the machair slopes at breath-taking speeds while the baby gurgled happily on the green sward chewing on daisies or buttercups or whatever else took his fancy. 'We better keep the little bugger clear of rabbit droppings,' said Gillespie, 'or your mother will knock the devil out of us if he goes home with his mouth black with shit.' We were beginning to pride ourselves on a fluent adult vocabulary which we were careful to exercise only privately between ourselves. We had worked hard to win my mother's confidence, and she had ceased to worry when we began to disappear with our charge over the lip of the big hollow down on the seaward edge of the machair. She was less inclined to agitate when she knew that we were within hearing distance if she shouted; she would have been less joco had she seen her newest infant being dumped the moment we were out of sight, and his carriage being converted into our version of *Bluebird* – which had rocketed Sir Malcolm Campbell to fame on Salt Lake Flats, Utah, a year or two before. I think it was fun with the go-chair which had first and finally broken down my childish jealousy of the baby, and now, watching him retch his little heart out, I felt sorry for him and more than a little afraid.

The drama must have been in progress for some time before I wakened and slithered out of bed in my shirt-tails to watch the puking infant who was, by now, beginning to slump with sheer exhaustion in my mother's arms. She was wiping away the froth that kept forming on his lips while my father mopped away half-heartedly at the remains of the sickness on the bedclothes, leaving behind an unmistakable red tinge.

'He's lost an awful lot of blood,' said my mother hoarsely. 'Go for the doctor right away; I'm scared another bout will be the end of him. O God what's brought this on us?'

Deep down in the islander's conscience there still remained in those days, and to a certain extent even now, the lingering superstition that physical ailment is some form of Divine retribution.

'Don't let me hear you talk like that, woman.' My father's gruffness was a pretence at confidence which even I could sense wasn't very surely founded, and an effort to bolster up her morale. 'It'll turn out to be something he's eaten, and tomorrow we'll be laughing at ourselves. But I'll go for the doctor just to put your mind at ease; and just to make sure he comes I'll go for him myself. You,' he said, turning to me in a sudden burst of decision, 'get your trousers on and go and borrow James's bicycle for me and then get yourself and your brother ready for school!'

The doctor! He obviously thought the matter was serious when it was the doctor he was thinking of summoning and not the nurse. And James's bicycle! I didn't know that my father could ride a bicycle. But I yanked my trousers and jersey on, remembering in the nick of time to slip my old sandshoes on as well, and I set off running down the road.

'The baby's dying,' I yelled to Farquhar the roadman who was trudging along with his pick and shovel on his shoulder and a cloud of his aromatic pipe tobacco trailing along behind him on the brittle autumn air. 'Father wants James's bicycle to go for the doctor.' I was aware of him stopping and trying to find words to say, but words didn't come quickly to him and I sped on.

'The baby's dying,' I gasped to my cousin Mary when she came to the door with sleep still gumming her eyes. 'Father wants James's bicycle to go for the doctor!'

'God save us,' she said. 'It's out in the shed. Be quick with you. I'll be along in a minute to see your poor mother.'

My highly developed sense of the dramatic combined with a new sense of my own importance, blending into a feeling of exhilaration which completely submerged the gravity of the situation; but nothing could dim the sheer ecstasy of having James's coveted bicycle all to myself with his own, or at least his wife's permission. Had James been at home he would rushed it to my father in his underpants rather than let me lay a finger on it; on half a dozen occasions he had threatened to cut my ears off if he ever saw me as much as touching it, after

112

I had bent his mudguards trying to master the act of riding it while he had been visiting our house. Latterly he had taken to chaining it to the gatepost whenever he called; but James was now in the Persian Gulf, wherever that might be, and the gleaming Raleigh and I were legitimately alone. It seemed only sensible to try to get some practice in. My experiments were not entirely successful and I have no idea which was more scraped, the bike or I, by the time I became aware of my father striding towards me flushed with anger. 'I might have known it!' he thundered. 'Just wait till I get back home, and then wait again till James comes back from sea!' He snatched the bicycle from me and whipped it round. I stared open mouthed as he put his left foot on the pedal, kicked twice with his right, swung himself effortlessly into the saddle and with the slightest of preliminary wobbles set off scorching down the road, sending the gravel flying in his wake. Old men had hidden talents, I mused to myself as I made my crestfallen way home.

My brother was finishing his breakfast as I got in. Mother was up and dressed and much more composed, although I could see that she was still worried as she mixed my bowl of brose, sprinkled some sugar on it and drowned it in milk. 'What in the name of Goodness have you been telling people?' she asked. 'Farquhar the roadman's been here wanting to go for a minister. Before I know where I am the neighbours will be crowding here as if for a wake. I wish you would learn to stop making a saga out of an incident! Get your brose inside you and get to school!' She picked up a plate of something and went through to the bedroom while I sat down by my brose trying to ignore the smug grin that my brother always reserved for my moments of greatest discomfiture.

We had missed 'the line' by the time we got to school but, uncharacteristically, the schoolteacher made no comment as we slid into our seats, and she asked for no explanations. 'Stand up,' she said. 'And close your eyes.' And we launched into the Lord's Prayer as usual, and rattled through it with the incoherence which the Lord, in his infinite mercy, must long since have decided to ignore. 'Take out your Bibles!' It was obvious that nothing was going to be allowed to interfere with the normal routine of the classroom, and I began to feel that my place in the limelight was going to elude me. Had nobody heard? Did crisis and even impending death not matter any more?

The Bible lesson stretched out to its inexorable half hour, but when it was over 'Conversation', appeared for a moment as if it was going to retrieve the situation. 'Farquhar the roadman says that Mrs Macdonald's baby is going to die!' chirruped one of the girls from the Higher Infants, jumping her place in the queue in her excitement to be first with the news, and probably grateful for a Heaven-sent piece of information that would conceal the fact that she had forgotten to prepare a sentence the night before. For a while there had been a rule that sentences produced for 'Conversation' had to begin with the words 'I read in the newspaper . . .' but the rule had been relaxed since money had begun to get scarce and most families had had to forgo the daily paper habit which had just begun to get a hold. There was a gratifying buzz of interest.

'That's enough of that,' snapped Miss Martin. 'Who said it was your turn, Shona? I don't want to hear any more of that kind of talk. We all know that the doctor is going to see the baby and the baby is going to be perfectly all right. Now I want to hear the sentences that you've all prepared!' The dreary routine of fabricated news items went on, with those who had forgotten to do their homework resorting to the usual ruses – trying to get away with mundane comments on the weather of the day or of the week, or trying to slip in a sentence that had been used by somebody days before in the hope that the teacher had forgotten. 'Right,' she said when it was all over. 'It's perfectly obvious I'm going to have to start giving out subjects; some of these sentences are perfectly dreadful. But we'll leave that for the moment and move on. Everybody! What's our morning word?' I felt my face getting hot as the school chorused it.

'Spell it, Finlay!' At least I could do that.

'H-y-g-e-n-e.'

'Wrong! You should be ashamed of yourself. Maggie Jean?'

'H-y-g-i-e-n-e,' simpered a girl two years my junior, and I didn't need the teacher to confirm that she was right.

Hygiene was a concept which had become epidemic in our school in the last few weeks. It had started the year before when a financially crippled Local Authority, forced by national stringency to make us make do with secondhand schoolbooks, had suddenly conjured up enough money to install chemical lavatories which nobody would use, and a row of white wash basins which nobody wanted but which Wm B. Morrison of Glasgow had been eager to supply. In their wake, in the new term, as if alerted to the fact that Scarista School now had brass taps gushing water, a firm called D. & W. Gibbs Ltd had decided to mark the occasion by launching a campaign to save the nation's teeth. And our school was in the firing line.

It was a brilliantly orchestrated operation. It started, if I remember rightly, with the enrolment of all of us as *Crusaders* (with enamel badges to prove our membership) dedicated to the task of defending our *Ivory Castles* against *Giant Decay*! (I hope whoever dreamt up the idea lived to reap an ample share in the profits which have subsequently accrued to D. & W. Gibbs Ltd, even if he did cause me a certain amount of confusion when I came to read of the Christian campaigns in the Holy Land in the eleventh to fourteenth centuries). We had our own monthly newspaper called the *Crusaders' Own Paper*, in those days when our parents couldn't afford the *Daily Express*. It carried horrific stories about the ravages of decay on teeth, disguised of course as the assaults of the fearsome giant on ivory castles throughout the land; it carried articles by *Crusaders* in schools from Lerwick to Land's End, so that we were comforted to know that yellowing teeth were not a prerogative of the Outer Hebrides and that even little Fauntleroys in the Home Counties had gummy grannies too; it carried crosswords and competitions, all of which, subtly, had to do with teeth; but not the least of its journalistic brilliance was that it carried an elegant sufficiency of general news which could be deemed to widen our knowledge and even tempt our more literate parents to browse through it. But nothing was for nothing even then! In order to be a *Crusader* one had to invest in a toothbrush, and in a little round aluminum tin for which D. &. W. Gibbs Ltd were prepared to provide endless supplies of rather pleasant-tasting medallions of pink dentrifrice which we were under oath to use morning, noon, and night after meals. Along with each kit went monthly calendar cards marked 'a.m.', 'mid-day' and 'p.m.' for each day. Parents were put on their honour to tick off the appropriate spaces as proof of evening and weekend brushings, but the responsibility for the morning and mid-day performances was shouldered by schoolteachers up and down the country. And so when Miss Martin said 'Hygiene' and wee Maggie Jean spelt it, that was the signal for us to line up at the brass taps and brush our teeth so that the teacher, on Presbyterian soul and conscience, could put a hygienic little cross on our cards. Although she was prepared to call it a cross, since that was how the *Crusaders' Own Paper* referred to it, she was always careful to draw the symbol of confirmation as a definite *x* so as to absolve herself from any possible hint of fealty to Rome. It was no small tribute to the propaganda skills of the toothpaste company that they were able to involve the educational network of the United Kingdom in their campaign – that teachers could be enticed into supervising it, and, above all, that ragamuffin Hebridean schoolchildren could be cajoled into carting around toothbrushes and tins of dentifrice along with the literary paraphernalia of school. 'Please miss, I have forgotten my toothbrush' was as grievous an admission as 'Please miss, I've forgotten to do my homework.' Forgotten dentifrice wasn't such a desperate affair; a 'rub' could be scrounged from a friend.

But that morning, in the turmoil of the domestic crisis, my brother and I had not only forgotten our toothbrushes and our tins of dentifrice but we had forgotten our registration cards as well, with the result that we had no means of proving that we had fortified our *Ivory Castles* against *Giant Decay* the night before. If truth be told, the fact that we didn't have our cards was reasonable proof that one or other of our parents had certified our fulfilment of our *Crusaders'* oath on the previous evening; otherwise, the cards would have been in among our schoolbooks to be certified by ourselves swiftly and secretly under the lids of our desks or in the privacy of one of the new toilets. Naturally one could hardly lead that as evidence.

This may seem a matter of remarkably small significance to have imprinted itself in such detail on the mind of a man from a lineage of non-toothbrushers which had thitherto reached back to Eden. But it happened to be a very important morning. Each month the *Crusaders' Own Paper* ran an essay competition, divided into sections for defined age groups, on subjects chosen to suit those various groupings; for those qualifying as infants the subject might be as simple as "The pet I would like best" and, for all I remember, there may have been a top grade contest for white-toothed geniuses on "Einstein's Theory of Relativity and its applications to dental hygiene"; what was of particular interest to me was that the prize offered to my age group was, from time to time, a bicycle – the thing which I coveted more than anything else in the whole wide world. Hitherto the subjects had been ones of urban significance in which a school, such as ours, with its total complement of 13, was singularly disadvantaged. But here, at last, was a subject with which everybody could have an equal chance. I can't recall the exact title, and neither, unfortunately, can Messrs Gibbs because their files were destroyed during the Blitz, but it was something like "The Place Where I Live". It was right up my street, if one may be allowed a highly inappropriate phrase, because I had loved and savoured our new village from the moment I had caught my first glimpse of it those seemingly many years ago. I had had a month's notice of the subject because it had been announced in the issue before last, and I had devoted a lot of thought to it. Now here, at last, was the designated morning of the competition, and here was I without the one essential qualification – a fully completed dental card attesting that I had brushed my teeth up and down, and backwards and forwards, morning, noon and night for a whole month. The teacher knew that essay writing was one of my better skills; she knew that I had at least a sporting chance of being in the prize list and a place in the prize list would have been an honour for the school; she knew that I had set my heart on winning. But she had to sign a declaration at the foot of the entry paper that she had, in her possession, the fully completed monthly dental chart of each competing *Crusader* to testify that the contestant had honoured the *Crusaders'* code. She was also on her honour to organize the competition under school examination conditions, starting it punctually at eleven o'clock and uplifting the essays, completed or otherwise, at twelve. And here was her prize contestant without his certificate, with only five minutes to go!

When I saw the teacher glancing at her watch I knew immediately what was going through her mind; she was debating whether, in view of the uncertain circumstances at home, she could give me permission to sprint back to the house, collect my own and my brother's cards, and come back to start my 'piece' – as my journalist friends would now call it – five or ten minutes late. I was on the point of encouraging her towards that decision when she heard the rattle of an approaching car and she looked out of the window. In those days, and particularly on our roads, cars did rattle and they were few and far enough between to cause a minor stampede to doors and windows in most homes. Not in school, of course. Only the teacher could keep track of the passing traffic from her vantage point at her desk.

'Too late, Finlay,' she said. 'I was going to suggest that you could run home and bring your cards, but that was the doctor's car and it wouldn't be right to disturb the family just now.' She paused and communed with her conscience. 'I'll tell you what we'll do though,' she said after one final decisive look at her wrist. 'You'll all get on with your compositions as if everything was normal and then, at dinner time, you, Finlay, will run home for the cards and I'll send a note along with the entries explaining the circumstances and that will keep things in order.' With that she began to hand out the foolscap entry forms so that the last one was dispensed on the stroke of eleven o'clock. It didn't cross my mind to wonder at the complicated brouhaha or to doubt for a moment whether the exalted editor of the *Crusaders' Own Paper* would really sit at his desk in London scanning thousands of hopeful essay entries from all corners of the kingdom and deciding for himself that F. Macdonald of Scaristavore did not ring as true a *Crusader* as his female contemporary M. Roberts of Grantham. What did flash across my mind with a tingle of excitement was that the teacher must have a fair amount of confidence in me to cause her to go to such extremes of effort to align her conscience with the rules; because, after all, not all the entries from every school in Britain were going to cascade into the headquarters of Gibbs – each teacher had to select what was, in her opinion (all teachers were female as far as I was aware then) the best entry in each class and submit it to represent the school. The glory would be the school's but, I suddenly felt sure, the prize bicycle would be mine. And all the tribulations of the morning went out of my mind as I began to write.

The school, like many schools in the Western Isles, had a large oaken bookcase with a brass plaque on it announcing that the library which it contained had been presented, for some reason which I have never been able to discover, by Messrs J. & P. Coats, a famous firm of thread manufacturers in the town of Paisley. It may have been that Messrs Coats had, early on, cottoned on to the benefits of 'diversification' and had decided to invest in some convoluted way in the book trade, and were going to pains to ensure a literate clientèle for the future; or their reasons may have been as obscure and subtle as those which nowadays prompt giant scaffolding companies to branch out into the marketing of books. But, whatever the reason, there is no doubt that that particular area of the beneficence of Coats helped me on my weary journey towards literacy in English and gave me the love of books which has been with me all my life. During our occasional Leisure Periods (euphemistic disguises for occasions when the teacher had private business of her own to transact) we were encouraged to browse through the library, and, under the impression that it was a book of pictures I had seized on one called *Sketch Book* by Washington Irving. It dealt with the adventures of one Rip Van Winkle, personified for me, by old Hector MacGeachan. Washington Irving's lovable hero had also lived in the shadow of the mountains and if I hadn't known that the Catskill Mountains were in another continent I would have sworn from their description that they were the hills of home. It was all there – the blue haze and the mystery which our own mountains represented for me – and the description was so masterly that it seemed wasteful of time and effort for me to try to improve on it, particularly as I was fairly certain that the teacher had never read *Sketch Book* and my instinct told me that the editorial staff of D. & W. Gibbs had not done so either.

And so I laboured lovingly for an hour, adding an original touch and a Gaelic place name here and there and by the time I had finished, having filled both sides of the foolscap page, the essay destined for the desk of the editor of the *Crusaders' Own Paper* was a masterly description of "The Place Where I Live" in my handwriting but in the style and language of Washington Irving – who had almost certainly never brushed his teeth in his life.

The schoolmistress declared a two hour dinner period in reward for our efforts but, probably, also because she wanted to hear news of the baby's welfare and the doctor's diagnosis. I was bidden to run all the way home and come straight back again with my dental record card, my dentifrice, and my toothbrush so that the formalities could be honourably concluded.

As soon as I entered the house I knew that all was well. The baby was sitting on his hunkers in the middle of the floor chewing at a hard crust of bread from the jar in which my mother always stored stuff that would help him with his teething; my father was sitting at the end of the table smoking his pipe and reading a copy of the *Daily Express*, so he had obviously intercepted Calum the Post with the dole Money Order and cashed it; my mother, looking considerably more cheerful than I had seen her for some days, was rolling sliced liver in flour in preparation for frying it for dinner. My brother struck the only discordant note in the otherwise harmonious scene; he was sitting hunched and grim faced on the corner of St Clement's Bench, having raced home while I was being given my final instructions by the teacher.

'How's the baby?' I asked.

'My father didn't look up from his paper. 'The baby's all right, little thanks to you two!'

'Little thanks to us?' I said in genuine perplexity, noticing, nevertheless, that my mother was being singularly uncommunicative as she stood at the table with her back to me. I looked at my brother but he just stared glumly ahead.

'What have we done wrong?'

My father came out from behind his paper and removed his pipe.

'You and your damn tooth scrubbing! That's what's wrong. Your Great Aunt Rachel wouldn't know a toothbrush from a hairbrush and she's as fit as a fiddle at sixty-nine. . . .'

'But Great Aunt Rachel has false teeth that she puts in on Sundays.' I could never resist contradicting him even when I knew it unfailingly made matters worse.

'Shut up! And how often have I told you not to leave things where the wee one can reach them, even though I think he's sometimes got as much sense as the two of you put together. The baby ate two whole damn cakes of that pink dentifrice of yours – that's what the matter was. It's no thanks to you that he's all right, but I've been made to look a fool in front of the whole of South Harris – bicycling off for the doctor at the crack of dawn while Farquhar the roadman's been going round the place telling people the baby's got a plague of some sort! I'm going to be a laughing-stock for weeks, I can tell you; this is one case the doctor won't be afraid to discuss with his cronies!'

'If he's eaten the dentifrice how can I brush my teeth for the competition?'

'I don't care if you brush your teeth in the pee-tub! Get out of my sight!'

He jammed his pipe back in his mouth and got back behind his paper. Then I had the sense to let the argument drop and I seized my toothbrush and my record card and slunk off, red faced, to break the news to the teacher. She was standing anxiously at the schoolhouse door when I arrived.

'You've been a long time; is the baby all right?'

'Yes miss, he's fine . . .' and I proceeded to blurt out the whole story while she stood with her jaw muscle twitching as she struggled to keep her face straight.

'O well,' she said when I was finished. 'There's a good word for this kind of situation; it's *emergency*. I think this is an emergency which you and I can deal with without involving

121

the *Crusaders' Own Paper*. You come in and I'll give you a spare cake of dentifrice and when you've brushed your teeth I'll certify your card.'

She was already sealing a large brown envelope when I came back from the washroom.

'There's another cake of dentifrice for your brother. You'd better tell him to keep it out of the baby's reach. Run away for your dinner now; I don't suppose having brushed your teeth *before* your meal will do you any harm for once!'

'Thank you, miss.' I muttered as I made for the door.

'O by the way . . .' She paused as I stood half-way through the doorway. 'I shouldn't say it, perhaps, but I think your essay is very good indeed. Very original.'

I raced off home thanking God and Washington Irving in turn.

Chapter Eleven

T HE anatomy of cruelty is something that men will go on dissecting till the holocaust. What the city man will regard as cruelty in the country man, may be part of the essential fabric of survival for the latter – whether it be the killing of a fox to protect his flock or the cutting of a sheep's throat to provide food for his family. The latter is forbidden by law now for reasons of hygiene apart from anything else, although certain immigrant communities have it as a tenet of their religion that the animal to be eaten must be bled to death. The same people who devise these laws and are prepared to force them on minorities against the cherished beliefs of those minorities are, themselves, quite happy to don red jackets and follow hounds or sit in laboratories and refine the qualities of napalm. The computations of the contradictions are endless and, in support of an apparent cruelty, somebody will always find or invent a justification. One of the few *real* thrashings that I remember ever getting from my mother was for killing a baby rabbit. She hadn't been very happy about my keeping it in a cage anyway because, she assured me, it probably still required its mother's milk even although I had caught it while it was incautiously nibbling at some blades of grass in a corner from which it couldn't escape. But she let me try. For several days I kept trying to tempt the little thing with grass and cabbage leaves, and even tried to force some warm cow's milk down its throat; it was no good and, eventually, it became clear to me that the thing was dying. Instead of being sorry for it I became insanely angry with it, and I was in the process of hammering it to death with a kitchen shovel when my mother came round the corner and caught me. She didn't say a word. She picked the rabbit up and deftly threw its neck, took me into the house, lowered my trousers and belted me till I screamed. 'Let that be a lesson to you,' she said. 'And if I catch you being cruel to an animal again you'll get that three times over. She herself would wring a cockerel's neck without a thought or walk past a sheep being slaughtered without turning a hair. The difference is clear enough now, but it was a long time before it became clear to the young mind.

It never occurred to anybody that gin-trapping was cruel, and certainly it didn't for a moment occur to me even although the memory of the thrashing was still with me. Today I would unhesitatingly report anybody I found using a gin trap or anything resembling it, but then it was a legitimate part of the hunt and had all the primeval thrill of pitting cunning against cunning. The warrens in the sand-dunes made ferreting difficult because it was almost impossible to spot which were the bolt-holes, and one could fill in half a dozen and still leave one escape open. For the same reason, though to a lesser extent, trapping presented its own problems; by early winter even the youngest litters of the new season's crop of rabbits had their survival instincts honed to a fine degree, and the least disturbance at the mouth of a burrow, the tiniest trace of metal showing or the smell of sweaty hands was enough to make them divert to one of their 'back doors'; wily old bucks wouldn't even bother to do that, choosing instead to jump clean over the trap and hop back in over it again. There was nothing more humiliating than seeing the marks of their landing heavily imprinted at each end of the trap with the sand over the fangs of the gin trap undisturbed. My brother and I knew all that on the first evening that we set our dozen traps, and although it took us hours we eliminated every possible trace of our activities. The idea of the gin trap is devilishly simple. The hinged serrated jaws run through a hole in a strong spring which, when pressed down, allows the jaws to fall open; a simple catch drops over one of the jaws and is clipped into a notched flange on the edge of a two inch square 'tongue', and the upward pressure of the spring against the tongue and catch keeps one jaw open under pressure while the other flaps flat. When any pressure is put on the tongue it yields and releases the catch allowing the spring to snap the jaws viciously together. The first secret is to set the plate and the catch so finely that the faintest pressure releases the spring; the second secret is in the careful spreading of soil over the trap using the palm of the hand with the fingers spread wide so that if the trap springs accidentally the vicious teeth glide over the taut skin of the palm. Somebody with small hands has to be doubly careful.

The cruelty, of course, is that the animal caught by a foreleg is held there helplessly, because the trap is securely pegged into the ground at the end of a short chain. The beast caught on the way to his evening feed is held in agony all night long with its instinct telling it that death will come sooner or later; the more fortunate one is caught on his way to the dawn graze so he doesn't have to wait so long; the occasionally very fortunate one is the one who struggles so hard that he severs one of his legs and gets away to live on three.

We were up at the crack of dawn and raced each other down to the warrens. At the first trap we stopped in horror. It contained our ageing cat, Tiger. Had either of us been alone he would have cried. It wasn't in Tiger's nature to go hunting in winter, and going into rabbit burrows was certainly not the nature of his attack. He must have scented us and allowed his curiosity get the better of him. A strange cat in a rabbit trap can be ferociously dangerous; poor old Tiger's instinct must have told him that it was all a mistake, and he waited patiently while we released him. He was lucky that he was a strong-limbed brute and had chanced into an old trap in which the spring was weakening, so he got off with only broken skin and a very sore paw. The next ten traps were unsprung as we had left them. The last one contained a dogfish!

We gaped at each other in astonishment and total disbelief. We were two hundred yards from the sands, far less the sea – which was another quarter of a mile away. We knew that eels travelled overland, but they had never been known to molest anything. We knew that dogfish would eat anything, but nobody had ever heard of a dogfish leaving the sea of his own accord. We sat down to think it out. And when the truth dawned on us it was humiliating. Gillespie's mother had devised the fishing method of setting yards of long line with innumerable baited hooks stretched out along the sands when the tide was at its lowest, allowing the tide to come in and cover the line, and then – as soon as the tide had receded again – she would be down at the ebb to collect her catch before the sea-birds got it. It was a primitive form of fishing, but it worked. The only trouble was that our coast was swarming with dogfish which either took the bait themselves or else took a goodly proportion of the fish that she had caught. She must have been down at her lines at first light, and the dogfish was her way of saying that our technique was so amateur that even a casual passer-by could spot our traps. And if she could, what chance did we have against wily rabbits? We went home bitterly ashamed, and when we told my father he laughed his head off!

Had we found 12 unsprung traps we might have given up in disgust, but being made to look foolish made us even more determined and we decided to go back that evening and re-set all our dozen gin traps; in our chagrin we hadn't even bothered to re-spring the two that had been so humiliatingly closed. And when we did go back, to our joy three of our traps from the night before had three fat rabbits in them – two three-quarter grown ones, and a buck with a neck like leather.

From them on we never looked back. We set our traps night and morning, except Saturday nights and Sundays, and we had rabbit meat and to spare. But a new factor emerged, significant yet again of the fact that, although we didn't know it, the 'slump' as it was called in those days was on the turn. Various firms began to advertise for rabbit skins, notably one in Appleby, offering tuppence a skin plus the cost of postage. The skin had to be removed whole and uncut, head and all, all the tallow removed from it, and hung up by the nose to dry till it was crispy hard. Before long we were despatching bundles of three dozen skins a week and postal orders for six shillings began arriving in addition to the dole. And then advertisements for whelks began to appear. It was a cold, weary job collecting whelks from the rock-pools; it was too cold and wet for us as children, but our parents went at it like people who had found gold, and all along the road by the sea-shore piles of bags of whelks began to appear for the market in a place called Billingsgate. Whenever I see a stall on the pavement selling whelks in Soho I make a point of buying a packet and a pin for old times' sake, because it was thanks to rabbit skins and whelks sold in far off, unheard of places, that I got my pair of winter boots that year.

Then, for the umpteenth time, my father announced that he was going to get a loom, and the usual argument ensued.

'A loom? Now, of all times? You must be out of your mind. What use is a loom to you when the house is stacked with unsold tweeds?' My mother was well accustomed to this old aspiration of my father's. 'And anyway you can't weave.'

'I was talking to my father when I was in Tarbert last week, and he knows somebody who's selling a loom and would be willing to wait for payment. He's coming down for a few days next week to teach me. I think times are getting better. They're even saying that there's going to be a Harris Tweed stall at the Empire Exhibition in Glasgow, and a competition for the best weaver.'

'And you'll be winning it?'

'I wouldn't be surprised!'

My mother dropped the subject; she was learning not to rise to what she manifestly regarded as his off-beat sense of humour.

'And where are you putting this wonderful loom that's going to weave us gold? In the bedroom with us and four children?' She glanced hastily in the direction of my brother and myself, but she needn't have bothered. We had overheard one of the village women teasing her with some of the crude, spicey, humour that always accompanied references to pregnancy, and we even knew that the new arrival was only a couple of weeks away.

Father had obviously put a lot of thought into this latest scheme of his without mentioning it to anyone, probably because he knew that most people would laugh him out of court for going into the weaving business when the Harris Tweed market was as stagnant as a pool left behind by a summer high tide. He had arranged to get some corrugated iron from somewhere and, although she didn't know it, my mother's own brother – the ship's carpenter with Sopwith – was home on holiday and had agreed to come and put up a lean-to hut against the rear of our little house. Like all Sopwith's crewmen he was very much a local hero; although *Endeavour 11* had failed ingloriously in her challenge for the America's Cup she had caused a sensation and earned herself yards of breathtaking press publicity by breaking her tow with *Philante* on her homeward journey, losing all communication for days on end, and finally making immaculate landfall in Ireland. Visits by Uncle Alex and Wee Grandfather in the same winter were highlights, and listening to grown-up conversation late into the night one began to get a feeling that better times were ahead. My father wasn't the only person in the village who was optimistic. The last of our bachelor ex-servicemen had, to everybody's surprise, by-passed the traditional system of building himself a temporary house and had gone straight ahead with a beautiful stone and lime one instead.

The loom was to represent a major change in our lives. Where my father had been lacking in enthusiasm for the croft, and had seen it only as a place of living, not a *way* of living, he found in the loom a chance to express himself; and perhaps it's not too fanciful to think that it allowed him express the poetry that was undoubtedly in him, and which would have found its expression in writing had he been born in another place or even two generations later on. He believed that when the market did revive there would be a demand for genuine Harris Tweed (already mill-spun yarn was creeping into such tweeds as were being made, and there were rumours that 'Harris Tweed' was even being made in Japan) and also that there was a need for greater innovation. There was a tendency to stick to traditional designs and colours; even although synthetic dyes were fast pushing out the more laborious and time-consuming natural dyes, there was still an inclination to cling to the simplest and best tried colour schemes like crotal and white.

Not that crotal and white was as humdrum as a simple

definition of it as 'brown and white' implies. Crotal was the grey lichen which, over hundreds of years, had grown over the moorland rocks particularly; it seemed to get a better hold in the dry moor air than down in the moister atmosphere of the coastal crofts. Or it may be, of course, that, over generations, the nearer rocks had been scraped clean and that years enough hadn't passed for the crotal to renew itself. In the summer it ripened and, at the same time as the wool began to rise from the sheep ready for shearing, the grey crotal eased itself off the mother rock. That was when the women went for it, equipped only with an old soup spoon off which one corner had been filed to leave it with a scraping edge and a sharp point to get into the crevices – because crotal was scarce enough to make it prudent to scrape each rock clean. In a long day, punctuated only by a picnic meal, two women could fill a sizeable sack; one woman could carry it because the best crotal was as light as down. When the shearing was done and the new fleeces brought home, a dry summer day would be chosen for the first dyeing day. Each croft wife had a huge three legged pot, capable of taking two or three fleeces, and all year round it sat outside beside a crude little rectangle of stones scorched black over the years. On the day, a peat fire would be lit in the stones, and the big pot filled. First a layer of washed fleece, then a good thick sprinkling of crotal, another layer of fleece and another layer of crotal and so on, tier upon tier, till the pot was almost full, leaving just room for water. The whole cauldron was then boiled for several hours with the addition of only extra water to keep it from boiling dry and one handful of common sorrel to fasten the dye. At the end of the day the fleeces were a rich dark red and they were tipped into the river for the flowing water to take away waste red liquid and the lichen which was now bleached white, having surrendered its colour.

You could tell that it was dyeing day in a village long before you came in sight of the houses. The open air peat fires added their stronger aroma to the peat smell that hung heavy from the domestic fires anyway. But the boiling crotal, marrying with the wool, added its own peculiar tartness; it was a smell that lingered in the nostrils, lingered unmistakably in the tweed into which the crotal wool would be woven, into the distant future when the tweed itself wore out; it was a smell that still lingers in the memory of any Harrisman born before the 1930s. Since the war most of the crotal on the rocks has been left to grow in peace, and, here and there, rocks that were scraped clean by women long since forgotten are beginning to grow a crop that will never be disturbed by an old kitchen spoon.

But it wasn't the smell alone. There was also the sight. Through the villages, during the drying days of summer and autumn, the dry-stone dykes and the modern new fences were draped with fleeces of many colours, for the range of dyes that centuries of expertise had imagined out of every sprig of vegetable matter spanned far beyond the rainbow. But, without question, the shades that drew the eye because of their preponderance were the dark red of the crotal and the one that wasn't a colour at all, the pure white. The white it was that had married with the lichen to make the crotal colour; they would intertwine again to produce many combinations. A handful of crotal-dyed wool teased in among a lot of white would give a light oatmeal colour; a stronger addition of crotal would give a richer brown. And then, of course, as spun threads they would be brought together in the loom according to the tweed-maker's design — two by two brown and white, dog-tooth brown and white, or the one checked or double-checked on the other. It didn't matter what the combination, the general name was still 'crotal and white', and the variations on the theme could be as diverse as whim; its shades as light or dark as thought. Just as the taste of crowdie and cream has been for me the lingering taste of the bitter-sweet of childhood, so the very word tweed evokes the phrase *crotal and white* and it, in turn, evokes the memory of the year we got the loom, and the year that things began to get better.

I think my mother really began to believe that things were on the mend when she sold her first tweed in many months, just shortly after her fourth boy was born. It was as if Providence had at last stepped in to ease a burden that was becoming too heavy. My father's pleasure in the loom was having an enlightening effect on the whole household; he hadn't yet actually started weaving full lengths of tweed on it, there was a big enough stockpile in the house to keep us going even if the market surged instead of just beginning slowly to gain momentum. So he spent his time practising and experimenting with patterns, and when he wasn't at the loom he was his old good-humoured self again. Perhaps the fact that he now seemed to be able to afford a regular supply of tobacco for his pipe had something to do with it, or perhaps the fact that he was able to resume getting his daily paper again. A regular daily bus service from Stornoway had started to challenge our own thrice weekly one, and the Stornoway bus had begun delivering papers. 'Delivering' is, perhaps, a slightly sophisticated word for the system; what happened, in fact, was that the driver rolled up the paper and without as much as touching his brake flung it out of the bus door as he passed each client's house.

The *Daily Record* had stepped up its challenge to the *Daily Express*, but the villagers' response – frequently influenced by the demands of the younger members of the family – was to agree on which household was to get which paper and then swop them round next day. Thus the adults got the benefit of the different news angles and the *Daily Record*'s strip cartoons, while the younger ones, who were still loyal to Rupert Bear, were able to keep track of their tartan-trousered hero. Rupert's trousers haven't changed over the years although he has lost out on column inches, and my memory of those days still makes me think of them as tartan although sense tells me now that they're check. When the *Express* moves into greater areas of colour they may turn out to be crotal and white, who knows?

As far as I was concerned, the *Daily Express* had the edge on its rival for a totally different reason. It had begun to serialize stories and, occasionally, books. It was there that I made my first acquaintance with A. J. Cronin's novels, such as *The Citadel*, although I would have to search that journal's files to find the year. But I know that it was in the year of the run-up to my bursary examination (the turning point of my life) that the daily paper became a bone of contention between my father and myself. I was under instructions from him to read the paper from cover to cover because he maintained, while it might not be great literature it was a goldmine of background information which I might be able to put to advantage in my test papers; and I was, he kept assuring me, 'reading history as it was being made' – because he was convinced that we were now coming up to a war. Mussolini had paid a State Visit to Hitler, and father's reading of events was that the three dictators, Hitler, Mussolini and Franco would carve up Europe between them and then swallow up Russia before beginning to swallow up each other. 'It will be the Roman Empire all over again,' he maintained. 'Europe will be one huge empire and then become too big for itself and begin to fall apart!' I was inclined to believe anything he had to say that concerned the Roman Empire, no matter how indirectly, because, by now, I was convinced that he knew Gibbon off by heart in much the same way as he had managed to coax me into learning off by heart a substantial portion of Macaulay's *Lays of Ancient Rome*. Not that that was any hardship. Mamilius and Herminius were more exciting antagonists by far than David and Goliath, and Horatius left Joshua right out in the cold.

But it was becoming noticeable to me that my father's enthusiasm for me to read the paper was always in inverse proportion to the degree of interest he happened to have in it himself. If I hadn't been able to get my hands on the paper by the time he came in from the loom, then it would suddenly become much more important that I should study my formal school books than that I should waste time on the paper 'which hasn't got much fresh to say for itself these days'.

Matters came to a head over one particular serial, the name of which I can't even now remember. But I do remember that it finished each day on a cliff-hanger and I could barely concentrate on anything else in or out of school till I got home and laid hands on the *Daily Express*. That is unless my father laid his hands on it first. Although he kept protesting that it was a poor look-out for me if I got so involved in a piece of cheap fiction that it occupied time when I should be concentrating on my preparations for the bursary, it was patently obvious that he himself was prepared to slip in from the loom as soon as the rattle of the Stornoway bus passing the gate indicated that the paper had arrived. And it was equally obvious that, unusually for him, he skipped hastily over the news on Page One and sat with his pipe clenched in his teeth and his jaw muscle twitching as he ploughed stolidly through Pages Six and Seven, which were the double-page spread of the story.

The plot was so simple that I remember it clearly although I have long since forgotten the twists and turns of it. It was about a man who had fallen off a liner in the middle of the Pacific Ocean at an early hour of the dawn and his absence hadn't been noticed till night. The liner put round immediately of course, but from the beginning, it seemed fairly obvious that it was going to be touch and go, but that, by dint of brilliant navigation and with a large element of good luck, the man would be found just before a shark got him or else he went down for the third and last time. I had begun to figure out the mechanisms of the suspense story.

But this one turned differently. Attention barely focused on the liner at all. Instead of that we stayed with the man. As soon as he had hit the water and failed to make his cries for help heard, he worked it out for himself that his safety lay in keeping calm and keeping afloat. Just that. Keeping afloat. He was a powerful swimmer but he knew that any exertion would be worse than futile; any movement on his part would not only drain his energy but take him further from the place where the liner would ultimately come to search for him. And so he kicked off his shoes and just floated for hour after hour after hour.

The hours spread into a couple of days and, of course, they spread over many days in the *Daily Express*. The man's life, in time-honoured tradition, floated slowly through his mind as his hope began to fade. Everything, good or bad, that he had done drifted through his failing consciousness because heat and thirst and sheer immersion were taking their toll. The climax, as far as the *Daily Express* was concerned, came on Saturday, with the last episode; but whatever agonies of suspense were being suffered by mainland readers they were multiplied for us because, despite the improved delivery of the bus, we still didn't get the daily paper till the day after publication. And, of course, we didn't get Saturday's paper till Monday. On Monday it was touch and go whether the bus arrived a few minutes before or a few minutes after school was dismissed and I sat through the Monday afternoon unable to concentrate on anything going on around me, wondering about the fate of the man in the middle of the Pacific. The bus passed me on my way home from school and I could see my father walking smartly down to the gate and practically catching the paper in its flight like a cricketer in the slips. I knew there was no point in hurrying. By the time I got into the house he was propped in his favourite position at the head of the table, with his back jammed against the corner of the table and the wall, with his feet up against the edge of the big cupboard. I sat on St Clement's bench and waited.

At long last he handed over the paper with a smile, lit his pipe and puffed patiently away at it watching my every reaction. And I must have gone through the gamut. The suspense was magnificently built up; the man reached one agony of despair in the penultimate line, then jack-knifed and sank.

I was stunned. I had been convinced that he would be rescued. But there it was in large letters, THE END. I put the paper down and became aware of my father looking over at me and smiling quizzically.

'Bit disappointing isn't it?'

'Disappointing!' I couldn't believe I was hearing him properly. 'Disappointing? You mean that he wasn't saved?'

'No. That it turned out to be such a bad story.'

'A bad story!' I felt angry on behalf of the man, the *Daily Express* and myself. 'It was a great story – it got more exciting every day right up to the end. It was one of the best stories I've ever read!'

He reached across for the paper and folded it back to Page One. 'You're forgetting something; really great fiction is stuff which a man invents but which could just be true.'

'But that could be true . . . every word of it. How do you think it couldn't?'

'Just tell me this, then. If he was all alone there all those days, with nobody to talk to and nobody to know even how he

134

died, how could they know what he was thinking just before he went down?'

I felt utterly deflated, and considerably let down. Angry with myself too that I hadn't worked that out for myself. I got up to go outside, and just as I reached the door I remembered something.

'Will you explain something to me then?'

'Yes. What?' He was just drifting into his paper.

'If they couldn't know what that man was thinking, how could they know what that woman was dreaming during the French Revolution when she dropped dead in her sleep when her maid tapped her neck with her fan during her dream?'

The muscle in his jaw twitched. But I could see him squeezing a smile back as he lifted up the *Daily Express* between us.

'O that!' he said. 'O that was different!'

I didn't pursue the argument, but I knew that for the first time the round had gone to me. And in every story I've ever written I've tried to make the plot at the very least such that 'it could just be true'!

Chapter Twelve

Nations and people aren't aware of pulling out of national Depressions and Recessions in one purposeful surge from a state of 'all's ill' to a glorious realization of 'all's well', no matter how much pundits interpret symptoms for them. It doesn't happen that way, any more than the man who is recovering from a long and weary illness suddenly sits up one day and says, 'Yesterday I was ill and dying; today, hallelujah, I am fit and well.' The only reason why we, in our new village, were aware of the recovery of the thirties probably more sharply than most of the rest of the kingdom was because a whole avalanche of progress and novelty overwhelmed us in a very short space of time. We were on the periphery of modernization in the early thirties, still without regular public transport, without electricity or gas, without running water in the vast majority of our homes, with 82 per cent of the population around us still suffering from tuberculosis, with no radio and with only the most rudimentary telephone service. Having advanced so little we couldn't slip back so very far, and what we were missing most were luxuries and conveniences to which we had barely had time to become accustomed. We had had, after all, a major local slump of our own in the mid-twenties when Lord Leverhulme's great plans for the industrialization of Harris had collapsed overnight, and all that remained of them now was the decaying town of Leverburgh – named after the great magnate.

When the world and the nearest bit of it to us, the mainland, began to pull out of the Depression, the effects of the mainland recovery had no immediate impact on us; but when it began to have, it began to have it very noticeably. When the cities could again afford fish, the fishing of the Northlands boomed; when the cities began to afford luxuries again and when the nation began to export, the Harris Tweed industry boomed: it is an industry that collapsed and boomed very rapidly in those days, and because it was so cottage-based its fluctuations were felt immediately. And then, within the space of a couple of years, radio, the aeroplane, daily bus service, mobile vans, and people to teach us how to make the most of life all began to descend on us at the same time. The markets of the south were obviously bursting at the seams and Calum the Post's van began to sag on its springs under the weight of advertising that poured in on our newly discovered land. Even the margarine companies convinced themselves that there was a market in a part of the world where every house had at least one cow, and most frequently two, and an unending supply of free fresh butter. The remarkable thing was that the margarine companies had spectacular success, not because people particularly liked their products but because people liked the varieties of gifts and bonuses that they were prepared to dish out in a bid to cut each others' throats and profits.

It was a matter of puzzlement and, indeed envy, for my own family when the last of the ex-servicemen forged ahead and built his new stone house leaving us standing – by now the only one of the temporary shacks that hadn't been replaced. It was beginning to rankle with me as a boy. I was beginning to feel that my father had somehow let us down, as we became more and more overcrowded in our tiny two rooms without amenity of any kind; and yet here was a bachelor, without any family at all, moving into his spacious new house. Many years later when he was on his death-bed I was able to put the question to that one-time bachelor who was, by then, widowed and being looked after by a devoted family.

'Was my father a bad crofter?' I asked him.

There is nobody as skilled as the Hebridean at the gentle answer that turneth away hurt.

'Your father was a very good neighbour,' he replied.

'But am I right in thinking he wasn't a very good crofter?'

'He was very well liked in this village.'

Finally I decided to try the blunt approach.

'Tell me then, how were you able to build this nice home while we never got out of the temporary house?'

'Ah well, you see, you needed a bit of capital even with the grants and loans, and your father wasn't able to accumulate the capital.'

'But what about you? How did you manage to accumulate capital? You didn't even have a loom except for a very short time.'

'Ah but I won that competition!'

I didn't know what he was talking about.

'What competition was that?'

'The margarine company, don't you remember? You had to buy a half pound of margarine with a wee coupon on the wrapper. And you had to complete a slogan which began *A pound of Echo margarine is equal to* . . . in less than six words. Ach, people were putting in all sorts of daft things, but I just put in *equal to a pound of butter* (God help me, I didn't even like margarine!) and I won a hundred pounds. That was a lot of money in those days. . . .'

It certainly was. About a third of the total price of a new house with an upstairs and a bathroom out of the cold!

That sort of luck didn't come our way, but a lot of good fortune did. My father decided early on that the shape of the Harris Tweed trade as a cottage industry must be re-thought if it was to survive as the sort of industry he felt it should be – a small domestic craft producing a very high quality of material, not so much in the vast rolls of before but as short suit and costume lengths for the tourists who were then beginning to discover us in their hundreds as their own financial circumstances in the cities and in the stockbroker belts improved. We represented adventure. Primitive people living in primitive conditions speaking a 'foreign' language, and with a great aura of romance surrounding us. Some were tempted to come and see 'the people living in poverty in poor hovels strung out along the roadside' that Louis MacNeice had written about in *I crossed the Minch*. Many more were being lured by the romantic world that had been portrayed for over a hundred years in the writings of Sir Walter Scott, and perpetuated by people like Marjorie Kennedy Fraser whose harp-accompanied "Songs of the Hebrides" were the rage in the salons of London. It was a far cry from six sweating women thumping a heavy soggy tweed – soaked in mature urine – on a wooden trestle, accompanied by their own rather raucous singing, to the elegance of a gowned lady singing a polished version of that same tune in the drawing room of Londonderry House. But no matter. Those who were tempted to search out the country of origin of the songs couldn't be disappointed. Either they saw the red sunsets and heard the fairy songs and went away happy, or they saw what was 'primitive poverty' by their standards and their pleasure was not the less sweet for being vicarious.

Those who went to the trouble of calling on us and meeting us were, without exception, extremely nice people. I remember only one case of offence being given and taken unwittingly, and that was over the head of me. I was seated at the end of the table reading a book one day when two English ladies arrived and were invited in by my mother. They tried to engage me in conversation and I was singularly and unusually unwilling to respond. I kept my head buried in my book and they weren't to notice that I wasn't turning the pages because the book was in fact a complete shielding of a deep resentment of my own which my mother was either unwilling or unable to explain. Three months earlier the *Crusaders' Own Paper* had announced that the response to their competition for an article on "The Place Where I Live" had been so sensationally large that the editor had decided in his wisdom to award three prizes and that, in time-honoured fashion, they would print the third-prize winner's composition first and announce his prize – which would reach him along with the issue carrying his article – and meantime would we all continue polishing our *Ivory Castles* with Gibb's dentifrice while we were grinding them with excitement? The anticipation was acute. The third-prize winner had written about life in some part of London of which we had never heard, but I was glad I hadn't won the prize because it was some Encyclopaedia or other, and I had set my heart on a bicycle. A month later the second prize was announced and the article it was won with was published, but I haven't the vaguest recollection where the winner came from or what the prize was – except that it wasn't a bicycle. And then came the day of the first prize, and when the teacher walked into the class-room I didn't have to be told. The beam on her face said everything. Not only had I won, but I'd received exceptional commendation and my piece was given what a newspaperman would call a Page One lead – its title and my first by-line splurged right across the page under the mast-head of the paper itself. But what was this? What was the box the teacher was holding in her hand? I was summoned out to stand in front of the class to listen to a speech praising me in terms that I had never heard before, and only half heard then, because I knew that whatever that box held it did not contain a bicycle, and my best guess was a wrist-watch – which I didn't own and didn't particularly want. I hadn't been given time to read the editor's commendation before being summoned out to the teacher's desk, but one or two of my class-mates had been reading it while the teacher had been speaking and I could see broad smirks appearing on their faces. At last I was allowed to rip the parcel open, and then the rather beautiful presentation box inside sprang apart at the press of a button to show, nestling on a bed of velvet, a thing called a *Chromatic Harmonica* or what was, by the only name that I knew for it, a very large and very elaborate mouth-organ of the type that Mr Larry Adler had almost certainly not yet aspired to. Even if Miss Ethel Bassin hadn't so definitely put my musicianship into such negative perspective I would have known that not in a hundred years could I have mastered that monstrosity with a sprung button at the end of it for changing keys, which I couldn't even hear far less play. That had been yesterday, and I hadn't spoken to anybody since.

'I think that boy's a bookworm,' one of the lady tourists had remarked as she left and my mother had flushed scarlet. She might have been saving up her wrath to give me a row for my rudeness as soon as the visitors left, but that saved my skin. Nobody was going to call her eldest son a worm. The visitors must have wondered why their hostess had suddenly turned so chilly as they left, just as I was left to wonder why she had suddenly become so charming and affectionate to me. I have no idea where that musical monstrosity went; to her eternal credit the teacher never even referred to it again.

Our little house had suddenly become a mecca for tourists who came to bathe on our white beaches. My father had become a very proficient weaver, and his policy of weaving short suit lengths was paying off. He loved company, and when the tourists arrived he would spend as much time as they cared to spare – regardless of the possibilities of a sale – instructing them in the subtleties of creating the dyes from various plants; he had a little pan on a paraffin stove on which he could demonstrate the dyeing of crotal. He would then show them how a tweed was 'framed' to decide the lay-out and design of the warp (the longways threads) and demonstrate how the shuttle carried the woof across to create the ultimate pattern or sett. His loom was one of the newer, heavy, kind known, appropriately, as *the big loom* and the operation of it was a very complicated business. Its four long wooden pedals had to be depressed and released in a pre-ordained order and with metronomic precision so that the warp was open when the weaver's beam was thrust furthest away with the left hand, to let the right hand fire the shuttle carrying the woof through the parted threads just a split second before the beam was thudded forwards towards the weaver to ram the cross threads into position. And then one foot moved the next appropriate pedal to lock the cross thread into place. It sounds complicated. It was. It was an operation which required split-second timing and perfect co-ordination between feet and hands, with each of the four limbs operating entirely independently of each other. But when the good weaver got into his rhythm, the shuttle clacked and the beam thudded in perfect harmony and with astonishing speed, and you could see the cloth growing inch by inch.

My father was a good weaver by any standards but, what was sometimes even more important on such occasions, he was an inveterate showman and his demonstrations were carried out to a running commentary which beguiled his watchers as a conjurer's patter disguises his sleight of hand. And then he would get off his narrow wooden seat.

141

'There's nothing to it as you can see. Here, weave a yard or two yourself and you'll be able to tell your friends that you're wearing a tweed that you wove yourself!' The unsuspecting tourist, who up to that point probably hadn't had the faintest intention of buying any tweed, would slip self-consciously on to the seat and proceed to get into a tangle of thread and machinery out of which Houdini couldn't have extricated himself, and in the end he, or she, would admit defeat in confusion – reduced to a nervous apologetic wreck in the case of a man, and to a giggling, blushing St Trinianite in the case of a woman.

'Would you like a wee shot at the wife's spinning wheel?' father would ask innocently.

'O Lord, no thanks! The time has flown and we simply must get back to – er – get back. . . . It's been a marvellous experience. Will your loom be all right?'

'Och probably! Don't you worry about that.'

Father always escorted them courteously down to the main road, and if there happened to be a sheep around he'd remark, 'That could well be the sheep that provided the wool for your tweed,' and the tourists could be seen to be storing up another piece of lore for recitation in the pub or the club back home. Father never stated that it *was* the sheep, only that it *could* be; nor did he have time to add that the sheep which had originally worn the wool could equally well be roaming the mountain tops two miles up, or have been eaten last winter.

The tourist industry can be a dangerous area of social economy, and there is an element of truth in the Highland argument that it can change a country into a nation of waiters. But we were fortunate in the calibre of person who came along in those pre-war days. Sometimes they never bought tweed. And nobody minded. By and large the people who came our way were professional people (whether they were initially attracted by the romantic idea or by curiosity) and with many of them my parents forged friendships that were to last for a lifetime. Some of them came back from time to time; many of them never returned again, probably because they had enjoyed the one holiday of a lifetime and couldn't afford the trip a second time. A substantial number kept up a correspondence for years, and sometimes we wouldn't hear from them except when a present arrived at Christmastime and their cards went to make Calum the Post's job harder. Some kept my father supplied with books, which he appreciated more than anything else.

The subtler influence which they exercised on us younger ones was much more far-reaching. As I've suggested throughout these pages the whole education system in our little 13-pupil school was geared to wean us away from our own culture and our own traditions. Our whole teaching was conducted in English and we could be punished for talking Gaelic in the playground. It was always stressed, in school and at home, that success meant qualifying to get away to College or University, or at the very least to a mainland job. Boys in particular were deemed to be failures if they left school at the age of fourteen (as they had to if they didn't pass the highly selective bursary examination) and became crofters or weavers or employees of some humble branch of Local Authority on their own home ground. To be a bus driver or a policeman or a commercial traveller in Glasgow carried a subtle social cachet, and more so if the person plying one or other of those trades got as far as Manchester or London. When such a person came home for a fortnight's holiday in summer he was rarely expected to give a helping hand with peat or with harvest; he was a gentleman, and invariably had pound notes to prove it. The tourists, unbeknown to themselves, were recruiting agents for those foreign fields – living examples of what we might hope to become if we worked at our books and 'got away'. When, belatedly, various organizations began to realize that we had a language and a culture worth preserving they began sending representatives round exhorting us to 'keep our language alive' and enlisting us in organizations for which we had to take solemn oaths promising 'to be a true Highlander as long as I live'. Up to that point we hadn't even been aware that our language was in danger of dying; we were merely learning an extra and more useful one. Nor were we aware that, as Highlanders, we were an endangered species. The effect of good intention was counter-productive and, not only were we now being encouraged to go away for the valid purposes of education, but we were creatures from the reservation being treated as special cases like other aboriginal tribes who rubbed noses and did things civilized people regarded as quaint.

Although the last holiday at Big Grandfather's had not been an unqualified success, it had given a new zest to the idea of 'getting away'. To go to school in a village of three hundred people with thirteen shops, a bank, two churches, a pier where ships came and went, was as alluring a prospect as London has been for people from all over Britain through the ages. The idea of attending a school where each class was as big as our entire village school was a bit daunting, but the thought of being taught new subjects by men was very challenging and promising. There was only one way of getting there and that was by winning the bursary. I don't know how many bursaries were available in the whole county of Inverness-shire but not more than half a dozen pupils could hope to win bursaries out of the whole of the Southlands, in which there were some ten or eleven schools. The standard of teaching and the parental outlook in some of those villages was such that some schools would not present candidates at all, but we were extremely fortunate in having a zealous teacher who could be depended on to present at least one pupil every year. I was in the crop of pupils who had come almost through the whole of our school lives, apart from the first disastrous year, with herself, and she was now preparing to put forward four of us to compete. Only two of us could possibly hope to win a bursary but two of us, including me, were young enough to have a second chance next year if we failed; but by then others would have caught up with us and the competition would be just as strong.

I was by now totally committed to winning. Various little successes, like the *Crusaders'* composition, had given me a certain confidence in myself. The subjects we had to compete in were English, Geography, History, and Arithmetic, with the accent very heavily on English – which was sub-divided into Essay, Interpretation and Parsing. I had a fair confidence in myself but I decided that a little help from the Divinity would not go amiss and so, each morning and evening for the

144

three months before the examination, I crept away to a quiet corner on my own and prayed. It was a very simple prayer which varied very little, but one sentence that didn't change one syllable was the sentence, 'Please God help me to win the bursary.' And I was pretty certain that He would!

The examination was scheduled to take place in May in the large school (large by our standards) of Leverburgh, five miles away. This was to be my first visit to Leverburgh, and it was decided that my father would walk down with me the evening before and that we would both stay in the house of a far-out relative of his very near to the school so that nothing could possibly prevent me getting to my desk in time in the morning. For the very first time ever it was decided that I should have a bought suit and new pair of low cut sandal type shoes. I suspect that at the back of the parental minds was the thought that both suit and shoes would be suitable for the great day – when it came – when I should be leaving home to go to the Northlands to school; when, in effect, I would be leaving home for ever and be returning only as one of the stylish holiday visitors that we had come to envy.

We set off, my father and myself, in time to arrive at our host's house not too late for an evening meal. It was a beautiful evening, and as we walked past the school and the old manse and the graveyard I felt strangely lonely and a little sad. I remembered the night that Gillespie and I had stolen out of the house when we were supposed to be sound asleep and made our ways to the feast before the wedding of Mary and James. It was broad daylight now, but that night there had been a fat moon save in the dark shadow of the churchyard where fear had all but turned us back; and if it had we would have missed a rare old ceremony which I, certainly, would never have had the chance to see again. This was to be the parting of the ways for Gillespie and myself. He and his parents had decided that he would stay on at the village school till he was fourteen and then take the mainland trail in search of a job. Jobs were becoming easy to get in Glasgow, with the fear of war growing and preliminary preparations being made even although noises from London indicated that there was going to be peace in our time.

145

I could sense that my father was nervous himself. He chattered inconsequentially instead of trying to involve me in any of the discussions that he liked to lead me into with the sole purpose, I was beginning to realize, of passing on to me as much information as he had collected on his own way through life. This wasn't his eldest son going to sit this crucial examination; this was his alter ego. This was the young himself getting a chance in life, or else somebody representing his old self getting the chance that he had never had; it was perhaps the justification of what he had fought for, those four years in France – the chance of a new beginning for a new generation. The only reference he made to the future was the often repeated assertion that if he had his life to live again he would go to University and study English and be a journalist, and I knew that he had been trying to edge me in that direction from the age that I could even begin to comprehend – never with pressure, but with an influence much subtler than that. Strangely enough he didn't seem to take into consideration at all that once I had made the breach I would come into contact with other influences – in Tarbert School itself, in High School and in University.

The evening passed quickly in the company of a boy a year or two older than myself, who attended the school in which I was going to sit my exam. He took me down to show me the building, and I was overwhelmed by its size. It was only four or five rooms in fact, but huge by the standards of our little village school.

It felt even bigger next morning at nine o'clock as fifteen of us met – total strangers to each other apart from the four of us from my own school – and we were placed in single desks spaced far apart from each other under the eagle eye of an invigilating minister, who started off the morning with prayer, followed by a little homily on honesty, and then a rapid recitation of the elementary examination rules. 'There's a clock on the wall,' he said. 'It's probably the most important thing in the room. You must attempt to pace yourselves so that you answer every question and not just get bogged down in a long-winded answer to one question that you happen to find easy.' It was my very first experience of formal examination conditions, but there I was at no disadvantage compared with the rest. I remember distinctly writing my name and age, school and address, and then nothing else at all. The most important day of my life was over before I was fully aware that it had begun.

We had to report to our own school next morning so that the teacher could satisfy her own curiosity as to how we had done, but whatever conclusions she came to she kept to herself. We were given the rest of the day off as a special treat, but life seemed strangely empty and there seemed to be little point in having a day off with my brother and Gillespie at school.

It would be the middle of August before we would get the official results, but I didn't have to wait that long. In mid-July (the first July that I had not been at Big Grandfather's) a car drew up at the gate and a highly respected minister from a village south of us came out of it and was making his way to the house, when he noticed my father working in the stackyard – clearing it out and preparing it to dry out for the new harvest in September or October. Mother and I were curious to know why the minister had called and mother, noticing that he had made a point of ignoring the house and walking straight to my father in the stackyard, was convinced that it was some bad news connected with her family in the Northlands that the minister wanted to pass on to my father first. But after a little while he left, smiling and raising his hat to mother as he passed the window; and from the fact that father didn't come rushing in as soon as the minister's back was turned we concluded that, whatever the reason for the minister's call, it had been of minor importance. Or perhaps he had just called for a quick chat having noticed father in the stackyard; they had been close friends when they had both been young men, and before the dog collar had separated their stations.

As soon as the minister's car was out of sight father did come rushing in, and from the light in his eye and the smile on his face it was obvious that the minister had certainly not been the bearer of bad news. For the first time in his life my father walked over to me with his hand held out. 'Congratulations, my boy,' he said. 'You've done it; I knew you would! You've won the bursary!' And mother began to cry.

147

'But not a word to anybody, not even to your own young brother. The minister was on his way back from a meeting of the Education Committee in Inverness, and he was really breaking faith by telling us at all. But he knew how anxious we were. Not a word to anybody. It won't be easy, but you'll have to keep quiet till the official letter comes.'

After that the next three weeks passed like one week. Mother got her catalogues out and she and father began planning what they could afford in the way of wardrobe. I don't suppose I had ever been so helpful around the croft in my life, partly to show some kind of gratitude, partly to keep myself busy so as to avoid the temptation to tell Gillespie the news. But just as I had remembered to pray for success, I now remembered to say 'Thank you', and night and morning I thanked God for helping me to win the bursary.

As it drew near to the middle of August father made a point of staying back from Calum the Post's van and letting me go down to collect the mail myself. At last it arrived, and Calum twinkled as he handed it to me. 'There you are,' he said, 'I thought you'd be passing out on me with excitement. I'll call in on my way back and hear all about it!' It was Saturday, the only day on which Calum returned home after completing his delivery; normally he spent the night in lodgings at the far end of his run and did the southward trip in the morning collecting the mail.

I rushed into the living room where my father and mother were standing waiting with smiles on their faces. 'Open it yourself,' my father said. 'It's your life it's about after all.' I ripped the envelope open and read without thinking and without taking in what I was saying. There were only two lines, but they were like an epitaph.

We very much regret to inform you that you have not been successful in your application for a bursary.

My mother began to cry softly. But I couldn't.

Chapter Thirteen

'NEVER mind boy,' said my father forcing a smile, 'you've got another chance and that's the most important thing to have in life. I should never have told you something that was told me in confidence. And I should have known better than to believe a minister. . . .'

'John!'

That sort of remark never failed to snap my mother out of whatever kind of mood she was in; she was too good a woman to regard herself as being religious, but she certainly didn't subscribe to my father's belief that God didn't mind his leg being pulled and that it was 'the sanctimonious buggers he objected to!'

'It's perfectly true. Ministers are only like wirelesses; it's only when they're in the pulpit that they've got their aerials plugged in; for the rest of the time they're just full of interference!'

'I'm not going to listen to any more of this!' She snatched the kettle off the stove and proceeded to fill it although we had just had a cup of tea before Calum the Post had come; it was her automatic escape route from an uncomfortable corner. 'In any case, I thought you had a tweed to finish!'

'Ach you're quite right as usual.' He turned to pick his pipe off the mantelpiece. 'And perhaps Finlay will go and catch us that fry of brown trout he's been promising us. Eh?'

That was calculated to jerk me out of my depression. I had come back from the Northlands that last summer boasting about the number of brown trout my cousin and I had caught during the holidays; it was the annual recitative and never a

whit more inhibited by the truth than that of more sophisticated fishermen. My father's jibe was more than justified,
however; whatever modicum of success I might have had on
the lochs of the Northlands I had never caught one single
trout on the teeming lochs of the southern moors. And God
knows I had thrashed them the previous summer in my own
private obsession with keeping away from any road or track
that might suddenly conjure up a caravan of gipsy carts. I
decided to take my father at his word. I picked up my fishing
rod and whistled to Mark. I was now of an age where even my
mother didn't mind my tramping the moors alone but, without
ever having thought out why, I had assumed the countryman's
predilection for having a dog at heel on the mountains. Mark
wasn't a very good sheepdog, but he had the loyalty of his
breed and the courage of an Alsatian.

'Remember to come back in time to milk Hector's cow
before we do the greens!' I heard my father shouting after me.

Now and then as I climbed up the track, I stopped and
looked back, not for any definite reason except that old instinct
tells the man who is used to the mountains to stop before his
breath begins to quicken; that way he can go on for mile after
mile. It was a gentle afternoon, with just enough haze to take
away the horizon and give the Atlantic a feeling of infinity, but
not enough to dim the features of the country, sea, and
moorscape that was widening the higher I went. Not that I
was in much of a mood for noticing anything. I was downcast
but not depressed; depression is a penalty of middle-age. I was
sad that I wouldn't be going to the Northlands school after all,
and yet glad that I would be staying on with Gillespie and my
brother; I was annoyed with myself that I had let my parents
and the teacher down. And I was furious with God. *He* had let
me down. During those months of prayer – first of petition and
then of thanksgiving – I had learnt the truth which I have
heard so many preachers preach since, and that many men
who don't listen to preachers at all find out for themselves in
other ways, that by constant prayer one can establish a
connection with a Power beyond, as real as the closest human
relationship and more fulfilling, and the knowledge of the
existence of a Greater Being. It is a belief that I have never

lost, but a knowledge which I have not always remembered. What I didn't realize that day was that my prayers had been heard all right but that He had just decided to say 'No.'

It isn't difficult to believe, when one's in a place like that, and not in a hurry. I was taking the long way; I was going over the upper shoulder of Bleaval instead of over the hip which would have got me there just the same. And when I got to the top I could see as much as any man can see of the world from one spot. And not just my world alone, but the old world of generations stretching back to forgotten time. Miles down and away to the south-west, the islands of the Sound of Harris (all the ones that the people had seen in new perspective from that first aeroplane) Killegray, Ensay, Shellay and the mysterious island of Pabbay, meaning Priests' Island, still with its ancient ruined chapel standing long after people – far less priests – had been banished from it. On our side of the Sound, on the mainland of Harris itself, Temple Park with its aged temple dating back – according to legend – to Druidic times, but standing upon layer upon layer of older foundations still, showing that man had inhabited that site two thousand years before Christ. The eyes travelled along the white beaches and the empty Atlantic till they reached the standing stone on the fringe of our own new village; a simple standing stone off which nobody would ever have scraped crotal because one would have been defacing the surface of history itself; Steingreidh Stone stood in sight of its replica on Nisabost Point further north, which in turn stood in sight of another of the same on the island of Taransay . . . three simple stones that were links in a whole chain of centres of ancient religious observance, all of them in sight of each other, at one time forming an unbroken chain of vision that included larger centres like the Callernish Stones in Lewis, Brodgar in Orkney and then south again link by link till it reached Stonehenge. Nearer still, from where I sat I could just make out the tip of the spire of St Clement's Church in Rodel (the church out of which that wooden bench at home had come), but although St Clement's is the only cruciform church in the Western Isles its foundations go back long long before the present building – which is only five centuries of age. Long before the modern St

Clement's was built by a Chief of Clan MacLeod in the fifteenth century, there had been a nunnery on the site and it was from there that the island I was going to visit now had derived its mystery and its name.

I had had no thought of visiting Eilean na Caillich when I left home. It was, after all, my father who had put the idea of going fishing into my head. But now that Loch Langabhat with all its wealth of elusive brown trout lay just a short walk down the hill I knew that I wasn't going to bother with the fish, who had so far not bothered with me, but I was certainly going to visit Eilean na Caillich which had been absolutely and firmly forbidden me all my life with no reason given.

In Gaelic the word *cailleach* (of which *caillich* is the possessive case) now means 'old woman' – although my grandparents would have been furious with me if I had used it in that sense, because they were aware of an older meaning still. In ancient times it meant holy woman or nun, and it was from such a person that the island had derived its name although nobody could be sure why. The legend was that, many centuries ago, a nun from the ancient nunnery which preceded St Clement's Church had been wrongly accused and convicted of some heinous sin or other and that she had been banished to the little island on Loch Langabhat for the rest of her days. If it was true it was a cruel banishment because the island is a mere patch in the middle of one of the loneliest lochs in the Hebrides. It isn't so lonely now because a road passes at the far end of it, but in those days of the holy woman's banishment it was in the middle of nowhere and on the uninhabited side of Harris.

Whenever I had asked why I wasn't allowed on to Eilean na Caillich I was just told that it was dangerous, and that was that. But there had always been something which had suggested that I was being fobbed off with a half truth. All I knew about the island, and I had gleaned that accidentally by overhearing somebody mention it, was that there was an underwater causeway to it with a stone that rattled when one stood on it. Now, islands with causeways with warning stones are ten-a-penny throughout the country; usually they were defensive islands, even with fortified castles on them sometimes, and the warning stone was, in effect, an early warning system to give the inhabitants notice of an approaching enemy. But by no stretch of the imagination could Eilean na Caillich be such a place. It was no larger in size than a suburban garden, and part of the punishment for the poor prisoner on it was that she would barely have room to stretch her legs. But why the mystery about it? Why the total ban on our visiting it as children? The subject hadn't arisen for a long time because I had always been in the Northlands during the months of holiday and weather when one might have been most tempted to go stravaiging the moors, and so it would be reasonable to plead – if the need arose – that one had assumed the ban to have lapsed. And what did it matter anyway? I was too big for the fetter rope now. The last time my father had thrashed me I had gritted my teeth and hadn't cried, and as I'd hitched up my trousers with apparent contempt I knew that he was the one who had suffered the greater ignominy and that that form of punishment would never be tried again. I called Mark and set off down the far side of the hill.

It took me longer than I thought to reach the shore of the loch and quite a long time to find the end of the causeway. When I did find it, all the mystery seemed to vanish, and it appeared to be fairly obvious why parents wouldn't want a child on his own tackling the passage. The old stones of the causeway had become worn and rounded with the years – with the wearing of feet in early times maybe, but mostly with the gentle but insistent action of the water, because the wind funnelling down the side of the mountain could raise quite a disturbance in the long narrow loch. And in addition to the wear and tear, the peaty water had caused a slippery slime to form. I knew it would have been dangerous to try the crossing a year or two earlier but now, with more caution and experience and with my rod to use as a balancing pole, I should have no trouble. I set off and soon found it wasn't just as easy as it looked, and I had to abandon all thought of getting across in any kind of dignified way. The only possible way to save myself from a ducking (or worse, since like most islanders I couldn't swim) was to get down to a crouch, balance myself using my rod as a pole in my right hand, and get whatever grip I could with my left hand on the stones of the pathway just under the surface. That way I made slow and steady progress, till suddenly a stone underfoot rocked violently and a crack like a shotgun echoed through the hills. The fright and the lurch nearly landed me in the water, and certainly gave me the fright of my life. But that wasn't all. Was it my imagination? Or was the day darkening over? I felt the beginnings of panic and suddenly realized that I was terribly alone. I looked around and saw Mark standing at the end of the causeway with his tail stiff and the hair of his ruff standing on end. I called to him, but he paid no attention. He put his nose in the air and began to bay; a series of slow eerie whines that echoed back from the rocks. I called him again but he paid no attention. I shouted in anger but he didn't even look my way. Suddenly I felt the beginnings of fear, which is a different thing altogether from fright. I knew that that dog must come with me whether he liked it or not. I felt that unreasonable, uncontrollable feeling of anger against a dumb brute coming over me, that I hadn't experienced since that day I'd been caught hammering the baby rabbit to death because he couldn't live. Forgetting all about danger I plunged back to the shore and grabbed Mark by the neck.

It was madness of course, without rhyme or reason to it. There was nobody to scoff at me for failing to make the crossing; there was nobody to help if I fell in, and I knew that the soggy peaty bottom of the loch could hold one by the ankles. I'd seen sheep's carcasses through the water with their wool and flesh all but gone and their feet still held firm; and I'd seen what had once been a hind.

A dog less loyal than Mark, or worse tempered, would have turned on me and broken away and headed for home. But he didn't. He struggled and protested, but I got him into the water, in which he was normally as happy as a seal; and, using him as a support in my left hand, with my rod still in my right, I started the crazy crossing again. This time I was ready for the warning stone, and when it cracked I didn't even startle. After that the rest of the crossing was quick and required only care. Exhausted, I stumbled on to Eilean na Caillich at last and flopped breathless on the heather. Mark shook himself dry and began to run round the circumference of the tiny island as if he was crazed, barking and baying in turn. I cursed him and threatened him, and at last he lay down as far from me as he could and put his head on his outstretched fore-paws and watched me. I had almost been happier with his noise. As his last whimper died away a total silence came down on the loch and the hills, and the sun stayed behind whichever rain-cloud had obscured it.

After a few minutes my breathing settled down and the strange feeling of eeriness seemed to lift. I began to explore the island, such as it was. At first glance it looked like one of the old rumples of stones peeping through the moorland heather where homes had stood once, except that this particular pile was peeping out of the waters of the loch with one stunted rowan tree growing out of a crevice among the bits of moss and heather.

After I had stood and looked for a few moments, now only feeling a slightly chill curiosity, I could see that there was more shape to the pile of stones than was immediately apparent. As I got used to the contours of them, and was able to eliminate the overgrowing moss and heather from my mind's eye I could make out, quite clearly, the outlines of what had once been the walls of a tiny little cell; I could see where the door had been, and as I went round, on my hands and knees now, I found a long flat stone that had once been a crude lintel. And then my hand went on to a jagged clutch of bones and I choked back a cry and stopped in time and very nearly opted for vomiting instead.

A split second later I was laughing, and the noise of my laughing set the dog whining again till I silenced him. They were bones all right, big bones, but there were feathers among them, and I realized that I was looking down at a heron's nest which I had never seen before close at hand. But instead of my mind being put at ease as I looked, a new apprehension came over me. The nest had two eggs in it, still whole but very very cold and, it didn't require much imagination to conclude, very addled. And I realized that they weren't the bones of one bird but of two, because the skulls and the long beaks were still there. Nor was that all. When I gave up trying to make any sense out of two large dead birds, obviously caught out by death while one was sitting on the nest and one beside it, I noticed another nest with exactly the same set-up. And another just a few yards along. In all a total of 6 herons and, I assume, 6 eggs although they weren't all whole; and all the birds dead. There was no sign of how or why and I just stood silently trying to imagine. And then I heard a voice. Or rather, felt a voice. It came from my ears but at the same time it came from within my head. It said, 'Put off thy shoes from off thy feet for the place whereon thou standest is holy ground.' I felt my knees beginning to give way and my tongue sticking to the roof of my mouth. But I didn't stop to think any more. I yelled 'Mark' and set off rushing over the slippery stones of the causeway, forgetting my rod to support me and making no attempt to cling on to the dog. Not that he waited. This time he gave a yelp and jumped into the water and swam ashore as if he were fetching a stick as he used to do as a puppy. By the time I floundered across, fortunately never having lost foothold completely, he was shaking himself dry and prancing with happiness. I remembered that my rod was still on the island. It was only a simple bamboo rod but even if it had been split cane with a silver reel I wouldn't have gone back for it. Nor would I now.

As I reached the shoulder of the hill I came on the sun again and I convinced myself that it was only the dipping of it into the west in the afternoon that had cast the shadow that had set my imagination going in the first place. But I didn't stop to cast a look behind at Loch Langabhat or Eilean na Caillich, but instead made my way down the mountain, across the moor and home without stopping.

Father was just closing the door of the weaving-shed behind him as I reached the house.

'Were you not able to carry all the fish then? Ach never mind we'll take a creel and I'll go and give you a hand with them after we'd have some food to strengthen us!'

When I didn't respond to the hoary old joke he stopped and looked at me.

'Are you feeling all right?'

'Yes, fine.'

'You don't look it. Where were you?'

'Loch Langabhat.'

He stopped walking and when I looked at him I saw his eyes narrow, but there was no hint of a twinkle in them.

'Did you go on to Eilean na Caillich by any chance?'

'Yes.'

'Well, you had to – some day. I suppose the surest way of making you go was by telling you not to. I'm glad you did, but you were daft to go alone. One slip into that water and you could have been drowned.'

I felt the surprise on my face as I looked at him.

'Have you been?'

'Yes, of course.'

'What happened?'

Now he did smile.

'Come on with you! Every time I tell you a good story you accuse me of making it up. But you're going up to milk Old Hector MacGeachan's cow as usual, aren't you? Why don't you ask him? And you're very pally with George MacLellan. Why don't you tell him that you were on the island and ask him what he feels about it.'

Ever since his sister had died, the village women – and some of the older boys – had taken it in turn to milk old Hector's cow for him. But since the summer holidays had begun the job had devolved more and more on me, just because I was nearer and because I had nothing else to do. So now the morning and evening milking of old Hector's cow was routine. The simple truth, although he would never admit it, was that he was scared of her himself, and one couldn't really blame him because he was getting arthritic and old. One day somebody would tell him to put the cow away and that the villagers would keep him supplied with milk night and morning, but not yet. Although he had no croft of his own the cow represented his independence for Old Hector, and he was glad that the minister who had died had given him a lifetime's grazing rights on the church's land. Which the minister had no right to do because he had no authority to make any promises that could be binding on his successor. But it didn't matter. There had been no successor to the old minister and the Kirk Session had just let Old Hector carry on as before; and when a new minister did come, as was now imminent, it would be unlikely that the Session would allow him retract the old man's only perquisite in life. Just as unlikely as it would be that our village would ever appoint a minister who would be the kind of man who would try.

Although nobody knew it, milking Old Hector's cow was, indirectly, a perquisite for me. The old man had given me his solemn promise that he wouldn't tell anybody that I smoked and so, every night, after I had strained and set the milk for him, I would light up and sit across the fire from him and smoke in comfort instead of crouching behind a dyke out of sight of our own house.

That night I broached the subject of the island after we had both lit up, and immediately I sensed his wariness.

'I wouldn't go near that place if I were you,' he said, 'there's something unchancy about it and there always has been.'

'What happened when you were there?'

'It's not a place I like talking about, especially now that I'm alone in this house.'

That jolted me. The old man obviously felt that whatever he had sensed on Eilean na Caillich could reach out to him in his own house. But that didn't really surprise me. Old Hector belonged to a generation for which the dividing line between superstition and religion was a very narrow one indeed, and very fudged in some areas. I wheedled him, and told him that my father had been on to the island and that it was he who had asked me to speak to him about it. I didn't let slip that I'd been myself because I knew he would question me inside out and that I would end up hearing nothing from him. At last he gave way and told me the story of how he'd been on the island many years before. He'd gone ashore from a rowing boat when he was a ghillie on the loch so he hadn't had to negotiate the causeway, but his story was none the less interesting for that.

When I saw George MacLellan a few days later he was much more forthcoming. George was an extrovert and, now that it was years in the past, he was prepared to laugh the whole thing off as imagination. But he wouldn't go back there again.

The stories the two men told weren't really stories as such at all. Just simple straightforward accounts of the legend of the island and how they had felt an eerie feeling. Neither of them had had anything like the extra gruesome touch of the herons that I'd experienced and still can't explain. What was interesting – and why I wouldn't go back – was that one sentence was common to all the stories. 'Put off thy shoes from off thy feet for the place whereon thou standest is holy ground.'

As I left Old Hector's house on the night that he told me, I remembered that the neighbour immediately next door to us had just got a wireless set, and I called in hoping that they might be listening. They were, and they had company because – instead of destroying social life as radio and television were to do in the years to come – the wireless was an attraction in our village in those days. Very few people had a set, but the few sets there were tended to attract evening visitors to hear what was going on in the world outside, and after the news (listening was carefully rationed because the power was supplied by wet batteries which had to be sent away for re-charge) people tended to sit on and exchange news and conduct village business. The news of the time was of the recruiting of volunteers for the Territorial Army, and it was becoming obvious that the rumours of war had not been so empty after all.

'Sorry to hear you didn't get the bursary,' somebody said, and I was glad it was out in the open. 'Never mind, you'll get another chance next year. In any case if a war starts there won't be much sense in boys going on to High School; they'll just be called up anyway before they're finished.'

'Nonsense,' the man of the house said. 'If there is a war it'll be over in a few months this time, and our boys will be too young to get involved.'

It turned out that two boys from our school had got bursaries – the youngest and the eldest of the candidates. Neither of them belonged to one of the eight families who had set up the new village. Our coterie was still intact, except for two much older girls who had been on the point of leaving before the new village began. And the places vacated by the two successful boys were soon to be filled. Yet another estate on the west coast was being divided into crofts and, till they got a school of their own the children were going to be 'bussed' to us.

Times were, indeed, moving on. The whole of the rich west coast of Harris was now subdivided from being farms into being small-holdings, and the new batch of people coming from the east were really 'returning home' as we ourselves had done, not so long before.

Chapter Fourteen

B Y the time I got back from listening to the men talking
about the possibilities of war, mother had gone through
to settle the baby and father was alone in the living
room.

'Where's Donald?' I asked.

'Where you should be. In bed!'

Gone was the sympathy for my disappointment over the
bursary result; gone was the feeling of bond on which we had
parted when he had been so mysterious about Eilean na
Caillich. I was fairly confident that I hadn't done anything
wrong – for the simple reason that I hadn't been in the house
– and I racked my brains to think of something that I had
done in the recent past that was just redounding on me now.
But no. My conscience was relatively clear and, in any case,
the fact that Donald was in bed early suggested that it was he
who had stirred up some trouble for which everybody else was
suffering now.

'Has Donald been doing something wrong?' I asked hopefully.

'Probably. But I haven't discovered it yet.' It was a bad sign
when he was being unforthcoming.

'Well, I haven't done anything; I haven't been in.'

'Precisely. Do you remember me asking you to do the greens
before you went off gallivanting and nearly getting yourself
drowned today? The last thing I said to you before you left
was to do the greens when you came back. But I didn't mean
when you came back at eleven o'clock at night with the
Sabbath only an hour away!'

So that was it! And yet he had given me the get-out himself.

'Well that's all right, isn't it? Nobody's going to play golf on Sunday, and even if somebody does play on Monday it won't be till evening. Hardly anybody plays on Monday.'

'Smart thinking. But not smart enough. Monday's a Bank Holiday and there's a match starting at ten o'clock. That means I've got to be up at five in the morning to get the greens done before they arrive. I'll tell you something; you're going to be up too!'

It was on the tip of my tongue to point out that, after all, he was the one who was being paid to do the greens although I doubted if he could find Number Five without taking them in sequence, but I knew where to draw the line when he was in that kind of mood, and in any case I had more to lose than I had to gain by continuing the argument. I decided to slip off to bed where he couldn't score any fresh points without wakening the baby. The greens had been a source of argument for two years now.

I have always maintained that, away back in the days of Creation, the Almighty, when he had finally remembered to place the Hebrides at all, had intended the undulating swathes of machair land which we had so unimaginatively commandeered for common grazing land, as a golf course. But it took a long time for anybody to cotton on to the Almighty's purpose – a failure of communication which is not altogether peculiar to the Western Isles. But when the revelation came, it came (as the Good Book itself forever stresses) in an unexpected quarter. The doctor, the bank manager, the landlord, the road surveyor, and sundry other members of the leisured classes decided that our Atlantic coast should and would, indeed, be made into a golf course. And the policeman (for all that he was left-handed) concurred. But the *Gentry*, as they deemed themselves, were stymied before the first club was swung; indeed before the first green was made.

While the Articles of Surrender (or whatever they were called) drawn up between the dispossessed landlord and the Board of Agriculture decreed that the former retained the fishing and shooting rights on what had once been his land, in all other respects the jurisdiction over that land now rested with the democratically elected Grazings Committee which represented the crofters. And, while they could not stop the landlord exercising his wild animal and mineral rights, there was not – in that constitution – one fragment of clause which gave anybody the right to march over the common grazing firing hard white balls which could kill a spring lamb or damage an expectant sheep, or, come to that, an expectant mother who might conceivably be milking a cow in the middle of a fairway. So, fired with their newfound enthusiasm, there was nothing the gentry and the policeman could do except come cap in hand to the Grazings Committee to plead their case to a gaggle of horny-handed crofters who knew nothing about golf except that it involved a lot of balls. And, unfortunately, they chose an evening when the crofters were suffering from a dose of bad English. For once, in a manner of speaking, the ball was in their court.

Nowadays everybody in the country knows more about golf than the late Harry Vardon did, for the same reason that even frail old ladies clutching the Queen's telegram can see a snooker developing in the eyes of the man bending over the cue. But it is very difficult to define golf to people who have been conditioned to think all their lives that the highest score wins; it can be obscenely difficult to describe it in a language as capable of ambiguity as English to Gaelic-speaking natives who are accustomed to a language which calls a spade a spade and in which round objects have to be very specifically defined. But, at last, the general idea got through.

And the gentlemen could guarantee that this ball could always be made to travel in a dead straight line?

Well – er – not always, but pretty nearly always.

So there was a danger – just a slight danger – that this hard white ball could wander on to a croft and hit a hen or, Heaven forbid, a child?

The chances were minimal; like winning the football pools.

Like what?

There is a great deal to be said for bi-lingualism, and not least is the legitimate excuse it gives to plead for time to think in one language when one is talking in another. And so the crofters pled for time, which the gentry dreaded as an elastic

163

commodity in the Hebrides; and the men of means began to see their chances of seaside links slipping away. So they tried the last resource of the moneyed classes. Money. Which was what the crofters had been waiting for; but, naturally, they couldn't resolve such a delicate problem haphazardly, however much might be on offer. They didn't want to spoil anybody's pleasure, and it wasn't as if this meant any great loss of amenity; not as if any of the grazing had to be scythed or anything like that.

Well, as a matter of fact, now that somebody had mentioned it there was a small matter of greens. Yes that had nearly been overlooked.

Greens?

Yes. Mown patches round those wee holes that the balls were ultimately going to land in.

But they could be down among the marram grass – the long stiff stuff growing out of the sand where there was no grazing for the sheep anyway.

Well, no. Not quite. It wasn't as easy as that. There had to be a fairly unobstructed run up to the – er – greens somewhere on this side of the marram, so that the marram could be a hazard for any balls which might, very occasionally, fly off course; just as it had been agreed that the crofts would be out of bounds for any balls which, once or twice a year, might go off course in that direction.

It was all becoming clearer now. Ideally the gentlemen wanted those green mown patches at intervals down the middle of the best green grazing. Was that it?

Well, that was one way of putting it.

But of course the greens – these mown patches – they would be very small?

O indeed yes. About – er – ten yards by ten.

About a hundred square yards?

That *was* another way of looking at it, yes.

And how many such patches would there be, very roughly?

That was *one* point there was no 'very roughly' about; there would be exactly nine. And nine things called tees which would be about sixteen square yards, but they wouldn't be mown as often as the greens. The divots usually saw to that.

The what?

Now, under pressure, divots *are* a bit difficult to explain without making them sound like miniature efforts at ploughing, and the gentlemen could not swear that occasional divots might not be uplifted accidentally from sundry other parts of the best grazing as well as from the designated area of the tees. All in all this was beginning to sound like a game with a fair incident of accident. But an accommodation could surely be reached. In all fairness to the gentlemen though, they were overlooking some problems which might be more complicated to solve. For example, if those mown greens had to be so very smooth and flat, would the ever increasing incidence of rabbits (those very productive strong Dutch ones which had been introduced by the landlord himself) be rather a nuisance especially when they started making little practice burrows in the smoothly mown sward?

The landlord squirmed. He was now isolated. Not even his own cronies could be expected to support him when it came to an argument about the advantages of rabbits digging little shallow holes in golfing greens, and so it ended up with him practically pleading with the crofters to trap them, snare them, or ferret them, or do whatever the hell they liked with them. And that, except for the embarrassing business of the money, was all – apart from the matter of the flimsy little wooden bridge which the crofters had, at great cost to themselves, put across the river on the common grazing; but the golfers would be willing to wade (wouldn't they?) because these planks couldn't stand up to constant traffic.

The district surveyor was a forceful man with access to wood and joiners. He was also getting fed up with the whole protracted argument. Yes, he would personally see to it that a solid new arched wooden bridge would be built across the river and would be regarded as a right of way. Now what about a token rental?

A crofter with an astonishingly good head for figures had worked out that nine hundred square yards (including of course those little tees) was not far off a quarter of an acre give or take a few square yards and those divot things, and put that way it sounded quite a lot. But, in view of the generosity of the gentlemen with regard to the bridge and the rabbits, a token rental of fifty-six pounds a year, payable to the Grazings Committee, would seem to be a modest sort of figure.

Fifty-six pounds a year! Good Heavens, that was about the total sum of the rental paid by the total sum of the eight crofters!

Well, well! Put that way, so it was!

And the crofters would be living rent free?

Only in a manner of speaking; the money would go into the coffers of the Grazings Committee. Naturally each crofter would hand over his own rent at term day as usual. But of course, if a score or so of salaried gentlemen were going to find it difficult to raise a pound and a couple of shillings a week between them . . .

Good Lord, there was no question of that. Of course the gentlemen would pay fifty-six pounds a year for the sake of good-will and all the rest of it . . . .

Once the deal had been struck the only other thing that had to be seen to was the appointment of a greenkeeper whose function it would be to keep the nine greens neatly mown, and to keep any little rabbit holes which might appear on the greens from time to time neatly patched up, especially on Saturdays and Bank Holidays which were the only days on which salaried men could admit to being free to play golf – Sunday, of course, being out of the question. The role and salary of greenkeeper were, for reasons which I have never fathomed, allocated to my father, and, in due course the Golfing Committee presented the most unmechanically minded man I have ever known with a complicated petrol motor mower and an instrument for making neat round holes. The latter was to revolutionize the planting of early potatoes.

If my father was unmechanically minded, the boys of the village certainly were not, and if they'd had money they would have paid for the privilege of chuntering along behind a motor machine mowing large square and round patches called greens. We'd have mown the fairways too given a chance, but the Grazings Committee was adamant that that particular chore had to be left to the sheep since the sheepstock was still

relatively important, now with the tweed trade improving –
even to a crofting community living, technically, rent free.

It was an excellent golf course by any standards, designed,
as I have indicated, by the Great Architect Himself. Not one
single bunker nor artificial hazard of any kind had to be
created. But natural hazards there were in plenty, ranging
from wide-mouthed rabbit holes which could no longer be
guaranteed not to have gin traps in them, to sand dunes and
sand pits and stretches of thick marram grass. To say nothing
of the river and sundry little burns. Perhaps the most discon-
certing hazard of all was a psychological one in the shape of a
tiny knot of eagle-eyed urchins who followed each golfing pair
or foursome at a safe distance and in total silence, watching
and noting where each golf ball went, but sadly bereft of
English when it came to telling. When the last golfer went
home, we descended on the course. We kept the best of the
recovered balls for ourselves, and, on the following Saturday
sold the surplus ones to the most generous payers. We became
rapidly addicted to the game. At first we had to make do with
heavy walking sticks with the handles shaved to represent club
faces, and with odd bits of light iron fencing droppers appropriately shaped. But, over the months, we managed to
accumulate a motley set of clubs – usually hickory-shafted
ones donated by the younger and friendlier members of the
Golf Club; the landlord, in fact, presented a large selection of
steel-shafted clubs to the school so that we could play in the
intervals. By the time my first attempt at the bursary examination had come round I was playing off scratch even although
my style might horrify Niklaus and amuse Trevino.

Occasionally, in the summer and autumn, after I'd received
the news of my failure, a flashy car would roll up at our gate
and a well dressed tourist in plus-fours would come to enquire
from my father, in his capacity as greenkeeper, if he could
suggest somebody who might caddy and guide him round the
course. The tourist was invariably accompanied by a lady,
who was – or purported to be – his wife, whom he was always
bent on impressing. His jaw would sag ever so slightly when
my father produced me – in ragged trousers and muddy bare

feet; in all my years of primary school we never graduated to shoes in summer or to long trousers at all.

These were, I think, the games I enjoyed most in all my golfing life. And the pattern of them was always remarkably the same. We would arrive on the first tee in silence, with the playing couple exchanging little doubtful upper-class glances which, translated in any language meant 'What the hell have we got here?'

Once on the tee I would point out where the first green was – a treacherous one on the lip of a twenty foot deep sandy crater – and I would warn them about the sundry other hazards that lay ahead. The gentleman would always drive off first with great self-confidence; and regardless of whether he hooked, or sliced, or chopped a short one down the middle, he would throw his partner a smug little look which said 'Follow that if you can!' And, of course, she never could – or wouldn't dare.

The light on an Atlantic golf course is very deceptive for someone used to inland courses or east coast links. And golf on an unknown course with unmown fairways is a different ball-game from that on manicured expanses like Turnberry or Lytham St Anne's. I always mentally took my hat off to anybody getting down in under seven on that first green of ours on his first time out; of course I never saw a tourist play a second round. On the second tee I would timidly suggest that it might be quicker if I were allowed to play and indicate the lie of the fairways that way (all for the joy of being able to handle beautifully matched clubs) and the suggestion was always greeted sceptically till, invariably, the lady, if she was of the motherly type at all, would intercede on my behalf. From then on it was fun. I knew every blade of grass on that course, and I had the tremendous psychological advantage that plus-foured gentlemen never expected bare-foot scruffy and ungainly ragamuffins to play golf – far less play well. As the round progressed and I got used to the clubs my confidence would increase, and my opponent's morale would visibly begin to crumble, not only because he was being humiliated in front of his partner (who usually said 'O Charles!' or something to that effect every time he was one down) but because he was being beaten by somebody he was going to have to pay at the end of the round. In all my caddying days I rarely played golf with a good sportsman; in my adult life I played only once with a bad one. And I think the moral has something to do with ragged trousers and bare feet.

But, as that autumn wore on and the ground became waterlogged, my spirits got heavier too as pressure from parents and teacher kept reminding me that I was now on my last chance; it was only by a matter of weeks that I had managed to meet the maximum age requirement that enabled me to have a second attempt at the bursary examination. This time if I failed, my option was quite clear; I would stay on at the village school and then leave to be a crofter or a weaver till such time as I found a job on the mainland. If I wanted a world of books I had eight months in which to ensure a glimpse of it. At the back of my mind I had begun to develop a feeling that though God might be a great designer of golf courses maybe he didn't see them as a guaranteed aid to scholastic success. And although my father had never said 'I told you so' after the shock of the first failure and the way it had come, it did linger in my young memory that on that August Bank Holiday morning – as we mowed the greens together in the dawn – he had said 'Golf's a bit like life you know; it's not getting to the green that really matters – it's how little fiddling about you have to do once you get there. You're on the green now and you've only got a short putt to sink! Remember that and be glad you've got another round to play.'

That was a long time ago. And now May was here again.

Oddly enough I can't remember how or when I went to Leverburgh for the second time. I remember nothing about the examination, except the rules that the teacher had made me learn by heart the day before. I can recite them still. 'Read the paper twice through. Make sure you understand the questions and then read it again. Choose the essay subject you know most about and don't try to write fancy stuff. Leave yourself time to read over what you've written. If you have to make a correction, make it carefully and neatly.'

The memory of Eilean na Caillich had stayed with me over the months and, peculiarly enough, it did something to wipe out the anger that I had felt for having had my prayers ignored. And so I had prayed again as diligently as before, and had found myself struggling hard to push away the thought 'but I'm not leaving it all to You this time'. Perhaps that's what worked.

This time there was no time for rumours. On 8 July I walked out of the village school for the last time as a pupil knowing that I had won, and that I would be going to Tarbert school and the future on 28 August.

On the evening before I left to take up lodgings with Big Grandfather I felt suddenly homesick for a home that I hadn't yet left, and I did what I always did when I wanted to be alone whether for joy or sadness. I walked up the peat road beside the river till I reached the old stone dyke which was the boundary of the croft, as, in the old days it had been the boundary of the big landlords who had held the people in thrall. The stone dyke enclosed, as it still does, the choicest piece of land on the west coast of Harris, known as Scarista Park, but by then the park had been divided between two of the men from the Great War – my father from the army, with a navyman beside him. The river ran down the middle of our croft and then became the boundary between us and the navyman on the left. At the point where I stood and looked back there was a worn step above a gully where my father had placed his feet every second day for nine years with a heavy bag of peat on his back, plodding his way through the kind of life that he had tried to teach me to escape in order that I might live the life he would have chosen for himself. A little further down from me, the river forked before meeting again round what my brother and I had always called 'the big island', where we played at crofts and planted 6 potatoes to represent a field, and a handful of corn to represent a harvest; they had always grown. Then on the river twisted to the spout in the cleft rock at which we filled the water pails; down past the little rectangle of stones with the three legged pot beside it where the white fleeces were dyed crotal to be married with the others in some blend of crotal and white.

Peeping up through a clump of nettles was a cairn of stones that I had forgotten all about; on that August Bank Holiday a year before, while the golf match was in progress, my father in a bout of enthusiasm – or perhaps wanting to take my mind off my failure – had decided that we should begin to collect stones for our new white house. I had laboured with a will for an hour or two and then something had diverted his attention, as had so often happened before. In Scotland cairns are frequently little memorials that people build on mountain tops to prove that they have climbed them; sometimes they're not . . . .

Further down, the river passed the house and the pool where my mother used to rinse out the heavy tweeds when they had been thumped and cleaned and shrunk to the width beyond which they would shrink no more on moorland or on golf course. Then it left us, and passed below the road which hadn't been there when we came to the new village – or at least only the foundations of it had – and as the water reached the machair it widened out into a series of deep pools where we fished for sticklebacks. Two planks used to span it; now the golfers had supplied a beautiful arched bridge of wood which made it more than ever the Tiber of my imaginings from the poem that father had fired my imagination with when I was struggling with English years ago.

With weeping and with laughter
Still is the story told . . . .

Unlike the Tiber, our river never reached the sea. Just after it got down to the white sands it filtered down into them to create patches of dangerous quicksands which one had to get to know, and not only know but try to keep a note of how they changed with excessive floods. You could read them when you got to know them. The quicksands weren't the ridged patches with treacherous looking shallow ditches of water lying between them. No, the quicksands were the peaceful looking flats that caught the light and looked as if one could step on them in perfect safety.

There had been 4 of us when father had built the little temporary house down below me; now we were 6 and the fact that I was moving out and, from now on, would only be coming home for holidays would take a bit of pressure off till father got round to building the new house now that things were getting better. And they were getting better. In 9 years a new village had grown up round the school and the church and the old manse up on the hill. The old manse which had seen the place change from an empty coast to an overcrowded coast, and then swing back to emptiness again, had seen the beginnings of a new village facing a new way of life with new hope. Now here it was, with all the amenities that were modern of their time – an aeroplane landing regularly on its white sands, radio in almost every home, a golf course, and a successful school with a brilliant teacher who could be guaranteed to send at least two pupils out into the world every year. Here was I leaving now – the first boy of the new village. Molly, the first girl, had gone. The trickle was to grow into a steady stream that would grow bigger and bigger, searching for its own bit of sea somewhere. Streams can grow into rivers for sure; they can reach their sea, or like ours sink into the sand. They rarely flow back because that way the hill is against them.

BOOK THREE
THE CORNCRAKE AND THE LYSANDER

For Deirdre and Gillie

Chapter One

Not many people have seen an ox felled. But I have. And this is what happens. The would-be assassin stands two short paces to the side of his victim's head, and far enough forward to be able to look him straight in the nearest eye while he murmurs blandishments to the beast to reassure him and distract his attention from the long-handled fourteen-pound hammer which the man is dangling gently in the manner of a golfer addressing a ball. When the moment is right, and a degree of mutual confidence has been established, the man lifts the hammer to regulation hockey-stick height and then swings it forward with rhythmic force so that the business end of it makes contact square between the eyes. The ox jerks. For a split second he looks (not unsurprisingly) mildly surprised. And then he buckles at the knees and folds to the ground.

That was exactly how Old Hector reacted to my proposal except that he couldn't fall to the ground because he was sitting in a chair with arms on it – which is a different thing altogether from an armchair. But, unlike the ox, Hector recovered. And, very much unlike an ox, the blow was to prove the best thing that had ever happened to him in a life not, hitherto, crowded with good things.

Old Hector always described himself as 'an ex-mariner' although the one and only voyage of his youth had ended ignominiously in Singapore after a marathon night on the booze. Unsympathetic sailors (themselves hardened to the

7

hazards of the East) used to hint that Hector wasn't telling the whole truth; they would make sly mutterings about there being 'black houses furth of the Outer Hebrides' and that some Chinese fellow had misunderstood Hector when he had asked for directions to the local Free Kirk. But the jokes had stopped long since and people had accepted that a couple of innocent pints had merely accelerated the onset of a severe bout of malaria, which had blighted the poor man's life and left him with a slightly shaky pair of legs and a very firm aversion to manual labour. For sure, for a few years after his premature retirement from the sea, he had worked for several seasons as a ghillie to wealthy English fishermen visiting the Big House, but that had only compounded his problems; he had ended up with rheumatism and a chronic twitch towards his cap whenever he met someone whom he considered to be above his own station in life. The former would have given him a valid reason for resisting permanent employment even if the 1930s hadn't come along; the latter had made him an easy victim for his sister Maggie, who considered herself above most people on the strength of having spent four summers as a chambermaid in a hotel in Oban. Matrimony had evaded her even in Oban, and so, when she deemed Hector's resistance to be at its lowest, she announced that she was going to sacrifice her hopes and her future to looking after him. And that, in all fairness, she did. She cooked his meals and patched his clothes; she worked their little patch of land on the moor's edge and milked the cow morning and night; she even carried home a daily creel of peat on her back every afternoon of every day, summer and winter. Hector spent his life pottering around doing humble little jobs about the house, carting the byre and feeding the hens; in the evenings he did the rounds of the village houses, yarning and drinking innumerable cups of tea – careful always to be back in his own home at whatever hour Maggie stipulated. On the rare occasion when he stepped out of line Maggie would exact fearful retribution by forgetting to buy his weekly quota of tobacco when she made her weekly visit to the Duchess's shop or kept her regular rendezvous with the grocery van. Hector not only smoked an evil-looking cutty-pipe but he also chewed nibbles of tobacco which he bit off a damp length of Bogey Roll he kept in his waistcoat pocket. He was so addicted to his daily dosage of nicotine that he had been known to smoke his waistcoat pocket during a period of enforced abstinence when Maggie's memory had conveniently forsaken her.

The way I have put it there makes Maggie sound a virago. She was. But it also makes Old Hector sound a pickthank – which he wasn't. It was just that he found it easier to float along on his sister's modest approval rather than face up to the tirades which he knew would be provoked by any self-assertion on his part. He was also very shrewd and he knew that a large part of the sympathy and good-will which he enjoyed among the villagers was a by-product of their attitude to Maggie, who was no more sparing of her tongue to them than she was to Hector.

But Maggie had died a long year ago, in the summer that the first aeroplane had landed in Harris. She had come home from the high moorlands with a sack of peat on her back and black thoughts in her heart for Hector, who was never to be found, by her way of it, when there was work to be done or peat to be ferried. She had dumped her burden at the end of the 'black house' as people called the crude thatched cottage out of which she and Hector had never moved, although the vast majority of people had forsaken those primitive dwellings for modern stone and lime houses or corrugated iron ones which, like our own, were supposed to be temporary till a 'white house' could be built. The black house, for all that it was primitive by advancing standards, was cosy; the fire sat in the middle of the beaten earthen floor and the smoke (or most of it) escaped through a hole situated obliquely above it so that any rain coming in didn't douse the fire beneath; the walls were seven feet thick, of dry stone build, and the only source of light was one small, deeply recessed, window. The combination of lingering smoke and limited light made for a gloomy interior in day time, but for a soft warm atmosphere when the lamp was lit at night.

But it was bright sunshine outside when Maggie huffed her way into the house that day, half expecting to find Hector sitting puffing his pipe now that the danger of having to go for the peat was over. She made her way into a darkness rendered blacker by the transition from sunshine to dim interior – and found herself confronted by a pair of large white eyes and a set of gleaming white teeth apparently suspended in nothingness three feet above the floor. It would have taken an imagination brisker by far than Maggie's to have puzzled out that a very dark-skinned Indian peddlar in a black suit was sitting on the fireside stool waiting patiently for her in the forlorn hope of selling her some items of finery from his bulky suitcase. But Maggie didn't even attempt to seek a rationalisation. She collapsed into a faint and Hector only discovered her when he fell on top of her, plunging his hand into the burning embers which Maggie had mercifully escaped. It was his yell of pain which had brought her back to consciousness but by the time they disentangled themselves the man whose name was not Mohammed had long since vanished from the village, presumably terrified lest he be arraigned in a foreign land for a capital crime.

We never found out who he was, or whether indeed he returned as one of the many Indian peddlars, who seemed to be discovering our village each summer, feeling safe in the camouflage of dark skin which made his kind look alike to us. Maggie lived for long enough to tell her story with superstitious enthusiasm and nobody had the heart to tell her the truth. What had happened was that the Indian peddlar in search of custom among the croft houses had bumped into one of the notorious pranksters of the village who had sent him climbing up the hill to Hector's house with the assurance that Maggie was desperate to buy a dress for a fictitious wedding. 'She's out at the peat,' said Sandy Cravat, who had earned his soubriquet from having acquired a certain amount of style during his seasons at the Tay salmon fishing. 'But she made me promise to be sure to tell you to go into the house and wait for her. Good luck, Mohammed –'

'I have told you, please, my name is not Mohammed –'

'Never you mind what your name is; just you go in and wait for Miss MacGeachan whose name is Maggie!'

None of that had come out, of course, till after poor Maggie had taken her stroke and died. Nobody ever thought of blaming anybody, even when the truth was told and her story of the teeth and eyes was, at last, believed. If there was blame at all it was directed at Sandy Cravat whose warped sense of humour had been the undoing of others ere then. Long after Sandy had settled into the sedating grip of matrimony there lingered on the legend he had created of the man of no name except 'the man whose name was not Mohammed'!

For the three days of Maggie's lying people had discovered nice things to say about her, in the way that people from Rome to Rodel find with the newly dead, but even then there were those who couldn't help putting a saw-edge on their sympathy. 'Poor woman,' they said. 'With that temper of hers it's a miracle that she didn't burst a blood vessel long since.' But the bizarre way of her final departure put an end even to the most veiled hints of criticism of her.

Her funeral was interrupted by no less an event than the landing on the beach of the first aeroplane, and those of the mourners who had the agility to match their curiosity had forsaken the grave-side to join the throng which had assembled on the beach to goggle at the silver De Havilland Rapide. Indeed one or two of them had taken advantage of the pilot's offer of 'a quick flip' before returning to consign Maggie to eternity. My father had been one of the curious and, although he didn't join in the free public relations rides, my mother's displeasure was no less vehement.

'A judgment will come on you people for your behaviour today. Mrs MacRae was in here and she'd been watching the whole thing from the Back of Scarista Hill. She said you looked for all the world like a stream of black cockroaches making for a dead sheep's carcase. It was easy to see that it was the missionary and not the minister conducting the funeral service, Mrs MacRae was saying, or he wouldn't have tolerated the gang of you rushing off to an aeroplane before poor Maggie MacGeachan's soul had been laid to rest. Mrs MacRae was horrified, and I'm not surprised!'

That was the point at which my father should have held his wheest. But he didn't.

'If God sends an aeroplane for Hetty MacRae's soul the way he did for Maggie's I'll be surprised!'

'John!'

And that was the last word before the long silence which lasted till early evening when, to the surprise of all of us, my mother went through to the bedroom and changed into her

11

Sunday frock. 'You two boys wash the dishes before you do anything else,' she said after she had made a cup of tea with more than the usual clatter of crockery. And then, without even looking at my father, 'And will you remember to milk the cow; I'm going out!'

'I didn't think you had taken to dressing in your finery for milking the cow. Although, mind you, she'd probably give an extra pint for seeing you looking as nice as that.'

She couldn't resist that, and I could see her twitching back a smile.

'That's what Hetty MacRae called in about. There's a sewing class in Drumpound tonight, and she doesn't like coming back alone past the cemetery after dark. Especially on an evening when there's been a funeral.'

'And since when did you start feeling so joco about coming past the churchyard at night?'

'We'll be all right with the two of us there – and there's a moon.'

'Ach well, you always got on quite well with Maggie, and she and Hetty haven't spoken to each other for two years so I doubt whether they'll start tonight.'

Her lips tightened again, but she decided not to rise to the bait.

'You be sure the baby's given a plate of semolina before he goes to sleep, and make sure he's dry.'

I was sent up the hill to bring the cow home as soon as mother and Mrs MacRae had set off for their sewing bee. It was only Spotty who was in milk; Rosie, having seen us through the winter, had now begun to go dry and soon the bull would be taking an interest in her. I found them both up at the little burn that separated the moorland pasture from the mountain grazing and they ambled gently down the slope in front of me – Spotty with her udder swinging heavily as she headed for the paddock gate. It was only in the last week or so that the township had started leaving the milking cows out on the moors overnight, and they still hadn't got into the rhythm of making their own ways home for milking. Soon they would arrive at the paddock gate precisely at eight o'clock – so punctually that you could set your watch to time by them.

When father came home with the milk pail, and after he had

12

strained and set the milk in its basins to cream, he settled down with a newspaper. He lit his pipe and propped his feet against the tall cupboard which served as dishes press, food store and pantry, taking up a substantial proportion of a living room which had been small enough for four but was, by now, getting claustrophobic since the new baby had brought the family up to five. While he had been at the milking I had embarked on an essay which the teacher had set us on the subject of the first landing of the aeroplane, and I was determined to finish it without help from him if I could. If ever I did invoke his help with an essay it brought out the frustrated writer in him, and once he got his teeth into a subject he took over completely even if it meant that the work on the croft or the loom went hang: invariably I had to spend more time rewriting and simplifying his compositions, in order to conceal their true authorship from the teacher, than it would have taken me if I'd written the whole thing from the beginning myself. But the subject of the aeroplane and its possible implications for the future of the community was proving more complex than I had thought and, in the end, I had to turn to him for assistance. His eyes lit up and he swung his feet down from the cupboard, but before he could get his pipe going to his satisfaction a knock came to the door, and he went to answer it with a puzzled look on his face; people didn't knock on doors in our village, they normally just walked in, and a knock at night-time usually suggested a stranger or a crisis of some kind. I was totally mystified when I heard our next-door-neighbour's voice talking urgently and so quietly that I couldn't make out what he was saying. I could hear expressions of concern and dismay from my father, and his face was white and strained when he came back for his cap.

'I'm afraid you'll have to finish your composition on your own, my boy. And remember to feed and change the baby. If your mother comes back before I do, just tell her I've had to go out and that I won't be long.' My instinct told me it would be unwise to question him and so, with my hope of an interesting 'new angle' having vanished I licked my pencil and got down to writing my essay on my own. By good grace I had just finished it when the door opened and my mother and Hetty MacRae burst in, clinging to each other and ashen faced.

'Where's your father?'

'He's out. Why? What's wrong?'

It was Hetty MacRae who answered, with her voice quivering and her eyes popping.

'Evil. That's what's wrong. I knew evil would come of this day when I saw men rushing from the blessed churchyard to view the devil's contraption on the beach. There are men digging in the cemetery. Digging! At dead of night. We didn't believe our eyes at first, but they're there all right. And I could swear it's Maggie MacGeachan's new grave they're at. What men of evil can't let the poor woman rest in peace? I wish your father would hurry up; I daren't walk home alone ...'

It wasn't in fact long before my father did arrive, and I could see that he was patently reluctant to talk in front of me. But he realised he had no option when he saw me staring at his boots. It was a tragi-comical story looked at from the vantage point of later years. A simple story – although it was serious of its time among people in whom religion and superstition were still fudging each other's lines of demarcation. Somebody fastened the coffin lid who shouldn't have done, and the result was that when Old Hector MacGeachan got home at last, having been fed by some kindly neighbour, but wearied and dispirited after the ordeals of the funeral service and the burial, he found Maggie still lying in bed; and he was too spent to take comfort from the fact that her jaw was firmly bound.

What was a simple community to do? There was no undertaker, no policeman, and certainly no Home Secretary in our new village, and so they took the only sensible course; they quietly dug up the empty coffin at dead of night and made sure that Maggie was in when they buried it again. They also made very sure that no murmur of the story got abroad, because the newspapers would have revelled in yet another story that smacked of 'Hielandism' and 'teuchterism'.

And so, Maggie had finally been laid to rest. She hadn't lived to see another man whose name *was* Mohammed take up his place as a respected member of our island community; she hadn't seen the village taking its greatest strides forward as the breakdown of the barriers separating the Hebrides from the mainland accelerated, and a weekly air service developed with the silver Rapide fluttering between mainland airports and our

14

beach, providing fast if not comfortable travel for those who could afford it and a life-line in time of medical emergency; she hadn't seen the growth of a twice-daily bus service linking us to Stornoway; she hadn't seen the slow acceptance of the wireless by the few who could afford one of the ornate walnut sets requiring a dry battery and an accumulator to give them voice; and she hadn't heard the insidious influx of English words that radio was beginning to feed into our native Gaelic. She probably wouldn't have been impressed anyway because she professed a disdain for all new-fangled things, dismissing them with a sniff and claiming that she had 'seen all that sort of thing in Oban'.

After her death the village had rallied round Old Hector: the men had cut his peat for him and planted his potatoes; the women had taken it in turn to do his shopping for him with the result that he was never again driven to smoking his waistcoat, and they had taken it in turn to milk his cow for him morning and evening. In short, Maggie's death had been the beginning of life for Hector and it hadn't taken him long to wipe away the last obligatory tear.

The memory of those events of last year were idling through my mind as I made my way up the path past the graveyard in which Maggie slept, and I tried to push them away so that I could frame the words in which I would deliver my ultimatum.

In some mysterious way the job of milking Hector's cow had devolved on me since that day in May when I had sat the County Council Bursary examination for the second time. I had sat it knowing it was my last chance, and in the full knowledge that without the annual grant which was the reward of success there was no hope that my parents could afford to send me on to High School. Without the bursary I would leave school at fourteen and take a job as a roadman or a weaver or a jobster of some kind till such time as I might win away to the mainland to become something sophisticated like a commercial traveller. It had been drummed into me that there was no alternative to 'going away'; to remain in my own community, false prophets were assuring my young generation, was to be a failure. But at the beginning of July I had heard that I had won the coveted bursary and I would soon be leaving the village to

15

embark on the first stages of that glittering higher education which would mould me for whatever future lay ahead. I had no idea what that future would be. Only dreams and fancies. I had been to the tailor in the Northlands and had been measured for a jacket; my first pairs of long trousers had been ordered from one of the Manchester mail order stores; a pair of 'Lornes' had been ordered from Northampton instead of the traditional winter boots. In three weeks' time I'd be boarding the blue bus, having left my home-spun, home-sewn image behind; I'd be leaving my brothers and Gillespie and the small world of friends in which I had been cosy and cocooned and in which the hard years of the thirties had been happy although, almost half a century later, I was to learn to talk of them glibly as 'bad'.

It was only when I put my foot on a thistle and stood, stork-like, on one leg to remove the thorns from a naked sole that I realised that I had been day-dreaming and had forgotten to frame the form of the words with which I would put my scheme to the old man whom I could see leaning against the dry-stane lintel of his doorway, puffing at his cutty, and waiting hopefully for any tidbits of news I might have collected for him. He'd been suffering from a summer cold and he had been keeping to the house, fearful of an onset of one of his occasional malarial bouts.

'Here you are at last,' he said as I reached him. 'I thought you were never going to come. Was that a thorn you got in your bare foot? Never mind, this will be your last barefoot summer; it'll be shoes for you all the year round now that you're going off to the High School like a posh young gentleman. Are you coming in for a puff before you do the milking?' He prattled on – his impatience at my late arrival already dissolved. 'Here you are. Five Woodbines I got Calum the Post to bring me, pretending they were for myself. It'll be a hell of a row I'll be getting from your mother if she spots that I'm allowing you to smoke here on the q.t. – and it's bankrupt you'll be yourself if you go on paying three pence every time you want five of these things. Three pence! You could buy three inches of Bogey Roll for that and it would keep you going for a week –'

'Och Hector, you shouldn't have done that. But thank you

very much.' I pocketed the flimsy green packet and then, remembering that I would buckle it when I squatted to milk the cow, I transferred it from my trouser pocket into my sleeve. 'I won't come in just now. I'll just get the pail and milk Primrose before she becomes restless and wanders away. I'll come in for a smoke afterwards.'

One of the rewards for the moil of milking Hector's cow was that I could smoke in comfort in Hector's house. I had started sampling the occasional cigarette when I was ten, but there was little satisfaction and no kudos in skulking with a cigarette behind a dyke or down among the seashore rocks on the odd occasion when one of 'the bloods' (the swaggering lumps of advanced teenagers) slipped me a dout, or a seaman cousin home on leave gave me a couple of fags from his duty-free pack; and so I hadn't really become addicted to nicotine – only to the idea, and the feeling of sophistication. My parents would have flayed me alive if they had found out, and this was one vice which none of the village parents would condone or conceal. But Old Hector wasn't a parent, and he got some kind of simple pleasure out of being able to share a plot with a youngster once he had got used to the idea. 'Ach, you'll be all right here,' he would say, reaching for his own pipe. 'I'll light up myself and if anybody comes in they won't be able to smell the cigarettes through my thick black.' This was the first time that anybody had ever given me a full pack (albeit of five) and I knew perfectly well that the old man couldn't afford thruppence. It wasn't meant as payment or reward, but it was that and more; it was a gesture of friendship, and a luxury for himself to feel that there was one small thing he could do for a fellow being. I felt a glow of affection for him welling in me as I sat in the peace of the dusk with my head tucked into Primrose's flank with the two jets of milk converging into one steady stream in the middle of the froth in the pail. Three continuous months of milking had strengthened my wrists so that they didn't get sore any more, and normally I got a lot of satisfaction out of trying to refine the rhythm of my pull. Now I was subconsciously aware that I was in perfect tune with Primrose because I could hear the matching rhythm of her cud, but my mind was far from being at ease …

'Man alive, that's quite a pailful!' he said, taking the handle in

17

both his rheumaticky hands. 'That cow's milking better this summer than she's ever done. You sit over there and light up. I'll set out the basins later on; I haven't skimmed the creamed ones yet, but I'll do it before I go to bed. At this rate I'll have enough salt butter to see me through the winter …' He prattled on as I sat down and lit a Woodbine and watched him trimming and lighting his single wick paraffin lamp; although it was still lazy daylight outside, the deeply recessed window of the black house didn't let in enough to light the faraway wall far less Hector's face. But by the time he had the soft light from the paraffin lamp trimmed to his satisfaction and was seated behind his pipe in the glow of the peat fire the scene was fit for Rembrandt.

We chatted backwards and forwards, and for once he had more news than I had because he had been talking to Calum the Post, who had become a richer source of information than ever since he had become the possessor of a wireless set. We discussed the news of the world, then the news of the village, but, at last, I had to come to the point which was worrying me.

'Hector,' I said, nipping my cigarette and carefully pocketing the dout for another time, 'you will have to start milking your own cow soon.'

He didn't say anything for a minute or two, nor did his eyes leave the fire. But at last he removed his pipe and spat accurately into the middle of the flames.

'O aye,' he said. 'You're not telling me anything that comes as news to me. I knew that you had to win the bursary this year; and I knew that you could and would win it because you've got a good head on you …' He paused, and I waited for his eyes to moisten as I knew they would. He could control his tear ducts in a way that would be worth money to a television actor. When they were neatly brimming he carried on. 'Ah well, that's the way of life. And I'm glad for your sake that you'll be getting on in the world. You just go off to High School in your good suit and your posh shoes, and nobody will wish you better than I do; nor will I ever let anybody say that you didn't do your best for me while you had time. There's no way I can be milking the cow – me with my bad legs – so I'll just face up to things and sell her, even although I can't expect to get much for her with prices the way they are –' He paused for a moment of effect

18

and rubbed one eye with the heel of his hand. 'This is what comes of being old and a widower.'

Mentally, to myself, I conceded the age bit because fifty-six did seem like a ripeness of years then; and people did refer to him as 'Old Hector' although, in retrospect, that was because he acted old and sported a struggle of black beard with a white tip to it as if he had dipped it accidentally into a basin of flour. I couldn't find words quickly enough to point out to him that the loss of a spinster sister did not confer on an elderly bachelor the status of widowhood, and I couldn't bring myself to be totally unsympathetic to his affliction and hint that a man's legs were of minimal importance in the milking process. I knew that the real truth of Hector's present dilemma was that he was scared stiff of his quiet old cow, who didn't know what horns were for; and I also knew that if he did sell Primrose the crofters would see to it that he was supplied with milk for the rest of his life. But a cow was a status symbol in a crofting community, and Hector needed all the status symbols he could get. I allowed all these thoughts to fleet past because I had worked out my plan and I was going to stick to it.

'You'll have to get a wife – and quickly!'

I didn't know whether he was going to spit out his cutty or swallow it. He did neither. He bit on the stem till his jaw muscles quivered. He then snatched it out of his mouth and spat wide.

'A wife!' he croaked at last. 'I've heard tell that education could turn a man's head but I didn't realise till this moment that it made a bloody idiot of him into the bargain. Even if I wanted a *woman* in this place where would I find one, far less one who would look at *me*? And what woman in her sane senses would come into a black house with an earthen floor when there are houses with slate roofs and linoleum springing up all over the place? You're mad, that's what you are. Education and cigarettes have driven out any sense that you may have been born with.' He licked his finger and thumb and picked a small burning ember of peat from the fire and popped it into his pipe. He glared at me before he began to puff. 'And what's more you're not very respectful to a frail old man who sins his soul to make it possible for you to smoke.'

I had foreseen all his arguments, and I knew that there was a certain validity in them; desperate women were in short supply

19

in our part of the island. But I had also worked out my next move, and I re-lit my cigarette stub to fortify myself.

'I'll tell you what, Hector; we'll advertise!'

That was when he did his imitation of the stunned ox.

His eyes widened first. Then his mouth – and he didn't even attempt to catch his cutty as it fell to the floor. He was sitting in his Taransay chair – a severe wooden frame, with a high slatted back and plain stout arm rests, which made a mild concession to comfort in the form of a plaited marram grass seat. He gripped the arms to steady himself.

'Advertise!' he mouthed. 'Advertise for a woman –'

'No. For a wife.'

He gobbled silently for a moment or two and then, in a burst of energy, picked up his pipe from the floor and pointed it at me like an upside-down pistol.

'Go!' he said. 'Go and take your fancy ideas home with you and don't come darkening my door again or I'll tell your mother you were smoking *cigarettes*.' He made the word sound positively evil.

I shrugged and set off down the hillside, but I hadn't gone two hundred yards when I heard a querulous voice shouting to me that the cow had to be milked in the morning. I paid no attention.

It had been a daft idea I admitted, grudgingly, to myself, and I should never have upset the old man with it. Certainly I had seen adverts like that from time to time in some of the magazines that friendly tourists occasionally sent my mother when they regained the safety of their cities, and on rare occasions similar pleas had appeared in the local paper but people had usually laughed at the latter and assumed them to be jokes. For a day or two I had, indeed, convinced myself that it might be the answer to Hector's dilemma but now, having seen his reaction, I realised that even as a joke it would have failed. I glanced nervously to my left as I passed the cemetery, half expecting to hear the sharp voice of Maggie upbraiding me from where she lay under one of the anonymous hummocks over which the nettles were creeping. A corncrake rasped and I nearly jumped out of my skin, but the faraway answering call restored reality and gave its peace back to the dusk. My father was just reaching for the Bible when I got in, preparing to read the mandatory psalm and chapter so that my mother could get to bed and he could go back to the *Daily Express*.

'How was Old Hector?'

'Fine. A bit quiet when I left.'

'The poor old soul,' said my mother, putting away yet another sock that was destined for my suitcase. 'He's bound to get a bit lonely up there in that dark house.'

'He's all right,' my father said, yawning as he always did before embarking on his reading. 'Maggie's not so very far away – and she's quiet now.'

'John! How can you talk like that with the Bible in your hand?'

He smiled and began to mumble his way through whichever psalm the Bible had fallen open at. By the time I had opened my eyes after his quick little prayer my conscience had cleared itself and my thoughts had turned again to the prospect of going to High School. But I wouldn't have slept so soundly if I'd known that Hector was still awake.

Next morning I was halfway through the milking when I became aware of him hovering around, carefully keeping away from both ends of Primrose. I was surprised because when I had found the clean empty milkpail sitting outside his door I had assumed it to be silent reproach; normally I went into the house and collected the pail and, as often as not, had to wash it myself in the burn on my way to the impatient cow. Not quite knowing how to handle the situation I merely mumbled something about another fine morning, and when he didn't respond I guessed that the night hadn't soothed him any. I paid no more attention to him and took a tantalisingly long time stripping the cow. When I had squeezed the last possible drop of milk into the pail I whipped the fetter-rope off her legs and made my way back to the house with Old Hector waddling along behind me in silence. It was only when I'd set out the milk in two large basins and filled a jug for his brose and his tea that he summoned up the courage to speak.

'I've got a cigarette here that I scrounged off the shepherd this morning pretending that I was out of tobacco. It's a Capstan. There's not much of a smoke in those wee Woodbines. Sit down and light up like a good lad.'

I sat down, puzzled as to why he was now making such

21

friendly overtures when he had been so upset – with perfectly good reason – a mere twelve hours before. He pulled out of his pocket the wadge of newspaper he always carried with him for spill, tore off a strip, twisted it with great deliberation, lit it and offered me a light before getting his own pipe going. He tamped it and sucked it till it was drawing to his satisfaction and then he looked at me with a new twinkle of confidence in his eyes.

'I haven't slept a wink all night, boy. At first I thought you were mocking me and I was angry; then I thought you were pulling my leg and I was annoyed at myself for not taking a joke; and then, dammity, I got round to thinking that if I was wanting a housekeeper like they do in the manse and the Big House I wouldn't think twice about advertising, would I? And after all it's a kind of a housekeeper I'm wanting – er – at first anyway.' He chuckled and leant over and poked me in the ribs. 'I know they all think I'm a bit soft in the head, and, for all I know, the malaria may have got me there as well as my legs; but I'll tell you this, my lad, the malaria didn't hit me everywhere!' He gave me another poke in the ribs that nearly pushed me off the low stool on which I was crouched and he fell back in the Taransay chair chortling his head off. For a moment I wondered if he could possibly have been drinking, but then as he began to concentrate on re-lighting his pipe I could see that his eyes had gone deadly serious. I hadn't said a word, but I felt my throat tightening as it began to dawn on me that I might be hoist with my own petard.

'You're not being serious, are you?'

'What are talking about, lad? Weren't you being serious last night?'

'Well – er – yes, in a way, but –'

'I should hope so. I don't mind a joke but I'd be annoyed if I thought I'd wasted a whole night thinking and then discovered you were pulling my leg after all.' He bellowed his cheeks a couple of times to keep his pipe going and then went on in a crisp, decisive manner of which I didn't ever think he was capable. 'You're a clever fellow and you know about those things. You would know how to put an advert in the *Gazette* so that nobody would know who it was from, wouldn't you?'

By chance I did know. For the last couple of years I'd been obsessed with the idea of getting a bicycle of my own even although I knew that my parents' resources hadn't yet recovered sufficiently for them to contemplate even a humble outlay such as a second-hand bicycle would represent. But I had toyed with the idea of testing the market and, feigning curiosity, I had found out from my father how one sent an advertisement (as short as possible) along with payment and one's name and address requesting the paper to withhold identification and allocate a Box Number. I had abandoned the whole idea when I discovered that I couldn't afford the advertisement far less the price of the most decrepit bicycle which, my friend Gillespie assured me, would be equivalent to a whole quarter's rent for the croft. And that was that. But the Gaelic proverb 'Keep a thing for seven years and you'll find a use for it' was proving itself once again. My accumulated, and hitherto useless, knowledge of the ways of the advertising world was now going to come in useful in a totally unexpected way. My qualms began to disappear and I warmed to the business of explaining the ins and outs of small ads to Old Hector.

'That buggers it!' he said, and it flashed across my mind that I had never heard him using the mildest of strong language before. 'If I've got to give my name and address the whole story will be winging from the Butt of Lewis to the Sound of Harris before they've even cashed my postal order, and that'll be quick enough!'

I assured him that the whole thing was as secret as the ballot box. 'All you need,' I said, with my confidence rapidly returning, 'is writing paper and an envelope, half-a-crown for a postal order and commission and a stamp.'

'Right,' he said, reaching under the Taransay chair where he must have concealed a writing pad and envelopes, 'here are the first two of those. You do the rest.' He looked at me slyly. 'It's a good job that boys who smoke cigarettes don't give away secrets.' I could sense blackmail without having it spelt out to me. I borrowed his tobacco knife to sharpen the stub of pencil that he produced from his waistcoat pocket and we moved over to the table at the window to begin the first of many drafts.

'Who's the postal order for?' the Duchess asked when I went to her shop, ostensibly for a half ounce of Bogey Roll for Old Hector. We didn't get the newspaper from her any more since

23

the driver of the daily bus had taken to flinging ordered copies out of his driving window at the croft-houses along his route.

'Old Hector,' I replied glibly. 'He's sending off for a bottle of linament for this rheumatism; it's a new kind that he saw advertised in *The Witness*.' He and I had rehearsed the lie so well that I could look her straight in the eye without blushing.

'Him and his linament,' she said as she thumped a stamp on the postal order. 'Tell him from me that Kruschen Salts is the latest thing for rheumatism; linament's out of date.'

The rest was easy. Calum the Post must have been surprised to find a stamped letter in the red pillar-box across the road from the schoolhouse because people usually just hailed him as he passed and handed him their letters with the appropriate sum of money to cover the postage. But if he ever associated the events that followed with an envelope carefully addressed in block capitals, he never let on.

Our letter must have been beautifully coincident with the paper's printings, because there, in the very next issue, was the result of our joint composition.

Retired seaman wants woman used to croft work with a view to matrumony. Reply Box 427

'May the good Lord look down on us,' said Old Hector, unable to conceal the tremor in his hands. '*Retired seaman*, sounds like a captain when you see it in proper print; all I ever was was a deckhand and that only for two months.' He smiled nervously as he folded the paper away. 'The only consolation is that only a halfwit would answer an advertisement like that.'

I couldn't quite see how he could glean consolation from that particular line of reasoning. But I was half inclined to agree with him. And, in the end, he turned out to be rather more than half right.

Chapter Two

August was a slow month in the village – a time suspended between two seasons; between the dying notes of the corncrake and the forlorn bleating of the orphaned lambs.

The corncrake came in May when the wild iris was tall enough for her to hide. In our parts the sandy-oat crop, from which the experts had not yet weaned the crofters, was too late and too thin to provide cover for the supreme camouflage expert of all the birds, and so she made her nest where the bracken ended and where the iris began, with the result that the brown remains of last year's foliage among this year's green made her well-nigh invisible when she was crouched on her nest, and her eggs totally indiscernible when she was away. I spent long hours of boyhood searching for her – stalking her croaks as she held rasping conversations with faraway echoes, and once I found her lying dead on her back, as I thought, with her pale green belly matched to the iris and her striped legs pointing upwards, but when I bent down to pick her up she was away through the flag like a shuttle through thread and when she hawked a few moments later there was a laugh in her throat.

'You shouldn't have disturbed her,' Old Aunt Rachel said when I told her. 'Don't you know that it's millions of crakes lying on their backs with their feet up that keep the sky in place? And it's the strain of it that's made their singing hoarse over the thousands of years. Only fools hunt the corncrake,' she went on. 'And those with little to do. But the wise man listens to her and holds back the Spring work till her first croak tells them that the frost is over for good; nor will he take his scythe from the rafters till her chorus is ended. It was the coming of the scythe that made her start taking to below the water for the winter, don't you know? And if you don't believe me keep your eye on the moor lochs during the spring and you might catch her coming out from under the water after her winter sleep with a white patch on her forehead from the cold.' She chortled. 'In any case your chances of seeing her then are as good as your ever seeing another one; already you've seen as many in your short life as I've seen in my long one!'

Great Aunt Rachel was a lady for whom my father had instilled in me the equal feelings of awe and affection with which he regarded her himself. She was his aunt on his mother's side. Her pedigree stretched back to the 1780s – to a man with a broken leg who had been found half dead in the ebb on the beach below the old village on the foundations of which our new village had been built. In thankfulness for his deliverance the man, whose name was MacKay, devoted himself to the service of the church and, in due course, had begotten the family known as the Clerics from whom my father had inherited the love of education which he was so intent on handing on to me. Aunt Rachel was, for her time, well educated and well read but she had a vivid imagination which, over the years, had led her to believe that the man who escaped the sea on our shore was a survivor of the Spanish Armada, despite a minor chronological discrepancy of two centuries. If anybody was ever bold enough to challenge her with the apparent flaw in her history she would merely sigh pityingly, close her eyes, rock gently in her chair and recall Holy Writ –

A thousand ages in Thy sight
Are like an evening gone ...

To that there was rarely any reply. But although the whimsies of the centuries always tended to get mixed up with Great Aunt Rachel there was always a glisk of truth where one least suspected it, and to this day I like to believe that, away back in my ancestry, a Spaniard lurks somewhere. Perhaps one day I will stumble across the truth of him just as I stumbled, very recently, across the old Highland myth that the corncrake hibernated underwater in winter and emerged in spring with a white spot on her forehead from the cold. The corncrake – in the less glamorous ornithological truth – migrates to Africa; the Highland legend confused the corncrake with her relation, the water rail. Of such facts and fancies were Great Aunt Rachel's dogmas compounded.

But she was right about the elusiveness of the crake. I never saw one again. But their stridulations from light dusk to brief dark in the summer evenings of boyhood were to become as implanted in the memory as the sound of the sea itself. I'm told that an occasional one can still be heard from time to time, but it's many years since they were loud enough to make the preacher raise his voice at evening service. I know now that the coming of the fertiliser landry was the beginning of the end of the crake.

We had long since got used to vans. Calum the Post's had always been with us, but it was not till the new road had been given a fine coating of gravel that people who had to pay for their own tyres and springs began to challenge the Duchess's monopoly with grocery vans and a fish van. The former didn't last long because a combination of wear and tear and tick made their profits minimal and their overheads astronomical. But the fish van had no competition either from the Duchess or the unfishable seas of our coasts; the fact that he was a Lewisman gave the fishman an age-old incentive to screw the last ha'penny out of his less worldly-wise Harris neighbours, and, although he only charged a shilling for a cod whose tail swept the ground when you carried him along by the head, Montgomery (who never had a first name) made enough to keep him going from his fish and saucer-sized biscuits which were hard enough to have been salvaged from the Mary Celeste. It may have been Montgomery's success that prompted his fellow islander to undertake a venture as bizarre as any entrepreneurial enterprise since the Icelander who sold the Aurora Borealis to the Edinburgh man.

Shortfield was a businessman who had crossed the Minch to live in Stornoway, but in all other respects he was reckoned to be sane. Till he conceived the idea of establishing a mobile

27

laundry service – in the shape of a large van which was scheduled to leave Stornoway on a Monday morning, travel down the west coast to Harris and back up the east coast, stopping at each croft house and picking up dirty washing which would, in two days' time, be returned crisply laundered to the grateful owners who would pay for it and replace it with more soiled linen destined for the same treatment. There was nothing wrong with the theory. Sitting in a warm office in Stornoway it seemed no more than reasonable to assume that harassed Harris housewives with large families, living in weather conditions where the most reasonable certainty was rain, would jump at the idea of ridding themselves of their washtubs, their scrubbing boards and their smoothing irons forever. Having, presumably, satisfied himself as to the cost-effectiveness of his dream, Shortfield (whose greatest asset was that he had an Old Testament first name) invested in a sizeable green van and a Lewis driver of inestimable charm and set them on the road to what he was convinced would be his fortune. Thus it was that on a Monday morning which I remember well, there appeared over the Back of Scarista Hill the laundry van which was to be known henceforth in the local dialect as 'the landry'.

But poor Shortfield overlooked three problems, and the third of them was probably the most insurmountable. First of all in those days very few women in Harris could contemplate the cost of sending their duddies away to be washed; in the second place not many of them had enough shifts to be able to send one set flittering off to Stornoway, and, thirdly and most certainly not one of them would be prepared to send her flannelette bloomers (far less her old man's long johns) to be held up and joked about by some lipsticked hussy in Stornoway. And so it was that, week after week, twice a week, the landry chuntered round its hundred mile circular route collecting nary a stich save, perhaps, an occasional linen table-cloth from one of the several manses and the few toff houses on its way. But the driver became a mini-celebrity. He was young and good-looking and cheerful, and so he endeared himself to blushing crofterettes and matrons alike; he always had some morsel of news from the burgeoning metropolis of Stornoway and so the men enjoyed his visits. But, more importantly, he was as obliging as Calum the Post and had all the time in the world to indulge in errandry, and so every time he returned to Stornoway he had a couple of his master's laundry labels full of orders for the chemist, the ironmonger, and the newly-opened Woolworth's Sixpenny Store. En route – because of the size and the emptiness of the van – he was able to carry much more in the way of heavy goods than Calum could carry; he could take half a dozen bags of peat, a couple of sacks of grain, several gallons of paraffin and a couple of newborn calves, without his van even looking low on its springs. Unlike Calum he was breaking no Government law; like Calum he was defrauding nobody since he was charging no fee for the services of a vehicle belonging to a master who was not in that form of transport business anyway. The landry took no time at all to become a valued institution.

Shortfield had the patience of the race from which he must have, sometime, inherited the name of Isaac; but he had none of that race's legendary business acumen. It can't have taken him long to realise that the laundry service wasn't making a profit; it took him a couple of months to accept that it never would. But, finally, he prepared to end something which anybody in his full senses would never have started.

But it wasn't as easy as that. The crofters had begun to like the idea of amenity. Calum the Post's van had paved the way for public transport in the shape of the twice daily bus; the various grocery vans (short-lived though some them were) had whetted the appetite for convenience; the fishman's van had proved a marvellous boon. But the landry had proved the greatest convenience of all – and here it was, suddenly, being withdrawn. There was uproar. Somebody wrote a letter to the local paper denouncing Shortfield for Tory, and repressive, and anti-social and all sorts of things; but the writer was careful to refer to the landry as 'the laundry service'. Poor Shortfield replied, claiming a white conscience and a red bank balance. But to no avail. The next letter was signed by the Clerks of half a dozen Grazings Committees trying to prove that a laundry service had become a social asset, and that by the very act of having instituted it the proprietor was under a moral if not legal obligation to keep it going, in much the same way as a landlord who concedes right of way is obliged to observe it forevermore …

Of course it didn't work! No enterprise, even as private as Shortfield's, can be forced to go on making a loss in a public weal for which there is no public purse, and, suddenly, the laundry service was, as they say nowadays, axed. The jeremiad was brief, because crofters are resilient by nature, but what did remain was a new word. The word *landry* had entered the local Gaelic vocabulary as the generic term for a vehicle which carried for free goods other than those for which it was commercially intended. Thus, when the Scottish Co-operative Wholesale Society launched a mobile grocery service, with a spacious van and an obliging driver, the vehicle became known as the *Co-op Landry*; when the Post Office decided to overhaul the telephone system and gave its engineers a big green pantechnicon with room to spare it became, inevitably, the *Telephone Landry*; and when the Department of Agriculture decided to upgrade the traditional and fairly primitive agricultural methods of the new villages, the lorry which they sent round at regular intervals with fertilisers and new-fangled weed-killers became the *Fertiliser Landry*. And all of them provided supplementary free services which ensured that no professional road haulier need ever contemplate profitable venturing into the Southlands of Harris.

It was the Fertiliser Landry which began to put the seal on the fate of the corncrake as the hitherto fallow fields began to be put under ryegrass for early harvesting and as the boundaries of the bracken and the wild iris began to be pushed back and farther back. But the process was only beginning as my days in the village were ending; and during the whole of that August before High School the crake was in chorus still.

Perhaps it was a pity that it was too early in the afternoon for the corncrake to have raised her voice when the people from the six parishes assembled in our village to celebrate the first ever pastoral visit to our corner of the Hebrides of The Right Reverend, The Moderator of the General Assembly of the Church of Scotland – whose very title, to this day, is his protection against the sort of sexual assault which the literati of the lavatories invoke against the Pope. The Moderatorship is the highest honour that the Church of Scotland can confer on any of her servants but, unlike the Pope, the Moderator's term

30

of office is one year only – his appointment lasting from one month of May till the next. Like the Pontiff he is larded with pomp and ceremony and, nowadays, is expected to undertake ceremonial tours all over the world, blessing the poor and the benighted; kissing innocent babies; and chiding errant rulers for their misdeeds, having partaken of their hospitality. Nowadays every Moderator is expected to jet to foreign parts like a born-again American trouble-shooter; in those days before the war our new village (although not quite so new by then) probably qualified as an 'emerging state' and – having been without a pastor of our own for a few years – we almost certainly were deemed to be in need of rehabilitation and blessing.

The news of the impending visitation had been received early on in the summer and had been greeted with great excitement by the womenfolk, who hadn't even had a wedding to stir up excitement for the last long while. It was immediately foreseen as an occasion for new hats and outfits; a few mail orders were dispatched by the older ladies, but the younger ones had, by now, got into the way of taking advantage of the daily return bus journey to Stornoway to plunder the emporia of fashion which were laying tentative foundations in the town. Some of the less secretive wives organised 'excursions' and hired one of our own Southland buses for a day-trip which would include a visit to the Picture House. The men were less enthusiastic. 'Sure as bloody hell he'll come on the finest day of August,' somebody said. 'The day that the Grazing Committee will have set aside for the lifting of the lambs.' And his prophecy was to prove true.

We had been selected as the focal point for the Moderatorial visitation because the new village had grown up round the huge church which, for more than two centuries, had been Harris Church – the Protestant ecclesiastical centre of the island from the days when the arable rolling Southlands had been the only really populated part of the island. The balance of population had swung during the eighteenth and nineteenth centuries when the population had been evicted overseas to Canada, or to the rocky coasts of the north and east which couldn't be exploited for sheepfarming. Slowly the Northlands in particular had evolved a different way of life, based on fishing and weaving. Round the magnificent anchorage of East Loch Tarbert a large village had been gouged out of the rocky hillside and it had matured into the administrative capital of the island with a dozen shops, a sizeable bank, a High School and the sundry other appurtenances of local government. Tarbert had two churches of different denominations, one of which belonged to the Church of Scotland and was thronged and active, but ours was still the traditional Parish Church even although a mere twenty people shuffled into its cavernous depths on the average Sunday. Tradition is cherished as much in the heart of the West Highlander as it is in the most aged institutions of the realm and the Harris Church had to be the scene of Moderator's pageant even although the organisation of it would be as inconvenient as would be the staging of the Coronation in a country village in Dorset.

Those who thought that the visit would be a matter of 'Hello' and 'God Bless' were quickly disillusioned. For that one day our tiny village was to be a centre of pilgrimage for a substantial hunk of the four thousand population of the island, and it was obvious that even the most dyed-in-the-wool fundamentalists from the other churches could not refrain from coming to watch the Church of Scotlanders worshipping their golden images and frolicking their way to perdition. By now it was common knowledge that, for this official visit, the Moderator would be costumed in the tricorn hat, lace ruffles, knee-breeches and silver buckled shoon of his office – the type of frivolity which would doubtless be preached against for weeks to come in the pulpits of the Free Church and the Free Presbyterian Church, both of whom held the Established Church as being only one step away from Rome and two from Hell. Nevertheless, come the day, the most ardent adherents of those creeds would undoubtedly turn out for the entertainment and would, if necessary, purge the sin of curiosity in some way later. Meantime, not only did they unobtrusively prepare to bedeck themselves suitably for the occasion but they contributed generously in cash and in kind to the preparations for the great day.

The Moderator was coming in a year when it was being borne home to people that the grim days of the slump and depression were really over. Incomes from all sources had increased. The price of sheep and cattle had improved, and no longer was it more economical for crofters to kill off their newborn calves than to rear them for sale. Roadworks were being re-started in various parts of the island and tarmacadam surfaces were being laid on the busier roads of the Northlands around Tarbert. Fishing was becoming profitable again although that didn't concern us in the Southlands. But what did concern us very much was that tweed was once more in great demand at good prices; in fact ten times as much Harris Tweed was being produced in the Hebrides as had been produced in the lean years of the early thirties and, in our village, there was a loom in almost every home. My own father had stuck to his policy of concentrating on short lengths and suit-lengths for the network of customers he had built up from the ever-increasing flow of tourists; mother was able to buy occasional luxuries from the grocery vans now, but she kept on the job of school cleaner which she had been glad to get when money had been desperately tight and poverty had been our nearest neighbour. It was as school cleaner that she had to fulfil a role in preparation for the visit. It had long since become obvious that the hospitality of the village could not possibly cope with the sudden surge of gawpers, and since it was tempting Providence to bank on another multiplication of loaves and fishes even in the presence of the titular head of the Church of Scotland, it was decided to turn the schoolroom and schoolhouse into a temporary canteen. On and off since the beginning of July my mother and the women of the village had scrubbed and polished and planned, and when the Moderator did finally arrive they were handsomely rewarded with praise for their efforts.

The women managed to organise their part of the celebration with surprisingly little fuss and no formality. But the men kept organising themselves into committees which held endless and sociable meetings in different houses, but they had to keep re-forming themselves and appointing new chairmen when they fell out on some point or other. One of the main problems was that none of the men considered themselves good enough to be full members of the church (or communicants) and so they couldn't be office bearers. We therefore had the paradoxical situation of a Parish Church without minister or elders, and it wasn't always convenient for elders from neighbouring congregations to travel to haphazardly arranged committee meetings. Murdo Mor was by way of being a professional committee chairman by dint of his enthusiasm for public speaking and by virtue of his having acquired a knowledge of procedures of all kinds while he was some kind of salesman in Manchester; he was also an elder – but, unfortunately, of a small church which had long since broken off diplomatic relations with the Church of Scotland as a result of a deep theological disagreement as to whether Jonah had been swallowed by a Blue Whale or a White Whale. But Murdo Mor was a conscientious pillar of the community and he agreed to lend his experience and his gifts of organisation to ensuring the success of the social side of the great event, provided he wasn't expected to perform any duties that could be determined 'religious'.

Under Murdo Mor's chairmanship the 'steering committee' had performed remarkable feats of fund-raising, and it was known that at least a hundred pounds had been collected by the beginning of July for the purposes of organising transport for the old and the decrepit, for the printing of leaflets giving the orders of procedure and of service, and for the dozens of other things which required hard cash rather than volunteer labour. Yet he himself caused the first splintering of the co-operative spirit when he suggested hiring two marquees for use as public toilets. That was too much like posh for some people who hadn't themselves aspired as yet to interior plumbing in their own homes and, in the heat of debate, somebody was heard to say that if the Moderator couldn't organise himself sufficiently to have a shit before he left his Stornoway hotel then it was no wonder that the Church of Scotland was in constant schism. Murdo didn't hold any brief for the Church of Scotland but his years in Manchester had inculcated in him a certain delicacy where references to the bowel were concerned, and he promptly resigned his chairmanship for the first of many times. In the end, the matter of comfort was resolved when somebody remembered that the County Council had spent a large sum of money installing dry closets in the school playground (conveniences which the pupils had disdained for two years) and a small sum of money was set aside for their rehabilitation, and an amiable lad called 'Daft Jimmie' from Drumpound was given five shillings to paint appropriate signs – but principally to keep him out of mischief.

Although I hadn't realised it, the pastoral visit had been scheduled fifteen months before – as soon as it was known that the Moderator Designate was a Gaelic speaker – and the staff at the Head Office of the Church of Scotland in Edinburgh had been quietly organising things with the sort of practised ease that the Lord Chamberlain's office brings to functions of Royal life and death. Unfortunately they didn't consider it necessary to keep the local community fully informed, and, consequently much duplicated effort led to occasional embarrassment. At least two ministers had spent their summer weeks preparing welcoming addresses – at the invitation of two separate parish committees – while the man who was eventually to deliver it had been, in fact, appointed by the Presbytery months before. It was only by the grace of God that three Divines weren't jostling for the pulpit when the day came.

'Mark my words,' Old Hector had said to me the day after I had posted the letter with his advertisement to the *Gazette*. 'There will be such a stramash here for the next three weeks that we could be putting a notice in the school window advertising for a wife and nobody would be noticing it.' He had been trying to bolster his own flagging confidence, but he wasn't far wrong. *Moderator fever* was beginning to grip the village and the most pious were not always the ones who were enjoying it most. Apart from the fact that strong drink was never considered as an ingredient, the whole event was taking on an air of carnival which bade fair to put into the shade the coronation of George VI and the wedding of James to my father's cousin Mary. The latter had been the first wedding in the village and my crony Gillespie and I had been banned from it because it would have been unseemly for five-year-olds to witness their parents abandoning themselves to carousal. But Gillespie and I had sneaked in on the proceedings unnoticed and – not for the last time, though for other reasons – I had spent a convivial evening under a table. But there were no exclusions from the kirk soiree. 'Suffer the little children ...' and all the rest of it, provided they were willing to put some effort into the preparations. A couple of members of the Grazings

35

Committee had tentatively suggested that the lambs could be lifted before the Moderator's day, but they were chided for being so worldly that they could even think of lambs with the man of God about to descend on us. Instead, the Grazings Committee was put to the task of coaxing six crofters to volunteer to donate a farrow sheep each to be slaughtered to feed the multitudes, and when Sandy Cravat had tried to make some facetious remark about loaves and fishes when one of his father's fattest sheep was earmarked for slaughter, Murdo Mor roasted him with a fusillade of biblical quotations that would have done justice to a concordance. The sacrifice of fat sheep seemed highly appropriate and in the best traditions of the Old Testament – except to those who were expected to forego the price that such sheep could command at the autumn sales.

There hadn't been many festive occasions since the village had been founded. Two weddings (of which I remember only James's), the Silver Jubilee in 1935 (still commemorated on countless tea caddies), and the Coronation. These had been celebrated with song and dance, music and flags; but there was a general feeling that the first three of those were not appropriate to an ecclesiastical visitation even if it was taking place on a weekday. But there were still yards of bunting lying around in odd corners, and dyed pillow-cases and table-cloths; even the occasional Union Jack. Were they appropriate or not? That was one of the questions which vexed the village organising committee and not even Murdo Mor knew the answer since the Moderator of the Church of Scotland had never been known to visit Manchester. The widow MacQueen was on the village committee as an ex-officio member by virtue of the fact that she had once been active in the now dormant branch of the WRI, but she had never been known to voice an opinion – having had it explained to her that 'ex-officio' meant 'beholding with charity, and listening in silence'. But when she watched the committee getting into a brangle over the matter of flags she could contain herself no longer. She heaved herself to her feet.

'We will rejoice in thy salvation, and in the name of our God we will set up our banners.'

She sat down, adding as she did so, 'Psalm 20, Verse 5'.

There was a moment of surprised silence. Murdo Mor

glanced left and right as if looking for guidance and then put his fingertips together and looked up at the ceiling which, of course, is where he should have looked in the first place.

'Seconded,' he said. 'Lift ye up a banner upon the high mountain … Isaiah, Chapter 13, Verse 2.'

That decided it; and if Murdo Mor hadn't remembered, in the nick of time, to say, 'Any other business?' everybody would have rushed home to scrabble in odd corners for flags and bamboo fishing rods to hoist them on. However he did remember, and he put the question as he closed the book where he kept his meticulous minutes, fully expecting the usual shuffle of feet and the rush for the door. But instead, the gentlest, quietest man in the Southlands got to his feet – a man who had never been known to utter in public, partly because of his own retiring nature and partly because he was burdened with an impediment of which he was painfully self-conscious.

'Wh-wh-wh-what,' he said, 'about a c-c-c-car for the M-M-M-M-?'

There was no need for him to struggle further. Those who had stood up sat down again, and those who had been silent all evening broke into hubbub. Murdo Mor looked like a man caught with his trousers round his ankles. 'Yes,' he said, 'er – yes …' But he was saved further embarrassment by big George MacLellan, normally not his best friend because MacLellan was a staunch Liberal while Murdo considered the Tory Party more in keeping with his standing as a retired ex-salesman who read the *Glasgow Herald*.

'I'll tell you one thing,' said big Geordie, lumbering to his feet. 'There's no bloody Lewisman going to come the hoity-toity on us by driving the Moderator to Harris; not even if I have to go for him in the Armstrong myself for free.' He sat down amid a ripple of interest, indeed relief. Geordie was the proud possessor of an aged Armstrong Siddley which had once belonged to a Clan Chief who had fallen on evil times. It was far too big for our roads and it took all George's strength to pull it round hairpin bends, but it was an impressive vehicle with hide upholstery (which he pronounced eupholstery) and, occasionally, he hired himself and the car to an unsuspecting tourist or a commercial traveller incautious enough not to check his charges in advance. Usually he used it to ferry

37

livestock between his own and his father's crofts. Nobody had ever known him to offer it to anybody for free.

'And would you promise to give it a polish and a clean inside, George?' asked the Widow MacQueen, encouraged by her earlier first foray into public debate.

The question assumed that Geordie's offer would be accepted, and made it impossible for it to be refused. Geordie not only promised to have the Armstrong polished 'till you couldn't tell it from a bloody Rolls-Royce' but he undertook to wear his Sunday suit and use his Sunday language. Once that was established the whole business of the Moderatorial visit seemed to be complete, and the meeting was on the point of skailing when the Widow MacQueen (who appeared to be smitten by a bug of public oratory) suggested that the meeting be closed with prayer. That is one of the few requests that it is impossible to deny.

On the evening before the day the western sky was red with promise; here and there men went quietly about the business of hauling up flags which just folded back peacefully against their poles; it was so quiet that you could hear a faraway man whistling quietly to himself as he worked, and even the sandpiper sounded sleepy for a change. Over the village hung an aroma of roasting mutton like the sleepy smell of incense over the Plains of Lasithi on the eve of the festival of Agias Zónis. The only note of discord was sounded by the hammer of 'Daft Jimmie' from Drumpound as he laboured at the schoolhouse to fix up two garish notices reading LADDIES and JENTS.

By mid-morning the first of the spectators began to arrive. Few came as strangers because the village had, after all, been created from different parts of the island and grafted on to an indigenous population from which, in turn, relatives had branched out over previous generations. But only the elderly availed themselves of the hospitality of the village homes; most of the visitors came en fête and headed for the school (where Jimmie's notices had been hastily draped with a Lion Rampant and a Union Jack) and there they revelled in tea and coffee and home baking with scant regard for their appetites for the full meal which would follow in the afternoon. The lively frocks of the younger women, mixing with the sedate Sunday suits of the men, reflected exactly the blend of festivity and solemnity which the occasion warranted and got. As the afternoon tiptoed in people moved, automatically, towards the stone-pillared gate leading up to the church on the hillside, and there must have been well over five hundred people assembled there, quietly jostling for the better view, as Big Geordie's Armstrong Siddley appeared, gleaming, over the top of Back of Scarista Hill. He had a feeling for the theatrical moment, had Geordie, and he drove at a carefully measured speed which was halfway between the one he would choose for a wedding and that demanded for a funeral. A silence drifted over the crowd as the big car eased to a halt. Geordie jumped out with a smooth agility of which nobody had ever suspected him. As he opened the rear door nearest the church gates he touched his forehead and stood back waiting for his passenger to get out. The crowd instinctively eased back as a tall, athletic man in a dark coat and a crisp black Anthony Eden hat stepped out and stood surveying the crowd for a moment before addressing George.

'What the bloody hell's going on here?'

The silence froze ten degrees further, except for the aged Agnes MacKenzie from Obbe who spoke no English. She murmured 'Amen'.

Chapter Three

There was no tradition of lynching parties in Harris, there being no trees. But big Geordie would have escaped anyway by divine intervention because, before the crowd had time to draw its corporate breath, there was a suggestion of huzza from somewhere and when we turned to look there was the kenspeckle stately Daimler from Stornoway cruising down the hill, followed by a tail of assorted cars which turned out to contain a whole witness of assorted ministers. This time the assembled company didn't have time to prepare its reaction; as the Daimler drew up the passenger door swung open and a cheery-faced, silver-haired man stepped smartly out, waving a tricorn hat and calling a good humoured Gaelic greeting to the throng. He struck a laughing theatrical pose for a few moments, giving people time to admire his lace jabot and cuffs, frock-coat, breeches, and silver buckled shoes, then he turned round with a sweep of his arm towards the spread of white beach and Atlantic. 'What a lovely place you have here,' he said. 'It's almost as nice as Tiree.' With that, a bodyguard of clerics forcing rusty smiles closed round him and began to urge him through the company towards the church.

No amount of shoe-horn tactics could possibly get everybody into the church although it had been built to accommodate four hundred in the days of its greatness, but somebody managed to open windows that hadn't opened for generations and soon the spine-tingling sound of precented

Gaelic psalm welled out from the ancient walls and was lifted by the crowd outside to the older hills. In moments of memory, when the noises of the village drift back to me across the years – the corncrake, the bleat of lambs, the clack of looms, soughing winds and grumbling sea – there peeps through, just once in a sacred while, an echo of 'Ye gates lift up your heads on high ...' as it rose to the skies that day.

When the Moderator climbed to the pulpit he took as his text, 'But when ye hear of wars and commotions, be not terrified.' And he preached a sermon of peace and comfort on the subject that men were trying to push to the back of their minds at that time. He knew what he was talking about because he had been through the same war as the men who had founded our village, and, like them, he hoped not to see another.

The service was short – or, at least, felt short in comparison with the ones to which we had become accustomed from a series of lay preachers during the period of our own kirk's fallowness – and when it was over, he broke away from his entourage and wandered among the people, cracking jokes in his own native Gaelic, which had a tinge of foreignness to us. Old ladies who had moulded their faces in preparation for an eminence of divinity found their legs being pulled about this and that; he attempted to swop hats with the Widow MacQueen, but hers was anchored to her head with a pin that would have held a sail in a storm; he asked a blushing teenager if she was married and offered to send her a list of eligible bachelors from Tiree; and in his more serious moments he revealed a remarkable knowledge of the affairs of the parish and hoped that we would find a minister of our own soon. At last one of his companions tugged his sleeve anxiously and suggested that they were falling behind schedule and should be getting on their way. 'What!' he said. 'And not sample that cooking I smelt as we passed the school?' And that, in itself, was enough to endear him to the women who had devoted time and care to preparing the spread.

Down in the school the two-seater desks had been draped in white cloths and were laden with enough food to feed a multitude without the invocation of miracle. The Moderator wandered among them, picking a mutton sandwich from one, a buttered oatcake here and a pancake there, and demanding constant re-fills of tea. The only man who did more justice to the bill of fare was a tall, athletic man, incongruously dressed for the sunshine in a dark coat and a black Anthony Eden hat, who had uttered only one sentence since he had arrived in the village, but it was destined to be remembered more vividly than the Moderator's text from St Luke.

'Who the hell's that?' somebody at last managed to whisper to big Geordie MacLellan, who had gone through the proceedings with a sullen expression that had hung like a thunder-cloud on a sunny day.

'I don't know who the bugger is,' gritted Geordie. 'He was standing outside St Columba Church in Stornoway with a suitcase, and when I stopped he asked me if I was the driver from Scarista. I couldn't get a word out of him the whole way down except grumbles about how long the journey was taking, and the poor bloody Armstrong doing forty –' He twitched on a smile that didn't reach his eyes as the Moderator drifted over and asked him what he did for a living.

'Who's the bloody half-wit with the Armstrong Siddley?' asked the man in the Anthony Eden hat when he felt that the Moderator was out of earshot.

The Boer War veteran pretended that he didn't know.

'I was standing on the pavement outside the County Hotel when he pulled up and when I asked him if he was the driver from Scaliscro he told me he was. I was due at an important meeting at Scaliscro Lodge at midday, but that fellow's getting me back there if it's midnight when we arrive. God knows what trouble he's caused!'

'Ach well, so long as you enjoyed yourself. I saw them giving you a seat at the front of the church seeing you were a stranger –'

'I happen to be a Roman Catholic. And I don't speak Gaelic!'

'And what's a man without Gaelic doing in these parts?' The Boer War veteran was a chatty, friendly man.

'I'm from the War Department.'

'Ach well,' said the old man tamping his pipe to hide the twinkle in his eye. 'Just once in a while it can be a good thing not to understand Gaelic.'

The man from the War Department looked puzzled, but decided to move towards the sandwiches while the Boer War veteran continued smiling to himself, remembering that the County Hotel and St Columba Church were, indeed, on the same street in Stornoway and that, in Geordie MacLellan's vocabulary 'outside' was an elastic sort of a word.

At long last the Moderator yielded to the supplications of his acolytes and allowed himself to be propelled gently towards the waiting Daimler which eased him off in the direction of his next appointment, having won for himself the love of a whole community and leaving behind him an aura of blessing and goodwill. As soon as his car moved off the company erupted into a chatter of relief and self-congratulation and the comparing of notes. Nobody paid any attention to the children descending on the remains of the feast; and only the Boer War veteran had noticed the agility with which the man in the Anthony Eden hat had flung himself into the back of the Armstrong Siddley as big Geordie tried to make his escape in the wake of the Moderator's convoy. In their twos and threes the visitors from other villages began to say their farewells; hired buses revved their engines and belched smoke, impatiently summoning their respective detachments of Women's Rural Institutes, Fishermen's Associations, and Congregational Boards to climb aboard. Grandparents and uncles and aunts would linger on for a day or two, taking advantage of the rare excuse for a holiday in the Southlands; but, by and large, the excitement which had taken weeks to bring its climax was ebbing pleasurably around us as we stood.

It was Farquhar the roadman who finally brought reality thudding back. 'Hey, children!' he shouted. 'Don't scoff every last morsel just because it's there; leave some over for the fank tomorrow. The least you can do is save your poor mothers some work after all they've been through already, and into the bargain give us a better picnic than usual at the fank.' There was a murmur of approval from adults of both sexes and the men loosened their ties and flung off their jackets as they began to give a hand restoring the schoolroom to normal as the women folded away table-cloths and napery for washing or else packed the remaining food into parcels for the next day.

43

'Do you think the weather's going to hold then?' somebody asked Farquhar, who had the reputation of being good at reading the skies.

'No doubt about it,' he replied. 'The Moderator's going to be in the islands for two days yet, and he's the kind for whom good weather lasts!'

It was a great tribute for a man who had a reputation for being 'worldly' and grudging a sunny Sabbath as a wasted working day.

When the last remains of the food had been rescued from them, the youngsters scattered away to play. For my part I was left awaiting a request to help here or there, but for the most part just listening, or answering the occasional question that someone might occasionally fling my way. More and more the awkward loneliness of adolescence was beginning to haunt me; I was very tall for my age and what was referred to despairingly by teacher and parents alike as my 'slouch' was, I suspect in retrospect, a self-conscious effort to conceal the fact that I was a head taller than my contemporaries; each winter my boot size had jumped by two so that, by now, I was wearing a full size larger than my father. For lack of anything better to do I would still, occasionally, seek to join in the pastimes of my younger brothers and their contemporaries but I couldn't help but be contemptuous of their attempts at whatever imaginary edifices or citadels they were trying to create, nor could I avoid using crude logic to scorn their fantasies; the result was that they evolved ways of making it clear that they didn't want my company and I would be left to wander off on my own like a gawky pup rejected by frolicking kittens – hurt more by the snub than the scratches.

Because I had failed to win the bursary to High School at my first attempt my pride was hurt anyway, but what made things worse was that my immediate contemporaries, who had either left school or had moved on to High School, had suddenly become denizens of another world – a world of adulthood in which they were either labourers in vineyards in which they earned their keep, or, what was even more difficult to accept, knowledgeable snobs who came back to the village on holiday, wearing good shoes and using English swear-words even, occasionally, in front of their parents; and though their

44

smoking was still secret they held their cigarettes elegantly between the tips of their first and second fingers and blew the smoke out slowly through their noses. I marvelled at how quickly higher education lifted people into a different social class and I could only steel myself to wait for the day when I could join it.

At home things were little better. My father – who had been parent and friend and subtle mentor – had been delighted when I had won the scholarship, but, almost overnight, the relationship between us had changed; he became impatient with my attempts at adult conversation, sceptical of my arguments, and angry at my contradictions. Was I too much of a gentleman to wind bobbins for his loom? Would I deign to weave a couple of yards of tweed while he did some croftwork, and if I did would it be too much to expect that if I got a false 'cross-thread' I would spare time to correct it rather than ruin his reputation as a weaver? Would it ruin my golf swing if I exercised my back to bring home a sack of peat from the hillside? Sometimes I felt the blood rush to my face and the tears swelling my eyelids as I bit them back and wished that he would just ask me to do things wheedlingly or sly-humouredly as he used to do: at other times I was angry with myself that I couldn't keep an edge of insolence out of the tone in which I spoke to him. My mother's attitude had altered less, except that, occasionally, she got tired of getting caught in the cross-fire and she would order me to get out from under her feet when she found me, after yet another brush with my father, crouched in a corner with a book.

Books were becoming an essential leaven of my being instead of just the indulgence of pleasure to which my father himself had led me; but because we had never got out of the small hut which had been supposed to be temporary when it had been built ten years before, and because the family had increased in number and in bulk, privacy was hard to find. On fine days I could occasionally escape down to the rocky shore of the Blue Skerries with the volume of the moment tucked under my ganzie, and I would lose track of time and place till the pangs of hunger or the prickles of conscience would urge me home. Books were an escape from everything, even though they were few and far between; Edgar Wallace, Algernon

45

Blackwood, Annie S Swan, O Douglas, Leslie Charteris all plucked at different chords of the imagination as they became available in the wooden crates delivered to the school by the County Lending Library; those moulded and catered for the admissible curiosities: the ever gnawing pangs of sexuality which could find no physical outlet in the village, nor prurient gratification in the carefully vetted volumes of the library, had to be satisfied by the occasional dog-eared volume brought home by one of my seaman cousins – literary titillates like *No Orchids for Miss Blandish* or *The Awful Confessions of Maria Monk.*

The abrasion of the special relationship with my father saddened me although I didn't understand it as sadness then; the only sadness now is that it never got a chance to heal because of time and inexorable circumstances – except for a brief spell, and through unusual circumstances, four years later. I learnt – as every man learns in time – that part of the tension was the inevitable father and son spasm of puberty; it took me longer to understand that there was an Oedipus strand in reverse, and that it was bitter for him to see his own son escaping from what he was beginning to accept as his own imprisonment. God knows what reactions to those years of war had deluded him into thinking that a new croft in a new land would ever provide the fulfilment for which he craved; whatever they were they were as illusory as the geographical change for the alcoholic. He was, heart and mind, a man of books and letters, and it was only natural that his joy would be tempered with envy, and his own frustration more sharply focussed, by seeing the first of his family getting the chance to embark on the sort of life for which he himself craved, and in which he would have thrived.

Conversely, my relationships in the village strengthened in those difficult weeks during which my enforced idleness and my suspension between two worlds were both factors exacerbating the difficulties between my father and myself. Other parents are always more able to sympathise with the problems of other people's children than they are with those of their own, and where I was finding it increasingly difficult to communicate with my father I was finding it easier to talk to people like the Boer War veteran, who had a smile for every boy. There was the man who had decided to emigrate to Patagonia in his own boyhood, but had seized on the offer of a government-sponsored free passage to return home to volunteer for the navy in 1914; when other people were preaching the gospel of 'get up and get out and get on' he alone was adamant that there was a future for young people in our own island. 'After all,' he used to say. 'I've been and I've seen, and the grass was no greener.' The man with the hole in his cheek was a listener of infinite patience and the mark of the bullet always made me feel that the brush with death had given a new dimension to his wisdom: his wife was one of the early innocent loves of my life. She could keep up a sparkling conversation without making one feel callow, and she always had all the time in the world although she never sat down in a house where everything always shone. Whenever I pass the home where she lived, as I do all too rarely now, I can still imagine the taste of the Atholl Brose (sans alcohol) that she conjured from fine oatmeal and the freshest of fresh cream that she distilled from unfermented milk with the new-fangled separator in which she had invested to the astonishment of older women who had spent their days setting basins and waiting for the cream to rise. Alas I can only imagine the taste because she died long, long ago, and far too young. There were others too – men and women I had known from the day that the new village had begun on the site of the old one. Most of all, there was, of course, Old Hector whose life consisted entirely of spare time.

On the day of the Moderator's visit I had made several efforts to catch Old Hector on his own so that I could find out whether the postman had brought a reply to our advertisement. But he seemed to be in popular demand and every time I got within earshot of him somebody else intervened and engaged him in conversation. I tried catching his eye and raising my eyebrows in question, but all I got back was an exasperating blank stare. I could hardly wait for milking time to come, and when I did finally prepare to set off my father remarked, 'You're in a devil of a hurry to milk Hector's cow tonight; I wish I could see you jumping to it when I ask you to do something around the croft.' I couldn't think of a reply and left the house, conscious once again, that by not responding I

47

had created, quite unintentionally, a suggestion of deliberate insolence. It was always the way things seemed to work out. But, for sure, I couldn't tell him why I was so keen to see Old Hector.

He was sitting crouched over his fire in the middle of the floor when I arrived; he was looking very morose, and my first reaction was that he had received a rejection.

'Are you going off your head? How the devil could I get a refusal when nobody knows what I did? I'm the only proposer in history who can only get an acceptance, and that's what's worrying me. I didn't get anything. That bloody Calum the Post could conjure up a holiday out of a summer shower! As soon as he heard of the Moderator's visit he was going round the place declaring a public holiday for himself, and saying it wouldn't be right for a public servant to be trundling the roads in a red van during a religious festival. Religious festival my backside! He doesn't even belong to the Church of Scotland ...' He spat towards the fire and missed – sure proof that he was out of kilter. I hadn't realised that there hadn't been a mail delivery that day, but it didn't surprise me; Calum didn't require much excuse to cancel his northward delivery trip and jam his delivery and collection trips into the following day. He was a man of measured tread in a community upon which the Royal Mail had not impressed urgency. But the old man's next question did catch me unawares.

'What made you tell your mother?'

'Me! I didn't tell my mother or anybody else.' I bridled at the very thought that he could suspect me. 'What on earth makes you think such a rotten thought?'

'I heard her discussing it with Hetty MacInnes – that's what. Down in the schoolhouse when they were waiting for the Moderator to arrive for his tea. I wasn't able to get into the church so I thought I might as well make something of the day, and I slipped down to the school to make sure that I got a bite to eat at least. And the two of them were in spate and laughing their heads off; they shut up as soon as they saw me.'

'What were they saying?'

'Your mother was going on about there being no fool like an old fool; and Hetty was saying "There's something romantic about it too; him up there all alone in his wee house waiting for

48

a letter from the woman of his dreams –" and she stopped and went as red as a beetroot when she saw me ...'

I burst out laughing before he could finish his sentence. I had been short of reading material and I'd been following the serial in the *People's Friend*, the weekly women's magazine which my mother and Hetty shared. I recognised the description of the ageing Dr Dalhousie waiting to hear from the childhood sweetheart with whom he had managed to make contact after forty years, to find that she was still unmarried.

'You may be right in thinking of yourself as an old fool,' I said. 'But you've got a great conceit to be thinking you're the only one. My mother and Hetty were talking about a story from a women's magazine!'

He looked relieved, but I felt a qualm of conscience yet again as it was brought home to me how much the whole thing was preying on Old Hector's mind. He was obviously going through his every day fearful of the result of what I always regarded as 'our advertisement' and even more fearful that any of the villagers would guess at the identity of 427. What I did appreciate (and he didn't) was that every post office in the Hebrides was not necessarily thronged with eager females jostling to catch the first postal collection with an acceptance of a vague and rather dubious proposal of marriage from some unknown person with a number instead of a name. But, on the other hand, I hadn't foreseen some of the problems that had suggested themselves to Hector during his sleepless hours.

'What happens if the most promising reply comes from a Roman Catholic?'

'You ignore it. You tear up the letter.'

'Very smart. But do you really think she's going to say right away that she's a Catholic; after all, you didn't say we wanted a Protestant woman, did you?'

I was thoroughly tired of the way the burden of responsibility was thrust on me whenever he got jittery.

'I didn't say I wanted anybody; I'm not a *retired seaman*. If the best reply comes from a Roman Catholic you'll just have to convert – that's that!'

'Damnation, you really are out of your senses. There's been only one Roman Catholic in Harris ever, and I'm not going to be the third. In any case I'd have to convert *to* the Church of

49

Scotland before I could convert out of it. I've never been anything special – just a fellow who goes to church on a Sunday if the day's good –'

I wasn't quick enough to point out to him that becoming a Catholic would absolve him from even casual attendance since there was no Catholic Church in the island. In any case, I had just remembered another problem, and I cut in before he could expand on his church attitudes.

'Hey, just wait. There's something else. Do you realise that the *Gazette* doesn't sell only in the Outer Hebrides; it goes to Glasgow and London and Canada? And my auntie sends her copy to a cousin in West Africa when she's read it herself.'

He looked at me to see if I was joking, and decided that I wasn't.'

'So now you're trying to tell me she could be Catholic and black!'

'No, I'm not saying that. Although it could be true it's not likely. What I'm trying to say is that the mail takes a long time crossing the Atlantic and you might have to wait a month or more for a letter from, say, Canada –'

His eyes were glittering and he had allowed his pipe to go out. I knew he was getting angry, but I couldn't find a way out of a conversation which he himself had started. But I did, quite sincerely, have a vision (improbable though it might be) of Hector finding himself a nice, decent, wife with a streak of jealousy in her who would have to add to the other hazards of her early marriage a steady trickle of letters from the four corners of the world, from panting females of varying creeds and contours offering to marry her husband and bring a dowry of diamonds. I had seen enough old copies of the *News of the World* to know that ever-increasing hazards beset passionate marriages made in Heaven far less postal ones made in Harris.

He stabbed in my direction with his cutty pipe.

'Look here, my boy. Just get this into your head. If any woman is damn fool enough to answer that advertisement, I will size her up from her letter and if I don't like the sound of her the letter goes into the fire there, and I know enough to know that nobody could sue a number for breach of promise even if a promise had been made.' That got that off his chest and he began to re-light his pipe with his modest self-assurance

50

restored. 'And I'll tell you another thing – you yourself have put my mind at ease although that's not what you meant to do; you said that if I got a letter from a Catholic I could tear it up. Well, I can tear up every damn letter that comes if I feel like it. I don't know why I let myself get into these fits of depression – it's from being alone too much. Go and milk the cow!'

I had never heard him being so decisive in his life. I got up without saying a word, picked up the pail, and went out to find Primrose. It was a mark of his new-found self-confidence that he didn't bother to waddle out after me. As I got down to the business of milking I thought to myself that if Old Hector did, by some strange chance, find himself a wife, she'd have to wait a week or two before she found the real Hector. I found myself hoping that the miracle would happen and that a nice woman would come along. Somewhere, there must be one who would be prepared to put up with his shortcomings from the goodness of her heart and *for* the goodness of his. I realised that my affection for him was deeper than pity, and kinder than pity by far.

When I got back into the house he had the little black teapot nestling on a bed of peat embers, and he began to pour as I set the milk. I searched out a reasonably long cigarette dout from behind the plate in his dresser where I kept a secreted supply. He held out the spill with which he had kindled his own pipe.

'Do you know,' he said, 'I was sitting here thinking while you were out at the milking. You were joking about me and a Catholic earlier on, and the thought came to me that maybe the Catholics have something after all. They go in for all that pomp and ceremonial and fancy stuff that the Presbyterians miscall them for, but did you notice how people liked the Moderator today – in all his fancy lace and buckled shoes. I think people secretly fancy a wee bit of colour in their lives, and we're too black and white altogether. Just you look at the Bible which I read more than you think when I'm alone here – it hasn't got a single bad word to say against beauty. It talks about the beauty of the lilies of the field, and the beauty of holiness, and the temple which is called Beautiful. And wasn't it three things of beauty that the wise men brought to the infant Christ?' He stopped and stared into the fire for a long time, and let the pipe in his hand go out. 'And we're blessed with a beautiful village here, you know. We forget it sometimes; it's only when I remember my boyhood that I remember the village as being beautiful – for most of the time I take it for granted; but I remembered the beauty of it that time when I thought I was dying in Singapore – by Jove I remembered it then ...

'You see, boy, I remember this place long before there was any thought of you people coming and settling in it, and it wasn't just beauty we had but happiness too although we were poor and had no land of our own. And one reason was that the kind of minister we had here was always a man of the soil – a man who worked his glebe there, and tended his sheep during the week just like any farmer. He knew what he was talking about. He was never a narrow-minded man ... And then, when you people came, your men were men who had seen danger and war and they wouldn't have put up with bloody-minded holiness. I think that's why there's a problem finding a minister now; the right kind don't come by the dozen. In the end it won't be us who'll find a minister; the right man will find us ...'

He struggled to his feet.

'And that's the gospel according to Old Hector. And that's the end of it ... it's time you were off home, and be back here for Calum the Post coming in the morning!' He patted my shoulder and ushered me out.

My way back home was down past the empty manse and the empty church, and I realised that I had got used to the idea that we didn't have a minister. I'd got used to the village being without one. I didn't even know if they were still looking for one.

As I reached the road the Armstrong Siddley came towards me and passed; the driver never looked my way and I only caught a glimpse of his white face staring straight ahead, but I knew that the look on big Geordie MacLellan's face was the look of a man who had done two hires to Stornoway for free.

I was still smiling to myself when I got into the house.

'Hello lad,' said my father. 'You're looking in a good mood and it's just as well – because we're a man short for the sheep-gathering tomorrow and you're going to have to do the south shoulder with me.'

I stared at him.

'No need to sulk now. A day on the hill will do your lungs a

52

power of good – and your mind too, before you set off to a gentleman's life in High School.'

That was typical of his misunderstanding of my every reaction nowadays. I wasn't sulking. I liked the hill. But I knew that if I went to the hill my mother would have to milk Hector's cow, and I wondered what on earth she would think when Calum the Post arrived with a sack of mail for a man who hadn't been known to receive a letter in years.

Chapter Four

The dawn is always cold underfoot although people with boots don't realise it. It was the rasping of my soles together to get the circulation going that brought my father out of his morning reverie.

'Shouldn't you be putting a pair of boots on for the hill? The heather's beginning to harden and you'll be hobbling like a duck on stubble before the day's half through.'

'I'll be O.K. – I'll be all right.' I corrected myself hastily; O.K. was beginning to creep into Gaelic usage and my father abominated the increasing use of 'Ganglish' which was already beginning to erode our language of every day, and dismissed the younger generation who were succumbing to it as 'illiterates in two languages'.

We were sitting together over our bowls of oatmeal brose and skimmed milk with the kettle beginning to hiss towards a new boil for tea. Although the days of hardship were relatively in the past our diet was still the diet of poverty which has become the diet of many fortunes in modern times. Weekday breakfasts were still oatmeal brose, or porridge, with skimmed milk (the cream being saved up for butter-making) with a boiled egg and oatcakes to follow. The main meal of the day was invariably salt herring and potatoes during the winter, with a switch to fresh fish during the summer depending on the regularity of the 'fish landry' as Montgomery's van had now come to be known. Normally Sunday was the only meat day although, perceptibly, Fray Bentos was not only creeping onto the menu but also into the vocabulary of our every day as the synonym for tinned meat regardless of its constituents or manufacturer. It is interesting but sad to look back over the years and realise that one was present when a language began to go into its death throes. Gaelic had survived the deliberate Government policy which had tried to extinguish it over a century and a half but, in the thirties, the acceleration of scientific progress with its new vernacular, the opening up of the Highlands to tourists, the invasion of newspapers and attractive magazines in English, the importation of 'English' mini-bureaucrats to positions of key importance ... all these things were beginning to undermine people's confidence in their own native language and relegate it in their subconscious to a workaday status, like a worn-out pullover useful for 'around the house' while English was the Sunday suit for high-days and holidays. When packaged foods began to creep in as money became more plentiful they wrought their own particular destructions – why, for example, bother to adapt a Gaelic word when 'loff' was an easy-on-the-tongue corruption for the mainland bread that was arriving in ever-increasing quantities in increasingly attractive and hygienic waxed wrapping and rendering the baking board and the griddle obsolete. The process was just beginning to begin.

'You and your O.K.,' my father said. 'You'll be as bad as the Reverend George before you know where you are!' The 'Reverend George' was one of the lay preachers who came to us on circuit during the period of vacancy in our church; unlike many worthy men who shared the round with him, he had spent a few months at a college before systematically failing a series of exams, but not before acquiring a rare conceit of himself to which he gave expression by interlarding his conversations and sermons with reams of English. 'You get it into your head that your own language is a great and beautiful language,' father went on. 'Some people claim that it was the language spoken in the Garden of Eden but I suspect that that's as doubtful as some of the Reverend George's theology. And English is a language of great power too – and beauty, as you've heard in Lord MacAulay's poetry. But when you mix the two together it's like crossing a sheepdog and a greyhound – you get a mongrel that's good for neither one thing nor another.'

My spirits rose. My father was back to his old form, and in the kind of mood which, over the years, had drawn us most closely together. The day on the hill promised to be good.

As we set off together a wreath of mist was wrapped round the shoulders of Bleaval like a silken scarf. Below, the mountain was purplish brown where the bloom on the heather was already beginning to give way to the autumn. The top, which was chilly on the hottest summer day, was etched grey and back-lit by the sun, which had already risen but hadn't yet cleared the top of the mountain, and I knew that by the time we reached the highest point of the ridge we'd be glad of the bottles of whey my father was carrying in his make-shift knapsack. Neither of us spoke except that, once in a while, he'd mutter to Fraoch to keep to heel; the dog had been this way before and he was restless and twitching to get on with his job of rounding up the sheep. He was a loveable, loyal animal and would follow any of the family through fire, but my father was a notoriously bad trainer and poor Fraoch had none of those finely honed techniques that will take a sheepdog snaking over a mile of moorland, tuned in to whistles too silent for the human ear, to separate one particular sheep from a flock. We would walk three times the distance that some of the crofters would do; we would have to get behind the sheep in order to drive them in while some of the more skilled neighbours would get their dogs to bring the sheep to them. For that reason, I suspected, we were given the easiest beat, and it was face-saving good fortune that it happened to be the one most geographically convenient to our croft. Now and again, in the distance, I could hear an occasional cough or a discreet whistle: I knew that along the foot of the mountain eight men were climbing, careful not to disturb the sheep till they were able to cordon them off at the mountain top in order to sweep them back down before them towards the fank at the Brown Shore.

When our village had been founded, the Board of Agriculture had ordained a souming of fifty sheep per crofter; that being calculated to be the number – a total of five hundred and fifty including the landlord's hundred and the minister's fifty – that the in-bye and the moorland grazing could sustain.

But recent landlords hadn't been interested in sheep and we'd had no minister for a while so the more adventurous crofters had quietly allowed their sheepstock to expand; even the less adventurous couldn't be expected to be highly numerate when it suited themselves not to be and the souming was now given only token observance. That day we would expect to bring some eight hundred sheep off the hill, including the season's lambs. In the townsman's legend sheep are stupid animals, but that is far from being the case, as any shepherd knows who has seen the understanding look in a sheep's eye as he tries to help her with a difficult lambing. And they have a highly developed sense of territory. Although we were bounded on three sides by other townships, there were no boundary fences; yet it was rarely that one of our sheep strayed off our mountain or one of our neighbours' animals wandered over to us. And when one did, it was, often as not, a sheep that had been sold from one township to another – or even its descendant – that was returning home. The sheep that we passed, nestled in the heather, on our way up the hill, were newly wakened and chewing their morning cud; they gazed at us incuriously without stirring, as much as to say, 'We know what you're up to; we'll see you on your way back!' Only the lambs, who were new to the game, showed flinches of panic and rushed to their dams.

The mist seemed to be retreating in front of us as we climbed, and when we finally reached the top edge of Bleaval's shoulder the day was crystal clear. Even while the sun was hot on the top of one's head one could feel the pinch of the mountain air on one's face. We had taken a good hour to reach our point of return, but it would take some of the men who were going to the summit another half-hour and they would take half an hour's rest then; so we had a good hour to wait. We sat down and my father unscrewed the top out of one of the bottles of whey. The scene was one that was familiar to me, and when I see it now, occasionally, from the cramped seat of an aeroplane, it comes as an illogical shock that it hasn't changed, and I fancy that if I could conjure up a whiff of that sharp mountain air time would roll back with the memory. But alas …

Behind us the back of Bleaval sloped down to the

fragmented, craggy coast and coves of the Eastlands and the shores of the Minch. Thither, a hundred years ago, our forebears from our village and its neighbours had been evicted to make way for the sheepfarms. There, among the selfish rocks, they had built up, laboriously over the years, with seaweed and scraped soil, the isolated little patches of fertility in which they had grown their potatoes and their tussocks of corn. Here and there they had drained small marshes and rescued slivers of arable land. With aching backs they had created oases among the Lewisian gneiss – enough to feed themselves along with the fish they could haul from the Minch. In the same way as we had returned ourselves to the west from the Northlands, so the descendants of those people had returned too, and created new villages along the coast from our own. But that had only been a thinning of the east coast population; down there in the morning light the patches among the rocks were still green with new corn, and smoke was rising from the modern new homes that had sprung up. But even then we knew that the Eastlands were living on loaned time, and without sufficient land and without any hopes of industry the population would age and shrink as life came to depend more and more on 'folding money'. The Minch was rich in fish still but, already, the rumbling and grumblings were beginning about invading trawlers scraping it clean.

Beyond the Minch lay the deceptive mountains of Skye – pale grey and listless in the morning light like old ladies resting on their elbows, but it needed only a gust of north wind ruffling down the Minch, or a scudding cloud across the sun to change them into hard-edged, lowering menace. I've seen it happening to them from that aeroplane seat, and that way too – even in their sudden ability to change – there is a continuity. And, behind the Coolins, the mountains of Ross and Sutherland, culminating in the grandeur of Cuil Beg, Cuil Mor, Arkle and Canisp … I never could get the order right, and there seems to be little need to now!

In front, one could have been looking out on another world. It was a surprise to be reminded how far we had climbed; our own huge beach that filled the entire view from the window of home was only one bay among several now, and the breakers on it that I knew to be high and foaming looked like a gentle white frill on a web of blue that stretched out to infinity, broken only here and there by specks of islands that the distance had stripped of character. To the right, peeping out from behind the Point of Huisinis but many miles away, the Flannan Isles; in the centre, Gaisgeir; and to the far left and furthest still away, St Kilda – empty by then, but once a valued piece of Clan MacLeod territory yielding rents that were well worth the collecting.

It was the movement that broke my day-dream as my father put the stopper back into the whey bottle, drew the back of his hand across his lips, and felt for his pipe. His eyes were narrowed as he gazed out across the miles to where the sea and sky met in such a compatibility of colour that there was no defined horizon. There was a crinkle of smile at the corner of his mouth, and I knew from experience that he was going to embark on one of his long discourses – yarn, fable, or theory, since there was no cause for exhortation or upbraiding.

'It's strange –' he said, and paused. 'Strange to think that somewhere away out there there's a whole country swallowed up with all its people by the sea.'

'What do you mean?'

He pretended to look surprised. 'What do you mean by "what do you mean?" You're not going to tell me you don't know about it?'

'No. I don't.'

'You've never heard of Neil-who-got-lost?'

'Never.'

'Well, well, well … It was my own grandfather who told me the story – the old man they called the Cleric – and I wouldn't be surprised if it was right on this spot that he told me. You see, I used to come here from the Northlands to visit my old grandfather on my mother's side in the same way as you've been going back to the Northlands to visit your Big Grandfather for the last few summers. And I used to climb Bleaval with him just as we've done today – not to gather sheep or anything like that, but just because the old man liked to come up to the top of the mountain and, as he got older, he used to say that I was good at finding the easiest ways to the top …

'According to him Neil-who-got-lost was one of the few

men who ever worked a boat out from these shores; as you know it's almost impossible to work a boat out from an exposed sandy beach like ours although I believe natives in the South Sea Islands manage to cope with bigger breakers than we ever see. Anyway, although Neil-who-got-lost (nobody knew any other name for him even in the Cleric's day) was a great dreamer and a great seaman at the same time and it's not often those two characteristics go together. He got himself a little boat – a coracle made with hides, which shows you how long ago it was – and he worked her out from the Red Geo where we fish for cuddies and saithe nowadays. God knows there's not much shelter there, but it's better than the open beach and the coracle was so light that he could climb up the rocks with it on his back like a snail with its shell.

'In those days men didn't have crofts to tie them down, and every day that was fine for fishing at all Neil-who-got-lost (that wasn't the name they knew him by then, of course) would launch his coracle and get out behind the breakers and sit fishing there in the middle of the bay, just catching enough shelter from Toe Head to make his long sit comfortable. Goodness only knows what he thought about, as he sat there for hour after hour with a line over the side, hauling in a cod now and again, or a lythe or a ling, because fish were plentiful in those days and with the coast being so bad hereabouts there was nobody to disturb them. Perhaps he made songs to pass the time for himself when the fish weren't biting – the old Cleric didn't know, because, of course, if he made songs they got lost with him. Sometimes on a particularly quiet day he would sit out in his coracle till the dusk came down and then he would row quietly back to the Red Geo. As you know yourself the sea is never quieter than when the tide is full on a still, calm evening.

'There came an evening, however, when Neil lost track of time and place all together, and when he came to himself he realised that a whiff of a breeze from the land had crept up on him unawares and that he was drifting away out past Toe Head. Not that that worried him at first; he was a good oarsman and he had been out that far often enough before. He thought that all he had to do was put the oars on her and pull a little harder than usual and keep pulling – the way any wise man does when things aren't going his way. But it wasn't just as easy for Neil as he thought. The sky had been darkening without his noticing it, and a stiff cold breeze was strengthening from the east and giving courage to the tide as they say, and, row as he might, Neil was making no headway and at last he realised that he'd be wise to save what strength he had left till he found a more hopeful purpose for it. He shipped his oars and lay down on the bottom of the boat so as to give the breeze less to get hold of.

'Now there isn't a sound in the world as sleep-making as the slip-slapping of the sea on the side of a boat if you're not the kind of person who worries about it; and Neil certainly wasn't that. Without knowing he was doing it he fell asleep, and when he woke up he thought he had just dozed off for a few moments because when you don't know whether the sun's in the east or in the west it's very difficult to tell the dusk from the dawn. But when the day began to get brighter instead of darker the man in the boat realised that he had slept the night through, and he wouldn't have been mortal if he hadn't been worried when he couldn't see a glimpse of land in front of him or behind him or on either side. There are, in life, times when there is nothing you can do to help yourself. People will tell you otherwise, but it's true – times in fact, when by trying to do something you are only making your state of affairs worse. That's where men who have a belief are lucky. They just sit back and let God take over, and, whatever happens – be it to their own good or their bad – they say that it was God's will.

'I don't know what Neil did, but, for sure, he drifted for three days and he could hardly believe his eyes when he woke up one morning and found himself almost ashore on a beautiful white strand on the greenest island he had ever seen. For a moment or two, when he saw the white beach, he thought he was back home again; but there was something about the green-ness of the land which convinced him that this was a place he had never seen in his life before. But what could he do? He wasn't going to push off and start rowing, was he? That would have been both the height and the depth of madness at the same time. No. He did what any man would do; he stepped ashore and pulled the coracle up behind him – so high up that no tide would reach it no matter how high

61

might be the tides that they had in a place like that.

'He was just on the point of wandering off to see what he could see when a light finger of fear touched him lest this might be the kind of place where mortals didn't thrive, and with the fear came memory of the knife in his pocket – a knife on which a wise old woman had once put a charm to protect him from evil, and just to be on the safe side he took the knife and buried it in the sand two paces to the left of the stone to which he had tied the coracle, and three paces ahead. And he set off on his search for whatever might be there that he couldn't see. He hadn't gone far when he met people who greeted him with smiles and with kindness, and gave him food to eat and drink to drink; but when he asked them where he was they just looked at him with faraway looks in their eyes and talked round his question without ever coming to the answer. And that's how it was for days. The farther he wandered the more beautiful the land became, and round each corner there was sunshine and never a trace of shadow.

'Well, I needn't tell you what happened. One of those days he met a woman who was as young as the rest but even more beautiful, and when she smiled at him it was as if he had known her all his life and wanted to get to know her more. And in due course they got married – not by a minister or a priest because there was no such person that he could see, but a man who seemed to be a little older than the rest; not in the way he looked or in the way he walked but, somehow, in the way he seemed to think. And the years went by – or the days, rather, because you can't count years when there are no winters. He was happy but not fully happy, and he kept wondering to himself why not; then one night a truth came to him out of the back of his mortal memory and he remembered that his happinesses from the past had been because he had always had sadnesses against which to measure them. And the more he thought about it, the more disjaskit his thinking became and he got to the stage when he couldn't sleep a full night nor keep awake a full day. Then, suddenly – and it was the first sudden thing that had happened to him in that place – he began to long for home, and for simple things like a glimpse of Bleaval on which we're sitting here, and a shower of rain, a flake of crotal on a rock, the sound of a storm, and the things that you and I take for granted and sometimes don't even like. The longing grew in him like a tubercle in the soul and, at last, he said to the woman of his life, *Come with me, back to my country and my people; I want to show them the beautiful bride that I've found for myself, and I want to show them to you.*

'She looked at him with her eyes full of the first clouding that he had ever seen there, and he felt a pain in his heart for having troubled her. *You've got the madness of mortals*, she said. *I'll go to the ends of our world here with you but not a step beyond, for I will never be part of that craziness that makes your kind want to go searching out sorrow the instant they've found content. And even if I wanted to go with you are you foolish enough to think that they'd let us?*

'In the very business of thinking human thoughts again, human cunning came back to him, and for the first time in their life together he set out to deceive her. *All right*, he said. *I accept the wisdom of what you're saying, and it was madness that made me talk the way I did. But at least come down to my boat with me and let's go for a plowter round the bay; I've got a great yearning to feel oars in my hands again.*

'She looked at him with love back in her eyes again. *If that'll make you happy it's not much to ask and even less for me to give. Let's do that thing for your happiness, but for your greater happiness, put out of your mind any hope or thought of hope that you'll ever get beyond the outer reef at the mouth of the bay. Perhaps the very tiredness of the oars in your hands will be the thing that'll teach you forevermore to be content with the good fortune you've got.*

'They went down together, and he was pleased beyond telling to see that his boat was just as he had left it, without any trace of rot or decay or sign of the length of time she had been there. Even the oars were just as he had placed them. He went to the stone to which he had tied the mooring rope, and he took two paces to the left of the stone and then turned and took three paces straight ahead of him, and when his companion wasn't looking he bent down and scooped the charmed knife out of the sand where he had hidden it and put it in his pocket. *Take a hold of one gunwale*, he said. *And together we'll carry her to the water.* She laughed and did as he told her. *It'll be the first and the last time of my life*, she said as she helped him carry the boat to the sea.

'No sooner had he started rowing than he felt the strange listlessness that he'd lived with for so long leaving him, and he felt his old strength coming back to him; and his old thoughts came back too, only this time the picture of Bleaval was crisp and clear in his mind, and he could almost feel the shower that he imagined to be sweeping across it at that very moment. He had always been a rower in a thousand, but that day he rowed with a strength that he had never imagined himself capable of, and in no time at all they were at the reef at the mouth of the bay.

'*This is where you turn back*, his companion said, smiling, but she didn't know about the charmed knife in his pocket nor the wise old woman's spell. *There's no turning back*, he said. *Not ever again!* And with that the coracle burst out of the bay past the reef and into the open sea which was ruffled with the kind of breeze that Neil hadn't felt on his face for as long as he could remember. And the fact that it was on his face, of course, meant that it was helping him on his journey. He didn't even notice that, for the first time since he had met her, there were tears in the eyes of the woman. And if he didn't notice them immediately there was no chance that he would notice them again, because she lifted the shawl from round her shoulders and buried her face in it. He was so busy with his rowing that he didn't notice her shoulders heaving as she sobbed.

'Nobody knows how long he rowed, but at last he made landfall and it was a beautiful evening just as it had been when he had been fishing for the cod and the lythe and the ling. The sea was flat calm, and he was in the hurry of a man at last in sight of home; he didn't even bother to go round the Blue Skerry to the Red Geo. He just let the boat ride the unbroken waves and beached her in the corner that you know – just where the sandy beach ends and the rocky shore begins. He hailed a man who was standing on the edge of the shore, and the man came down to look at him in wonder – looking at the stranger who had come out of the sea. And Neil couldn't believe that his eyes were seeing a stranger because from his boyhood he had known everybody who lived on that coast.

'*Who are you?* Neil asked in astonishment.

'*Who are you?* said the man on the shore, answering a

question with a question. *Who are you that comes out of the sea with the strange old woman?*

Neil turned round to look at his wife, and he felt the marrow draining from his bones. She had removed her shawl from her face and there, instead of the beautiful companion he had spent the unknown years with, was an ancient woman with a shrunken face and lines on it that could have been carved with a rusty knife. *Turn back while there is time*, she croaked. *Once before I gave you advice that you didn't take. In the name of all the spirits above and below the ocean take the advice that I'm giving you now. Turn your back to this shore of mortals and row with a mortal's strength while there is time. And let us get back to the land under the waves – to the land of the ever-young where my beauty will be restored to me; where we'll be young together in eternal sunshine. It is not often that a mortal is given a second chance of a happiness that he spurned. Turn back.*

'Neil looked sadly at Bleaval, and then at the frail-looking man standing at the sea's edge, and without another word he pushed his coracle back into the water. And the wind that had been in the west turned to the east and carried them both away out over the horizon. And the man on the shore stood looking after them in wonderment as they disappeared, and away at the back of his mind there stirred a story he had heard long ago about a man called Neil-who-was-lost.'

I had listened spell-bound. My father had always been a superb story teller, but it had been a long time since we had been close enough for him to tell me a story like that. Up there on the shoulder of Bleaval time had held its breath. My father laughed.

'I know what you're going to ask. You're going to use your clever brain and wonder how the story can be known if Neil-who-was-lost was really lost to another world. Well, one thing I'm going to tell you is that my grandfather, the Cleric, told me the story sitting here, or hereabouts, and he would have it that the man standing at the sea's edge was his own great-great-grandfather on his mother's side, and who was I to doubt him. And the other thing I'm going to tell you is that that story exists in one form or another in all sorts of parts of the world. Even the old Greeks had it, and they called their *land under the waves* Atlantis. But we have as good a claim to it as the Greeks ever had, because, if you look out there, you'll see St Kilda and the Flannan Isles on the horizon; and if the old Cleric was wrong when he told me that they are the tips of the mountains of that drowned land, then I'm only passing on to you a yarn that was passed on to me. But the funny thing is that men laugh at our Highland version of the story, but they call the Greek version a classic. That's the way of the world.'

From the top of Bleaval there came a whistle, signalling that the man with the hole in his cheek had reached the summit with his two good dogs and that the time had come to start driving the sheep down to the plain. My father got up and stretched himself, and felt for his pipe.

'You don't believe that story, do you?'

'No, of course I don't believe it, but –'

'Aye,' he said. 'That's always the way of it with boys when they reach your age. But I always think that a boy loses a lot when he learns to disbelieve.'

Chapter Five

The men of the village were mild of manner and moderate of language and, in the normal course of events, their most heated discussions would not have brought down the wrath of God on a vicarage. But on a sheep day it was different. It was as if the floodgates had been opened on the pent-up imprecations of frustrated weeks, and if the docile collies had been sensitive to the aspersions being hurled at the characters of themselves and their ancestors they would have leapt to follow the Gadarene swine. Instead, they slunk and stalked, and raced and froze, each with an inimical eye on his charges and a devoted one on his master. Unlike their owners the dogs worked silently, and for the first part of the drive the only sound was blasphemy. Then, slowly, the sheep began to raise echo; first the lambs in fear and then their mothers in reassurance. The older ones had been through it all before and, with a little encouragement, would probably have made their ways down to the fank in silent order; but the half-grown lambs were frightened and only the bravest of them would make a momentary stand and then, routed and embarrassed, would dive below his mother for a comforting teat, thumping her rear end up off the ground before being butted aside. Occasionally a seasoned old crock would glare defiance at a dog and thump her foreleg in challenge, and even the boldest dog would hang back for a moment till a skirl of Gaelic invective made him dart into the attack afresh.

My job, and that of the other young boys, was to mop up – to follow closely behind the dogs and search the scars and clefts in which wily old ewes and rams might have gone to ground in the hope of escaping the drive; although the principle aim of the August fank was to separate the lambs and forever wean them from their mothers, it was also in itself a 'cleaning up' operation designed to pull in beasts that had escaped shearing in the summer fanks, and lambs that had missed marking, or males that had been too young to castrate. It was also the fank at which farrow ewes and wethers would be taken to the croft and fattened for butchering at the beginning of winter. The drive had all the atmosphere of a cowboy round-up (sans horses) with whooping and shouting and the protest of the animals becoming more and more of a raucous chorus as they tightened into a semi-circle as we got nearer the fank by the shore. The fank itself was a large corral built of corrugated iron sheeting, showing patches of rust after ten years, with one big assembly area to receive the entire flock as it came off the hill, and with several smaller pens leading off it so that the sheep could be divided into their various categories and according to the various treatments being meted out to them. In my father's case, last year's crop would have his J brand burnt into their horns; young lambs overlooked in June would have their ears slit into his particular marking; all his beasts would have the blue spot of keel and the saddle-stripe of red renewed on the nape of their necks and on their backs respectively. There was a full day's work ahead, but, first of all, as the seven hundred sheep milled around the entrance there was much halloo-ing and beating of walking-sticks on the ground and frenzied barking as the dogs (who had worked silently till now) were given rein to use any method short of biting to coax a reluctant leader through the entrance of the main pen. Once one led the way, the rest – like the proverbial sheep – followed docilely.

Then, at last, time for the regaining of breath and the parcelling out of food. Sometimes, at that stage, the men would go home for a meal in order to give the sheep time to settle, but on that particular morning of sunshine there was plenty of left-over food from the Moderator's soiree and everybody sat on the rim of the shore for a picnic. It was one of the best-humoured fanks I could remember; there was a lot to talk about from the previous day – serious discussion and banter and a swopping of embellished yarns. The arrival of the drove had been seen from the village and various people who had not been on the hill themselves now drifted along either for the relaxation of a day out or to render extra assistance. One of them was Old Hector, and I was chagrined that he sat down at the far side of the group from me so that I couldn't satisfy my curiosity as to what (if anything) the mail-van had brought him. It was a dour-faced Geordie MacLellan who sat down without acknowledging the sarcastic salutations from left and right.

Once the business of the day got started there was no way in which I could button-hole Hector, but I did manage to mutter a hasty, 'Did the postman have anything?' as we brushed past one another, each of us astride a sheep being taken for belated clipping; it made my frustration worse to have him mutter a surly, 'Yes' out of the corner of his mouth just as somebody came to his rescue; manhandling a sheep is not a ploy for a man with gammy legs. I resigned myself to having to wait until the afternoon, when the most hectic part of the day's work would be easing off. But by the time that moment came Old Hector had been dispatched on one of the more unusual missions of his life.

When I referred to the moderation of the language of the crofters I exempted Tom-of-the-oaths because, at that time, he wasn't a resident of the village. I say resident, as opposed to native, because Tom-of-the-oaths was as native to the village as the crotal on the rocks. He was descended from a long and honourable line of people who had, for one reason or another, escaped the successive waves of evictions, but Tom himself had never settled down in the community because he had decided early on to become a professional shepherd and he had spent his life taking employment wherever it was offered to him. Occasionally it would be with a big farmer on the mainland; usually he found himself exiled to a hermit existence as keeper of the flock on one of the large, grassy, empty off-shore islands like Pabbay or Ensay or Kellegray – islands which had once been the homes of thriving populations but which had been emptied to make way for sheep-runs and had never been repopulated. It must have been on the mainland that Tom-of-the-oaths picked up his vocabulary, and it must have been in the loneliness of winters on the islands that he practised it. He had words that were unknown in our parts, but you could tell by the texture of them that they were potent curse-words; sometimes he stiffened them up even further by marrying them with four-letter English words with a cavalier illiteracy which rendered them all the more pungent; occasionally he melded them with our milder indigenous swear-words in a mutilating graft which could be awe-inspiring. 'I can't help you hearing Tom-of-the oaths,' my father used to say. 'But by God I can stop you from quoting him even if I have to leave the marks of my five fingers on your bare backside!'

His language was the only bad thing about Tom. In all other respects he was the kindliest and the gentlest of men; he was descended from one of the best poets that our island had ever produced and he could sing with a mellifluous voice not only his ancestor's songs but a vast anthology of the songs of the Hebrides. But shepherding was the love of his life, and although the great singing shepherd of the Old Testament would probably have disowned him as a fellow craftsman, Tom-of-the oaths had the cleaner conscience in the pursuits of the flesh. Otherwise I don't think my Great Aunt Rachel's sister would have married him when they were both rich in years.

Because shepherding was his hobby as much as his profession he attended every fank within travelling distance with the same sort of enthusiasm which some of his compatriots bestowed on revivalist meetings, and which modern aficionados confer on tennis tournaments. But it wasn't just as a spectator that he attended; he lent his skills wherever they were required, and his advice was as valuable as a vet's. In fact it was in an elementary veterinary capacity that he was most in demand. In those days there were no newfangled methods of castrating male lambs, nor any official practitioner to perform a task which had to be done unless the whole business of sheep-rearing was to dissolve into chaos since the balances of males to females was totally disproportionate in a species disinclined to monogamy. The

70

common way of castrating was for the owner of a young ram to hold the beast to his chest with the corresponding rear and forelegs firmly pinioned while the operator swiftly sliced off the top of the lamb's scrotum, pressed out one testicle till he could grip it with his teeth and swiftly and smoothly pull it out, spit it away, and then do the same with other. The whole business took less than half a minute and, strange as it may seem, the lamb bounded free and in seconds was frolicking with his fellow, unaware and, apparently, unwounded. It was not a job which many men relished doing, because of the associations, psychological and otherwise; but to Tom-of-the-oaths it was all in the day's work and, for that reason even if for no other, his presence was always appreciated at the summer fanks.

Part of the 'mopping up' aspect of the August fank was the dealing with the occasional lamb who had escaped the knife in June which was when most of the budding rams were turned into wethers. That year, a couple of ours had had a reprieve and fate had only now caught up with them. My father had pointed them out to me and made it my responsibility to catch them and hold them for Tom-of-the-oaths when he became available. It's a job which I would find repellent now – even if it weren't prohibited by law in favour of an even more barbarous practice – but the country boy is introduced early to the work of men, and the less appealing aspects of farming and shepherding don't even register on his consciousness far less scar his psyche.

I was holding the second lamb for Tom and he had already spat out the first testicle. He had just extracted the second one, slowly and carefully, and was still holding it in his teeth when there was a sudden loud metallic click to the side of us. I flinced and Tom froze. Had his mouth fallen open in surprise it might have been better, but it hadn't; and before he could react in any way there was another click just as I turned round to see the second of two elegant, Pringled, lipsticked ladies lowering her camera while her companion stared at us in smiling fascination.

It all happened so quickly that I didn't see what Tom did with the testicle; his back was already turned to me as I bent down to release the lamb, who bounded off as if he had

71

enjoyed his moment of stardom; I was trapped, frozen where I stood.

'May I ask what you were doing with the little lamb?' asked the taller of the two ladies, in a voice tinged with smiling curiosity, and an accent redolent of Roedean. I stared at her. And even if I'd been a native English speaker I don't think I could have dreamt up a reply. Without a hint of graciousness I turned on my heel and ran over to my father. But Tom-of-the-oaths had got there ahead of me.

'I don't give a bugger what you do, but you better bloody well do something. It was your God-damned lamb, and if you think I'm going to have my picture splattered all over the *Sunday Post* with his ball hanging from my teeth you better bloody well start thinking again, John son of Finlay!'

My father knew better than to laugh because the shepherd had been known to use his fists with a dram in him, and he had worse than a dram in him now. He had embarrassment and cold fury – and an imagination so inflamed that he could impute to the homely *Sunday Post* actions which, if they were even contemplated, would have resulted in the sort of Press upheaval which was unheard of in those days, even on Fleet Street.

'Just calm down, Tom,' my father said. 'I'll talk to them and I'll send them home to Katie to see some spinning; that usually interests them and, with luck, Katie might be able to keep them occupied till I get home. We'll think of something. Or it will be the *News of the World* for sure –'

He moved off before Tom could conjure up even a swear-word and, a few moments later, he was deep in conversation with the two posh tourists. Somebody, unaware of what was going on, called on me to fetch a half-clad rogue sheep so that he could divest her of the tattered remains of her fleece, and by the time I looked again the two ladies were walking away from the fank chaperoned by Old Hector. I hoped that he could steer the conversation to Singapore, and at the same time felt annoyed that I would now have to wait till evening to find out what news Calum the Post had brought. Deep down I felt moderately certain that the tongue-tied bachelor Hector was not going to get himself involved in any conversation even remotely involving the objects of the ladies' inquisitiveness!

Two hours later the fank was over. All the odd jobs had been

72

done, and the main job of the day was on the point of being accomplished. All the lambs were segregated in one pen with the mothers in another. In a few minutes a man with two good dogs would drive the older sheep on to the lower moorland, and when the in-bye gate was securely fastened on them the lambs would be herded on to the machair (the golf course as it was now) and they would be equally securely impounded. They would cry despairingly for a night and a day, but would fall silent as the replies from the moor became fewer and fainter.

Normally, on the day of a fank, my father would swallow a cup of tea and stretch out for an hour on St Clement's bench in the living room before settling down to a proper meal, such would be his tiredness. But today I could see him squaring his shoulders as he walked up to the house from the gate, and switching on a smile as he opened the door. He had been unusually pre-occupied on his way home, and had snapped my head off when I asked him what he thought the tourists would do with their photographs of Tom-of-the-oaths.

'What do you mean – photographs? It was only one picture they took.'

'No. They took two anyway; maybe more.'

'O God, it's a bloody film show they'll be having!'

I thought to myself that his own vocabulary was rivalling Tom's but I felt it wiser to make no comment.

There was no sign of his asperity as he entered the living room where the two ladies were sitting primly on St Clement's bench, balancing empty cups and saucers on empty plates.

'Ah, there you are ladies; I see you've been sampling the wife's tea ... and her spinning too, by the looks of things!'

He glanced in my mother's direction, where she was sitting looking slightly flustered behind her wheel trying to unravel a tangle of thick thread from the hooks on the sheckle. Around her feet on the floor was enough mangled wool to make a cardigan. 'O, the ladies have been doing very well,' she said, adding with a slight glint of malice, 'I've been telling them that you would give them a few lessons on the loom when you came home.' The look in her eye meant 'that'll teach you to land your fancy visitors on me!'

'O that *would* be marvellous,' cooed the one who blushed.

73

'And then we'll be able to say that we've seen the whole Harris Tweed process from sheep to wearer –'

'The round-up was so fascinating,' the other one chipped in slightly apologetically. 'And the gentleman who escorted us here has had such an interesting life. He must find island life very quiet after the Far East.'

I wondered what legends of the Orient Old Hector had conjured out of one voyage to Singapore.

'Just a pity we didn't get a few more photographs, but Mr MacGeekan was convinced there was going to be a thunder-storm; I'm so glad he was wrong.'

My father hadn't sat down, and I could sense my mother daring him to do so. I knew that, at a conservative estimate, the visitors had been with her for two hours, and two hours with two enthusiastic English women in search of the Hebridean ethos could be an unnerving experience. The bare top of the stove was proof that she hadn't even been able to begin preparing the evening meal.

'Would you ladies like to have a go at the loom, then?' asked the man who wouldn't normally have looked at the loom for two days after a fank. With much oohing and fluttering they confirmed that they would. I had seen the routine many times before but, this time, I felt that I couldn't miss it and I slipped out to the weaving shed with them before my mother could dragoon me into dish washing or potato scrubbing. My three brothers were huddled on the red kist at the end of the table and two of them were old enough to take a share of the chores. I could almost hear my father's joints protesting as he eased himself on the hard wooden board which was his seat for the loom. While he was doing so the ladies were deciding that there was enough light to take a photograph if my father were to leave the door open – which, of course, he would.

There was nothing new about his performance except that it lacked a little of his usual energy. He pedalled his four pedals, swung the weaver's beam, shot the shuttle backwards and forwards through the meshing warp with deceptive ease. But his commentary lacked its customary sparkle and embellishment and he had woven a mere half yard when he stopped.

'Right then, which of you two ladies is going to have the first go; you look to me as if you had the legs and the arms of born

74

weavers.' He slipped off the wooden seat and surreptitiously winked at me but I couldn't for the life of me see why.

With giggles and protest and 'you go first, Madge' the tourists sorted themselves out and the one who blushed and was Madge pushed Susan onto the driving seat. After she had discovered that she could keep her skirt down over her knees *and* reach the pedals with her toes Susan attacked the loom with an abandon that would have qualified her for St Trinian's. As usual, with novices, the shuttle slithered over the top of the warp and not through it, but with such force that it left the beam altogether and if I hadn't jumped smartly aside I'd have suffered the fate of the photographed lamb.

'O dear! I've done something wrong, haven't I?'

'O Susan, you're far too impatient; didn't you notice that Mr Macdonald always had that wooden thing pushed away from him before he yanked the string?' Making allowance for her uncertain terminology, Madge did have a point and my father concurred as he retrieved the shuttle from the floor. He replaced it in the box nearer him, told Susan to push the beam away from her as far as she could (which she did, almost dislocating her pelvis), press her right foot down hard (which she did, and to her obvious astonishment the warp opened), jerk 'the string' to her right (which she did and the shuttle slid almost to the far end), pull the beam (which she did with a gasp) and, lo and behold, she had woven one thread at a speed which indicated that, if she maintained it, she might complete a full length of Harris Tweed by the time she attained the old age pension.

My father then had an inspiration. Why didn't Madge go and stand at the far side of the loom and look as if she were giving Susan a hint about her technique and he would take a photograph of them both so that they could prove to their friends in the deep south that they had, indeed, themselves woven a bit of the tweed they were going to buy – er – that is, of course, if they were going to buy it; something they were under no obligation whatsoever to do; the words had just slipped out. The two ladies weren't as soft as their giggliness indicated. They ignored the suggestion about buying, but they were most enthusiastic about the photograph and Madge slipped her camera off her shoulder before she took up a carefully studied pose at the other side of the loom. My father studied the camera and assured them that he had used the type before; which was news to me, because in no way did it resemble the ancient Box Brownie that my mother produced from the red kist once every summer. Just as he was on the point of raising it to his eye his finger appeared to slip and the back of the camera swung open.

'O Lord! I'm an idiot. What have I done? Have I ruined the film?'

His distress was such that the ladies recovered quickly from their initial flashes of annoyance; Susan slipped off the seat and Madge darted round from behind the loom to put him at his ease. It was nothing. It didn't matter. There were only three pictures on it – the ones taken at the 'round-up' – and they'd be bound to see another 'round-up' before they left the island. Of course, my father couldn't pay for the film; it was nice of him to suggest it; but, really and truly, it didn't matter. They had plenty of spools back in the hotel. After that my father relaxed, and, having saved the honour of Tom-of-the-oaths, decided to retrieve some of his own by giving Madge and Susan a long and good-humoured lesson in the art of weaving. They were surprisingly apt pupils, and once they got over their initial coyness each developed a remarkably determined set to her jaw and by the time they decided to set off for their hotel, although they had by no means mastered the art of weaving, they had mastered the theory of it. They called a cheery farewell to my mother as they made their ways down to the gate, escorted by my father, and they took a careful note of his address before they parted company with him.

'Well I'm dashed!' he was to say later when he got a letter requesting samples of Harris Tweed from a well-known London fashion house which listed among its directors two women whose first names were Madge and Susan. They were to remain good customers of his for a long time to come. But that was in the future. His immediate concern was to get down to the dinner which we could both smell as we reached the door.

'What on earth do you suppose Old Hector's up to?' my mother asked as we were half-way through the meal and had exhausted speculation about Madge and Susan.

'What do you mean?' I asked before my father could respond.

'The post arrived when I was milking his cow this morning. You know Calum the Post isn't such a bad character; he'll make us walk to the van to collect our mail but he got out today and walked the whole way up the hill to hand over Hector's letter to him. And that was just pure kindliness out of sympathy for the poor man's legs!'

'Pure curiosity more likely,' my father grunted. 'And I don't blame him in Hector's case; I don't suppose the old fellow's had a letter since Christmas. If Calum was doing his job he'd be walking up to every door with the letters as he would do if he worked in town. And what's more he wouldn't have a van if he were in town; he'd be tramping the streets with a big heavy sack on his back. He gets away with blue murder because he gives us lifts from time to time and brings the occasional box of groceries from Obbe!'

I couldn't care less about the postman's peccadilloes; I was dying to get up to Old Hector's but I knew I'd get my head in my hands if I suggested leaving the table before the rest were finished. And now that the strain of the tourists was off her shoulders my mother seemed determined to relax and let the evening slip by her.

'But you should have seen Hector. He got all flustered and excited, and dashed off to the end room with this large brown envelope as soon as Calum's back was turned. I think he was going to hide it; he certainly didn't have time to read the shortest of letters before he returned, and he couldn't wait to get me out of the house!'

'Perhaps he was getting some of those things they advertise under plain sealed wrappers.'

'John!'

I kept my face straight, pretending I didn't know what they were talking about.

'Anyway,' my mother went on, 'I'll have to milk Primrose tonight and tomorrow; Finlay's going to have other business on his hands.' She got up from the table and went across to the mantelpiece.

I had dropped out of the conversation because I had noticed that she kept referring to Old Hector as having received one

77

letter; in my imaginings I had come to believe that he would get a score at least. It took a second for her remark to register with me.

'What are you talking about, mammy? I'm going to milk Hector's cow as usual.'

'You're going to the doctor,' my brother burbled. 'You're going to Rodel to the doctor.'

'What's going on?' My father was as puzzled as I was.

My mother came back to the table with an official-looking brown letter in her hand. 'This came in the post today. Calum had to walk up to *this* house for once, because there was no-one here to meet him at the gate; he didn't know that I was to be in Hector's house or he'd have given it to me there. It's a letter from the Education Authority about your bursary for High School. You're to get a medical examination before you can register in Tarbert.'

'Right enough, we should have remembered that,' my father said, taking the letter from her. 'Jamie MacInnes had to have one; it's just a matter of form to make sure you haven't got T.B. or anything. You've got nothing to worry about on that score.' Tuberculosis was still endemic in the islands and every parent's dread was of 'that wee cough'.

'But what's that got to do with my milking Hector's cow?' I asked, trying to keep the exasperation out of my voice.

'I'll tell you what it's got to do with it.' My mother, for once, was carrying the burden of the argument; my father was studying the letter from Inverness. 'I've arranged with Geordie MacLellan to give you a lift to Rodel to the doctor tomorrow; he's got to collect some people at the hotel. And, if the doctor sees you right away you'll be able to get the bus back home at three o'clock –'

'I still don't see –'

'Will you keep quiet and stop interrupting me. You'll take the tin bath in from the end of the house and give yourself a good bath tonight; I'm not going to have you going to the doctor smelling of sheep and Hector's cow. What's all the excitement about Hector's cow anyway? You spend half your days grumbling about having to milk her; this is your chance to have the 'night off' that you keep pleading for – and a chance to have a good bath into the bargain! So I don't want to hear any more about it. Your father will keep me company up and down past the cemetery and maybe he can satisfy his curiosity about Hector's letter while he's up there.'

She got up from the table. 'I'll have to milk our own cows before I do Hector's; and I'll have to get the young ones to bed before I do anything else. You two boys can do the dishes.'

'There's nothing to this,' my father said, putting the letter back in its envelope. 'The doctor will just sound your chest and test your eyes – that's all. You put two big pans on the stove for hot water for yourself; I'm going to have a smoke.'

I was seething with anger and frustration, but I knew that there was no point in protesting further. At this rate I'm going to be away to High School before I know Hector's fate, I thought sulkily to myself as I began to haul in water from the river. Normally I would have jumped at the chance of a trip to Rodel on my own, but this was not a normal occasion. It was infuriating to be able to see Old Hector's light shining yellow on the hillside – he must have lit his lamp early in expectation of my visit – and be as incommunicado as if I were a hundred miles away. I couldn't even have a smoke because all my douts were in Hector's house. But I'd have given up smoking just to know what that brown envelope contained.

Chapter Six

I was bathed and clean and sulky when my parents returned from milking Hector's cow, and I had the mildest trace of an irritating giddiness which, I was to learn in years to come, was already the beginning of nicotine craving. Over the past six months or so hardly a day had passed without my having smoked at least one cigarette, and since the beginning of the summer holidays I'd had at least one after each morning milking and a couple as I relaxed with Hector after the evening chore. There was no suggestion of any of the much publicised diseases attributable to cigarette smoking nowadays but there was a vague unease that cigarettes might make one more susceptible to the 'wee cough'. Indeed many of the deaths which were put down to T.B. may well have been lung cancer although not diagnosed as such. But the simple fact was that, even at that early age, I was 'hooked', and on that particular day I had already missed out on my morning fix because of the fank. Niggling at my mind also was the thought that most of tomorrow would also be a smokeless day unless my parents decided to give me some spending money for my Rodel trip; Geordie MacLellan, with whom I was going to travel, was a smoker himself but he couldn't be trusted to keep my vice secret because he had boys of his own and, consequently, parental attitudes!

'How did you get on?' A slight fleeting frown on my mother's face showed that she had detected the surliness in my voice, but she decided to let it pass.

'Fine,' she said. 'Why not? I've milked a cow before. But I thought I was never going to get home once your father and Old Hector started blethering; I thought fanks were tiring affairs, but apparently they're only exhausting as far as doing work around the croft is concerned. When did Donald go to bed?'

My father saved me from having to tell a lie rather than admit that my younger brother had slipped off only when he heard the gate squeak.

'What's going on between Old Hector and yourself?' he asked. 'He barely thanked your mother for doing the milking for him, and you'd have thought somebody had stolen his last ha'penny when he heard that you wouldn't be going up in the morning either. Are the two of you plotting something? Although I can't imagine that –'

My mother cut in, saving me from replying. 'Loneliness,' she said. 'That's what it is. The poor man's going out of mind living on his own up on the hill there. Maggie may have given him a tonguing now and again but at least it was the sound of a human voice. And that house of his is becoming a real piggery. I offered to wash down the dresser for him but he nearly took my head off when he saw me going to touch a plate!'

Good for Hector! If my mother had started cleaning the dishes on the dresser she'd have come across my packet of Woodbines and my hoard of douts, and she wouldn't have required the two sights to know who had stashed them there.

'Pity we couldn't get a wife for him,' said my father, yawning and reaching for the Bible. 'There's no way he's going to be able to hang on to Primrose once Finlay goes off to High School; there's a limit to how long the women of the village can keep on doing his milking for him once winter comes in. I don't know why the hell he wants a cow anyway. There's nothing wrong with nessels when you get used to it and it's a damn sight cheaper than a cow in the long run.' 'Nessels' was another word that had been adopted into Gaelic, regardless of whether or not the product had been produced by the famous Swiss firm; the other word that was creeping in was 'idal' for the version of tinned milk trade-named 'Ideal'.

My mother had come back down from the hill when big

81

Geordie drew up at the gate in the Armstrong. 'Now,' my father was instructing me, 'you'll do exactly as I say. Geordie will take you to the door of the bar and if he goes in for a pint himself he'll keep you right. But if he doesn't, you'll go in on your own even if you're not the age. There won't be many people there at that hour, and you'll be able to spot the doctor without any bother. He's tall and as bald as a baby's backside, and he'll be leaning against the far end of the bar with a pint at his elbow. You'll go up to him and explain what you want and hand him that form. He'll tell you the rest, and when he's filled in the form you'll hand him that half crown and tell him that your father wants him to have a dram. Understand?'

I nodded and took the half crown and the envelope containing the Education Committee form.

'And there's a half crown for yourself. The bus will cost you sixpence, and that means you can spend two shillings in the shop. Don't spend it all on sweets or your mother will kill me; get a couple of pencils or something, and bring back a bar of toffee for Donald.' Geordie's klaxon sounded impatiently. 'Off with you or Geordie'll be away without you! And don't lose that form whatever you do …'

Fine! I was rich. Eight pence would buy twenty Red Label Woodbine which were newly on the market, and the cheapest by far, and a box of matches would be a ha'penny. I'd have enough left over for a token pencil and a bar of toffee for Donald forbye.

My father's instructions with regard to the doctor may sound bizarre to today's reader, but they were no more so than the haphazard medical system which prevailed in parts of the West Highlands at that time. Although the Southlands had now been completely repopulated for three or four years, we still didn't have a permanent doctor of our own. Not that he was necessary; the District Nurse and the old wives who were skilful in the arts of midwifery normally fulfilled the needs of the district and a doctor was rarely summoned except in cases of serious accident and for the signing of death certificates and the filling in of rare official documents like my own. The result was that the series of locums who processed through the Southlands while the authorities were debating the need for a full-time doctor, tended to be people who, by being exiled to us from the main, were suffering a fate second only to being struck off the medical register, gentlemen who were fanatical anglers, or, occasionally, newly qualified men fired with Hippocratic enthusiasm. Whichever category they belonged to, they found themselves with more time on their hands than they had hitherto imagined to exist, and if they weren't careful they found themselves fighting an increasingly difficult battle against alcoholism. Most of them decided to escape in the nick of time. Dr Frankinson, the present incumbent, had decided to surrender.

He was an extremely popular man, and a marvellous raconteur. When he had money he was extremely generous in the bar; when he hadn't, his position in society afforded him a length of 'slate' which the proprietor would never have allowed a local. For many years now, the Rodel Hotel has been presided over by one of the great characters of the West Highlands – a Hebridean with a personality which would have taken him to the top in any profession, and a heart of gold; not the least of his qualities is that he treats all men the same, except the less able, whom he treats even better. But his predecessor was in a different mould, and tended to touch his cap to 'society', and since the doctor fell into that category he was able to use the hotel as his club. Dr Frankinson went one better – during his short stay he used the bar as his surgery as well! And that was where I found him when my eyes got used to the gloom after the August sunshine. He was standing exactly as my father had described – bald and impressive, and elegant in a well cut tweed suit which was so worn that only a member of the aristocracy or a millionaire would have been seen dead in it.

'Well laddie,' he said, in a rich rolling mainland accent. 'You've got the look of a man looking for the doctor. But it's not for yourself – that's for sure – you're as healthy as a stirk. Who is it that thinks he's dying? Tell him he'll get better, and if not he'll be better off!' The twinkle in his eye took any suggestion of heartlessness out of his talk.

'It's nobody,' I said, shoving the envelope with my form at him. 'It's the form for High School; I've got to have it signed by a doctor.'

'Ah! One of those.' He studied the form for a while. 'So

you're off to High School, eh? And what are you going to do with all the fine education you'll collect there? A minister, eh? Or a schoolmaster? Or a damn fool doctor like me?'

'A banker,' I said. It wasn't a subject to which I'd given much thought of late. I'd had vague notions of writing for newspapers at one time, but most people to whom I'd mentioned it had dismissed it as flim-flam. A secure job with a salary and a pension was the thing to go for; 'a schoolmaster in the city' – now there was something to aim for. But recently a second cousin of mine had got himself a job in the bank in Tarbert without having had to go through the whole hassle of a University degree, and from his very first day he was never seen in old clothes again, and in no time he had acquired a spanking new motor bicycle. Everybody maintained that he 'wouldn't be stuck in Tarbert for long; that he would get on in the bank and get away'. The 'getting away' idea had been deeply instilled in me from my earliest days in school, and the bank seemed to offer a shorter cut than either the ministry or teaching.

'A banker! Don't be daft. Only little Hitlers want to be bankers and bank managers; they want to sit behind big desks and bully people like me who are better at subtraction than at multiplication!' I hadn't the faintest idea what he was talking about; I hadn't learn't to recognise the symptoms of an overdraft.

'You go and get yourself a good education and come back here and take over your old man's croft. He's no damn good as a crofter; I don't know what put the idea into his head. He should have been in parliament, or writing poetry, or something daft like that.'

'Do you know my father?'

"Course I do. We were in the army together. He wouldn't mention that, of course. Lucky John, we used to call him – well, we were both lucky I guess. Tell him I'll be up to see him one of those days. But you come back home when you get your education and take over the croft!'

I was dying to ask him more about the army and my father's part in it, but I could sense that he had deliberately put a full stop to that part of the conversation.

'But I wouldn't need to go away to school to do that,' I

ventured. 'You don't need education to be a crofter.'

'And what bloody fool told you that? Not your father, that's for sure. Education isn't for *being* something, boy; education is for enjoying whatever you are. The only thing you have to *be* in life is yourself. There are only two ways to enjoy yourself – one is to have a good education so that you can understand how much worse off you could be; the other way is to have no education at all, and not be discontented with your lot in the first place. Bloody banker! Huh! If I thought that's what you'd become I'd give you a medical certificate that wouldn't get you anywhere except into a hospital. Come here!'

He led the way out into the back yard where the empty beer barrels were stacked and he smoothed out the medical form on the top of one. He produced a fountain pen and filled it in from top to bottom without glancing once at me or asking one single question. 'There you are,' he said when he had signed his name with a flourish; 'that'll see you right. Nobody will ever read the damn thing anyway – they're just a lot of little Hitlers there, in Inverness – just like bankers, bossing people around!' He handed me the form and was turning away when I remembered the half crown.

'My father said to give you that; he said you were to have a dram.'

He smiled. 'Is that what he said? Well, you tell him from me that that doesn't cover what he owes me for the last job I did for him!' He took the half crown and put it in his pocket, and solemnly handed me back two shillings. 'You don't have to mention any other sums of money,' he winked. 'Just tell him I took the half crown and that way you won't be telling a word of a lie!'

'But –'

'Only goats and rams butt!' He turned on his heel but stopped again. 'Are you going home on the bus?'

'Yes.'

'Then you've got two hours to spare. See that road there? Go up there till you come to a little cottage with a red roof on it. Knock on the door and tell them the doctor asked you to get the key to St Clement's, and when you get it go and spend an hour prowling there among your people's history; there's education for you.' He made to go and hesitated yet again. 'O,

85

by the way, I've put in your form that you've got a very slight weakness of the eyes, and that you'll soon be needing spectacles like your father.'

'My father hasn't got spectacles –'

'No. But he needs them. Otherwise he'd have noticed the yellow staining on the tips of the first two fingers of your right hand. If I didn't know better I'd have sworn it was nicotine – that's the English for the poison in cigarettes!' And with that he strode back into the bar. I stood looking after him for a moment, remembering some of the things I'd heard people say about him. 'Brilliant;' they used to say. 'He's a better doctor drunk than others are sober.' I was to get to know that for myself one day, when he came to save my life. But that was a long way ahead. I decided I'd take his advice and go to St Clement's; there would be time to get cigarettes later on. The morning craving had passed, and as I fingered the florin piece in my pocket alongside my other half crown I had the comforting thought that I could afford Capstan for once.

It was bitterly cold in St Clement's; the centuries old church hadn't absorbed enough of the summer heat to last it through the wet July that we'd had, and it wasn't responding to the paler sun of a Hebridean August. And it was dark, except where shafts of light cut through from the narrow windows. But it had an atmosphere that I had felt only once before, not in a church but on a lonely island in a moorland loch. Just inside the door I found a large wooden spatula with the church's story sketchily outlined on it, telling how it was the oldest cruciform church in the Western Isles, probably contemporary with Iona Abbey. That didn't mean very much to me, but I was transfixed in front of the tomb of Alasdair Crotach, the fierce chief of Clan Macleod who had rebuilt the church four hundred years ago and re-dedicated it to the patron saint of sea-farers. He had been a ruthless chief, Alasdair Crotach (called Alasdair Humpbacked because of a sword wound that had disfigured him), and yet he found it in his heart to re-build a great church and build for himself a tomb inside it. I stood staring at his effigy carved in stone, with his sword in his hand and his dogs at his feet, and felt the cold atmosphere around me disappearing. Dr Frankinson had been right; this was history, pulsing and living even although there couldn't be bones down there after four hundred years; the dust would have returned to dust – just as it would have done whether the man had been saint or sinner, and this, obviously from the potted history, had been both. The same tourist guide, on the wooden hand board, reminded me that, of course, St Clement's had been thatched in Alasdair Crotach's day – much in the same style, I thought, as Old Hector's house and the few other old black houses on the moor's edge. It had been Lady Dunmore in the nineteenth century (the laird's wife who had founded the Harris Tweed industry) who had rescued the church from ruin again, and had replaced the old thatch with slate. Generation after generation had made an effort to leave its own little notch of remembrance on a building which stood on a site of worship that was older than Christianity. I had begun to feel quite the young man as the days of High School were approaching; now, suddenly, I felt very young indeed.

Outside, I wandered around among the ancient tombstones – the railed sepulchres of landlords of vanity, craving for their immortality, and the once ornate monuments of grandeur looked tawdry beside the simple dignity of St Clement's. More dignified by far were the flat stones on which the simple inscriptions had long since faded; one of them, my guide notes told me, covered the grave of one of the great poets of the nineteenth century; another (nobody could be sure which) lay on the grave of one of the greatest bards of the whole Highlands – Mary MacLeod of the seventeenth century, whose songs live on as memorials more lasting than stone.

I went back inside the church again and climbed the narrow circular stairway built into the wall, and came out at the top. From there, the whole history fell into place. From there I could see why Rodel had been the Harris capital of the Macleods, who are, to this day the Macleods of Harris although their castle is in Skye. Down below me was the harbour, landlocked almost so that the chief's war galleys could find shelter from the worst storms and a defensible refuge from enemies. and just by turning left towards the east I could see Skye itself in the distance and I could tell that it wouldn't take a galley, under sail or under sixteen oars, long to link the chief's two strongholds – giving him virtual control of the Minch separating the Outer Hebrides from Skye and the mainland. My school books had taught me that history was something that happened elsewhere – in far away places like Lucknow and Cawnpore; in Omdurman and Khartoum; in Kimberley and Ladysmith ... the books had taught me that history had to be monumental to be important, and that the making of empire was history's chief end.

Yes, Dr Frankinson was right. But the sudden recollection of the doctor reminded me of his jibe about my nicotine-stained fingers, and that, in turn, reminded me that I had better hurry if I were to get to the shop in time to catch the bus. I left St Clement's behind me for thirty years ...

The woman in the shop looked at me as if she ought to know me, but, fortunately, she decided that she didn't and the sight of the silver in my palm allayed her qualms about selling cigarettes to somebody who was manifestly under age. When she handed me a flat twenty packet of Capstan I asked her for two packets of ten instead. She looked puzzled. 'Why do you want two packets? That'll cost you a shilling whereas you'll get a full twenty for eleven pence ha'penny leaving you a ha'penny for a box of matches.'

'They're for different people.' I said, marvelling at how glibly the lie came. But I couldn't explain to her that two packets of ten could be concealed, one in each trouser pocket, while a packet of twenty couldn't. Certainly a twenty pack would have looked manly and impressive but, unfortunately, this was one thing which I couldn't use to impress. The old lady looked relieved not to be breaking the law, and she went on happily to serve with me with slabs of toffee and a couple of pencils. I had made a mental calculation to be careful; Dr Frankinson had warned me not to tell that he had taken only sixpence for his consultation, so I had to be sure that such purchases as I could produce at home were no more than I could cover from the money my father had given me.

To my delight the bus was empty when I boarded it back at the hotel and, what was more, the driver was 'a trusty' – the hero of every youngster in the island. He was only in his early twenties and yet here he was heaving a long blue bus that could take thirty passengers round the island's hairpin bends day in and day out. And he did it with style too – appearing to lean with his bus like a racing driver and managing to give an appearance of dash and speed while keeping up a constant flow of racy anecdote.

'Have a fag,' I said nonchalantly, using yet another word that had become a fashionable Gaelic noun. 'I'll light it for you.' And to my delight he took it as if it were the most natural thing in the world for me to be offering it; it made me feel sixteen at least. We chatted about this and that as the bus threaded its way through gentle Rodel glen, with me hiding – under the most casual air – the fact that I was scanning the road ahead, ready to extinguish my cigarette if I saw an adult flagging down the bus. Meanwhile Jackie flung out of his driver's window a copy of the *Daily Express* here and a *Daily Record* there at the gates of those who had placed orders. And that was almost every gate, because the rumours of war were building up steadily as news filtered through of crisis meetings, and as Germany annexed more and more of Europe. Whenever I glanced behind me through the rear window of the bus I could see people trotting down their paths – people who had obviously been watching from their windows, waiting for their daily dose of news. Many of them had wireless sets by then, but the newspapers were more solid, somehow, and more credible than the disembodied voice from the box.

Rodel glen is the nearest to parkland that I know in the whole of the Hebrides. And not without reason. Its name in Gaelic means 'the choicest of dales' and it was for many years the home farm of the chief of MacLeod, and one of the last of their lands that the MacLeods parted with when their estates were sold off to meet debts in the eighteenth and nineteenth centuries. The petrified remains of dead forest still clung on to the hillside on our left as we drove north, and through the ghostly skeletal remains of trees from which the sap had departed, like the blood from old ladies' corpses, I could see a clearly etched ridge of green which looked like the manicured border of a huge path.

'Is that another road over there, Jackie?'

Jackie didn't have to look.

'Well, it is and it isn't. They tell me that was a drive-way once, and one passenger (I can't remember who it was) was saying that his grandmother could remember ladies driving along through the woods there in a carriage drawn by four horses. It

89

must have been quite a sight. Lord Dunmore it must have been. They say that the night he died, though he was away from the island then, a mighty big thunderstorm broke out – just when his soul was passing on – and every one of the great trees died where it stood. Makes you think doesn't it?'

It made me think that Jackie was more of a poet than I had suspected, but a few moments later as we crested the hill above Obbe, I had reason to revert to my original assessment.

'Look at this bloody son-of-a-bitch here; he's going to bring that ram aboard the bus and I won't ever get a fare for it. All I'll get will be hell when the boss finds sheep shit all over the bus!'

Sure enough, there was a hefty crofter whom I knew by sight although I didn't know his name, standing with a massive ram at the road-side and, slightly self-consciously, flagging down the bus.

'Hello, Jackie. I'm sorry to bother you, but I missed the Board of Agriculture landry; the wife was saying that you wouldn't mind giving me a wee lift as far as Borve?'

'I don't mind giving you a wee lift for a wee fare, but I'll get my books if I take that bloody beast aboard! You know that perfectly well!'

'Indeed I do Jackie; it was just seeing you with your uncle's calf in the bus a couple of weeks ago that made me think the rules had, maybe, been softened a bit. But if you'd rather not –'

Considering the ram was already aboard, Jackie didn't have much option.

'I'll tell you one thing for sure – I'll be charging you a ticket for him then. A full ticket!'

'Dammit man,' said the crofter. 'Do you think I'd be scrounging him on for free; but the snag is I've only got my own fare neat, and I was just going to ask if you would get the office to send me a wee account?'

Jackie spluttered.

'How the hell can I get the office to send a wee account for something that's not supposed to be aboard anyway? Keep the bloody thing under control then,' he yelped as the ram attacked a seat with his massive head. And he slammed the bus into gear sending the crofter flying on top of his beast.

'A terribly hasty temper that fellow's got,' the new passenger said to me, shaking his head. 'He'll have an accident one of those days!' He sat down and lit his pipe, and Jackie drove on in silence.

As we reached the village I glanced up towards the hill and I could see Old Hector plowtering about at the end of his house. I toyed with the idea of getting off at his road end, but it was only four o'clock and I knew that my mother would be anxious for news of my visit to the doctor. Having waited so far, I could bide in patience for another few hours. Jackie pulled up at our gate and handed me my father's *Daily Express* as I fumbled for my sixpence.

'Ach forget it, boy; at least you don't shit in my bus!'

Running public service transport profitably in a close-knit community was a problem in the Hebrides in those days. And still is.

'How was Dr Frankinson?' asked my father as he prepared to settle down to his *Express*.

'Fine,' I said. 'He filled in the form.'

'And did he take the half crown?'

'Yes,' I said, with moderate truth. 'But he said to tell you it didn't cover what you owed him. What did he mean?'

'O!' He looked a little nonplussed, but he smiled as his hand wandered unconsciously to the scar on the top of his head – a scar which he always claimed was the result of an accident long ago. He checked his hand. 'I don't know,' he said, biting his lip. 'I don't know at all. He's got a funny sense of humour, has Fred.' And with that he lost himself in the paper. Whatever Dr Frankinson meant, I never found out; nor did I ever hear reference again from either of them to their having been together in the war.

My brother came charging in demanding to know whether I'd brought him his bar of toffee; my mother came in from feeding the chickens wanting to know whom I'd seen and how I'd got on. It was soon the hour for the evening meal, and, one way and another, the time passed till it was reasonable for me to suggest that I'd better go and milk Hector's cow.

'Aye, you'd better,' my mother said. 'I hope you get more thanks than I got. That man gets more crotchety every day; it's just as well there's nobody with him who has to put up with him!'

I wondered if that situation might not be on the point of changing. I would soon know.

Chapter Seven

Old Hector was standing outside his door shifting impatiently from foot to foot, which for him was a more cumbersome effort than for most. He didn't say anything as I arrived, panting from my jog up the hill; he waited till we were inside where there was no danger that his voice could carry down to the village over the August evening that was so still that a fleck of down would have fallen straight to earth. But when we did get inside he exploded. He was a mild-mannered man, as I've taken pains to establish, but I knew that he had a secret store of pungent vocabulary picked up on his only voyage. Now he unleashed it.

'You're a son-of-a-bitch, that's what you are – and an ungrateful one at that. For all these months I've plied you with cigarettes and kept your bad habits secret forbye. And what do you do to me? You blackmail me into trouble, and as soon as I'm in it up to my arse you start having baths and buggering off to Rodel. I'll tell you this – for two pins I'd have let your mother start "clean-springing" the house and let her find your filthy Woodbines hiding behind my best crockery –'

I made several attempts to check his rhetoric but I might as well have tried, single-handed, to stop a flock of sheep in stampede. At long last he began to run out of energy and he flopped down into the Taransay chair. I suspected that he was beginning to feel better.

'I know you had to go and see the doctor. I know you had to

have a bath because that's the sort of thing that fancy boys going off to High School have to get used to. Your mother told me all that; but even if you couldn't have milked the cow you could have found some way of slipping up here for two minutes when you must have known that I was getting a nervous break-down all alone on this bloody hill –'

At last I was able to jump into a pause as he took two breaths instead of one, and I tried to explain to him that there was no way that I could slip out of the house for the time I knew would be required without turning my parents' puzzlement into suspicion. And how, I asked him, would he have liked it if they had elicited some clue that would have allowed them to stumble on to his secret?

No – he wouldn't have liked that at all; of course he wouldn't. 'But you could have fixed it so that they wouldn't suspect. You were quick enough to find a way for yourself and Gillespie to get to James's wedding, and back home again, without your parents finding out! That was all very well; that was something *you* wanted to fix for that Gillespie and yourself, but when it came to doing something for poor old Hector it was too much trouble to put your brains to work –'

'How?' I spluttered and stopped! How on earth had he found out about that escapade of mine and Gillespie's all those years ago? I had forgotten about it myself. Gillespie and I covered our tracks so well that when we did, occasionally and accidentally, let slip some reference to the wedding feast that we had attended as invisible guests people had imagined that we were either telling lies or else creating fantasies out of bits and pieces of information that we had overheard. Yet here was Hector after all this time casually referring to the incident as if it had been common knowledge all the time. I had drifted away momentarily into a puzzled dwam and I'd lost track of Hector's ravings and rantings till one fragment of reproach scythed through my dismay '… but of course for all you cared those three women could have come charging up the hill in their Sunday hats and nothing else, and started fighting over me like crows over carrion –'

'*Three* women! What do you mean, *three* women? Did you get three replies?'

'Hah! I thought that would get through to the little bit of

conscience that you've got left. Yes, I got three replies. Isn't that what's been driving me into the crazy house? Wondering how I could barricade myself in if I saw the three of them hopping out of Mitchell's bus down at the road there. I'll tell you this – when I looked out of the window this morning and saw your mother coming up the hill with a scarf round her head I thought that my heart coming up would meet my porridge going down! What the hell are you laughing at?'

I couldn't tell him that it was the word 'hopping' that had kittled my fancy. Never in my most optimistic imaginings had I envisaged any potential candidate of an age and an agility that would permit her to *hop* off a three inch doorstep far less off Mitchell's tall bus. At best I had hoped for one desperate woman with at least one hand sufficiently free of rheumatism and arthritis to enable her to milk a cow; in fact, in all my thinking, the need for a milker for Primrose had rated higher than a bride for Hector, but my common sense told me that our only chance of securing the former was by procuring the latter.

'I wasn't laughing at you,' I assured him. 'I was laughing at the idea of you mistaking my mother for a woman who would reply to the advertisement. And in any case why can't you get it into your head that nobody's going to come chasing after you? No sane woman would climb on to Mitchell's bus and ask Jackie to take her to 427's house. You're only a number, so far!'

'Aye – a back number; and that's what I'm going to remain. If I were a drinking man I'd convince myself I'd have the excuse of having been drunk when I allowed you to talk me into this whole mad business. Just think of it – picking a woman from a list of applicants, as if you were picking a pair of boots from a catalogue! If those letters did nothing else they brought me to my senses.'

I hadn't wanted to push him towards the subject of the letters although I'd been dying to see them; but this was my cue. I pulled one of my packets of Capstan out of my pocket and lit a cigarette as casually as I could. I saw his eyes going to the crisp new packet of ten but he didn't say anything; instead he was reminded to light his own pipe.

'Are you not going to show me the letters, then?'

He waited till his pipe was glowing and then got up, shakily,

94

and went over to the dresser. He rummaged deep into the back of a drawer, and it was obvious that he had hidden the letters so carefully that even he was having difficulty finding them. Finally he turned round with three rather grimy small envelopes in his hand; either the writers weren't unduly beset by cleanliness or Old Hector had spent the last two days thumbing them over and over again. I suspected that the latter was the more likely. He handed over the letters with a suggestion of embarrassment but, at least, he had recovered his equanimity for the time being. 'Poor souls,' he said. 'I wonder if any one of them would have written if she had a clue about what a poor bargain she was chasing; it would be a cruel joke if there was a chance of one of them ever finding out.'

I ignored the implication of his remark.

'My mother said it was one brown envelope you had received; that's why I was surprised when you mentioned *three* women.'

'O, your mother told you that did she? That's just what I mean about the danger of this whole thing becoming known in the village; I'd be a laughing stock for the rest of my born days. There are plenty of them think I've got a weakness in the head as it is. However, your mother was right; it was a brown envelope all those wee ones came in, but you don't think I was going to be daft enough to leave it lying around for anybody to see – addressed to me as plain as plain could be. Not on your life; I burnt it the moment your mother's back was turned.'

I began to wonder if he had a 'weakness in the head' after all: he had burnt a perfectly innocuous envelope with his name and address on it (an envelope which could have contained anything from a mail order catalogue to a copy of the Church of Scotland's *Life and Work*) but he had clung on to three white envelopes (or, to be precise, two white ones and a blue one) clearly addressed Box 427, Stornoway Gazette, Stornoway. It wouldn't have taken Dixon Hawke or The Saint long to conclude that Old Hector had been advertising for something.

Two of the letters were terse and to the point. The first one read, 'Dear Sir, regarding your advertissment for a wife in the Gazette I would be much oblidged if you could send me more information. I am used to living on a croft. Please reply by return. Your obdt servant …'

The second one was in the same sort of vein. 'Dear Sir, i have been reading your advert. And i would like to say that i would like to offer myself if the conditions of employment is right, i am a respectfully unmarried woman not that i haven't had plenty of men after me but not yet one i would look at but I would like to see a fotograf or yourself. Your sincerely …'

Both those were from neighbouring Lewis and both approximately an hour and a half's bus journey away. The third one, in the blue envelope, was from one of the smaller off-shore islands which it is better, even now, to leave unidentified. 'Dear Mr 427,' it read, 'If you advertisement was a legpul it doesnt matter but if you are a nice man and serious I would like you to know that I am to. I will be fifty years of age next year and my life is very lonely sometimes. If you would like to meet me you are welcome to come and see me here but if it is your idea to make a fool of some poor woman then He who forgives all things will forgive that too. Yours faithfully …'

'I think this one from the island is the one,' I said. 'She's the only one who can make a reasonable attempt at spelling; and she sounds a good woman.'

He looked at me with the same sort of stunned expression as I'd seen on his face when I had suggested advertising in the first place, now almost a fortnight ago. He looked at me, glanced at his pipe, looked into my eyes again as if trying to detect some madness there; he gave a dry half laugh and automatically reached into his pocket for the piece of paper which he kept for spills for lighting his pipe. 'You're being serious,' he said. 'I thought I was the madman for agreeing with you when you had this crazy idea in the first place, but then I thought that you were pulling my leg and that I'd be a poor sport if I didn't go along with you. But now that you've landed me in this dung heap you really do think I'll go along with you. Well, I'll tell you my lad – the fun's over.' He bent down over the fire and got his pipe going; he then plucked the letters out of my hand. 'We'll just forget that this ever happened; just you go and milk Primrose and when you're finished come in and have a cigarette and we'll just yarn away like old times.'

'What about breach of promise?' I asked, casually, as I

turned to get the milking pail. 'It won't be one case you'll have to defend but three.'

Breach of promise was forever featuring in the popular papers of the day as one of the more lurid hazards of High Society, and even in the Scottish Highlands more than one fine fellow had trudged to the altar under threat.

'At least they can't take the house from you,' I said as I reached the door. 'But the best price that you can get for Primrose won't seem much when it's divided between three angry women.'

'Get out!' he said. But I noticed out of the corner of my eye that he didn't throw the three letters into the fire as I was fully expecting him to do. Instead he went over to the dresser where he was obviously going to restore them to their hiding place.

Primrose was twitching her tail impatiently as I reached her, and the firm chomp of her cud indicated that she wanted this whole tedious operation over and done with as quickly as possible so that she could get moving from under the attack of the midges. They were out for blood that night and I couldn't get a two handed rhythm into the milking because, every few moments, I had to disengage one hand and rub my face to get rid of the half-sting, half-itch, of the greatest August menace in the West Highlands. For once in my life I was grateful when Primrose switched her tail and caught me a wallop on the side of the face; normally it made me swear at her but tonight it was as if she were trying to protect us both. Over on the far edge of the moor I could see a cow which looked for all the world as if it had been fitted with a puffing chimney, and I knew that Gillespie's father was crouched in the same situation as myself but using a deterrent that wasn't available to me. I wished I could chance lighting up but I knew that if my mother or father happened to go to the river for a pail of water they would see the smoke rising just as I was seeing it rising from behind our neighbour's cow; and they would know for certain that Hector's pipe would never achieve such proximity to hoof or horns. That reminded me that Old Hector hadn't come near me since I'd started milking, and that meant that he wasn't interested in opening peace negotiations. Normally, after one of our tiffs, he found some excuse to come slinking to the dyke and he would launch on some conversation far removed from the point at issue. The fact that he didn't appear might well mean that his annoyance had been genuine. That made me begin to think seriously for the first time about the implications of what I had initiated. I had never in fact, I admitted to myself, decided whether I was having fun at Hector's expense or whether something had prompted me towards a genuine solution to a problem to which the old man (as I still considered him) was going to have to face up much sooner than he appreciated.

As I returned to the original pair of teats for the second round I found myself wondering if the idea of a 'plotted' marriage was such a crazy one after all. Even then I had begun to wonder if the great 'romantic' idea of love as an indispensible ingredient of marriage was such a valid idea after all; it seemed to me that the hardest headed, least lovey-dovey, business-like couples that I knew seemed to be faring a dashed sight better than the ones who clucked and petted and called each other 'my dear' even when they were arguing; and the *Royal Crown Reader, Book VI*, from which I had recently parted company, had a long chapter on the frightfully 'un-British' custom of arranged marriages in places like India. Nobody had arranged much for Hector hitherto; perhaps it was time somebody did.

I squeezed the last couple of squirts from Primrose, felt that her udder was as empty as a collapsed bagpipe, and whipped the fetter-rope from around her ankles. She lifted her legs into the air like a frisky calf and set off to wage her own private war with the midges. As I hurried back to the smokey shelter of Hector's house I could see that the demons were drowning themselves in their hundreds in the froth on the top of my milking pail; it was some slight consolation for a face that was beginning to feel swollen.

I decided that I'd had enough of badinage for a night and after I had strained the milk and set the basins I concealed my new consignment of cigarettes behind the plate on the dresser, and sat down to smoke two of the douts left over from two nights before.

'Do you remember that queer fellow who arrived at the Moderator's soiree by mistake?' Hector asked. And I knew by his tone that he was determined to move the conversation away from any controversial ground; I settled back in my chair, placing my second dout where I could reach it comfortably and, when the time came, re-light it from the stub end of the other in the sophisticated manner known as 'chain-smoking'.

'Yes, of course I remember him; nobody will ever forget him. I tried to ask Geordie MacLellan about him yesterday but he nearly took my head off. Why do you ask?'

Hector chuckled. 'O, yes. Big Geordie wouldn't want to talk about that fellow; he made Geordie take him all the way back to Stornoway for free and, what was worse, kept Geordie waiting at the Tarbert Hotel for an hour while he himself was knocking back whiskies with one of the Tarbert nobs. Never even invited Geordie in from the car. But listen to what I'm going to tell you. I saw Big Neil today and he had been talking to the stranger in the school after church; the fellow said he was from the War Department. That was that, but the rumour is going round now that he was doing a tour of the islands trying to get some of the landlords and people like that to form a part-time regiment of soldiers. Big Neil doesn't like the idea at all!'

'I know; I heard my father and him talking about it. My father thinks Hitler's making fools of us, and that we should stand up to him right now.'

'Let's hope they're wrong. Big Neil has seen two wars already and your father has seen one – and that's enough for both of them. I suppose I've been one of the lucky ones. Nobody ever thought it worthwhile to call me up, and if they didn't think it last time they certainly won't think it now. Mind you, I'm the kind they should take – the kind that's no good for anything else!'

I thought he was going to embark on one of his self-pitying monologues. But no. Old Hector, whose opinion few people ever sought and who was normally too retiring to volunteer it, was clearly an avid reader of the newspapers although he made great play of his own lack of education. For the next half hour I was treated to a simple lecture on the rise of Nazi Germany, and it was only the descent of the dark that finally brought me to my feet. On my way out I noticed his navy blue serge jacket draped over the back of a chair.

'Why have you got your Sunday suit hanging out? Are you going somewhere?' I was only pulling his leg, because Hector had never been known to leave the village since he stopped ghillying. I noticed but didn't really register that what I could see of his face in the dark looked vaguely shifty for a moment. 'Oh, that,' he said. And then, quickly recovering his old easy manner, 'Are you forgetting the Moderator's visit? With one thing and another I haven't had time to put it back in the trunk.' I left him and went racing down the hill, suddenly filled with excitement at the prospect of a war on the horizon. None of the implications of it worried my young mind of course but, suddenly, the idea seemed rather splendid. The wars of my schoolbooks were wars of heroics and romance and totally unreal; my father's war was shrouded in silence and as unreal as the rest. But the prospect of a war on my own doorstep and in my own time was exhilarating, and I found myself wishing that I were older – ready to don a khaki uniform with brass buttons on the shoulders, or a navy blue one with gold plastered on the cap; the airforce didn't have a very glamorous tradition as yet, but I remembered what my father had said the day the first aeroplane landed on the sands, the day Maggie MacGeachan had been buried. 'These are the things of the new wars,' he had said. 'These are the things with the power of good and evil; they'll be lifting people to the beach down there to the hospital when there's an emergency like a burst appendix or something, and somewhere else they'll be dropping death on people from the skies.'

'Is there going to be a war?' I asked him when I got home.

'Probably,' he said. 'And the sooner the better!'

'John!' There was no mistaking the horror in my mother's face.

'It's true,' he said. 'Every extra day we give that madman the more powerful he'll become; and this damn government we've got thinks it'll buy him off with sweet and reasonable arguments. We're always the same, hoping things will work out. We're too used to winning, that's our trouble; this time we might be in for a big surprise.'

'You're not saying we'll lose!' My chauvinism was well founded in the glories of the Empire.

'No, because we've also got a habit of winning. But it's not going to be as easy as some people think. Some fool in the newspaper was talking of the united world crushing Hitler in a few weeks if war breaks out. Some hopes. For a start the Yanks

100

will come in and pick up the medals when somebody else has done the dirty work. Anyway, who wants to talk of war? You've got a whole new world opening up for you in a week's time. Tarbert may be only a tuppeny-ha'penny village as far as the rest of the world is concerned, but for you it's the golden gates.'

He went back to repairing a boot which he had wedged on to a three-headed last; he had finished pinning on a new leather sole and now he was trimming it with a knife and a rasp. I knew that he wouldn't hear anything else even if I tried to pursue the conversation; when he did start on a job his concentration was total. My brother hadn't even looked up when I came in; he was equally deeply involved in a jig-saw puzzle that some visiting relative had given him and, in any case, as the time for my departure drew nearer the same gulf seemed to be developing between him and me as between me and Gillespie, who had opted not to continue with school after fourteen. Over on St Clement's bench my mother was putting the last stitches into a jacket which had been handed down to me from my young banker cousin, and apart from that one word of remonstration to my father she had remained engrossed in her own task – but, I could sense from the automatic rhythm of her stitching, lost in a private world of her own too. We had recently acquired a double wick oil-lamp of the kind that clipped on to the wall and from its height it cast a semi-circular pool of light which spread out to take in the three of them as they bent over their different tasks. Where I sat, just inside the door, the edge of the light had begun to diffuse with the darkness and I found myself feeling like a stranger looking in on a world of other people, and I suddenly felt lonely at the thought of the golden gates.

Next morning I was winding my way as usual to milk Primrose, revived by a night's sleep and the thought that this was one chore that I would be leaving behind me. I was trudging along with my eyes on my toes and so I was almost beside him when I noticed Old Hector standing at the roadside, obviously waiting for the morning bus that travelled northwards to Tarbert and on to Stornoway in Lewis. I suddenly realised that he'd been lying to me (or at least being devious) about the Sunday suit the night before. Because now he was wearing it – dressed to the nines in fact, in a white celluloid collar and tie, a crotal and white Harris Tweed cap, and a polished pair of delicate shoes that he probably hadn't worn since Singapore. He was leaning on a hefty walking stick, puffing at his pipe and staring into the distance like a man with doom on his mind.

'Wh – where are you going?' I asked.

'On the bus,' he said sarcastically without removing his pipe. 'I've reached an age when I'm allowed out on my own.' I felt myself flushing at the snub, but I decided to make no retort and moved up the hill to find Primrose.

'Where was Old Hector going?' everybody I met that day asked me, and I seemed to meet half the village. 'He hasn't left the village in years. Where was he going?'

'Woolworth's,' I replied, not liking to admit that he hadn't let me into his confidence.

'Woolworth's! What the devil can he want in Woolworth's that Jackie the driver couldn't bring him, or the tweed landry?' The Harris Tweed trade had begun to boom to such an extent that a regular lorry now came round from a Stornoway textile mill to supply the weavers with yarn for contracted-out tweeds, and it, of course, was contributing its share to the well-being of the villages as an unofficial public service vehicle. 'Woolworth's!' said somebody else. 'It's well seen his sister Maggie isn't alive or he wouldn't be going off gallivanting and spending money in Woolworth's.'

If Maggie was alive he wouldn't be needing to go on the bus, I thought to myself as I made my way through a long and guilty day.

The return bus from Stornoway wasn't due back till long after the evening milking, so after I'd seen to Primrose I decided to stay on in Hector's house and keep the fire in for his return and have the kettle boiling. The first warning I had of his arrival was the thud of his walking-stick as he flung it into a corner, and the softer flump of his cap as he threw it on to the wooden seat below the window.

'How did it go?' I asked, thankful that the walking-stick was out of his hand.

'Go?' he said. 'Go!' He obviously didn't remember that I didn't know officially where he was; he was also confirming that he had been exactly where I thought he had been. But it was a relief to know that his anger wasn't directed at me for once; in fact he was almost appealing to me to join in his wrath.

'I've never been so insulted in my life! She was sixty if she was a day and, judging by the streaky red hair of her, there was tinker blood in her. For sure there was plenty tinker in her talk. And if God ever gave a man a warning it was there in the shape of her mother who will never see ninety-eight again – all fankled up with arthritis except for her tongue … and she had the nerve to make remarks about my legs!'

'So you're not taking the daughter?' I ventured.

'Take her!' he spluttered. 'It was a job lot man. Whoever is fool enough to take that one has to take the mother as well. It wasn't a man she was wanting, it was a caretaker! We didn't say in our advertisement that we wanted a woman who would come and live here; she was all set to have me move in there. Me live in Lewis! I'd be a laughing-stock for the few days that I survived …'

He said a lot more than that, but I had relaxed once I'd heard him refer to the advert as 'our advertisement'. I was relieved to know that he wasn't holding me personally responsible for the day, and, after that all I had to do was to keep a straight face till he got the anger out of his system.

'Would you like a cup of tea?' I asked. 'The kettle's boiling.'

'Ach you're a good lad. See, Jackie the driver offered me a cigarette and I took it and slipped it into my pocket for you.' For a moment I could have sworn that I caught a whiff of whisky as he patted me on the shoulder and sat down in his own chair for the first time since he came in. 'Aye,' he said. 'A cup of tea would be just fine; it's more than I was offered in that place.'

I should have left things at that, I suppose, but some devil must have prompted me.

'And when are you going to see the next one?' I asked – unfortunately just as he took a large mouthful of tea. I thought I was going to have to thump him on the back to get him breathing again. But he recovered.

'The next one!' he gasped. 'You must be out of your mind or you must think I'm out of mine. There's going to be no next one! I'd rather sell Primrose and make do with nessels for the rest of my life.'

'Are you forgetting breach of promise? And the price of Primrose won't be the half of what you'll have to pay.'

'What the devil have you done to me?' gasped Hector, putting his teacup on the floor and his head in his hands. I

103

slipped off home without replying.

'Woolworth's must have put a spell on Hector MacGeachan,' somebody said to me a few days later. The atmosphere between us had been distinctly chilly for the last few days and it was only on the evening before his second safari that he had told me, almost casually, that he was setting off on his travels again. He encouraged no discussion. On the evening of his second journey I took care to have the milking finished and be clear of his house before the night bus came back from Stornoway, and next morning it was with a certain amount of trepidation that I wound my way up the hill. To my astonishment he was waiting for me in great good form with a letter in his hand. But neither then nor ever after did he refer to his trip, and it will become easy to see why I couldn't possibly raise the subject.

'Here, I want you to post this letter for me. Here's a penny ha'penny to buy a stamp, and I want you to put the letter in the pillar-box yourself and *not* hand it to Calum the Post. I'm writing as you can see to that woman on the island, and if she'll have me I'm taking her, as they say, "unseen".'

'You can't do that!'

'Stop telling me what I can and can't do,' he growled. 'I survived all these years with my sister Maggie, so I reckon that I can cope with most things now. I'm going off for a sack of peat. You get on with the milking of Primrose. And don't mention that letter to a living soul.'

The inter-islands post was uncertain and slow in those days, and I knew that Hector couldn't possibly get a reply before I left for High School.

'What'll happen to Old Hector and Primrose?' I asked my mother as she packed my case the night before the day. 'You won't be able to milk her night and morning, day in day out.'

'Don't you worry about Old Hector; I've been talking to the women and we'll take it in turns to milk the cow for him till he gets her sold at the October sales. And after that we'll see to it that he's all right for milk; despite what your father says I don't see Hector adapting to nessels at his age.'

I smiled to myself. I had an idea that Hector was going to have to adapt to rather more than condensed milk in the next month or two.

Chapter Eight

Every year since school began I had gone to the Northlands to Big Grandfather's for the whole duration of the summer holiday and in recent years, since a regular bus service had been established, I had travelled each way alone. This time my father was going to accompany me; it was as if I was being ceremonially handed over into fosterage. I suppose that's how it must have felt to my parents too. High School was only sixteen miles away and today, if the circumstances were the same, I would be expected to commute – travelling twenty minutes each way by school bus. But times were different; the state of the road was vastly different; buses were different and their regularity uncertain. Therefore, from now on, I would be coming home only for the statutory school holidays and for occasional long week-ends. From that August day onward it would be from the outside that I would see the village ageing – the village which I love more than any place on earth. And that is how it has been. It has always been as a visitor that I have returned … and, increasingly, as a stranger.

My parents must have realised that. They must have known that only failure (in terms of the island philosophy of the time) would bring me back to a life in the village. I had 'done my homework' … I had learnt 'to talk English' … I had 'won the bursary' … I had done all the things that would launch me for far shores. And I was as excited as any man setting off on a voyage – too young to care that I was leaving the people who had moulded my life … my parents themselves, Great Aunt Rachel, the Boer War veteran, the man with the hole in his cheek, Old Hector and all the others whom I know now to have shaped my character and my attitudes. Others would wield their different influences in times to come, but they would be only adding daubs and touches of better and worse. It was the knowledge of the beginning of finality that made my mother give me a hasty peck on the cheek, and made my father sound brusque as he picked up my case and said 'Here comes the bus; come along!' We walked down to the gate dressed as if we were setting off to some formal function. He had his good plus-four suit on; I was in my first pair of long trousers which made me feel as if I was walking with my knees in splints.

The bus was long for the roads and Jackie was out to impress a larger complement of passengers than usual. Every time we hit a pot-hole – and there were plenty of them – we were detonated six inches off our seats to come back down with a thud; here and there a man muttered an expletive and a couple of holy women groaned. Jackie was trying to make up time, waging a losing battle with the unpunctuality which his employers were trying to iron out of him, knowing that his stops would be more frequent than usual because of the 'scholars' going back to school. Four times he stopped before leaving the village behind him, each time to pick up a well-dressed boy or girl with a suitcase; they were the ones who had gone the bursary road before me.

I was setting out on the journey to my future and yet, in a sense, it was a journey back in time. A century before, helpless and hopeless bands of people must have plodded northwards on a track along that same route; they were the displaced persons of their time, callously thrown off the lush agricultural ground of the Southlands by overlords who decided to follow the profitable fashion of the mainland and turn their estates into sheepfarms. Sheepfarming didn't require large numbers of workers; on the contrary tenants were taking up valuable land that could be put under sheep, and so the people were shunted out of their homelands and crowded into the dour rocky north. Generations later I was born in those Northlands just as the trend was at last being reversed, and as a child I had travelled south with my parents as they set out to reclaim the

106

old lands and build a new village. A decade had now passed since we jolted in a decrepit bus on our journey to our promised land. The Atlantic had been on our right then and we had threaded our way through empty country – a country which became greener and more inviting the farther south we went. Now, those ten years later, the sea was on the left and I was travelling the route northwards – through new villages that had sprouted along the shore in quick succession after the apparently successful establishment of our own. Only their names were old – memorials to the ancient Viking exploration of those lands. Horgabost, Crago, Seileabost, and finally Luskentyre strung out along one of the most spectacular beaches in Britain. These were the villages of the people who had returned to reclaim the good land for themselves and they were now out to prove that they could coax prosperity from it. Time would tell.

After the Luskentyre road-end the landscape changed as the bland machair lands of the south gave way to the dour Northlands with acres of grey rock resisting the tough stunted heather which didn't have enough soil beneath it to allow it to grow into cover. Here and there miniscular peatbanks had been discovered by the men of the north who would labour to pick out seams that would each surrender only a couple of creels of winter fuel. It was a landscape I had passed through many times without noticing it, but now I was seeing it with fresh eyes and comparing those scars of peat with the long trenches on our own moorlands. Here and there hessian sacks of peat were stacked by the roadside waiting to be transported by lorry to Tarbert; now and again a man and wife would wave to the bus before bending back to the business of filling more sacks to add to their pile.

Just before the wicked crook of road known as The Devil's Elbow the bus crested the high hill and the view burst open on to the bays of Miavag and Kendebig and, further on, the mouth of East Loch Tarbert with the island of Scalpay sitting squat bastion against the Minch. I was looking down on peopled territory once again and I could see the chequered pattern those people had dug out of the heather with spade and pick to give themselves tillable patches around their homes. And for all the poverty of the land there was an air of gentle prosperity; well-established white houses had steadily displaced most of the thatched houses. They owed nothing to the land, those houses; they had been built with money from fishing or, most usually, with money sent home by sailor sons, and daughters in service in the mansions of the mainland cities. It was no shame to be in service. Far from it. Those girls, like their sailor brothers, were repaying their debt to ageing parents to whom some would, themselves, return one day with some of the city's sophistication showing in their manners and their clothes and their luggage. They wouldn't all come back, of course. Many of the girls, in particular, would marry city husbands and swell the Highland coteries of Glasgow and Edinburgh and London: each one who did return would marry, not too late in life, a man from home and rear a family into which she would instill a longing for the bright lights.

As the bus moved carefully down the Heel of Kendebig its progress became easier and conversation was allowed to develop, not only because the bumping stopped, but because passengers who have no private sorrows always become more voluble with relief at the approach of the journey's end. The reason for the greater comfort was that we were now on the new tarmacadam surface which was gently snaking its way out south from Tarbert where it had begun in the time honoured tradition that improvement always begins at the centre of local government and at the doorsteps of its representatives. The marvel of the 'tar road' was a subject for conversation in itself; it was a miracle of our time although it had taken six score years to reach us.

On the right we passed Wee Grandfather's house from where my family had set out on our odyssey ten years ago; my father looked into the middle distance and bit on his pipe but I would never know whether he wondered if his move had been a wise one. I knew that my mother had never got over her longing for the Northlands, but I never knew with him.

On the left was the flat no man's land where the tinkers camped in summer; I felt my face flushing as I remembered my encounter with the crude siren of their tribe. In the moonlight the coppery red of her hair and her silhouette had convinced me that she must be the glamorous accommodating maid from the doctor's house. Accommodating she had proved to be but, alas, more willing than I was able and I had been unable to verify whether the Johnsonian dictum regarding the chambermaid and the Duchess applied to the tinker girl and the doctor's maid. I was mightily relieved to see that the gipsy encampment had been uplifted for the winter. Would she recognise me again, I wondered? And hoped not.

My father drew my attention to the water-driven wool mill which two enterprising brothers had opened in neat time for the latest boom in Harris Tweed; there the crofters sent the raw fleeces to be combed and carded and sent back as long thin sausages of soft wool for hand-spinning; the very boom that had made them was on the point of breaking them because the demand for tweed now far exceeded what the hand-spinners could satisfy and, more and more, the mills of Stornoway were turning out ready-spun thread and the spinning wheels would soon be making their ways to the antique shops of the cities. 'That's progress for you,' my father said. 'Soon they'll be making Harris Tweed in Japan and that'll be that.' As he finished speaking he put his pipe in his pocket and put his cap on. We were approaching the red gate which my grandfather felt obliged to keep painted red since it had become a landmark, and I could see the old man standing waiting for us.

The uneasy relationship which I remembered from boyhood had disappeared from between my father and the old man, and a vague mutual respect had taken its place; it never flourished into friendship because Big Grandfather had never, I think, fully accepted that the match had ever been worthy of my mother. Grandfather was a pragmatist who had built around himself a solid core of respectability; he had moved his family from black house to white; he had saved enough money from his days at sea to be able to surround himself with the trappings of modest comfort; he had built up a sheepstock against the odds in a barren land, and he had become an expert on sheep-rearing; he had seen his elder daughter through school and college into the teaching profession in days when education had not yet achieved predominant importance; he had seen a strong, intelligent son develop into a master craftsman as a cabinet-maker. Backed up by Wee Grannie whose roly-poly appearance belied a very sharp, shrewd brain he had built up a pillarship of community from which my mother had been plucked by a man of books and dreams. In the early days Big Grandfather had courteously upbraided and cajoled, and my father had smiled and remained unruffled. Now each accepted the other for the quality of total honesty that they had in common.

'Well, I've brought him to you,' my father said. 'He's been warned to do what he's told and to be a help to you around the place.'

'He's never been any trouble here,' said my grandfather, leading the way down the winding path to the house by the shore. 'He's never been any trouble to his grandmother or myself.' I was glad that the old man seemed to have forgotten my visit of the previous summer when I had put the effervescent salts into the pee-pot below the bed being occupied by two holy lady visitors and caused them to flood or, rather, froth the house! Grandfather had confined me to barracks for a week then, vowing that the shame of my behaviour would haunt him forever. The shame had obviously been exorcised. 'So long as he's home before dark and keeps away from the craobhag ... that's all I'll expect from him. And that he brings home a trout from the burn now and again.'

'And gets stuck into his books,' said my father pointedly.

'Hum!' said the old man, and changed the conversation to talk of the weather and the sheep-stock, to which my father responded with as much enthusiasm as he could muster. I knew that he would stay for a meal and then make his way back to his own parents' house where he would spend the night before catching the morning bus back to the Southlands; there was a finality about the prospect which gave me slight stirrings of apprehension; but they disappeared as the smell of Wee Grannie's cooking wafted to meet us while we were still a hundred yards from the house.

'We'll just take your case straight up the stairs and your grandmother will show you where to put your things later on.'

My father went into the living room and I could hear Wee Grannie and himself exchanging pleasantries as I followed grandfather upstairs. Over the years, under the guidance of my uncle who was now away in Southampton, he'd had the house modernised. In addition to the very comfortable living room downstairs there was also a drawing-room-cum-dining-room 'for best' furnished with a magnificent red mahogany expanding table which could pull out to seat twelve on occasions like the twice yearly communions, twelve mahogany chairs covered in horse-hair that used to prickle the backs of my knees but wouldn't any more now that I was in long trousers for good, and a large elegant side-board with a tall mirror; in addition, it had two comfortable armchairs on each side of a maroon-tiled fireplace flanked by two spotted china dogs and brass fire-irons. Heavy Victorian velvet curtains gave it a slightly gloomy air in summer but made it cosy in winter, and they trapped the heady smell of the geraniums which my grandmother nurtured carefully from year to year.

The stairs in themselves were a fascination for me – brought up in the over-crowded little corrugated-iron two-roomed house in the Southlands; they led up to two large bedrooms which had recently been made even more spacious by having had dormer windows added to them; in their own room my grandparents had decided to retain the closed in box-beds, but the spare room had been refurbished in a crisp modern style and had a musty camphory smell except when it was aired for visitors. My room was the small coomb-ceilinged one between the other two; it had a bed with brass knobs on it, and I would have it all to myself; on the opposite wall from it was a bookcase fashioned out of two orange-boxes with white lace draped over them, with a brass oil-lamp sitting on top; the chest-of-drawers for my clothes was placed with a mirror on it right under a sky-light which, when it was propped open, let in the smell of the shore, the call of the seabirds and the morning and evening chugging of the fishing boats coming in to Tarbert pier. As grandfather threw open the door I could see that the whole room had been papered and painted afresh against my arrival, and a neat little woollen rug had been placed in front of the bed to protect my feet from the cold of the linoleum. I stopped and stared. This was to be my room – my very own, private room – for three years, and the thrill of its comfort and its privacy was something I have never captured since even in the plushest hotel.

'What's that?' I asked, pointing to a small pile of clothes and a leather harness-type satchel on the quilt.

'O, your Great-Aunt Christina brought these for you; the

twins had them when they were in school.' The twins were two manly second cousins of mine (one of them was now the banker who had prompted my reply to the doctor); they were quite a few years older than I was and it might take me a little time to grow into their well-kept school clothes, but the satchel was something which would come in useful right away. I fingered it, trying to look casual, but deep down I was thrilled; up till then I had always carried my books to school in a bundle tied with string – tucking them under my jersey to keep them dry when it rained. The satchel was yet another symbol of the new age!

'Right, we'd better go back downstairs or you'll be getting a sharp touch of your grannie's tongue before you're an hour in the house if you're not ready to sit at the table when she lifts the meal. And there's something I want to show you privately.'

He led me downstairs but instead of turning into the living room where I could hear my father and grandmother in animated conversation about Harris Tweed he turned right and opened the door into a closet which had always been a junk room – although as with everything else in grandfather's house, tidily ordered – the room in which I had occasionally been made to camp when the house was full of communion or cattle-sale visitors. I couldn't imagine what there could be to see in the closet. But when Big Grandfather opened the door, it was a junk room no longer. Instead it had a wash basin with two taps, a flush toilet and a full length bath. I'd had no idea that the old man had had 'the water brought in' as it was popularly known, and this was a totally new dimension to my world – a slightly embarrassing one. Although some of the new white houses in our own village had had interior plumbing installed, we hadn't, and I'd never had occasion to experiment with bath or toilet. Taps, yes. When our school had been modernised the outhouses had been fitted with chemical toilets but nobody had ever used them, and the brass taps in the cloakrooms gushed only cold water. In neighbours' houses a visitor would never have dreamt of making indelicate use of the facilities and one didn't go visiting in order to wash one's hands. While I was admiring the black and white tiled linoleum and marvelling at the clinical appearance of it all, grandfather was turning the taps on and off and talking about a bath every Saturday night.

'And now look here,' he said. 'This is something your grannie can't very well explain to you. We've got no river on this croft as you have at home so that water from a well up at the back has to be stored in a big concrete tank that you'll see out there on the hillock behind the house. The tank takes a long time to fill up so we have to conserve the water as much as possible. You'll still be pee-ing outside, of course, unless you're caught short at night but don't pull the plug after a pee. You do your shitties in here, and you use that paper there afterwards; that's when you must be sure to press this lever here.' And he demonstrated by flushing the toilet. I seemed to be entering into several new worlds all at once.

My father stopped to relieve himself at the end of the byre as he set off to his own parents' house after the meal. 'Did you see the new bathroom?' I asked him.

'Aye,' he said. 'You'll be taking unkindly to using the outside when you come home at Christmas. That's progress for you. There was an old man in Lewis whose son married a stylish girl from the mainland and she insisted on turning one of the rooms of the house into a bathroom. Very stylish she was and not at all used to the ways of Lewis. One thing she couldn't stand was the smell of salt herring boiling and didn't she insist that if the old man wanted to continue eating potatoes and salt herring he had to eat them outside. One of the neighbours couldn't believe it one day when he came along and found the old fellow outside at the end of the house with a big platter of potatoes and salt herring on his knee. *What the devil are you doing eating outside?* the neighbour asked. *It's the way of the new world, man,* the old fellow replied. *There was a time when I ate inside and shat outside, but now I shit inside and eat out!*'

'That's not true,' I laughed.

'Maybe not,' he said. 'But there's truth in it. A lot of your world is going to be turned upside down and inside out from tomorrow; and most of it will be for the best. Ach well –' He dug into his pocket. 'I know your mother has given you a bit of money for your pocket and she'll be sending you some in the post from time to time. Here's half-a-crown for extra.' He paused and his eyes crinkled in a way that he had. 'Well, so long my boy – and good luck'. He shook hands with me for the first time in his life, and walked briskly away without looking back. I stood looking after him till the dusk closed round him at the red gate. I was alone on the pathway in the gloom; the house was out of sight round an elbow of the path. A few lights twinkled far away across the bay on the island of Scalpay, accentuating the utter solitude. I felt the chill of the evening and a prickling at the back of my eyes, and I could almost see in my mind's eye my mother and my three brothers in the hot little living room back in the village.

A little tin oil-lamp, hanging on the wall, lit up the stair down which my grandmother was making her slow progress as I got in. She was breathing heavily and carefully putting the same foot in front of her on each new tread as she came down, and, for the first time, I realised that she was getting very old.

'I've been putting a hot bottle in your bed just for tonight,' she said. 'And I've laid out your clothes for school tomorrow. There's a glass of milk and some oatcakes on the table, and your grandfather's waiting to take the book when you're finished.' The usual phrase for morning and evening prayers was 'taking the books' but Wee Grandmother, for some reason that I've never fathomed, spoke her native Gaelic with immaculate purity and rhythm but with occasional archaisms and highly individual usages. The bible was 'the book' one and indivisible stretching from the Genesis to her present moment of time. Grandfather treated God with immaculate courtesy but was precise as to the time set aside for Him. He conducted morning worship at quarter past eight (at home we hadn't ever held morning prayers) and at night he invariably reached for the bible and his gold rimmed spectacles at half past ten. He had his own tall mahogany chair with slim arms on it on one side of the fire; Grannie had a Taransay chair with a plaited straw seat on the other; I sat on the newly acquired modern couch which they both called a 'dive in'. Prayers that night were as they would be every night for three years. Grandfather prayed, sitting in his chair; he then read a psalm and a chapter which he always seemed to know almost word perfectly, but if he faltered Grannie would prompt him from her memory; when he was finished he gave exactly the same kind of sigh every night and we all got down on our knees while he prayed – first to a set formula and then, discursively, taking in events of topical concern. When he was finished he straightened up and yawned and said 'Well, woman ...' and waited for her to

114

precede him upstairs after he had seen to his dogs in the scullery. 'You'll blow your own lamp out,' he said as he left the room. 'Don't fall asleep with it on or you'll smoke us all out.' I couldn't believe my ears. Father had a well-founded holy terror of fire and would never have dreamt of letting anybody put out the last flame of the evening without checking it himself. This was another freedom that I was going to enjoy.

I was wakened in the morning by the chugging of the fishing boats and the screeching of their escorts of gulls. I had no idea what the time was so I opened the skylight and just stood in my shirt tails staring out at a scene that couldn't possibly be more different from the one I was accustomed to at home. It wasn't a totally new scene to me; I had seen it at holiday times over the years but now I felt it, strangely, part of my life, whereas then I'd been a visitor and an onlooker. There were, I suppose, half a dozen boats in the bay with their Kelvin paraffin engines hammering out their staccatos, and through the alternating fury and exultation of the seagulls I could hear the men shouting to each other from boat to boat as they folded their nets and flung unwanted squid and shrimp and crab overboard to the frenzied birds; the morning was so still that I could hear their conversations as they compared news of their catches and bits of gossip. Occasionally they would break into English which, even to me, was painfully ungrammatical, as they included a boat which had an east coast number on her shoulder. I had completely forgotten the purpose of my morning till I heard Big Grandfather shouting from the foot of the stairs, demanding to know if I was deliberately trying to be late for my first morning of High School.

'You know where the school is?' he enquired as he spooned his brose.

'Man, your memory worries me,' Grannie said. 'Don't you remember the boy went to the infant school here for a while when the family had the measles that year?'

I had almost forgotten myself; or, rather, I hadn't associated that Primary School with the one I was going to join now. 'Yes, of course,' I said. 'Instead of turning right down through the town at the foot of Caw Brae I go straight on past the Doctor's manse to the east side.'

'It'll take you fifteen minutes if you run part of the way,' grandfather went on. 'And that means that you'll have to move smartly at the dinner hour if you're going to have time for a decent dinner –'

'Which you're going to have,' Grannie cut in firmly. 'You're not going to be spending money in Tommy's on rubbish at eleven o'clock and then coming home here without an appetite for your food!'

Tommy's shop! I'd forgotten that a shrewd distant relative of our own had opened up a little grocery store just across the road from the school, and it had developed into a tuck shop to which the Headmaster tended to turn a blind eye even though there was a strict school law that no pupils were to leave the school playground except at the lunch hour and at four o'clock. Few rules were honoured more in the breech … and I made a mental note to pop upstairs for some pennies before setting off. I thought Big Grandfather's morning prayers would never end but, at last, I found myself with my empty satchel on my back trotting up to the red gate and the main road. A small number of youngsters, all with the crispness of first day of term about them, were walking along the road in their ones and twos; they had a casual air about them that suggested that the journey was not a new one for them. But they were all strangers to me and I jogged on alone.

The best view of the town of Tarbert (for town it is called despite the fact that it's a village by mainland standards) is the view that was discovered by the first of the picture-postcard photographers many years ago. And it will never be improved on – from land, sea or air. It is the view as one stands at the top of the steep hill known as the Caw and leans over the stone dyke that protects one from the sheer drop down to the near shore of the bay. From there the town is seen in the entirety of it that matters – from the hotel on the far left the eye is drawn along the shore road known as 'the street' which edges the far side of the harbour and leads down to the pier. It isn't a crescent quite, but near enough. It is, despite what many people tend to think, the new town – the town that grew up when the mailboat began to ply across the Minch connecting Tarbert to the mainland, thereby making it the principal centre of commerce from which it grew into a capital. Tarbert is the Gaelic for isthmus and only a scrawny neck of land separates east loch from west. In the old days of Clan MacLeod and the big estate owners who bought them out, sea traffic had been down the west coast, down from Huisinis and Amhuinnsuidhe of the great castle, down by the off-shore islands of Scarp and Taransay and all the way to the rich green machair lands where the new villages of my own boyhood are now ageing. But with the opening of the steamer route and the building of the road all that had changed; West Tarbert had become a mini-suburbia and East Tarbert had begun to bustle.

There were fourteen shops in the year that I went to High School, for the town now served the whole hinterland with its scrabble of villages. As I paused at the top of Caw I could see the whole sweep of the town and from my memory of summer holidays I could identify all the shops. Nine of them were general stores – different from each other only according to the characters that their owners had stamped on them; in most of them you could buy anything from a foot of black-twist pipe tobacco to a tether for a cow or a bag of nails and a hammer. Five were special – the baker, the cobbler, the butcher, the watchmaker, and 'the black man's' – owned by Ali Mohammed, who was now an established member of the community and was called Alick. And there were the institutions – the large ones like the big white Bank of Scotland with the manager's house on top of it, the pier office, the Church of Scotland and the Free Presbyterian Church, each with its own manse. There were discreet offices too, like the one where a registrar lurked who put births and marriages and deaths on files; there were offices which were beginning to classify people into sick and deserving poor and the rest. People lived there too, above and beside their places of business. All the buildings, in a higgledy-piggledy of styles, hugged the one side of the street like a row of pensioners holding hands, and, alone on the nearside to me stood the tall war memorial with red fuchsia growing up round a lot of names.

The street still seemed asleep as I watched it, with the shop doors still closed. But smoke was beginning to rise and, here and there, a house door opened and someone with a satchel would slip out. Like the country road along which I'd come the street was beginning to move with the ones and twos heading for the school and I moved down the Caw to join the stream at the junction of the road and the street where the country met the town. Three boys were coming along together, chatting earnestly like old friends. One was lean and sophisticated with the air of someone who'd been around for a while and knew the ropes; one was large with an unruly mane and a white laugh; one was sturdy and serious looking, with a suggestion of a seaman's walk. They had the assurance of each other's company; I was the country mouse come to town. The older boy spoke to me and asked my name and where I came from, and I told him. It turned out that he was, indeed, in his final year and that his two companions were rookies like myself. They were to be my companions through the High School and beyond, till the time came about which people were then only beginning to worry.

Chapter Nine

There were more pupils assembled in the grounds of the High School on that morning in late August than the total of those who had passed through the doors of the old school that I had left in the Southlands in the forty-five years of its existence. Tarbert School was two schools in one: one section of it was the Primary School for the town and its hinterland, and the other the High School to which pupils graduated in their early teens from more than a score of village schools throughout the whole of Harris. It had a grand name, after a landlord who had been its benefactor at the end of last century, and the technical description of it was Junior Secondary School. But it was known as Tarbert School, and that was that.

Awe is the second-last thing to which a lump of a boy will admit, but if it wasn't with awe it was certainly with a great amount of wonderment and a flittering of trepidation, that I stared round the motley throng as I clung close to my new-found companions. The threads of the Hebridean tapestry were all there – the fair hair and the blue eyes of the Norse incomers of nine centuries ago, the brown-eyed Iberian strain which was my own, and the jet black hair and the blue eyes of the Celt. But it wasn't heredity or pedigree that occupied my mind, but the thought that any moment now I would be coming face to face with the Headmaster whose legend was monster for discipline – the man who had moulded the whole character of the school and given it a formidable reputation for learning although his own education was home-spun to the extent of his never having attended college or University. He had carved his way up from being a pupil-teacher in his youth, achieving the status of teacher through an informal apprenticeship long before the various education laws demanded diplomas or degrees. He had a reputation for choleric temper and ferocious Presbyterianism – a combination more explosive than Nobel's imaginings. I had never heard him referred to by his proper name; to the whole community (behind his back, of course) he was 'The Blus' because of his eccentric pronunciation of the arithmetical additional symbol; his character would never have permitted of him being called 'The Minors' although he had that one wrong too. I didn't have long to wait to meet him. An imperious whistle sounded, and when I turned round there he was at the top of the school steps – a sturdy figure in a well cut plus-four suit of much finer tweed than our Harris variety; he had a shock of greying hair, a strong face which looked as if it could hide a smile deep down for a special occasion, and shrewd hazel eyes behind gold-rimmed spectacles. As soon as the whistle sounded a silence fell over the playground and, herded by the veterans, we scuffed our ways into our respective male and female lines. As we filed in he stood like a traffic policeman directing us. Third year to the science room. Second year to the English room. First year to his own room. It didn't require much education to know that the last category was my own.

Angus Macdonald (for that was his real name) was the only example of the archetypal dominie that I ever came across; he was probably a member of the last generation of the species. His own subjects were Latin and Gaelic and he taught them both with a ferocity which he reinforced, as he did discipline, with a supple leather Lochgelly tawse. But he didn't ply it with the sadism in which that first teacher of my childhood had revelled; he used it as the third arm of authority. In my three years under his tutelage I heard him miscalled and cursed with adolescent enthusiasm but I never once heard him accused of unfairness. Every single line of the Goldsmith evocation applied to him; not least that

> ... he was kind; or if severe in aught
> The love he bore to learning was in fault.

120

Not the least of his influences on me was that he taught me, for the first time, that my own native language was a language of aged culture and literature and not a crude dialect to be scourged out of my consciousness as an aberration of heritage or as something 'of no commercial value, and a barrier to advancement in the world'.

'The Blus' (his name was never used without the definite article) was backed by two young men of totally different attitudes to teaching. They were in their twenties – youthful and enthusiastic – and they regarded their students as young adults with whom they could joke and laugh and for whom they could bring their respective class-room subjects to life. Their relationships with us were much more that of tutors than teachers. Over the years Alexander Nicholson was to build on the love of English and history which my primary teacher and my father had nurtured in me; Leslie Watson came to accept with unswerving good grace that the most he could ever hope to teach me from the rich realms of mathematics and science was that Pythagoras was the one who adorned triangles with squares and that Archimedes was the one who had the bath. What those two young men did find in me – which neither I nor anybody else had ever suspected – was that I had a sense of humour and, by encouraging it, they helped me grow out of the 'please miss, yes miss' attitudes of infant school and discover that learning was a process of doubting and questioning in which there could be fun.

It took remarkably little time to adjust to the size of the new school after the cosy menage of thirteen in which I had spent most of my school life hitherto. The most difficult thing to get used to was the formality of a large class in which everybody concentrated on the same subject instead of eight little units at different stages and involved in different themes. Gone was the hum of activity and the pervasive smell of chalk; in their place was an almost tangible feel of concentration. Gone too was the innocent informality of little boys and girls sharing desks; now the boys were grouped on one side of the room and on the other was a uniformity of gym-slips belted to suggest varying promises of chests.

Within a week or two I was marching from classroom to classroom at change-over time as if I had stridden those corridors all my life. The awe of the second and third year boys vanished as I packed into the urinal with them at the intervals to snatch quick smokes while somebody kept cave at the door. Occasionally The Blus would take it into his head to do a tour of the premises, but the most brazen of us merely cupped our cigarettes in our hands and pulled them up into our sleeves, swinging our arms to dispel the smoke while his head was thrust into the reeking hazy atmosphere demanding to know what we were doing 'crowded in here on a lovely day like this' as if he feared we might be getting up to some of the more unorthodox sophistications of the great Public Schools. One soon learnt that The Blus, for all this thundering, didn't really expect boys to behave themselves – he had seen too many boys for that – but he did expect them not to get caught. His rule and his role were equally extraordinary.

Most of the country pupils were in formal lodgings with landladies who meticulously took their money every Friday; a few like myself, for reasons of kinship and poverty, were guests with relatives who deemed it more blest to give than to receive. The lodgers set the pattern of life. They had to be back in their digs each evening at six o'clock for their meals and their landladies, who took their responsibilities seriously and were frequently in cahoots with the headmaster, expected their charges to remain indoors for the rest of the evening and do their homework unless there was an organised fishing trip or a rare social function. Between the hours of four and six the boys and girls were free to do as they chose although, in all conscience, there was little to do except parade up and down the street, look into the shop windows, or hang over the sea-wall watching the occasional fishing boat coming in with its covey of quarrelling gulls. Now and then a boat with unfamiliar registration lettering would attract us down to the pier itself and we would listen uncomprehendingly to the east coast chatter of men from faraway places like Peterhead or Stonehaven or Buckie as they spoke in a language that was almost English but not quite. On two evenings a week the mailboat *Lochmor* would shoulder her way in from the Minch and for an hour or so the village would be en fête as the bulk of the population congregated on the pier 'to meet the boat'. It was a ritual born out of the uniformity of daily life; it didn't matter that there was no visitor to meet or any item to collect – there were new faces to see even if they were only hanging over the railings as their wearers waited for the boat to chug on to its next port of call. 'Meeting the boat' continued to be a Hebridean pastime long after the frontiers of isolation had been demolished by accelerating communications and the years of war.

Those of us who lived 'out of town' soon convinced our relatives to adjust their meal hours to the hours of the Tarbert lodgers so that we could join our schoolmates in the promenade. We would deposit our school satchels in a friendly shop till it was time to take the road up Caw, and we would each join his or her own little pack. Boys and girls never walked together, of course. The girls teetered along in knots of three or four with their heads close together in secret conversation and giggling. The boys, in similar groups, swaggered with hands deep in pockets and shoulders swaying, pretending not to notice the girls unless, occasionally, to challenge them to outrageous and improbable assignations. Every now and again the smokers would melt into an alleyway for a drag, careful to post a look-out for The Blus, who was capable of thrusting his head into the most unexpected corner in search of misdeed. At half past five every day he would stalk down the street to the pier, his tweed cap sedately square over his forehead, swinging his silver-mounted walking stick; occasionally he would stop to exchange a sentence or two with one or two of the more solid citizens but, by and large, his only acknowledgment of the townsfolk was a nod and a grunt. At ten to six he would walk back up the street glancing into shop doors and probing into the occasional alley, and woe-betide the country boy or girl who wasn't off the street by then. He didn't bother about the pupils whose homes were in the town; they were the responsibility of their parents. But his duty, *in loco parentis*, was firmly fulfilled with regard to those of us who had no parents to supervise us. To the best of his ability he was trying to maintain a boarding school regime against some considerable odds. On Sundays he would sit in the aisle seat in the pew he had occupied for years, looking around and checking who was and who wasn't present, and the boy or girl who missed two Sundays in a row could expect to be summoned to his room at four o'clock on Monday. Any excuse had to be backed up by a note from landlady or guardian. Even the inventive third year boy who tried to plead on soul and conscience that he had decided to embrace the Muslim faith was told that he was a member of a free country and could be a Muslim for the five school days provided he stood up in class in front of his fellows and bowed thrice to Mecca; on Saturdays he could be whatever he wanted to be; on Sundays he would be in a pew in either the Church of Scotland or the Free Presbyterian Church. And that was that.

I was fortunate. Big Grandfather's house was a good mile out of town, and then a quarter of a mile down a track towards the seashore. Once there I could range the countryside with impunity provided I avoided the loch which The Blus occasionally fished for trout, and kept well clear of the main road along which he took frequent evening constitutionals. I got to know every sheeptrack on the shore crofts and I could follow them and even on the brightest autumn evening could reach Wee Grandfather's house without fear of detection. Once there, in the company of my cousin, life was my own. Together he and I fished the moorland lochs and streams to our hearts' content and, as the nights got longer and the trout got fewer, we visited the houses where we knew the locals met to exchange yarns and the news of the day. There was a whole enclave of my father's people still living round the bay to which their ancestors had been evicted from the Southlands long ago, a few of them still living in little black houses like the one that Old Hector lived in back home. They were all great story-tellers on my father's side, and the wireless had not yet killed out the pastime romanticised as *ceilidhing*. There is a deep-rooted conviction that Hebrideans spent (nay, spend) their evenings congregated round peat fires in selected houses drinking drams and singing Gaelic songs. Not in that part of the world. Not now. Not then. They congregated, for sure, if four or five comprised a congregation, but it was to talk of the times and the news of the world and occasionally to recall an old story with nary a dram in sight save at a wedding or, sometimes, at a wake. The talk was an education in itself, but not, necessarily, the form of education in which The Blus put his faith, nor the kind that my father fondly imagined I was imbibing. Big Grandfather didn't have my father's pre-occu-

124

pation with book-learning; his concern was with my physical well-fare and, if the evening was fine and the night not too dark, the only stipulation he made was that I should be home by ten. If he saw me, between then and bedtime, attempting to rush through a piece of school homework by the light of the hissing Tilley lamp – the brand new evaporating paraffin lamp which burnt a brilliant gauze filter, and which was beginning to supplant the yellow glowing old oil lamps in the more modern homes – he discouraged me lest I might strain my eyes. And Wee Grandmother would back him up with a quotation from the Bible to the effect that 'much reading was a weariness to the flesh'. The result was that most of my study was done in my little attic room by the light of a candle which I lit as soon as I heard Grandfather draw his first snore.

On Saturday night everybody went to town – everybody, that is, who was under middle age and unsmitten by matrimony or religion. Some of the older married men might make their ways to the pub for a couple of quiet pints and then adjourn to the cobbler's shop for an hour or two of conversation and discussion of community affairs but, by and large, family men and people of Big Grandfather's vintage spent the evening at home preparing for the Sabbath. Grandfather would do the milking, redd out the byre and the outhouses, and bring in four pails of spring water to supply the kitchen till Monday morning: although he now had a bathroom and running taps all the water for cooking and drinking was drawn from the cool, stone-lined well which had been dug and bottomed with filtering gravel by his father or, maybe, somebody long before that. When his chores were over he would betake himself to the bathroom and spend half an hour meticulously stropping his two beautiful Sheffield steel open razors; when they were so sharp that they would slice a hair dangling from his forefinger and thumb he would return one to its box and give himself a slow close shave with the other; he used his razors week about, maintaining that good steel rejuvenated itself if it was given rest. That was the last act of his 'working' week; cleaned and spruced he would make his way to his big mahogany chair in the living room, put on his gold spectacles and settle down to an hour with the *Stornoway Gazette*. Grannie, having completed her housework till every dish was tidily in the dresser, and the table set for Sunday breakfast, would wind the aged pendulum clock which had ticked its way through her long married life, and then she would put on her tortoise shell glasses and ease herself into the Taransay chair across the fire from her man, clutching some church magazine. Thus, peacefully and with the orderliness of years, their week drew gently to its close. For them the nights of going to the town were over.

Three roads converged in town. One from the south which passed the end of Grandfather's croft road, one from the west that threaded through a few hamlets before beginning to claw its lonely way up through the moors and over the towering Clisham on its way to Stornoway which was a real town, or so they said, with gas-light on its streets and a picture house instead of our cobbler's shop; the third road was a short gravel track, barely passable by car, which ended after a few miles eastwards in the tiny shore village of Kyles Scalpay. The communities living along those three roads not only had their own individual existences, they had their own inter-connections forming, as it were, three separate communes with their own distinctive characteristics. Only special occasions drew them together – like shearing or Sundays or Saturday nights. From the top of the hill above Caw where we boys sometimes congregated before descending to the town we could see the trickles of people from the three directions making their ways to town. The older men – older but still on the right side of middle age – wore their best suits and walked singly or in twos with the confidence of many Saturdays. The younger ones (our heroes) sported Harris Tweed jackets and grey flannels; there was an eagerness in their walk and a recklessness if they were on bicycles, and we knew that when we tagged on to them later on they would be smelling of beer and brilliantine. The girls walked in giggles of three or four and where they went we knew not because, in those days, only the most brazen hussy would go into the hotel and none at all into the pub. Most probably they collected in the kitchens of the big houses where sisters or cousins would be in service, or in the houses of friends, from which they would emerge after pub closing time for a discreet promenade – for an assignation, or in hope.

For us there was no point in rushing into town; we were too

young for anything worthwhile, and it was only after the pub skailed that the 'action' would begin and even then our pleasures would be vicarious. But, in due course, we scrambled down the hillside on to the main road and made our way into town anyway, just as the older night-outers melted into their various haunts and as our schoolmates emerged from their lodgings. In actual fact the first part of evening would be just a repeat of our normal après-school round except that it had the subtle excitement of Saturday, of the descending dark and the gentle fluorescing of lights in the windows of those shops whose owners were worldly enough to squeeze the last drips of profit out of the last hours before the Sabbath. They were invariably the ones who would be exchanging their crouch behind the tills for an upright stance behind the collection plate in one or other of the kirks tomorrow. Except for Ali, of course. His God was away on the dark side of the world, and since Ali hadn't as yet attached himself to either of the Tarbert churches there were no taboos for him to offend, and his shop could glow to within minutes of the midnight hour. And it glowed much brighter than the rest.

Ali had come to Harris as a packman several years before but, unlike his fellows who came and left with the swallows, he had decided, for some reason best known to himself, to settle down in our peat and heather island. Wicked rumour had it that he had decided to put several oceans between himself and a wife and scroosh of children but that was disproved to everybody's satisfaction – if slight surprise – when he elected to marry one of the most desirable young women in the community. In many another Scottish society in that age that would have been a sensational happening, but the Harrisman can be periodically pragmatic and within a very short space of time Ali and his bride had settled into a comfortable little house at the neck of the pier. He had discarded his pack and opened up a little shop in which he sold silks and satins and lotions and potions which were exotic by the standards of the established stores. He had a flair for display and, in the lamplight especially, his window glittered as if it were eternal Christmas. Bottles of eau de Cologne rubbed shoulders with improbably coloured bath salts which made discreet claims to ease rheumatism; bright red packets of Craven A cork-tipped cigarettes were stacked in pyramids and draped with silk handkerchiefs to suggest that the man who smoked Craven A had style; he reversed the usual trend of things by having scintillating beads on display for the white natives; there was an assortment of brilliantines and hair oils and pomades that turned schoolboy heads as we pressed up against his window with our manes sleeked back with God's good water. And other things besides.

'I bet you he's got French letters,' said a fellow on third year who knew a thing or two. He spoke in Gaelic with a bravado meant to impress the raw recruits from the country.

'Yes, plenty galore,' shouted Ali from behind the window in Gaelic only faintly tinged with Eastern blemish. 'You come in. You see!' he went on in English, bending down to pull a drawer on to the counter. 'Hurry up before Blus come!' He gave an imperious sideways flick of his head as he saw us hesitating. The very mention of The Blus was enough to galvanise us into some sort of action even in such an improbable situation; there were only two courses of action we could take, so we began to shuffle in – each one trying not to be first through the door and yet with an urgency of curiosity in our jostle. We ended up in a tight knot of five on one side of the counter with Ali, looking for all the world like a magician on the point of producing a rabbit, guddling in the drawer. And with a conjurer's flourish he produced a pink envelope.

'Look!' he said. 'A pack of three. One shilling.'

We looked and shuffled and said nothing.

Very deliberately he opened the envelope and produced a flat rubber medallion which he proceeded, very carefully, to unroll on to the second finger of his left hand. One was aware of heavy breathing all round, and an occasional gulp.

'You put on like this,' he said holding up the rubber-covered finger like a doctor about to make an unmentionable examination. 'Then you not get girl in trouble. But you not put on *finger* or you get girl in plenty trouble. You know where to put.'

We were all becoming acutely aware where to put, but there seemed to be no intelligent comment that any of us could make. To anybody who had chanced to look through the window the silent frozen tableau would have looked like an obscene postcard. But, fortunately, the street had not yet come to life.

'You buy?' said Ali thrusting an unopened packet towards the

128

fellow who had been so brash outside. Suddenly his self-confidence evaporated.

'N-n-no.' He managed to stammer at last. And then in desperation he flung a shilling on the counter. 'It was a packet of Craven A I wanted.' It was a desperate reaction from the only non-smoker in the company, but it got us off the hook and the prospect of sharing twenty Craven A between five of us compensated for Ali's laughter behind us as we tumbled out of the shop. It was a very chastened Farquhar Angus that we hustled into the nearest alleyway, and it was in vain that he pleaded that that was the last shilling of his pocket money.

By the time we had stamped out the burnt cork tips of our first full cigarette of the evening the public bar of the hotel had begun to skail.

The first to emerge were always the older, stone-cold sober men who wouldn't deign to wait to be hounded out by the landlord's shouts of 'Time!'. They had long since served their apprenticeships – some of them in bars far, far afield – and they threw back their nips and sipped their pints for pleasure, not for kicks. If there was anything to show that they had imbibed at all it was that they walked just a shade more sedately than before and by the time they had a ritual run-off against the wall behind Duncan's store they would be ready for an hour of serious discussion with their peers who had forsaken the bar completely as their youth had forsaken them, and had taken to making their only rendezvous the cobbler's little shop. The men with the beer on their breath would push their way in through the pipe-smoke, bringing with them new subjects for conversation. After their contributions had been analysed and discussed for a while somebody would glance at the ancient time-piece on the wall and say 'Which way is the clock?' and after a consultation of fob watches it would be decided whether it was fast or slow and, regardless of which, they would file slowly homewards secure in the knowledge that their heads and their consciences would be clear come the chiming of the church bell in the morning.

The brilliantine boys were different altogether. They would erupt from the pub in an exuberance of high spirits just a moment or two before they were due to be ejected. They would stagger to their bicycles with half bottle bulges on their breasts and screwtops of beer protruding from their hips. For them, optimistically, the best was yet to come as the young women – as if by coincidence – emerged from their places of visit. This was the highlight of the evening that we cockerels had waited for; this was where our longings became our vicariousness as we watched the teamings up and wondered who had paid a stealthy visit to Ali's shop and who was going to do 'that' to whom – and where? We hovered.

Down where the three roads met there was a wall of sitting height on one side, and on the other a big house with a shadow at the end of it. Since the three roads that led to everywhere met there it was a natural place at which to meet by accident!

'Hello Mary Ann, and are you wanting a cross-bar home?'

Since the fellow making the offer would be in a state of doubt as to whether he was propping the bike or the bike propping him, Mary Ann would be foolish in the extreme to accept the offer even if other doubts weren't put into her mind.

'Don't be daft, Mary Ann, it's more than a cross-bar you'll be getting if you go with him!'

'You'd fare better with Geordie Allan; the last time he gave Peggy Jean MacKenzie a cross-bar she was half way across the Huisinis road when she discovered it was a lady's bike he was riding.'

The ribaldry was fast and furious and the boyos from the pub in such effervescent form that a remark about the weather was good for a laugh. But it was the quiet ones that we watched – the couples who would slip into the shadow of the big house, whisper for a few moments, and slip off silently hand in hand. We would pick on a pair and stalk them carefully in the hope of catching them in the act which our salacity convinced us they were planning; but they had been at the game themselves and easily gave us the slip, or else they would ambush us and the fellow would give us a cuffing for our pains. Some of the bolder of us would hang about on the fringe of the crowd hoping for pickings in the shape of some plump teenager with a 'reputation'. But it never worked out that way and as the night wore on the assembly dissolved as couples paired and vanished, or the swains who had imbibed too freely sicked up their week's savings over the wall and set off ignominiously alone, wheeling their bikes erratically beside them. At last we'd be alone with our frustrations and our imaginings, and nothing left to do but trudge back home hoping for better luck next Saturday. My cousin and I walked the south road together.

'Boy, if only I'd got near the doctor's servant I'd have made it for sure. She's got tits like footballs, and she kept looking at me …'

I had heard it all before. He had some peculiar obsession with the doctor's maids; I'd heard him boasting about three of them, and had long since ceased believing him. In any case, by the time we reached the end of Big Grandfather's road my ardour would have subsided in the face of the prospect that I wouldn't be home in time for prayers. And on a Saturday night that would have been sin. Almost always I made it just as the pendulum clock struck half past ten; rarely did my lateness merit more than a pale stare over the top of my grandfather's gold spectacles. My oatcakes and milk would be sitting on a corner of the table alongside tomorrow's breakfast dishes.

'Anything fresh in town, boy?'

'No. Nothing at all.'

I would eat my supper in silence, with a strange home-longing coming over me as I listened to the aged clock wearily measuring time; no other sound except for an occasional sigh from my grandmother as she came across some reference that reminded her of the frailty of mortality – something which always weighed on her more heavily than usual on Saturday nights and Sundays. When Grandfather saw me picking up my dishes to carry them to the scullery he would begin to put away his paper and reach for the big Bible, and Grannie would tuck the *Christian Herald* or *The Witness* (as she still insisted on calling the church magazine although it had long since changed its name) below the cushion of her chair. By the time I had rinsed my cup and plate below the tap the old man would have the Bible open on his knee and he'd be polishing his spectacles, ready to bring down the curtain on another week.

And so, the routine went on as autumn gave way to winter.

For the first few days of term I had missed the village, and although a little attic room all to myself was an escape from the crowded little house in the Southlands, and a bathroom with running hot water a sophistication beyond my dreams, there

131

had still been an emptiness in being plucked out of a large warm family like a kitten suddenly sold from a litter. But as I began to find my feet in my new environment and get to know my way around in town my attitudes began to change. The loneliness gave way to a sense of freedom; it was marvellous never to be called on to do chores any more but be waited on, hand and foot, by Grandmother; the more I got into the swing of the gentlemanly life the better I liked it, and the company I kept was infinitely more swanky than the horny-handed men in the village and the bare-foot boys and girls of Primary School with darns in their jerseys. It was only on Saturday nights now that little twinges of that home-longing returned, but they would dispel when I got up to the attic room; I had discovered that I could smoke with impunity in my own room, once my grandparents were in bed, so long as I kept the skylight open a crack and made sure that the douts rolled down the slates into the guttering. I kept a copy of *The Pilgrim's Progress* and *The Works of Robert Louis Stevenson* beside my bed but, tucked in among my clothes, I had a store of lurid paperbacks from the mildly pornographic library which circulated surreptitiously from hand to hand below the desk lids in school. Propped up in bed with one of those and a glowing Woodbine the feeling of the good life quickly returned.

Every week since the very beginning of term I had received a letter from my mother by Tuesday morning's post enclosing two shillings carefully wrapped in newspaper because it was reckoned to be illegal to send coins through the post; but the two shillings must have strained her resources sufficiently without having to lay out the poundage charge on a postal order. At first, her bits and pieces of news were read and re-read with avid interest and when, in mid-September, she added a post-script saying 'I nearly forgot to tell you that Old Hector is going to get married ...' I wrote back immediately demanding to know more. She replied saying, '... they say she's a woman from Uist, but nobody knows for sure and nobody knows how he met her. I hope she's nice, but your father says that she must be wrong in the head to be marrying Hector but that isn't right. Hector's a very kind man, but if it's Uist she's from it'll be in Uist the wedding will be ...'

And so it was. Three weeks later she wrote to say that Hector had been quietly married in Uist and that his bride was, indeed, 'a nice, homely woman'. But by that time the world of Old Hector and the world of the village seemed a long way away and not so very important. My mother's letters were fast losing their interest too. They seemed to consist of catalogues of unimportant things like the price of heifers at sales, a pick-up in the Harris Tweed market, somebody expecting yet another baby, and all the other trivia of small village life. She was also allowing an irritating nag to creep into the correspondence. '… we're glad you caught twelve trout last week, but your father says that you must be sure to do your homework in the evening …' or '… we're sure it was very exciting in Tarbert on Saturday night with Alex John MacRae getting drunk, and it's only right that you should enjoy yourself, but remember that it's quite a strain keeping you in high school so that you get a better chance than poor Alex John ever had, and we hope that you're doing well at your lessons …'

Now we were well into bleak December and another week was over. Heavy rain had cast a gloom on the Saturday safari but even if the doctor's maid had made the most generous offer imaginable I doubt whether I could have summoned up the enthusiasm to take advantage of it. If there had been an alternative to a Saturday night alone with my grandparents I doubt whether I'd have gone to town at all. As it was I'd come back home as early as I dared do without risking questions from the old folk; I had had my supper and knelt through prayers that seemed even longer than usual and now, at last, I was safely in my room with a tasteless cigarette in my lips. For the umpteenth time I was reading through my school end-of-term report card with which The Blus had eventually presented me – after a half-hour session in his room on the previous evening, with the warning that it was to be taken home to my parents when I went back to the village for the Christmas break, and that it was to be brought back signed personally by my father. I had read and re-read the column of subject and marks but, always, my eyes returned to the last line. *Place in class – 32. Number in class 32.*

In two days' time I'd be going back to the village for my first holiday from High School. And meeting my father.

Chapter Ten

It was a strange feeling, to be returning to one's own home on holiday; it was made stranger still by the burden of apprehension and guilt that weighed in on me as I stood waiting for the bus at the red gate. My suitcase was heavy with the weight of cake and black pudding and freshly killed mutton that my grandparents were sending to my mother to supplement the Christmas table, and I had a parcel of hand-me-down jumpers and cardigans from an aunt who was married to a merchant and could afford to indulge her flair for style; packed in among the knitwear were an assortment of little packages which I guessed contained toys for my brothers' Christmas stocking and probably a pipe and pipe tobacco for my father. I was laden, in fact, with everything that would make for good cheer except good news. Deep down I hoped that my father would explode; I could stand that better than his tight silence and the deep hurt that could show in his eyes.

The bus was crowded. There were merchant navy men coming home for Christmas and New Year leave and it was obvious that they had already started celebrating; there were glamorous young ladies home on holiday from nursing or service in Glasgow; there was the usual hard core of men from the Southlands who had come north by the morning bus and were now on their way back home smelling of tweed and beer; and there were the three 'scholars' from my own village whom I knew to have fared well in their first term exams. All of those had one thing in common; they had something to feel happy about. For me it was a long and dreary journey, aggravated by the fact that I had to pretend good cheer and join the general bonhomie. The bus seemed to stop at every homestead between Tarbert and the new village before it finally drew up at the gate to my home. As I stepped off and took my heavy case from Jackie the driver who heaved it on to the running board for me, I could see my father coming down towards the road from the byre. I guessed that he had been hovering there, pretending to be doing odd jobs rather than be at his loom, so that he could keep a weather eye open for the bus coming over the Back of Scarista hill.

'Hullo my boy,' he said, offering his hand as he hefted my case with the other. 'It's grand having you back home with us again. And, Good Lord, I think you've put on a couple of inches in height; I'm having to look up to you already. O, and here's herself; she's been like a hen on a hot griddle since morning, and she'd have had me kill the fatted calf if there had been a fatted calf to kill.' My mother was standing at the door, wiping her hands on her apron. For a second I thought she was going to kiss me but she settled for squeezing my arm instead. 'You're looking well,' she said. 'Your grandmother's cooking must be agreeing with you; I'm afraid you'll be finding your poor mother's efforts a bit wishy-washy after all the fine fare in Dieraclate!' I knew by the smell from the stove that that was unlikely to be the case; the first whiff told me that some cockerel or hen had come to an untimely end.

'Grannie sent some mutton and black puddings and things; they're in my case. And there's a parcel from Auntie Mary; it's got clothes in it for you and Christmas presents for the boys.'

My three brothers, sitting in a row on St Clement's bench, merely wriggled their bottoms where they sat. The whole atmosphere was peculiarly unreal because the situation was totally new; never before had a member of the family been away from home for three and a half months, and, suddenly a strange gulf divided us. I was conscious that I was dressed much better than any of the rest; whatever I might have to say to my brothers later, there was nothing that I could think of to say to them in public. But above all else I felt uncomfortable because of the tininess of the room. It had been my home since

135

boyhood, and I had known little but happiness there even during the years of our poverty. But now, after the spaciousness of Big Grandfather's house, it seemed claustrophobic and – truth to tell – a little dingy and hovelly. My father guessed my thoughts.

'You'll be finding us a bit humble after the fine lodgings you've had. But never mind, boy – when you're finished at University with an M.A. and making a great name for yourself you'll be able to send us enough money to build a grand white house that will put Dieraclate in the shade.'

'Not at all,' said my mother. 'He'll be marrying a toff from the mainland as soon as he qualifies and we'll be lucky if he comes back for a week to the Rodel Hotel! But what's all this nonsense about anyway? Sit down there and let's see what you've got in your case and I'll get on with setting the table.'

The mention of marriage made my brothers laugh, and the atmosphere relaxed at last. I sat down beside them on the settle and began to open Auntie Mary's parcel and distribute her presents even though she had given strict instructions for the smaller packages to be left unopened till Christmas. By the time the meal was on the table conversation was flowing in torrents – my parents trying to enquire after relatives and about the excitements of Tarbert while my brothers talked each other down in the eagerness of each to be first with the news of school and the village.

Mother had always been a good cook and had managed to conjure up meals out of nothing during the Depression years, but she had really pulled all the stops out for my welcome home. Three courses, and tea and biscuits to round off. It was the sort of spread that one associated with weddings or Communion times.

'Well, well,' said my father as he pushed back his chair and felt for his pipe. 'I reckon we'll have to arrange for you to come home two or three times a term if it's going to mean a dinner like that.'

'Listen to him!' My mother was obviously flattered by his compliment. 'I slave over that stove for half my life and he never even notices what I put down in front of him.'

'And now some cheery news to round it all off, eh?' Father

136

had his pipe going. 'How's school coming along? How did the tests go?'

'I've got a report card you've to sign and send back to the Headmaster.'

I could feel my throat constricting and my voice sounded a whole tone higher; I sensed rather than saw a suspicious look coming into his eyes as I left the table and dug in my case for the buff envelope. I handed it to him without a word. My mother looked from me to him. My brothers felt there was something amiss and fell silent, staring at my father as he scanned the card. I could see his jaw muscle tightening as he clenched his pipe, and I saw his eyes move back to the top of the card as if he couldn't believe what he had read the first time. At last he laid the card on the table and took the pipe from his mouth.

'Well, by God, I suspected that something was wrong from the skimpy things that you chose to call letters when you deigned to send them. But not for a minute did I imagine anything like this –'

'John! What's wrong?'

'Wrong? I'll tell you what's wrong. Our bloody son has humiliated us in front of the whole of the goddamned island –'

'Watch your language in front of the children!'

'The children are going to hear every word I've got to say about the clown of a brother they've got. Our big man who parades the Tarbert street on a Saturday night as if he was God Almighty from what I hear. Our great fisherman who catches more trout than the landlord. Our nancy-boy who looked as if he had walked into a tinker's camp when he came in through that door. He has come *last* in his class – that's what he's done! He's come bloody last in a class that I happen to know contains a couple of the biggest dim-wits in Tarbert!' He turned on me with an anger in his eyes that I had never seen before – a steely, cold anger. 'I put all my hopes in you. I taught you everything I knew myself although God knows that wasn't much – I didn't have bursaries and daft parents to buy books for me. And you've thrown it all back in my face like a shovel of shit. What were you up to? Boozing, or smoking your lungs out, or trying to get below the skirts of every tarty servant girl in Tarbert?'

'John!'

137

'No! I'll not stop till I've had my say. And that's not much now. I stood by you, lad, when you failed to get the bursary the first time because I knew you had tried and nobody can do more than that. But now it's all I can do to keep my hands off you. Not just for my sake, but for your mother's. She's slaved for you; she's put money past herself when she hardly had clothes to put on her own back so that you could go to High School dressed like a gentleman. And what has she got in exchange? Humiliation in her native village, in front of her own people.'

He stopped and held my eyes.

'What have you got to say for yourself?'

There was nothing I could say.

'Nothing! Just as I thought! Well I've got one thing to say, and then I'm saying no more. I'm giving you till summer in Tarbert school and if, by that time, you're not in the first five places in that class you're going to come back home here and sit at that loom weaving tweed till you've got more callouses on your backside than all of your forefathers had corns on their feet. And that's my last word on it!'

And it was. He lit his pipe with a slight shake in his hand, picked up the *Daily Express*, which he hadn't opened since the bus driver left it tucked into the handle of my suitcase, and withdrew into a chilly concentration.

One by one my brothers slipped away from the table. My mother sat for a few moments staring down at her plate, and then stood up.

'I'd better get on with washing those dishes.'

It wasn't meant but that one sentence stung more than all of my father's wrath. The weariness in her tone conveyed her disappointment, and the reference to the dishes reminded me of all the trouble she had gone to in order to make me welcome back home.

'I'll dry for you.'

'No. You've got your good suit on.'

I got up and went over to St Clement's bench and sat silently wondering what I could do to occupy myself. I could think of nothing. And just sat. My father didn't say another word; nor ever again did he refer to the report card – not even when he handed it back to me, signed.

138

I don't know how the evening would have dragged on if my mother hadn't taken matters into her own hands. When she was lighting the lamp she turned to me – not with a smile but with a hint of sympathy in her voice. 'O Finlay, I nearly forgot … I met Old Hector last night and I swore to him that I would get you to call in on him tonight. His wife's called Catriona, by the way. She's a really nice woman.' I could have hugged mother for getting me out of the ice-box situation and I had to restrain myself from running out of the room.

When the cold air hit me I realised that I was bursting for a pee and, momentarily, I checked my step as I thought of going to the bathroom. But in the same split instant I remembered there wasn't one. As I stood relieving myself against the back wall of the house my resentment of earlier on surfaced momentarily as I realised that, for the next fortnight, I would be reverting to the old modes of life. No running water. No room of my own. No toilet and toilet paper; instead a cold squat on two rocks in a hidden crook of the river. My father was right. I'd have to get on with my school-work or I'd be shitting in the open and washing my face in a bucket for the rest of my life.

It was a new road I walked on the way to Hector's. A cold road. A pallid moon hung over the village and there was a gripe of frost in the air, but that wasn't the cold that I felt. It was a chill of the mind. As I walked past my old Primary School, where I'd been leathered by the sadistic Miss Dalbeith and coached and encouraged by Miss Martin, I realised how very small it was although it had seemed a huge building when I first approached it as a five year old trotting at my father's side. Now it had an unreal 'doll's house' quality about it, and none of the style and grandeur of the big school in the Northlands. It was impossible to believe that I had spent eight years of my life there, and I didn't even remember that I had spent a happy year there even before school began, when, as a family, we had lodged in the living-quarters end of it, sharing accommodation with the Boer War veteran and the Duchess and Molly who had tried to poison me. None of those memories came back as I hurried past lest Miss Martin might still be in residence and would pop out to ask me about the fulfilment of my promise in my new posh school. I had been one of her star pupils according to herself once, and thirty-second out of thirty-two would not sound exactly like the crowning of her ambitions for me.

It wasn't just the school that looked small. The village itself seemed to have shrunk and lost that burgeoning promise that it had clung to during the ten years since my parents and their neighbours had come and founded it in the confidence that they had reached their land of milk and honey. It had survived its growing pains as the pioneers made their mistakes and some strove for too much too soon; it survived the Depression when the natural resources of its sea and countryside saved it from the deprivation that beset the cities. It had heard the laughter of my boyhood generation. Now it was just a tired straggle of houses along a gravel road with the wind from the sea beginning to turn the crispness of the frost to damp. Our own corrugated iron shack out of which, by my father's mismanagement as I judged it in my present mood, we had never graduated, looked like a symbol of eternal poverty rather than the cosy family nest it had once been. There's something different about the village, I thought. Something has happened to it. But I didn't have the wits to see that the something was happening to me.

Time took a step backwards as I reached Old Hector's thatched black house. There it stood, with its two little windows recessed into its six foot thick walls and its roof of layered marram grass, like an old man with his bonnet pulled over his eyes. Whatever else had changed it hadn't. It stood now as it had stood when my Great Aunt Rachel was a girl and it had been old then. It had seen populations come and go, but it had crouched there in its timelessness untouched by any passing whim of society and untempted into the new age of amenity. I didn't think all that out as I stood there, of course. I didn't think of anything. But my depression and my mood of grudge melted away. I approached the door as if my last visit had been yesterday.

But something had changed – dramatically. The door opened as I reached it and I was greeted by a big strong woman with rosy cheeks and a twinkle that made one smile.

'Come in,' she said. 'I know who you are and I know all about you. Himself here was just wondering if you'd be along to see us. Maybe he'll be too grand now he was saying; but I knew you wouldn't be if you were the kind of fellow he had told me about!'

While she was talking she ushered me into the crouched old living room that I knew so well, but I wouldn't have known it now if somebody had put me inside, blindfold, and then uncovered my eyes. The gloom had disappeared. The peat-fire burnt brightly on the hearth; the interior stone walls had been white-washed so that they reflected the light from the oil-lamp and would do the same to the light from the deep little window in the daytime; there was a general impression of airiness and freshness, flecked here and there with chintzes of predominant reds and yellows. It was an incredible transformation and it was all I could do not to stand and gawp. But there was a greater transformation still. The old Taransay chair had been stripped of its layers of brown paint and varnish and repainted white; and, cushioned in it, was Old Hector in a clean shirt such as he had hitherto worn only for church or for funeral … and once, long ago, at the Christmas Treat. Beside him on a little table improvised from a three-legged milking stool were laid out his pipe, paper spills, a short rope of bogey roll and a knife for slicing it. This was the man who had been used all his life to being sent out to the end of the house for a smoke if his sister Maggie happened to be in bad form. The enormity of what I had done last mid-summer flashed through my mind as I remembered that advertisement which read *Retired seaman wants woman used to croft work with a view to matrimony. Reply Box 427.* Yet here was the outcome of it all – success by all appearances.

'You sit down there beside Hector while I dash out to the well for a fresh pail of water, and then we'll have a wee cup of tea.'

She placed a chair beside Hector's while he pumped my hand with both of his. He patted the seat of the chair.

'Sit down boy and light up. Catriona is as trusty as myself; she'll not be telling your parents you have a wee puff now and again, will you Catriona?'

'Of course I won't. But I'm not sure that I approve of young boys smoking though; it makes them grow into ugly old men like one I can think of.' She chuckled and went out. As soon as the door swung to behind her the smile went off Old Hector's

141

face; he lent towards me and gripped my arm, and he dropped his voice to a whisper.

'Quick. Listen to me before she comes back. There's only one lie I've ever told her; I told her the advertisement was all my own idea and that it came to me in a dream one night. I – er – well – er – I sort of let her think it was – well – some kind of message from on High … the kind of things that used to happen in the Old Testament. I didn't say it was that, but I sort of hinted at it. Oh! And I told her that she was the only one who replied. It wasn't much of a lie, was it?'

'It was two lies.'

'No it wasn't! I've thought that one out. It was two halves of one!'

I managed to keep my face straight, and pretended to be thinking out my attitude. His grip on my arm tightened.

'It wasn't much more of a deceit than not telling the truth about smoking, was it?'

The old blackmailer! I was glad that he hadn't changed too much after all.

'Ach no,' I said. 'And it isn't all that far from being the truth anyway.'

He relaxed.

'Do you know what she calls me when we're on our own?' He paused, and I shook my head. 'Four-two-seven! That's what she calls me.' He slapped his knee and, for the first time, I heard the old man laugh out loud. The old man? Somehow he didn't seem old any more. He lent towards me again. 'There's one thing; she's a wee bit too old to be having children; may be we should have put an age limit in the paper, eh?'

'Then Catriona wouldn't have replied.'

'Dammit man, that's what education does for you! I never thought of that.' He was still chuckling as Catriona came back from the well.

'And how are you getting on with Primrose?' I asked as we sat over tea and scones. 'Is she milking as well as ever?'

'Better, my boy. Better.' said Hector.

'And it's not just Primrose any more,' the new wife continued, and I noticed how effortlessly she took the conversation out of Hector's hands. 'I had a cow of my own and I brought her with me, and she and Primrose are both in

142

calf. We're thinking we'll keep one of the calves for rearing, if there's a female one, and sell the other with calf at foot.' It struck me that Hector hadn't only got himself a wife but a manageress into the bargain – a manageress with a cow at foot. The business of bringing on a new calf of good strain to be a milking cow was sound common sense, but I couldn't help hoping that Primrose would be the one to drop the female calf and thus be the one to stay. After all, but for Primrose that advertisement would never have been written.

The visit was long and late, and the moon had shrunk behind the haar when Old Hector accompanied me to the door. He had picked up a torch from the window sill as he passed.

'I'll walk you a bit down the path,' he said. 'Catriona tells me that those bandy legs of mine need exercise, and may be she's got a point.' I was going to expostulate but he stopped me. 'No, no. I'll be all right. And besides I want a yarn with you.'

We walked in silence for a while – and slowly because Hector's feet were bad.

'So school didn't go so well, then?'

I stopped dead.

'What do you mean? How do you know?'

'Ach, I've known you a long time. I've watched you growing up. When you're a bit of an oddity like me – whether it's bad legs or timidity or whatever – people let their guards down and reveal more of themselves than they would normally do to what they would think of as a whole man. And so I've seen more of you than even your parents have done; I've seen the deeper you where they've been concerned with other things – like your welfare, and your health, and your education and so on. But I learnt to read your eyes. Just after you came into the house I said something about what education does for a man and a cloud came over your eyes which told me everything. What went wrong?'

I told him everything – the disastrous examination results and my father's outburst. He listened without interrupting, except to touch my arm and make me resume our slow walk down the path beside the churchyard. When I finished he stopped again.

'As you know, my boy, I never got much in the way of

143

education, and even if I had done I'm not sure that I'd have known what to do with it. I've never worried about it. But your father's different; he's a clever man and if he'd had the chance the Lord only knows how he'd have ended up. But because he's intelligent enough to know what he missed he allowed a tiny little bit of bitterness to sow itself somewhere; perhaps he had too much time to think in that kind of war that he had. And a seed like that creates a canker in your mind just as a thorn in your thumb can cause an abscess. But then you came along and it so happens that you developed the same sort of interests as he had, and it was like a cure for him. He began to see all the things that he had hoped for for himself being fulfilled in you; and he thinks you've not only let him down but you've destroyed his hopes … and that's the worst thing you can do to a man. He'll come round when you begin to do better –'

'*If* I do better.'

Hector chortled and took a moment to light his cutty.

'You bloody well will – if only because you can't be thirty-third out of thirty-two!'

He became serious again.

'It's a difficult thing to be chucked into a brand new world. I remember that one and only trip of mine to Singapore … my God boy, nobody knows the half of it. I'd never been out of this village before, and even at home I'd always been in the shadow of my sister Maggie over there,' he nodded towards the grave-yard as casually as if she was standing a few feet away from us in the life, 'and when I got aboard ship I went wild. I had my freedom at last. I was loose in a shining new world where everything was better and bigger than it was here. I've never told you about some of the ports we called into on the way, and what I got up to. And I never will … But I'll tell you this – that bout of malaria that buggered up my legs was what saved my life. It stopped me dead in my tracks. And when I came home here, I made up my mind that I was never going to leave again and never again going to rush. That bad mark is your malaria; it's stopped you dead in your tracks, but, unlike me, you'll get moving again. Only remember this – don't go trying to start from a point out there. Start from here. Your education is out there, but this is where wisdom is. A tree grows from its roots – not from its highest branch, and roots aren't posh and glittery things; they're busy grubbing around in the soil and drawing the goodness from it that will eventually produce the blossom. That's all I'm going to say.'

And I could sense that it was. There was nothing I could say in response so I changed the subject.

'Isn't the beach quiet and empty? That's one thing I miss in the Northlands – the beach!'

He looked out towards the sea for a long time.

'Yes,' he said. 'The beach is quiet and empty but not for long, I'm afraid.'

'What do you mean?'

'I've been reading the papers a lot those last few weeks; Catriona keeps me supplied with them; she says they keep me from getting in her way. And I'll be surprised if we see the next year out without a war. I remember the last one. That beach down there was cluttered from end to end with flotsam that you've never seen the like of. Yes, and a body or two forbye. It was only when the bodies came that it was brought home to us that the sea casts up only what the sea has taken in the first place. And if it was bad last time, what will it be like next time with all the instruments of war they've been inventing while we've been thinking peace … Ach well …' He paused, and then pulled himself together with a visible jerk. 'Goodnight boy; Catriona will be getting worried.' And he turned on his heel and hirpled off up the path, following the spot of his torch. I stared after him in disbelief. It used to be a standing joke in the village that the only things Old Hector feared more than his sister Maggie were the dark and the churchyard at night. Yet there he was – oblivious to them both, and, come to think of it, to Maggie as well. Catriona was obviously a mighty powerful influence in her own twinkly way.

My father was alone in the living room when I got in, checking, as he had done every night of his life, that there was not the remotest chance of a live ember escaping from the dying stove. I felt a sag of relief when he turned round and smiled, and truth to tell, a prickling behind the eyes.

'Did you have a good evening? It was long enough anyway.'

There was no reproach in his voice, and it was obvious that he had been meaning to go to bed and leave the door open for me – something which he had never done before; it was a gesture of confidence which meant infinitely more than words.

'I had a great time. Catriona's very nice isn't she?'

'She's a fantastic woman; she's made a man of Hector in his middle age.' He picked the Bible off the table and returned it to its shelf. 'But how the devil did you talk Hector into putting that advert into the *Gazette*?'

I felt my jaw slackening and it took me all my time not to flop down on the bed that my mother had made up for me on St Clement's bench.

'Who … how … what …?'

'Don't worry. I'm the only one who knows. But then not even the teacher ever seemed to notice that you could never spell matrimony; and the damn fool editor of the *Gazette* obviously didn't notice either.'

He was chortling as he went through to the bedroom. And suddenly it felt as if the Christmas holidays weren't going to be so bad after all.

Chapter Eleven

Winter doesn't really begin till January in the Hebrides. There are November gales and scythings of frost in December and rain anytime, but it isn't till January that the earth has drunk its fill and become so water-logged that even the high ground squelches. Nowadays, modern houses with double glazing and central heating and airing-cupboards have taken the ultimate discomfort out of the pervasive damp but, in those days, even in Big Grandfather's well-fired, bathroomed house, the first three months of the year were dispiriting. Every day, from Monday till Friday, I walked the mile and a half between school and home four times a day – morning and night and each way each day at lunchtime; if I took the short-cut diagonally across Angus Donald Og's croft I had to pick my way through peatland and spongey sphagnum moss, and, sooner or later, a false step would lead to a water-logged boot about which I could do nothing except walk fast or run till the water warmed to body-heat, and, in class when it got cold, wiggle to bring it back to warmth again. If I took the gravel path to the main road then the sodden rushes drooping across the track whipped at my flannel trouser legs and there was nothing for it except to reconcile myself to the feeling of walking around as if my legs were lagged with cold porridge. Even if my father's ultimatum weren't still nagging at me, the thought of changing into dry clothes and going out again at night in order to get drenched afresh would have been enough to stem my ardour for the gallivant.

There is a certain limit to the amount of conversational tapestry that one can weave out of the three strands of God, the sheepstock, and the events of day in school – particularly when the interests of the three parties involved are fairly definitely defined. And so, as soon as the evening meal was over, I tended to head upstairs to my attic and try to muster some enthusiasm for my schoolwork. I found it hard to become addicted to Latin; mathematics and science froze my soul, but I found a new interest in learning to read and write my own native Gaelic for the first time, and, concurrently my old interest in English began to rekindle. I began to delve into the leather-bound volume of Robert Louis Stevenson's works which had lain unopened by my bedside for the whole of first term. I ploughed my way stolidly through the first few pages of *Kidnapped*, there is nothing more difficult than getting into the rhythm of good writing when one has been immersed in trash for a while, but I perservered and by the time David Balfour had recovered consciousness in the bowels of the brig *Covenant* I was in thrall. *Treasure Island* came next and I revelled in its bounding adventure. And then *The Body Snatcher*. It was on a blustery night when the skylight was rattling enough to make me jittery anyway that, after a long straight read, I came to the untying of the sack and the *light falling clear upon the dark well-moulded features and smooth shaven cheeks of a too familiar countenance*. I was glad to rush through the last lines of the story and make for the warmth and the company of downstairs.

The macabre and the supernatural tug at the same nerves and, in the Hebridean of my generation, the belief in the supernatural was submerged only under a very thin veneer of education and sophistication. Big Grandfather was as tough a man as one could meet on a long day's journey; if he met the devil in the dark he would send him on his way. And he had not the faintest doubt that there were more things in heaven and earth than Horatio or anybody else dreamt of. And when he talked of his own experiences in the undefinable realms he was as matter-of-fact as if he were discussing yesterday's most ordinary events. He would have been happier if the eerie light, seen by himself and many people, mysteriously flitting along the edge of craobhag were to fulfil its portent. The craobhag was the high crumbly sea-cliff, with a couple of rowan trees peeping from it, that fell away at the foot of his croft. For generations – once in a while and without warning or possible explanation – a white light would blaze out of nowhere and settle on the top of craobhag momentarily before beginning its restless patrolling along the cliff edge and then plunging into the sea. Grandfather had dreaded all his life that it presaged an accident to one of his own children but they had grown up and gone their ways without mishap. Now his fears were transferred to his grandchildren when they came a-visiting, and I was under strict orders never to go near craobhag edge, and never never at night to the short-cut that ran close to the cliff lest misdirection misguide me towards it. As far as I know the augury of the light has not, so far, been realised. Unlike the other light that I heard grandfather and other people tell of – the light on the white boat.

When he was a young man Big Grandfather, like most of his fellow crofters in the seaside communities, had a sturdy rowing boat which he kept moored at the foot of the croft. He was inordinately proud of his boat – a sixteen foot white skiff which he had bought on the mainland when he gave up a brief career as a seaman and settled down to married life.

In those days, before the arrival of motor transport, a boat was an essential for a sea-side crofter in the Northlands where both terrain and the difficulties of feeding made it impossible to use horses in the way that people in the gentler lands of the south used them. It was only by boat that a man could bring home his sacks of meal or flour, seed corn for sowing or barrels of salt herring for winter. His alternative would be to lug them on his back over miles of rough country. It was by boat that coffins were taken to Rodel churchyard in the south end of the island, since the rocky Northlands couldn't be dug for a cemetery. And a boat, of course, was necessary for fishing in a bay that was sheltered and teeming with fish. Grandfather was inordinately proud of a boat that was acknowledged to be one of the best in the neighbourhood, and he tended her with the meticulous care which he lavished on all the accoutrements of his croft.

Then rumours began to circulate that the white boat was haunted, and people began to be reluctant to work her or travel in her. At first – he admitted in later years – he put it down to mild envy on somebody's part, or even a crafty dodge to make him part with the boat at a knock-down price. Then, suddenly one night, he realised that the rumours, which he had never heard defined, were well founded. He was checking that the front door was closed, prior to going to bed, when he saw what he described as 'a pale light' leaving the white boat and travelling out into the middle of the bay. His first reaction was that poachers had borrowed the boat and he rushed down to the shore to check, only to find that the boat was safely moored as he had left her, while the light was disappearing into the distance on the far side of the bay.

He kept a sporadic look-out thereafter and, on many occasions, he and grandmother saw the light leaving the boat – always at the same late hour – and, from the higher vantage of the house they could watch it move out across the bay and turn gently into the narrow Sound of Scalpay before disappearing behind the headland. And two or three times in the late winter dawn he had seen the light return and slowly extinguish as it reached the mooring. From the beginning he accepted the happening for what he was convinced it was – a foreshadowing of tragedy of some kind … a drowning from the boat, or the loss of the boat itself. People urged him to get rid of her; my grandmother pled with him to sell. But he wouldn't. He maintained, quite simply, that what was predestined would be fulfilled regardless of any effort on his part. In later life, secure in her faith and mellow with experience, she would agree that he had been right and that she had been wrong.

Then, in January 1907 word came that the yacht on which grandfather's brother, Roderick, worked as a deckhand was putting in to anchor in Loch Erisort in Lewis and that Roderick was being allowed home for some days' leave. He never did come. When he and some of his mates were climbing from the yacht into the dinghy taking them ashore the yacht yawed in a sudden squall and swamped the dinghy. Four of the men disappeared. It was late at night when word of the tragedy reached my grandfather and the information that his brother's body was still unrecovered; immediately, he and some of his neighbours set off to join in the search, and, with a lantern in her prow, the white boat moved out into the middle of the bay.

150

From the window grandmother watched the lantern grow smaller as it reached the Sound of Scalpay and then disappeared round the headland as she had watched that light disappear many times before. She sat up all night waiting and, through the dawn, she saw the white boat rowing back into the bay with the lantern still burning in her stem – and Roderick's body aboard. The light was never seen again, but, a few years later grandfather sold the white boat – not for any reasons of superstition but because she reminded him of a grief.

I had heard the story from other people many times before I heard it from Big Grandfather himself.

'Man,' Grandmother said. 'You'll be giving the boy night-mares – telling him that sort of story; young people nowadays have more on their minds than that sort of thing.'

'But is it true, Grannie?'

'O, it's true all right; I saw the light many times myself although I saw it returning only the once. But things like that don't seem to happen nowadays – or else people don't notice them; they don't have time.'

I suspect that the old lady was near the truth. I caught the tail end of the generation which had time and an uncomplicated attitude to life and belief which made them more receptive – and, perhaps, perceptive. I was aware of the speed of change – one never is when one is at the heart of the vortex; but in that particular year, life in our part of the world was changing dramatically, and perhaps only people like my grandmother, watching from the higher vantage of the years and from a cushioned domesticity, were aware of it. Even Grandfather, when he railed against the increasing difficulties of getting a crew for the cutting of his peat, was inclined to put the problem down to 'laziness of the younger generation' rather than to a change in the social order.

The idea of 'crewing' the peat-cutting was a novelty to me, because it had already died out in the Southlands. It was an elementary form of traditional co-operation which had flourished for years in tight knit communities like those of the Northlands, but was less practicable in a place like our new village where, by virtue of the size of the crofts, people lived farther away from each other, and where, because they were a new community which had come together as strangers, people weren't so inclined to team together. Invariably my father cut his peat over several days of spring with the help of my mother or of a relative. In Dieraclate it was different. The men of the township would assemble on a given evening in late spring and decide on a rota. Then on the allotted day eight or ten of them would arrive with their peat irons and complete one croft's peat-cutting (the whole winter's supply) in one single day. Then, if the next day was fine, they would move on to the next croft; and so on till the peat for the entire village was cut and a few days were added for the widows or the disabled. It was a simple system, and all the more effective because it assumed mildly gala proportions.

Grandfather got up early every day, but particularly early on his own peat-cutting day. It was his responsibility to see that the peat-banks were skinned (the turf removed from the top of the peat proper) and that any collected water was drained away from the trench of the bank. He would lay out his own two cutting irons in case some villager came without one or, for that matter, in case some stranger from another village decided to come along to give a hand just for the joy of a good day out. The remains of last year's peat – such of it as hadn't already been consumed or stacked at the end of the house – had to be cleared back from the spreading area so that the new wet peat had a clear sward. Most of the preparatory work would have been done well before cutting day, but it was mandatory that everything should be checked so that when the men were assembled they would be able to get straight down to work. That was the theory.

While Grandfather was checking the preparation of his own domain, Grandmother was bustling about getting the house in order because she would have up to a dozen people to feed and that involved a lot of organisation even although, in the course of the morning, several village wives would arrive with baskets of home baking and cooked chickens and hunks of cold salt mutton. But these were extras. The onus was still on Grandmother to provide the basic meals so that, even if the neighbours failed to contribute (which was inconceivable), there would still be food to feed the multitude. It would never do to be seen to be beholden; and, devout and all as she was, Grannie preferred to perform her own miracles in advance! In the other years that I could remember, when I had been allowed to go north especially for the peat-cutting if it fell on a Saturday, one of the miracles for me had been Grannie's ashets of seafood. There were oysters in their hundreds down at the foot of the croft where the Yellow Skerry protected a channel of sea from any ruffling of the waters of the bay; and, farther along, below craobhag, there grew gigantic mussels (the size of my cupped hands) which were called 'wolf-mussels'. A pail of oysters and a pail of mussels were collected at the last low tide before the peat-cutting and kept in sea water till morning, when they were boiled till they opened and then rolled in oatmeal and fried. We didn't have oysters or wolf-mussels in the Southlands because the sea was too rough on such patches of rocky shore as we had between the sandy beaches, so Grannie's seafood platters (as the restaurants of later year taught me to call them) were special treats.

'Where are the oysters?' I asked her that beautiful spring morning when, happily for me, Grandfather's crew day had fallen on a Saturday.

'There aren't any this year.'

'Why not?'

'Ask the Good Lord that! I've never known it before. Your grandfather says there isn't a single oyster worth bringing home in the whole of the Yellow Skerry bed.'

'What about the wolf mussels, then? Can't we have them on their own?'

'I'm not chancing them. Chirsty Donald Og picked some a fortnight ago and she and Angus were very sick; she was saying that a couple of people in Caw were ill too, and they're blaming the wolf-mussels. There may be some shellfish disease – I don't know …'

I didn't know it then, but I was never going to taste a wolf-mussel or a Yellow Skerry oyster again. And neither Grandmother nor I could be expected to associate the mysterious disappearance of the shellfish with the fact that Grandfather's new bathroom was only one of the latest in a whole line of new bathrooms from which pipes led straight into the bay. Not only our beliefs and superstitions were being undermined by the onward skelter of progress.

'Dangitty! People are getting lazier and lazier,' Grandfather muttered for the third or fourth time. 'It's ten o'clock and not a sign of a peat-cutter yet; it's going to be dark by the time we finish – and this a Saturday too!'

'Man of the house,' said Grannie, deliberately using the formal address to be informal. 'You're getting more impatient with every passing year. Since when did a crew ever start assembling before ten o'clock? And even if they did, you'd be grumbling because they were kicking their heels waiting for the dew to lift on the spreading ground. Why don't you take the pail and go off for the beer?'

'The bar doesn't open till eleven o'clock, that's why. And it's not going to take me an hour to walk to the bar, bad and all as my feet are!'

'There's nothing wrong with your feet since Dr MacBeth fixed them. And in any case it's not your feet that will delay you but your tongue by the time you meet a score of people that you haven't met in a month. And there'll be plenty of those around, this being, as you say, Saturday.'

'They'll be a change from a female tongue anyway!' He winked at me as he picked up the enamelled pail and set off. Their badinage was unusual, but it was in keeping with the mood of the miniscular carnival which was the peat-crewing day; and the beer pail was part of the ritual. There was no reason why it should be; the word 'screw-top' had long since been absorbed into the vernacular and the Sabbath roadside tended to glint with the occasional empty bottle from Saturday night's 'carry-out'; but the middle-aged men of the peat-crewing would have regarded 'screw-tops' as boozing, or infra dig like corned beef for Sunday dinner, whereas a middle of the day mug from the pail of flat beer followed by a satisfied sigh and a rasp of the back of the hand across the chin was as much part of the tradition of peat day as was the custom that the man of the house cut only the first peat of the day from his own bank, and, for the rest of the time played host.

'Well, men, that was a good day's work well done,' said Big Grandfather after he put the amen to the grace after the long and sumptuous meal served up by Grannie and the helping village wives at the end of the day. 'I'm glad it's Sunday tomorrow and that I have a full day before I have to start repaying.' The fact that grandfather was making a little joke was proof that he was highly pleased with his crew's efforts.

'Fine for you,' said somebody of his own age. 'You got the Saturday cut and your peat will get their first day's drying while you're at your prayers. See and don't be studying their progress on your way to and from church!'

The conversation pursued its leisurely aimless course as the pipes were lit and the women got on with washing the dishes. It was Alasdair Norman from the Kyles Skerries crofts who, as usual, introduced a note of pessimism into the easy-osiness of the chat.

'Well, it's been getting harder and harder to get peat-crews together for the last year or two, but I doubt if we'll get one at all next year if what I hear is true –'

'What on earth are you talking about?'

'Do you remember that strange fellow who turned up by accident at the Moderator's day in Scarista?'

'What of him?' somebody asked while one or two chuckled as they remembered Geordie MacLellan's discomfiture.

'They're saying he was some kind of a spy from the Government, checking on the possibility of raising the militia again, and –'

'The Territorial Army,' said my second cousin Archie who with his twin brother Neil the Banker were the youngest members of the peat-crew. 'Somebody was telling Neil that there's been an army general going round the southern islands making a count of the young men who might be willing to volunteer. Just making a count.'

'Well I hope neither of you is fool enough to volunteer!' Neil and Archie glanced at each other but said nothing; they were so close that people used to say of them that they could carry on a conversation with each other without talking.

'War, war, war,' said my grandfather. 'If it comes to that it'll be the third one in my memory, but I pray that men will come to their senses. If it comes to war it'll be men who fought in the last one who'll start it, and that's just beyond belief.'

A few weeks later, Captain Derek Lang and Viscount Fincastle arrived in Harris to call for recruits for the 4th Battalion (the Territorial Battalion) of the Queen's Own Cameron Highlanders, and in one night eighty-nine young men from the small island of Harris volunteered. Archie and

Neil were among the first. Within a couple of weeks their numbers had grown to about a hundred. It had been a stroke of brilliant public relations to make Lord Fincastle Company Commander. His grandparents, Lord and Lady Dunmore, had been proprietors of the whole of Harris at the end of the last century. He had been a sympathetic and progressive landlord; she had seen the potential of local tweed and had established the Harris Tweed Industry, which was to become the foundation of the economy of the island, and despite its susceptibility to world market fluctuations had remained so for generations. The Dunmores had not only done much to counter the bitterness which their predecessors had engendered in Harris with policies of exploitation, repression and, frequently, eviction, but they had set a precedent for good landlordship for their successors and we were, as a result, reasonably free of the antipathy which sours relationships between landlords and crofters in other parts of the West Highlands. While the vast majority of our men would have spat at the idea of 'touching their bonnets to the laird' there lingered on two traditions which met when Captain Lang did his recruitment drive – the age-old instinct in the Highlander to respond to 'the call to arms' despite the disaster that that response had sometimes brought to his country and his race, and the equally aged instinct to look to the laird for the leadership as he would, once upon a time, have looked to his Clan Chief. Now, less than half a century on, that whole exposition may sound ridiculous; but it wasn't then. And it wasn't only 'Dubby' Fincastle that Captain Lang was fortunate in; the landlord of our new village was a peppery ex-Colonel who commanded a great deal of respect and his son Gavin (well-liked and handsome and, as events were to prove, heroic) became one of Lang's first officers. So the Harrismen were led from the beginning by men whose pedigrees they knew; and the non-commissioned infrastructure was local too – the popular 'Bunt' Macdonald of the local Bank of Scotland became Colour Sergeant and his colleague, my second cousin Neil, became Corporal. They even had one of the best pipers of the Hebrides in Peter Roses.

Of course the whole thing was a game. There was going to be no war. And the initial parades and exercises were a welcome diversion in a place where regular entertainment tended to begin and end with the Saturday promenade. When rifles and a Lewis Gun and hand-grenades began to arrive they only added piquancy to the ploy, and even the old women used to take their knitting out to the hillocks on lovely summer evenings and watch the lads shooting at targets and causing bangs and mini mushroom clouds of peat when they practised throwing their grenades into peat pools. When the uniforms arrived the whole thing took on a new theatricality; the populace of Tarbert would turn out to watch the Company march down the street with Peter Ross at their head with the bagpipe. Even the soldiers themselves weren't yet taking it all seriously; some of the dedicated ones would march with their eyes determinedly forward; a few of the more self-conscious would stumble and blush crimson to their bonnets when they heard a 'look at our Sandy' from a doting aunt or grannie; occasionally a cock-sure braggart would wink suggestively in the direction of a buxom area of the crowd without breaking step or concentration.

There was a time when these youths had been our idols and sometimes our friends. On Sunday afternoon walks we would be allowed to consort with them and scrounge cigarettes from them; in their own homes they would treat us as equals; up till now it was only on the Saturday promenade that they spurned us as we hung around on the edge of their courtings like pups vainly hoping for a nibble of the big dogs' bones. The uniforms and the rifles moved them out of our ken all together; even the third year girls who, hitherto, might have held out an occasional grape of Tantallus in our direction, now looked down their noses at us and, on manoeuvre evenings in particular, walked round the village with their gym-frock belts tightened to strangulation and looking stuck-up and stuck-out. It was galling, but, far from resenting the 'Terriers' as they had come to be called, it inflamed our chauvinism; we all wanted to be soldiers and get into uniform; we would have falsified our ages if that had been legally possible or physically credible. A few of the Tarbert boys were members of the local Boy Scout troop, and we country yokels had hitherto regarded them as nancy-boys. But suddenly their khaki hats and tunics and neckerchiefs represented a uniform. I rushed to the scoutmaster and enlisted – three days before he decided that his duties with the Territorials were taking up all his spare time, and, in the absence of anybody able and willing to take over from him, the troop was disbanded. I must be the shortest serving Boy Scout on record.

While the 'uniform fever' (it was by no stretch of the imagination war fever) gripped a large portion of the community, there was one section which reacted totally differently. The older men, those who had served in the 1914-18 war, with very few exceptions withdrew into a silence. They would occasionally turn out to watch an official march past or parade, but they watched it with none of the fun-of-the-fair attitude of the rest. When somebody occasionally committed a gaffe – and there were occasional ones since commands spat out in English did not always get a crisp accurate response from recruits who thought in Gaelic – the older men would smile with smiles that rarely reached their eyes. There was a subtle change in their social pattern too; they took to going to town two or three evenings a week and the traditional rendezvous in the cobbler's shop was abandoned. Instead they took to meeting in the watchmaker's shop where there was a modern efficient wireless set, and they would stand around and discuss and dissect the evening news bulletin before returning slowly back home. Such optimism as they clung to dissolved as they heard of the German-Russian Pact and the Dutch call-up; it vanished completely when the British Navy was mobilised. On Saturday 2nd September the whole community knew that the make-believe was over when the Territorials got telegrams telling them to prepare to embark on the cargo boat *Clydesdale* on Monday.

Nobody heard Chamberlain's formal declaration of war on the Sunday because, in the Hebrides in those days, radio sets were never switched on on Sunday – not even for the news. But they didn't need to hear.

Long before the normal hour of worship people were streaming along the three roads, some heading for the Free Presbyterian Church on the edge of the town; some for the Church of Scotland down at the shore. There wasn't an empty seat in either. The normal observation of family pews went by the board although, of course, families still crowded together even more than usual. Like the rest, Grandfather's pew had strangers in it and I, along with the other young folk, was ushered into the standing area below the gallery. Although the church was fuller than I had ever seen it even at communion time there was an atmosphere of hush, and the huge congregation even seemed to move in silence when they stood up for the prayers. It was only when the minister began to pray specifically for the boys who were going away 'to fight a just war' that there was a little noise from here and there as, here and there, a woman sobbed against her will …

The *Clydesdale* didn't arrive on Monday. Word came that she was threading her way up through the southern isles – Barra, South Uist, Benbecula and North Uist, picking up the Territorials from there. But, on Tuesday afternoon, Tarbert pier was packed with people from every airt of Harris. The Territorials had marched crisply the short distance from the Drill Hall to the pier with Piper Ross playing ahead of them, but now they had been stood down and each soldier, with his pack on his back and trailing his rifle, was standing surrounded by his family and relatives; here and there a girl friend had abandoned the secrecy of courtship and, probably for the first time, joined the boy's parents. The *Clydesdale* seemed to take an age from the time that she appeared behind the Minister's Islands at the mouth of the bay and the old tub, scheduled for retirement, was lower in the water than she had been for many a day. As she crept closer the sound of bagpipes came on ahead of her, long before one could hear the thud of her engines. 'The Uist boys' somebody said with a smile and, somehow or other, that eased the tension and the conversation spread out of its private knots. The Uistmen were, and are, superb pipers and ready to tune in to joy or sorrow. There were a lot of them playing but they fell silent as the ship tied up and scores of soldiers in their spick and span uniforms crowded the rails to cheer the Harris contingent as it marched, single file, up the gangway. In minutes the gangway was being lifted again and the Clydesdale's engines thudded astern. She began to creep carefully away from the jetty where there was now complete silence, but as the last hawser was thrown clear a solitary male voice began to precent a psalm in the traditional Gaelic way and from shore and ship voices welled up to chant the lines after him,

> 'God is our refuge and our strength
> In straits a present aid …'

Chapter Twelve

Laughter was slow to return; but it did. Just as bereavement, no matter how intense or how personal, has to surrender its sorrowful indulgence to the pressures of ordinary living, so a community has to adjust itself evén to the sudden creaming off of its most vibrant members. And there was no immediate tragedy to turn an international war into a family's war. The Territorials who left Tarbert pier on the *Clydesdale* had teamed up with a further contingent from Skye and had joined up in Inverness with other elements of the famous 51st Highland Division – the Seaforths, the Gordons, the Argylls and the Black Watch. That much we knew, despite the immediate censorship clamp-down, because most of the families of the Northlands had relatives in Inverness and their communications were not subject to scrutiny like the mail from the soldiers themselves. So, while the lads in Dochfour camp were desperately trying to invent codes to communicate what they were up to, the people at home knew their every movement through the good offices of the Invernessians. The West Highlands and the Western Isles were immediately declared a 'protected area' because of the number of naval establishments there and because the north of Scotland was fast becoming a rendezvous area for the Atlantic convoys. People needed 'passport' certificates to move out of the area, or more especially come into it, and that for a while became an irritation and gave a feeling that we were in mild state of seige. The Territorials came home for Christmas leave, not having been farther afield than Aldershot, and their very presence, first footing in their uniforms, and looking fit and cheerful, created a vague sort of feeling that our worries had been exaggerated and that nothing serious was going to befall them after all. Since periods and epochs aren't designated till afterwards we weren't to know that what we were going through was later to become known as 'the phoney war'.

Not that we were under any illusions about the reality of it for other people. We were hearing more and more about air raids on the southern cities; news like the fall of Warsaw (although it was only an unknown town in a far away country) warned us that the Germans were not being halted as easily as we fondly imagined they would be. The stunning news that the *Royal Oak* was sunk in Scapa Flow with a loss of 800 lives (the equivalent of a third of our total island population as someone put it) created an awesome fear in an island where the majority of families had somebody facing the war at sea; the vast majority of our serving men were, in fact, in the Merchant Service or in the Royal Navy; the war was crystallised for us round the army only because we had seen, with our own eyes, the departure of one hundred men in one compact unit. And for me, personally, that crystallisation was inevitable because Archie and Neil whom I hero worshipped were part of that unit. Grandfather and Grandmother had a much more personal interest which caused them more anxiety than they ever revealed; not only was their son (my uncle) at sea, but his wife and baby son were in Southampton and very much in the firing line as the air raids began to intensify.

Everywhere the word *news* was acquiring a new urgency and significance. 'What's the news?' no longer meant 'What's fresh in your part of the world?'; it meant 'What is the very latest that you have heard about the war?' It had taken us a long time to get used to the immediacy of the daily newspaper stories; as the war had been seen to be approaching the radio had speeded up information and made people feel that they should be abreast with the day; that same radio was now urging us into thinking of the world changing hour by hour. Radio was still a relative novelty and by no means every house had a set; Grandfather didn't, and my own parents back in the Southlands didn't. At first most people had thought it was a luxury they could afford to do without, and by the time they began to regard it as a necessity radio sets had become very hard to get because the nation's manufacturing resources were being channelled into the war effort. One was fortunate if one could buy a second hand set, and that remained the case till the pressures of public demand resulted in the famous 'utility sets' in their spartan white-wood as opposed to the sedate and luxurious walnuts and mahoganies and oaks of their forerunners.

In Tarbert the cobbler's shop had never recovered its place as the village council chamber; although the little old cobbler still crouched over his last by lamplight into the late hours of the night few of his former cronies now congregated around him and he began to look lonelier and lonelier. But the watchmaker's shop had boomed; one had to be early in the queue if one were to get reasonably near the loudspeaker (and one needed to be close because the quality of reception still left a lot to be desired) and when the black-out started one almost had to book a seat. It was only on a Friday or a Saturday night that I could hope to get to the watchmaker's anyway, because The Blus kept up his patrol in war as assiduously as he had done in the peace. When I did so I tried to store up every scrap of information that I heard so that I could relay the latest news to my grandparents when I got home.

Grandfather had given up going to town at night, and because most of the young men were away, he saw few visitors. His only regular link to the sources of immediate news was Ali who, if he had ever contemplated a return to his native land, was now firmly cut off from any such escape; as if a wife and family were not enough to anchor him he now had the whole naval resources of Nazi Germany between him and the vast homeland which was still just India in the British Raj. The one way in which Ali had not been able to take a full role in the crofting community was that he didn't have a cow. He had a few sheep which he was allowed to graze on the hill pastures and which some crofter or other would tend for him during lambing time. But, living in rented accommodation in Tarbert, it was not very practical for him to keep a cow. So, night after night, except Sunday, he trudged out to Big Grandfather's to buy milk – oblivious to winter gales or lightning or thunder. As soon as he had heard the nine o'clock news Ali set off for Grandfather's, occasionally giving a

162

lonely traveller the fright of his life when he smiled at him suddenly out of the dark, and, having arrived, he would plonk himself on the nearest chair and launch into a recitation of the nine o'clock bulletin. The only occasional preface he put to his monologue was, 'Tonight the news was told by Joseph MacLeod' as if the fact that he had the same surname as grandfather gave that distinguished newsreader's message an added validity. I was, by then, tolerably fluent in English but I had to strain my ears and my knowledge and my imagination to make some sense out of Ali's fractured rendering of the news. Grandfather, who spoke good English but whose ear wasn't attuned to the standard versions far less Ali's must have ended up with some rather bizarre impressions of the progress of the conflict, particularly when Lord Haw-Haw started broadcasting his propaganda bulletins, which Ali listened to and always edited into his recollections of the BBC version. Occasionally, when matters appeared to be getting out of hand, I would sit with a mournful Grandfather after Ali had left and try to explain to him that half the Royal Navy had not been sunk in Coventry, and could not possibly have been since Coventry was reasonably remote from the seas. That was when Ali had got some of Haw-Haw's more extravagant claims mixed up with the BBC's account of a bombing raid, or else Grandfather had failed to follow Ali's bad grammar and exotic accent.

The passing on of news by word of mouth through second and third parties is a hazardous business at the best of times, but doubly so when it is being sifted through two thought processes (one operating in Hindu and the other in Gaelic) before being reconstituted in broken English. Even back home in the Southlands the problems applied although not in the same way. Because our village had been founded by veterans from the First World War, our men were too old and their sons too young, by and large, for either generation to be called on to participate actively in the second one. But nobody can be totally exempt from war. And though our little village contributed only two or three people to the services there were relatives by the score in the army and even more in the merchant marine. For that reason news of every action was awaited anxiously, and because the first war was still fresh in the minds of the men who had survived it, the walls of every house were covered with the war maps which were being copiously supplied by various newspapers, and the movements of navies and armies were plotted with little pins as if Scaristavore were at the nerve centre of command. News was in demand, therefore, at two levels – at the professional level, by those who still had a lingering interest in the tactical disposition of military forces, and emotionally by those who had relatives or friends 'away'. In the Southlands wirelesses were in even shorter supply than they were among the more sophisticated citizenry of Tarbert. Calum the Post was getting old, but, just as he had always been our principal contact with the outside world, there now devolved on him the duty of chief war correspondent by virtue of the fact that he had the best radio set in the parish. He was more accurate than Ali with his reportage but much more temperamental, and if the mood took him he might, out of sheer cussedness, refuse to stop at a house unless he had a letter to deliver. 'I am paid to deliver news with a stamp on it' was his defence if anybody chided him for being neglectful.

Because there was no electricity in Harris then (outside establishments with their own private generators) all the wirelesses were powered by a large 'dry' battery which had a long and fairly predictable life, and by a 'wet' battery known as an accumulator which had to be taken to some generating centre, like the nearest wool mill, to be re-charged when it became exhausted. Accumulators were exasperating things. There was no way of anticipating their demise because the duration of each charge depended on the conscientiousness of the electrician administering it, and, of course, on the length of the period during which the radio set was in use. In a house where the younger members of the family had predilections for Scottish dance music, the sudden demise of the accumulator tended to have the sort of explosive effect that the telephone bill has nowadays on a house with daughters.

'What's the news today, Calum?' enquired a devout old lady who had a finely honed relish for grief.

It was the umpteenth time that Calum had been asked the same question that morning, and his patience wasn't elastic at the best of times.

'The accumulator's down!' he shouted, crashing his red van into gear so that he didn't hear the old lady's anguished moan of,

'God help us! I wonder how many island boys lost their lives on that one.' Since most things travelled faster than Calum, bad news certainly did, and, by the time he reached the ninth house on, having been overtaken by a couple of bicycles, the information was awaiting him that a large merchant ship had been sunk and scores of Hebridean seamen had been lost. Which news, for lack of any other, Calum passed on to the rest of the houses on his route. It took him a while to unravel why, two or three days later, he found himself being accused of the new crime of the age – 'spreading alarm and despondency', and why few people were inclined to believe him when he did pass on a piece of 'highly confidential information' to the effect that, in response to a personal appeal from the Government, Colonel Walker, the landlord, was going to mobilise the entire male population of the Southlands and form them into an armed defence regiment to be known as the LDV.

'Rubbish!' said most people.

'Why not?' wondered my father. 'If the Government thinks us important enough to give us our own wee Lysander to protect us, it's not beyond the bounds of possibility that they would think of sticking guns into our hands to protect ourselves. They don't know some of the people in this place!' The 'wee Lysander' to which he referred was a little spotter plane which was on permanent patrol in our area and as the U-boat attacks on merchant shipping became more menacing the sound of the Lysander became as familiar as the croak of the corncrake and its appearances much more common. As the menace of the war became more oppressive after the shattering news of Dunkirk, aircraft activity above the sea-lanes became more and more intense. Occasionally one would hear the tell-tale stop-start drone of an enemy plane and under those circumstances the homely chug of 'our own wee Lysander' was a comfort; a symbol of the impregnable ring of defence which we imagined to be surrounding us.

In the Northlands, I was only vaguely aware of the activities in the village, and such information as I did get was only sketchily conveyed by my mother in her letters, which still reached me regularly on Tuesdays. Her news tended to concentrate more on domestic issues – the nuisance of local merchants insisting on sticking rigidly to the 'points' allocated in the ration books, the record number of socks that a certain local woman had contributed to some area of the war effort; the fact that father was getting a new loom now that there was a dramatic upsurge in the sale of Harris Tweed. The news that tended to interest me most were the items introduced 'Your father says to tell you ...' and it was under that heading that I heard about Calum and the accumulator, the rumours about the arming of the village, and the sad news that the Golf Course was being closed down ... The distance between myself and the village was steadily getting greater although the miles remained the same. I was by way of becoming more and more a boy of the Northlands (whence, after all, I had originally come) and the pressures of schoolwork, which happily was now beginning to prove more congenial as I devoted more time to it, were adding to the distancing. The highlights and the tragedies of 'my war' were the ones which most deeply affected the Northlands and, consequently, most immediately, the young soldiers who had sailed from Tarbert Pier six months before. We knew they were now in France – in the Saar. We knew that because Archie had been home on leave.

Dunkirk came as numbing news. It was impossible to believe that the great British army was in retreat; Britain just didn't lose wars, according to the history books. But there it was, being relayed day by day for a whole week from the watchmaker's radio to the knot of people that now never seemed to leave the shop door. One could sense a slow depression spreading through the community; it wasn't that people discussed the business so much as the fact that they didn't smile so much any more. Even in school much of the laughter had gone out of the boys who still congregated in the lavatory for the morning and afternoon interval smokes, and the conversation wasn't any more the chit-chat of local happenings or the prurience of sexual fantasising. The incredible achievement of the evacuation didn't, for a long time, penetrate; the BBC might pump out heroic stories about rowing boats and pleasure yachts snatching men off the beaches under fire; the news might hint optimistically about the day when the British army would return. But, as far as we were concerned, the blunt truth was that a powerful army of 400,000 men had been defeated. There was one pathetic glimmer of hope. The 51st Division was still in France. The

Highlanders had not retreated. And were they not, after all, the kilted warriors that the Germans had dreaded most in that other war as 'the ladies from Hell?' When they fixed bayonets … when the pipers began to play … when … when … when …

It was a braggart euphoria, and the dispelling of it was doubly agonising because it was so slow. A week after Dunkirk had passed into the legend the news came that the 51st Highland Division had been captured at St Valery en Caux where all attempts at a Dunkirk type evacuation had been frustrated. This was reality. This was no longer a case of an army being routed or captured; these were our own kith and kin – the lads who had sailed on the Clydesdale from Tarbert. The agony was so much the worse because it contained a glimmer of hope; after all the dreaded telegram that told of death put an end to hope, but if a man was taken prisoner of war there was the knowledge that he would return home one day. The surrender hadn't happened without casualties – we knew that from the few telegrams that did come; the dreadful business was not knowing and the waiting, from day to day, till a list of prisoners would be announced. For many it was a long, long wait, and my own people were among those most desperately on the rack. There had been no news of Archie since he had gone back to France after that last leave of his, and nobody knew whether he and Neil were prisoners, or wounded, or dead. Rumours sprang out of the empty air, and they only served to make the waiting worse.

But, from St Valery on, the mood changed; the dull resignation gave way to bitterness and the war was no longer the war against Germany; as Hitler ranted about the total annihilation of the enemies of the Reich it became 'Hitler's war'. He, personally, it was who had been responsible for the loss of our hundred men – whether by imprisonment or death. The British propaganda machine was swinging effectively into action too and, as the threatened invasion didn't immediately materialise, the sense of sorrow gave way to a sense of defiance save in the individual grieving breast. 'Call-up' was yet another word that became absorbed into the Gaelic vocabulary and, week after week, an individual or a couple of individuals would board the mailboat in Sunday best and carrying a small suitcase; but never again was there to be a mass departure with pomp and ceremony such as there had been with the Terriers.

In school, some of the boys were now beginning to talk about the day when they would enlist. After all some of them were approaching sixteen and soon would be liable for conscription anyway; most of these would have volunteered there and then if they were allowed to, but there was no way that parents would tolerate a falsification of ages. Those parents who hadn't experienced the grimness of the battle-front in the first war, had experienced the traumas of bereavement or waiting and wondering in the second.

Bit by bit the Saturday night parade was re-establishing itself although there was now a marked accent on school pupils, but it was reviving because there was nothing better to do. The excitement had gone out of it except on the rare occasion when a small group of sailors happened to be home on leave, or when a naval vessel put into East Loch Tarbert and a swaggering group of ratings with strange accents came ashore in search of the kind of fun which, by and large, vanished behind closed doors as soon as fathers heard the chugging of the pinnaces. Whatever hopes the sailors clutched as they tied up at the pier soon vanished and they were left with only an all-male bar in which liquor supplies were running low, and a gaggle of scruffy schoolboys trying to scrounge cigarettes from them.

Yet another reason that the parade was losing its excitement was that the heart was going out of the shops as anything resembling luxury merchandise disappeared from the shelves. There was no longer any point in remaining open late on a Saturday night. Ali was doubly hit. His main customers for his vanity goods had sailed on the *Clydesdale* and although his window still shimmered with toiletry there was no profit to be made out of school children crushing their noses up against his window; worse still the increasingly strict black-out regulations meant that the glitter was killed stone dead when the blinds were dropped. At last he announced that he was going to close down and he approached a member of my school class to ask if he could muster a team of six strong lads for the following Saturday night to move his stock out of the shop into store. Poor innocent Ali!

When we descended on the shop at eight o'clock he had all his goods carefully packed into large cardboard cartons which, in his innocence, he didn't even bother to seal. There began a shuttle service of carriers from the little shop down to the store at the end of his house where his wife was waiting to take delivery of the boxes, and to check that the number of cartons that left the shop reached the store. What neither of them realised was that on the way down, half-way between the shop and the store and out of sight of both, there was an empty garage into which we had long-since forced entry so that we could use it as a smoking hide-away out of the ken of 'The Blus'. Every promising carton was carried into the garage and hastily ransacked for the luxuries that we had coveted in the shop window for months. Bottles of brilliantine, jars of hair-cream, scented soaps, after-shave lotion … everything that savoured of unattainable luxury was there. We pillaged ruthlessly but discreetly. We left the cigarettes alone because we knew that Ali was bound to have count of them; we were tempted by the condoms but should they ever be discovered in our possession we'd be in dire trouble; deep down we knew that the chances of our using them were slim indeed and when one of our number declared that a friend of his had said that their usage was 'like having a bath in an oilskin' that was a good enough face-saving formula. By the time we were finished there was a discreet hoard of toiletries hidden under a scrap of tarpaulin in a dark corner of the garage; the spoils ranged from solidified brilliantine to rather sophisticated eau-de-Cologne. At the end of the night we had the ill grace to accept twenty cigarettes and a shilling each from Ali before slipping back under cover of dark to the garage to divide the spoils. In all fairness we took only sufficient for our own long term needs and a little over to share with our friends.

Half-way down the path to my grandfather's house I met the old man on his way to look for me. I prayed that the Sabbath hadn't arrived. It hadn't, but it didn't make any difference; all the way down to the house I got a tongue lashing such as I had never suspected him to be capable of, but it was nothing compared to what Grannie had to say as I snuffled my way through supper careful not to jerk as I moved lest the tins and the bottles in my pockets rattled. I had meant to conceal my hoard among the hay in the byre on my way home but, by meeting me, Big Grandfather had foiled that. I had to sweat my way through Saturday night prayers, moving like a cripple lest I clank when it came to kneeling for the final prayer. I was what I imagined a nervous wreck must be by the time I got upstairs and got my loot concealed behind the most innocent looking books in my make-shift book-case. I left a tin of solid brilliantine beside the mirror on my dressing table, fairly certain that neither Grandmother nor Grandfather would assume that it was other than purchased out of my pocket money.

By Sunday morning the lateness of my home-coming was either forgotten or forgiven and Grandfather was mildly complimentary about the alacrity with which I had sprung out of bed as soon as I heard him shuffling downstairs. He even complimented me on my appearance as I sat at breakfast with my hair flattened under a weight of brilliantine; if he smelt the toilet water with which I had laved myself he made no comment. As we set off together for church, up the path on which he had met me in wrath twelve hours before, our normal relationship had been totally restored. It was a morning of glorious sunshine with a twittering harmony of birds, and, as we walked along chatting to friends and neighbours making their ways to worship, my conscience didn't trouble me a whit. It was like one of the Sundays of the year before except that the church bell was silent.

Church was crowded as it had been every Sabbath since the day the war began. The absence of the young men in the services was made up for many times over by parents and grandparents and relatives who came to offer up their prayers of supplication and of thanks. The boats from Scalpay, Drinishadder and Scadabay had tied up at the pier as we approached the church and their passengers had joined the leisurely column making its way up the path past Ali's house or else made their ways to the Free Presbyterian Church up the hill.

I had always associated the shore kirk with cool and camphor, but only the latter was in evidence that day as I sat hunched tightly between my grandfather and my stoutest aunt. The sun, beating through the kirk windows, appeared to have singled out our pew and the one in front in which sat two of my fellow looters from the night before. I noted that their hair was plastered flat like my own and both heads were gleaming like the flanks of well groomed horses. I knew that the other three were somewhere in the church, but I couldn't remember which were their landladies' pews and even if I had done I could no more swivel round to look for them than a sheaf of corn could have stood on end in an autumn stack. I was already trying a rhythm whereby I could breathe in when my aunt was breathing out. Apart from my partners in crime in front of me I was aware of only two faces at the end of their respective pews; one was The Blus whose jaw was twitching as he discreetly sucked at a peppermint; the other was Ali who was staring straight ahead of him with the impassivity of his race. The war had apparently converted him. At last the minister appeared through the door that opened into his pulpit, high above the one in which the precentor had long since taken his seat with much sighing and massaging of his eyes. The minister announced the first psalm and after the precentor had stood up and coughed discreetly a couple of times he led the congregation into a mighty volume of singing. He was, of course, the only one standing; I would have to await that relief till the first prayer. My aunt was a mighty singer and although my grandfather enunciated a note here and there he went through the whole chest expansion process as if he were tackling a Wagnerian aria; between them I felt like a baby mouse trapped in the bellows of an accordion. But my troubles were only beginning.

By the end of the first verse my Harris Tweed suit was beginning to pull at my body hairs as the lustiness of the singing seemed to generate heat additional to that of the beating sun. The second verse was half way through when I became aware of a rivulet of what I assumed to be sweat oozing down my temple and I realised to my horror that I didn't have a handkerchief. With my elbow wedged tightly between my aunt and myself I managed to get the tips of my fingers to my forehead before the perspiration reached my eye, but as soon as I felt the oily slitheriness I realised what was happening. My solid brilliantine was melting in the heat of the kirk; and I knew that there was nothing that I could do to stop it melting. My grandfather elbowed me sharply to stop me wriggling, and all I could do was look helplessly at my two friends in front to see how they were faring. Not much better. Except that they had handkerchiefs with which they could mop themselves discreetly from time to time, while I could only sit still and allow the oily rivulets to follow the contours of my face down into the collar of my shirt; I prayed God that the word VIOLET on the tin on my dressing-table referred to the scent and not the colour.

My aunt sniffed after she had lashed out at the last note of that interminable psalm. The minister sniffed and looked around the church before he called us to prayer, probably wondering if he had strayed into a chapel by some ghastly mistake. Somebody sniffed at the far end of the church during the prayer, and by the time the minister got round to his first reading the church sounded like an ill-mannered kindergarten smitten by flu. One fragile old lady left hastily clutching her handkerchief to her mouth, and one of the elders hurried out after her. The benediction brought to an end the longest church service I have ever known. Strangely enough the only person to make any comment was a navyman from Scalpay who turned to his companion as he got out of the door of the church and said, 'What the hell was going on in church today; the place smelt like a Hong Kong whorehouse!' Heads whipped round to look at him in disbelief and he fell silent.

It was the last Sunday of term, and on the Monday, after school, I smuggled my hoard out of the house and hid it in an unlikely corner of the byre where there was little chance of my grandfather discovering it. I could risk taking only one bottle of hair-dressing home with me without attracting questions and, worse still, giving the impression that I had pocket money to spare.

My arrival home for the long summer break was a happier one by far than that dreaded Christmas one which now seemed a life-time away. I had in my pocket the first report card which I had received since that disastrous preliminary one, and it showed a dramatic improvement – particularly in English, which I knew would please my father most. This was my fourth visit back home, including one long mid-term week-end, and nobody came to meet the bus any more with any special welcome. This time such shocks as were in store were for me. In what had hitherto been the front porch there stood a compact little iron loom with two pedals instead of four; I knew it to be the new Hattersley loom, popularly known as 'the automatic' to which many Hebridean weavers had finally been converted and which was already beginning to revolutionise the Harris Tweed industry. But there was a greater shock in store when I opened the door into the living room. My father was sitting at the end of the table filling in some official looking forms; he was in an ill-fitting khaki uniform, and behind him, propped up against the wall, was a rifle.

Chapter Thirteen

Nobody ever had 'a good war' and I can't imagine how anybody could coin the phrase in cynicism or in jest. But because, on the Atlantic coast of the Hebrides, we were about as remote from the 'action' as it was possible to be, we didn't suffer the horrors experienced, as time went on, by people living in Liverpool or London or Glasgow. Nor did we suffer the privations of day to day living to the same extent. Just as the sea and the land had saved us during the Depression years, so the natural resources of the countryside spared us from the stringency of rationing, and, by and large, we depended on the little buff ration books only for things which would have been considered luxuries in our part of the world two or three generations back. We had our own hens, our own eggs, milk, potatoes and fish; and every crofter had his own flock of sheep. There were stringent laws governing the butchering of sheep and cattle, but London laws were hard to enforce in the Western isles at the best of times and doubly hard when communications were doubly worse! No law could be invented that would prevent a wedder or a crock disappearing in a quagmire or falling over a cliff, and while Lord Woolton at the Ministry of Food was gaining plaudits for spreading resources so that the nation as a whole was reasonably nourished, there was little he could do to stop parts of it being better nourished than others. George Morrison, the celebrated humorist of the *Stornoway Gazette* defined the Government's dilemma in a poem which caused much hilarity at the time.

173

There's no wether on the tether
Where the wether used to be;
But there's meat upon the rafter
Which Lord Woolton must not see.
They say it was the weather
Which the wether couldn't stand –
That it died of influenza …
But the smell of it is grand.

We were deeply conscious of the shortages from which our cousins in the cities suffered and we tried to help. It was perhaps fortunate that Government officials were otherwise busily engaged and didn't have time to wonder at the steady stream of large parcels labelled 'Books with care' that left the islands by every mailboat as we sought to share our bounty of fresh mutton and poultry and black puddings with our less fortunate relations. But the smell of the roast coming from the oven that day was somehow unfamiliar.

'Good Lord, boy,' said my father. 'What are you doing here? The bus isn't due for an hour yet.'

I explained to him that the bus service had been cut from twice daily to thrice weekly to save petrol and this was its new schedule time.

'Nobody ever tells us anything. Your mother will be mortified that she's not home to meet you, and her with a nice haunch of venison roasting for your home-coming. I hear that you deserve more than the prodigal son's mere calf this time.' I had written to my mother telling her of the improvement in my marks and I could see that my lapse of the winter term had been forgiven.

'Where did the venison come from?'

'Och I've always said that Colonel Walker was a good landlord. I hear that some of the LDV boys on the mainland are going around with khaki bands on their arms and practising with hay-forks and pikes and things, but when Churchill heard that we had a ready-made full Colonel to lead us he ordered nine Welsh Guardsmen to be stripped of their uniforms and rifles so that they could be sent to us. "We must hold Harris," he said in the House of Commons …' My father smiled ruefully as he looked down at his midriff. 'Mind you, it must have been a devil of a big Welsh Guardsman who had this uniform; I could

174

take another fellow inside it with me.' I didn't care about the uniform. I couldn't take my eyes off the rifle. I couldn't take in the idea of my father with a rifle. Over the years he would never tolerate a gun in the house although I had pleaded, over and over again, to be allowed to borrow a neighbour's shot-gun to shoot rabits. Whatever he had gone through, during his four years as a sniper in the first war, had turned him bitterly against guns forever.

'Can I fire it some time?'

The question had come out automatically, and even when he heaved himself to his feet I couldn't believe that he was going to agree.

'Why not? Just once, seeing you did so well in your test in school, and seeing your mother isn't here to meet you. And besides I know that you'll never stop pestering me till I agree.' I stared in fascination as he pulled back the bolt and fed in two shells. 'One shot, mind you. And I'll probably get court-martialled!'

He stopped as we were going through the porch, which had now been converted into a weaving shed for the new Hattersley.

'You were quick enough to spot the rifle but you didn't say anything about the new loom. But I'll tell you something. This one shot is going to cost you ten yards of tweed woven on that loom as soon as I get a few minutes to show you how to use it. It'll be fun for you. It's just like pedalling a bicycle.' I'd have agreed to weave ten tweeds, far less ten yards.'

There were several round iron lids from sheep-dip pails lying out at the end of the house. He picked one up and, with a lump of the red keel that we used for marking sheep, he drew concentric rings on it till it began to look like a reasonable imitation of a target.

'Go and stand that up against the old mid-way dyke!'

'The mid-way dyke? Will it fire that far? That's four hundred yards!'

'A 303 bullet will travel a mile, even if not accurately. That's why you've always got to have your target up against a sand-bag or a hill or something. On you go!'

I went off like the wind and placed the target where he had instructed me; by the time I got back to him he was on his

175

stomach resting on his elbows and nestling the butt against his cheek.

'I'm warning you, you've got to hold the butt really tightly against your shoulder or she'll break your collar-bone when she kicks. The idea is to get the bead at the end of the barrel into the V of the back-sight; you start with your gun pointing at the bottom of the target and then you lift the barrel up gently till the V and the bead and the bulls-eye are in one line. Do you understand?' Before I could reply he had fired, completely casually, or so it seemed, and a hole appeared in the middle of the little spot which was the bulls-eye.

His eyes were strangely icy as he handed me the gun.

'One shot,' he snapped as he levered the bolt and cleared the breech.

I got down and aimed for all I was worth and ended up with a bruised shoulder and a target unscathed.

'See what I told you? Man, that bullet of yours is still travelling; it'll probably end up in the Minch.'

When he got inside he dropped the lead of the pull-through into the breech end of the barrel and got me to heave it through. When he was satisfied that it was as clean as new he put the rifle into the loft. I never saw him fire the gun again although he went off with it twice a week to drill. One of his fellow Home Guardsmen (as they came to be called) told me afterwards that, at rifle practice, father merely jerked the gun as the others fired but never pulled the trigger himself. Later, he slipped his unused bullets to whoever was due to go and investigate the deer forest next, on condition that he got the shell casings back so that he could claim his next allocation of bullets. Apparently Colonel Walker could never understand why a man who had been a soldier in the first war couldn't even hit the target. Poor Colonel Walker. It must have been a sore trial to him to be ordered by the Government to issue his tenants with a rifle and ammunition and then encourage them to improve their skill so that their aim would be all the more certain in the dusk among his own stags. Just before the war I remember seeing herds of up to twenty deer each grazing on the slopes of Bleaval; I'm told that now there are none. It's a pity but, fortunately, the red deer is not an endangered species and if the Bleaval ones made the supreme sacrifice during the early war years there is some comfort in the thought that they made it in the cause of peace and as a contribution to the training of our Home Guard.

I repaid my promise of ten yards of tweed many times over. The Hattersley Domestic loom had made its appearance in the Western Isles in the 1920s but the weavers of those early days were chary of change and, besides, there was a strong lobby which resisted anything that suggested a mechanisation of the old handloom weaving. Already both the warp and the weft were being spun in the mills and, by the time the war began, the spinning wheel – once a feature of every living room in Harris – was being relegated to the loft or the barn. The crofter would send his raw fleeces away to a mill with instructions regarding the colours he wanted and, in due course, he would receive back a sack of large bobbins of thread which he only had to thread into his old handloom and weave laboriously, swinging his weaver's beam with his left hand, firing his shuttle with his right, and meshing the threads of his warp by stamping on each of four sturdy wooden levers in the order demanded by his pattern. The Hattersley Domestic eliminated almost all of the back-break. The weaver set his pattern by selecting a combination of little steel plates which governed a box of six shuttles, each of which could carry a different colour of thread, and, once the loom was set up, all the weaver had to do was sit back and pedal two pedals and keep a careful eye on the warp and the weft lest a thread break. It was monotonous work but one could see the web of tweed steadily growing in front of one's eyes. In vain the older weavers protested that their tweeds were no longer hand-woven, that they were foot-woven. The war and an incredible upsurge in the demand for tweed swept aside their protests and the click-clack of the Hattersley was soon as familiar a noise as the rasp of the corncrake. The vast majority of people if asked to name the noise they associated with war would say 'gunfire'; for me it would be the chatter of the Hattersley and the twice daily drone of 'our own wee Lysander' overhead.

I don't know how many yards of tweed I would have been coaxed to contribute to the islands' annual turn-over of some three million yards in the early war years if I hadn't learnt long since that I must never be seen to be good at anything resembling physical labour. God knows it was difficult to be bad at weaving on the Hattersley when all I had to do was to sit and pedal, but I soon discovered that by altering the rhythm of the pedalling I could achieve a slackness in the weave which offended my father's pride of craftsmanship, and by failing to notice that the thread in a particular shuttle had broken, I could turn out a few yards of tweed which bore a vague resemblance to lace. There was only one way father could sort that out and that was by unravelling the tweed right back to the last correct section, re-setting the tension of the warp and starting all over again. His nerve couldn't take much of that, particularly since he couldn't be confident that the roll of tweed already woven and wrapped round the receiving roller wouldn't, when unrolled, reveal a few inches of something resembling a hairy broderie anglaise.

'For Heaven's sake keep away from that loom or my tweeds will be black-listed from John O' Groats to Lands End. Stick to your books and you might make a minister if nothing else. Meantime why don't you go down to the beach and see if anything has come ashore?'

Every coast dweller is an instinctive beachcomber, and it's a very narrow line of conscience that separates the ebb-searcher from the wrecker of the Cornish legends. Very early on in the war Old Hector's prophecy of the beach 'being covered in flotsam from end to end' came true, and whenever the tide ran with a westerly wind the Atlantic spewed up a whole assortment of stuff ranging from wooden pit-props to bales of exotic textiles. One didn't pause to think that these represented destruction – that they represented the cargoes of ships that had been torpedoed as they sought to cross the Atlantic east or west; they were the spoils of war without the immediate association of death and tragedy. Only on the very rare occasion (and the occasions were astonishingly rare considering the circumstances) when a body was washed ashore, did one really associate the spoils with the sorrow. And beachcombing became a fever, with people constantly scanning the horizon to spot a larger floating item, or else prowling the tide-line after the ebb. An official Receiver of Wrecks had been appointed to handle and report on any objects of interest or of value. And the Home Guard was given a certain amount of responsibility to contact the authorities regarding wreckage of a naval or military nature. But, in the end, it was the sharp eyed finder who decided for himself whether an object on the beach was of interest to any branch of His Majesty's Government. Patently a hogshead of rum which had been contaminated by sea-water was the total responsibility of some branch of the Government and the finder would hopefully claim salvage; on the other hand, if the contents of the hogshead were unadulterated, there was no way in which any amount of petty salvage reward could compensate for the intrinsic value of the commodity itself in a community which had only one public house peddling strictly rationed beer and the occasional dram of whisky. Our villagers were so far from the nearest bar that they had never become dedicated or regular drinkers, but if Fate threw up a barrel of good quality spirits on the shore it would have taken exceptional fortitude to spurn it or turn it over to some anonymous authority. It was very rarely that that particular problem arose. The stuff which was washed up was, usually, of little interest to Customs and Excise, but it could be of great community value. A sack of flour in salt water forms an inch of thick soggy crust round the inside of the bag thus making it waterproof and protecting ninety-five percent of the contents so that they are as dry and fresh as they were the day they were milled; half-hundredweight kebbucks of butter and lard are, by their very greasy nature, waterproof anyway, and the greatest damage that they suffered was that when they rolled on the lip of the depositing wave they collected overcoats of fine sand to a depth of an inch or so. In the normal course of events one wouldn't have bothered with the gritty exterior but wartime restrictions had induced an instinct for economy even where flotsam was concerned, and the outside layers of butter and lard were fed to the cattle who would, in due course, get rid of the sand in their own way; just to be on the safe side, in case the next half inch layer had been tainted by sea water it was used to grease the loom; only the fresh pure lard or butter from the core of the lump was reserved for human consumption. The Hattersley chattered smoothly with its greasing of lard and the cattle beasts never looked glossier. The only sufferers (and only for short periods) were the local merchants who must have wondered why people didn't bother to take up their rations of butter and cooking-fat.

One day my brother and I came home with a handful of beautiful pegs, each of about six inches in length, with which we

179

proceeded to decorate the front door. Nobody paid any attention to us, at first, but by the time we had achieved a clumsy figure 7 and a crude brass knocker my father couldn't fail but notice.

'What the devil are you doing to the door, and where did you find those things?'

We explained that an old anti-shipping mine had been washed up and that we had managed to screw some of the horns off it; we would go back later with a spanner and remove the rest.

'The first thing you will do is take a hammer and remove those damn things from the door. And then, if you haven't anything better to do wind some bobbins for the Hattersley so that I can finish off that tweed when I come back!'

We thought it injudicious to ask where he was going, and it didn't matter anyway because he never got there. Half-way to the gate he stopped, spun round on his heel and came racing back.

'What did you say? An old mine? How do you know it was old?'

'If it had been a new one it would have exploded when it hit the beach, wouldn't it?'

'And if it had exploded it wouldn't be there, would it? Don't you dare go near that beach today, and if you see anybody else going in the direction of the shore stop them. I'm going to contact the Coast Guard.'

This time there was no doubt where he was going – and in a hurry. He was going to the Duchess's shop and the phone.

Early that evening a large lorry with a dozen soldiers aboard roared into the village from Stornoway. They flung open the gate to the Common Grazing and trundled towards the beach, sending sheep and cattle scattering in every direction. From the hillock above the house my brother and I watched them spilling out of the lorry. Ten of them grouped round the vehicle while two moved cautiously towards the mine which was, by now, beginning to wobble gently in the incoming tide. They seemed to take only seconds to come to a decision, and after much gesticulating from the soldier who seemed to be in charge, the main body split up and soldiers fanned out towards the village houses while the two who had examined the mine began to uncoil a huge drum of cable from the back of the lorry. In no time at all each house in the village had been visited, and the occupants warned to keep clear of their windows. A soldier was posted at each entrance to the village to stop any traffic, and then the troop moved their vehicle in behind a large sand dune and crouched down round it. When the explosion came it shook every window in the township and the reverberation of it was felt in Drumpound, two miles away.

The cows were beginning to settle down and graze again as the army lorry drew up at our gate, and a sergeant marched smartly to the door. My father invited him in and handed him the eight brass pegs which we had dutifully prized off the door.

'You screwed these off the mine?' the sergeant asked, looking from me to my brother and back to me again.

'Yes. But we didn't think we were doing any harm.'

'And then you hammered them?'

We nodded.

'Bloody hell! I don't know whether it's God or the devil looking after you, but somebody is. If that mine had gone up when you were unscrewing these horns we wouldn't have found a trouser button off one of you. And how you got away with hammering them, I'll never know. Each of them contains a detonator which would, at the very least, have taken the hands off you if one of them had decided to explode!'

He looked at my parents, both of whom were ashen-faced. I don't know what reaction he was expecting, but my mother merely forced a tight smile and said 'Would you like to bring your boys in for a cup of tea?' It was her automatic reaction to any tense situation, but it diffused this one. The sergeant laughed.

'You Lewis women! If the devil himself appeared at the door you'd offer him a cup of tea.'

'I don't know what Lewis women would do,' said my father. 'The devil might well find them more approachable than Harris women.'

'O God, I'm sorry; I'll never get it right. O.K., O.K. I'm not in Britain, I'm in Scotland. And this end of the island is Harris and the other end is Lewis. And I don't know what a poor bloody Birmingham man is doing here anyway –'

'Never you mind –' My father was warming to the idea of

company. 'Just bring in the lads and the wife'll put the kettle on while she's forgiving you.'

'I can't do that; there are twelve of us!'

'Yourself and eleven disciples. We know what happened to the other one. Just you go and bring them in, and we'll find enough cups to go round.'

And so, a troop of hefty Royal Engineers crowded into our tiny living room and found themselves perches somehow or other. In no time at all I could hardly see their faces for smoke as they chatted and my mother plied the teapot.

'And what's the news on the war front?' my father asked when the banter died down and the subject of the mine was thankfully exhausted. My brother and I had been mercilessly ribbed. At first we had taken it in good part, thankful that nobody was taking a more serious view of our exploit, but now the whole thing was becoming tedious and we were grateful to my father for changing the direction of the conversation.

'News?' pondered the sergeant. 'I don't know. Nothing that you won't have heard on the radio. O, there was that bit of excitement at the beginning of the week. One of those little reconnaissance planes. One of our lads heard her engine cutting out suddenly and she just disappeared. It was very misty and nobody saw anything. The Coast Guard and some fishing boats spent two days searching round the coast, and we were turned out. But nothing's been found. Poor chap – probably thought himself lucky to be on a milk run, but that's the way it goes.'

'O, no!'

My father's tone made some of the soldiers turn to look at him. There was a sad kind of smile on his face.

'It would be our own wee Lysander,' he said. 'Sure as anything. I wondered why I hadn't heard it for a few days.'

'Your own what?' the sergeant asked.

'Nothing at all. I'd just got sort of used to the sound of that wee aeroplane. It was daft, but it made one feel kind of safe to have it around.'

'That's the way it goes,' shrugged the sergeant, handing his empty cup to my mother. 'Somebody somewhere will be missing him. Just hope he's washed ashore somewhere; it's not so bad when you know for sure what happened and when you know a chap's had a decent burial.' He chattered on as he rose

182

and put his cap on and waited for the company to get to its feet. 'Thanks for the tea, Missus. Twelve's a hell of a lot of teas out of your rations; next time there's a jeep down this way I'll get the boys to drop you off a couple of packets.'

'Not at all,' protested my mother as she followed them out to the door. 'It was a great pleasure.' Father got up but didn't say anything. I knew that he was thinking of the 'wee Lysander' which had become a strange symbol of something for him. I caught his eye as he went out after the rest, and he gave a hint of a wistful little smile. He never referred to 'our own wee Lysander' again; not even when one which looked to me identical took its place.

When the truck pulled away from the gate my brother turned to me. 'How many soldiers were in here?'

'Twelve. Why?'

'No. There were only eleven.'

'Don't be daft; the sergeant himself said twelve.'

'I know he did, but I counted eleven. And I counted twelve on the lorry when it went down to the beach. I think one of them got blown up!'

'Rubbish!' But I wasn't all that sure of myself. Donald was twelve and already beginning to show evidence of the thrawn-ness which was to serve him well in later life. I was much more inclined to accept a statement of fact without examining it, and the fact that the sergeant had said 'twelve' was enough for me. But I did know that Donald could count.

'Right then. Let's go down to the shore and have a look. Are you sure he didn't just stay behind in the lorry while the rest were having their tea?'

'No. I was trying to get into the lorry, but it was locked and there was nobody inside it.'

We slipped out to the back of the house and waited till father and mother returned from waving their unexpected guests farewell. As soon as they were indoors we set off for the beach like a couple of greyhounds out of their traps. My imagination had by now gone into top gear and I had visions of bits of flesh and khaki splattered over the rocks of the Blue Skerry.

But we weren't the first on the scene. As we reached the edge of the band of marram which separated the beach from the soft grazing we saw Gillespie waving frantically to us from the rim of one of the big sandy gouges which pitted the shore-line. Gillespie and I had been closer than brothers all our lives, and had been in countless scrapes together, but he had decided not to go on to High School and had now finally left school aged fourteen. Leaving school at fourteen meant being pitched into an early manhood, and already an indefinable maturity had come down on him and a little of the laughter had gone out. That, and the physical separation when I had moved out of the village to school in the Northlands, had dropped a gossamer of reticence between us, but that was reft now by the full hurtle of Gillespie's excitement.

'Hurry up! There's a dead soldier here.' I could detect a touch of nervousness in his exuberance. 'I found him,' he added as if, even with a corpse, finders were keepers.

'I told you there were only eleven,' my brother puffed as we reached the crater.

Sure enough, there, on the bottom of the sandpit beside an electrical plunger, lay a soldier face down. We stood high above him, staring down on him like three ragged vultures, and for my own part I felt the beginnings of fear coming over me. And then the corpse muttered something and turned over on his back with a smile on his face.

'Look at him,' Gillespie spluttered. 'He's not dead at all; he's found the place where Sandy Cravat hid his rum and he's blind drunk!' Sure enough, when the man rolled over we could see that he had been lying on top of a bottle which had slipped out of his fingers and now lay on its side with a damp patch of sand at its neck. Gillespie's assessment of the situation was manifestly right. Some weeks before, Sandy Cravat had found a large cask of rum on the beach and, unlike some of the liquor that came ashore, this was unadulterated by sea water and very strong. Unfortunately the local men, who weren't very devout drinkers anyway, didn't at all fancy rum and Sandy, who used to claim that he could drink turpentine with a spoonful of sugar in it, was left with a whole cask to himself. He solved his problem in a typically Sandy way; he filled and cached forty bottles for his own immediate needs, topped the cask with water and re-bunged it. He then claimed salvage, which he got along with a letter commending him for his honesty. The whole village knew roughly where the rum was hidden but it had remained undisturbed till the sapper with a thirst stumbled on it that day.

'We'd better get him to your house; your father will know what to do with him.'

The soldier raised his head cautiously when he heard Gillespie speaking in Gaelic and then, in perfect Gaelic, asked who the hell we were. That was a bit difficult to explain; we were just ourselves – unlike him in a place where we had every right to be. So instead of telling him about us we told him about him – how his comrades had gone off without him, and how we'd found him dead drunk, and how we'd telephone Stornoway and get them to send the lorry back for him.

'O God, don't do that,' he implored with his head in his hands. 'Give me time to think. If you phone Stornoway it'll be the bloody M.P.s they'll send down and I'll be on more charges than I have fingers. I'm the odd man out in the damn platoon; I'm the only Gaelic speaker in it and that sod of an English sergeant has his knife in me.'

That put a different complexion on things. This was one of our own men – from the island of South Uist as it turned out, and in that particular regiment because he had enlisted in London. We weren't going to let any English upstart get the better of him and so we began to oxter him towards our house. My brother, with more savvy than I would have given him credit for, buried the empty rum bottle in the sand and covered over the remainder of Sandy's cache which the South Uistman had unwittingly exposed.

Father's pipe nearly fell out of his mouth when we arrived at the house with three of us supporting something which must have looked like a marionette in a uniform.

'What the devil have you got there?'

'It's a soldier.'

'You could have fooled me; but it explains a lot about the way the war's going. Where did you find him? Washed up on the beach or blown down over the hill?'

'I beg your pardon, Sir.' The hapless soldier tried to pull himself together. We had informed him that my father had been a regular soldier (which he had been, more or less) and an officer in the Home Guard (which he wasn't). 'I got separated from my platoon and –'

185

'He comes from South Uist and he speaks Gaelic,' I chipped in.

'That explains even more.' The stench of rum was beginning to fill the room, and my mother, sizing up the situation, had already begun bustling with the kettle. I could see laughter in my father's eyes although he was still clipped and formal. He sniffed. 'You smell to me more like a navyman. Anyway, sit down. Perhaps a cup of tea will sober you up till we decide what we're going to do with you.'

Poor Private MacAulay, as we had discovered him to be, was not, I suspected, a very articulate person at the best of times and there was something about him which suggested that he had attained the highest rank that the army would ever consider bestowing on him. So the three of us took turns to tell his story for him while he laboured over his cup of tea; we spelt out in detail the fate that would befall him when the English sergeant discovered that he was missing. The idea of an English sergeant versus a South Uist private of limited resilience had the same chauvinistic effect on my father as it had had on ourselves. One could sense him switching his mind into action.

'Finlay. Run as fast as you can move your legs and get Sandy Cravat for me. Tell him I want him here in his Home Guard uniform in five minutes flat, and if he as much as opens his mouth in protest tell him that he'd better think up a good explanation for forty bottles of rum on which he has been paid salvage money.'

I was nothing loath to give Sandy, who could be a cocky devil, his come-uppance, and by the time I had embellished my father's message he couldn't get into the uniform fast enough even although there was very definite apprehension writ large all over him. By the time we reached our house, I could hear something that sounded suspiciously like the army truck rumbling up the Back of Scarista hill.

'Good for you, Sandy.' My father's manner was positively jubilant. 'And you remembered to bring your rifle with you; we'll make a soldier of you yet.'

That was the last thing Sandy wanted; he had applied for exemption on every ground from excema to insanity, and, with the help of the local doctor he had, so far, resisted the call to the Colours. He was in the Home Guard only because somebody

186

had told him they'd be holding regimental dances. He opened his mouth to protest or to query, but my father cut him short.

'We've no time to talk. Just remember forty bottles of illegal rum –'

'That's blackmail!'

'I know that. Powerful stuff sometimes. This is the soldier that you came across down at the Blue Skerry when you were out on patrol just about the time that they exploded the mine. From the way he was lurking in the sand dunes you thought he was a German spy and you knocked him out and locked him in the Scaristaveg barn and you waited till he came round from the terrible blow you had given him. You arrived here with him just as the army lorry was moving away, and you're here now because I told you that I was fairly certain the truck would come back.' My father heard the squeal of brakes at the gate and added, 'As it has done.'

'Bloody hell, what are you talking about. If this gets out people will think I'm mad!'

'Exactly. That's precisely what I'll tell the big sergeant who is approaching the door now. Who knows, this might get you your exemption. Just remember – you thought he was a German spy ... you knocked him out ... he took a long time to come round ... you brought him here –' The knock on the door cut him short, and he went out to open it. He closed the living room door behind him as he went, but we could hear every word.

'Hello, Sergeant, I'm glad to see you again –'

'Sorry to bother you, Mr Macdonald, but I've lost one of my men.'

'O dear, that's sad. And his poor next-of-kin probably thinking he was safe in these parts. Ah well, that's war for you –'

The sergeant chuckled. 'No, no. I don't mean lost in that sense. I mean he's wandered off somewhere and I can't find him. I wondered if you'd seen him around?'

'O! You mean you've mislaid him. Goodness me, in my day the Colonel would have had something to say about that. I hope our landlord, Colonel Walker, doesn't hear about it; he tends to think that he's still on active service. Where do you think you left your poor man?'

'I didn't just leave him. He – er – well – I thought he was with us and then when I checked – well –' The chuckle was gone from the sergeant's voice.

'Ach, yes, Sergeant. And twelve soldiers take a lot of counting. Keep your fingers crossed that they never land you with a whole regiment. But come in, anyway, and see what we've got here for you …'

The sergeant's face was purple when he came through the living room door, but a few extra veins popped into prominence when he saw Private MacAulay drooping beside Sandy Cravat. They looked for all the world like Stan Laurel (of film comedy fame) with a taller twin brother.

'What the hell's this? Can I have an explanation, Private MacAulay?' He looked at Sandy Cravat. 'And who the devil are you?'

I could sense that my mother was getting uneasy at the kind of language with which her brood had been regaled all afternoon, but her uneasiness was sophisticated confidence compared with Private MacAulay and Sandy Cravat. My father stepped hastily into the silence.

'Let me explain, Sergeant. This is Corporal Cravat of the Home Guard. He's got his stripes but his mother hasn't had time to sew them on for him. A great soldier – you might care to make a bid for him.' Sandy Cravat looked as if he would have done something with his rifle if it had been loaded. 'But Sandy met his match in your tough Private MacAulay. You see, Corporal Cravat was on Home Guard patrol round about the time you were fiddling with the mine and didn't he go and stumble across this suspicious looking character whom he assumed, naturally, on this kind of coast, to be one of those German spies that they're putting ashore from submarines.'

'What German spies are they putting ashore from submarines? Why the hell should they – O never mind, carry on.'

My father was enjoying himself.

'And when your man started talking about blowing up something Corporal Cravat became even more suspicious, especially when he noticed that the man's accent didn't belong to any category that we're familiar with in these parts. You see, Sergeant –'

188

'But dammit, man, Private MacAulay speaks Gaylick and Garlick or whatever you call it!'

'Precisely. And what language would a good German spy make a point of learning if he was going to try and infiltrate a community like this? Why, Gaelic of course. And unfortunately, coming from the island of South Uist Private MacAulay's Gaelic is not the most fluent variety compared to the poetic kind that we speak in these parts.' It was Private MacAulay's turn to squirm but he was on a spit from which he couldn't descend. 'In short,' my father went on, 'Private MacAulay's Gaelic has got the sort of guttural quality which you would expect from a German student of the language. Gaelic is very poetic, you see –'

'O for God's sake. I'm very sorry, Mr Macdonald, but I have no time to go into the finer points of your native language. I don't think the war's going to last long enough for me to learn it.'

'No, perhaps not. But if you don't learn to look after your men better, and count them from time to time, it'll maybe be German that we'll all have to be learning. Now, you'll be treating Private MacAulay well, I'm sure, when you take him away. You needn't worry about any of us spreading stories about how you lost him, so long as we know he's well looked after; he may be a South Uistman but he's an islander for all that and we islanders like to look after our own.'

'I can see that,' said the sergeant with the last vestiges of his patience gone. 'Come along Private MacAulay; we'll stop on the way and telephone to make sure that somebody has your bath run and ready for you. Good-bye, Mrs Macdonald.' He managed a half smile for my mother who had been silent during the whole scene. His 'Good-bye' to my father was much crisper, and thrown over his shoulder as he marched through the door with MacAulay in dazed pursuit. Father stood at the door watching them walking down the path, and he suddenly remembered something just as the sergeant hauled himself into the passenger seat of the truck leaving MacAulay to be hauled into the back by his comrades, who made no attempt to hide their impatience. 'Sergeant, be sure that you don't ask Private MacAulay to drive; I had to force a tumbler of rum down the poor chap's throat to bring him round after the mauling Sandy gave him.'

'I'll arrange a personal chauffeur for Private MacAulay,' shouted the sergeant as he slammed the door and the truck roared off.

My father was chuckling as he came back into the living room. 'I haven't enjoyed myself so much for a long time. You know, I haven't ever met a Birmingham man with a sense of humour. Sandy, after all that I don't think we'll have any bother getting you made a sergeant in the Home Guard. The more that man tells his story the better you'll come out of it, and once you're a sergeant in the Home Guard they'll have you into the real army in no time.'

'Bloody hell, I don't want to go into the real army. How often do I have to tell you? I don't want to be a hero. I want to stay at home here and look after my parents and run the croft. If you could get me kicked out of the Home Guard it would be the greatest favour you could do me.'

Father sat down on St Clement's bench and began to fill his pipe. 'Well, we might find a way to do that too – you never know. If you were to go and dig up a bottle of that rum of yours it might help us think.'

'Haven't you done enough blackmailing for a day, without putting the screws on me for a bottle of rum which I'd give you anyway, just for the polite asking.'

'You and your blackmail, Sandy. It's people like you who give blackmail a bad name; there's nothing wrong with it when it's used moderately and in a good cause.'

Sandy shuffled off muttering something about people who would sit happily on the right side of the law watching others doing their dirty work for them. He had a point. Nobody had lifted a finger to help him with the cask of rum (had it been whisky it would have been a different matter) but whenever the mood took somebody poor Sandy was sent off to dig up another of his bottles with the threat of exposure always hanging over his head. Just as Sandy arrived back with his bottle of rum Tom-of-the-Oaths and the Man with the hole in his cheek strolled up to the door as if on cue. They had come to discuss some township business but whatever it was got pushed further and further down the agenda as drams were poured from Sandy's bottle and father gave a highly embroidered account of Private MacAulay's adventures. From being non-existent

Sandy Cravat's role in the affair became more and more heroic, and the more he protested the more the newcomers were disposed to believe my father's invention. By the time the bottle was finished they were at the stage of discussing a letter to General Lang recommending Sandy for a commission in the Cameron Highlanders.

'Do that and I'll put a bullet through my foot the next time we're on Home Guard parade, and that'll make sure I'll fail the medical. That's how much I want to go into the bloody army!'

The Man with the hole in his cheek looked horrified.

'You'd do that!' he said. 'And you with your Home Guard boots on. They're the King's boots man. Nobody's going to worry about your foot, but if they hear that you're threatening to damage Government property even before you're in the army they'll have you on Court Martial even before you're in uniform!'

It was an evening which, in its cosiness, reminded me of our early years in the new house in the new village. There was laughter and teasing just as there had been then although the themes were different. For a brief while the gap which had been developing between me and the village had disappeared. These were my people – the people who had moulded my youth more than the school-teachers of the Southlands or the Northlands. What mattered it if the Northlands had shops, and Big Grandfather's house had a bathroom instead our 'end of the house' or 'outside'. Here was the warmth. And suddenly, out there in the dusk, a corncrake rasped a note of scorn as if she were saying, 'We'll see if the mood of the balmy evening will last through the chill of the dawn.' Sandy Cravat must have noticed a jerk in my mood; up to that point I'd been silent on the fringe of the banter.

'For God's sake Finlay, see and do well in that school of yours. Make sure you get to Portree, if only to get yourself away from this mob; they tell me if you go in for the kirk you're exempt from the army.'

Sandy's remark was a re-statement of the corncrake's fancied comment and it brought me back to reality with a thud. I was only at the beginning of my long road on which Tarbert school was only a milestone. Success in Tarbert meant that I would go on to a higher grade school in Portree in Skye. Success in

Portree would mean that I would go on to University in one of the cities. Success in University would mean that I would be unlikely to return to the community again since our community offered little scope for men with degrees. In short, success meant that this was one of the last evenings that I would spend in the village …

It was late when the men went away in great good form. The rum had mellowed everybody and even Sandy Cravat's equanimity had returned as the veterans assured him that not even an English regiment would look at him. Father was smiling to himself as he checked the dying embers before dousing the lamp. Then, in the stillness, there came the distant sound of an aeroplane and he paused and looked as if he were going to say something. But he shrugged and carried on with his chore.

I was dropping off to sleep when a thunderous knocking came to the door. I swung my feet off my make-shift bed and I could hear father thumping to the floor in the bedroom. 'Who is it?' he shouted.

'Don't worry,' said the familiar voice of the Boer War veteran. 'It's only myself. There's nothing wrong. It's just an air-raid warning and the rules say that I've got to let you know. Just go back to sleep. I'll waken you later with the All-clear.'

But he didn't. Not that night or the night after, nor on any of the nights that remained to me in the village before I set off again on that long road into the future. Perhaps, like myself, the Boer War veteran assumed that peace would reign in the village anyway whether an official All-clear was announced or not.

A DALESMAN'S DIARY

W. R. Mitchell

Bill Mitchell was born, grew up and has worked all his life in the Yorkshire Dales. His role as editor of *The Dalesman* (1968–1988) has taken him all over this idyllic country and in A DALESMAN'S DIARY he shares his authoritative knowledge and understanding with us. He takes the reader on a nostalgic and enthralling journey which records his intimate memories of this beautiful land still unsullied by modern urban society, and describes the traditional lifestyles and folkways of its natives. With photographs taken over many years, the author captures the unique charm of this unequivocal landscape.

'If you appreciate the countryside and the lifestyle led by the people who live there you won't be able to put this book down'
The Lady

'packed with stories of Dales traditions, landmarks, characters and humour'
Huddersfield Daily Examiner

IT'S A LONG WAY TO MUCKLE FLUGGA
Journeys in Northern Scotland

W. R. Mitchell

Bill Mitchell, for twenty years editor of *The Dalesman*, is known throughout the world for his love of his native Yorkshire Dales, but there is another place close to his heart: the remote parts of the Scottish Highlands and Islands.

Every spring, Bill and his friends head north across the Border to explore some region of Scotland – one year the Isle of Arran, another year the Great Glen – moving ever northwards to their ultimate goal: Muckle Flugga in the Shetlands.

They are drawn by the wild, lonely landscape, by the abundant bird and animal life and the flowers that bloom in forgotten places, by the people of the crofting communities and the simple philosophy of their hard lives.

This enthralling odyssey through an unspoilt wilderness will delight armchair dreamers as much as those who share the author's affinity with remote places. Readers will be captivated, from the day when the author and his friends sail out from Ardrossan on the Firth of Clyde, to the moment when they gaze spellbound at the rocky outpost of Muckle Flugga, the culmination of their dreams.

100 BEST ROUTES ON SCOTTISH MOUNTAINS

Ralph Storer

From gentle afternoon strolls to challenging scrambles in remote mountain sanctuaries – a major new guide to walks in the magnificent Scottish Highlands.

* All walks are circular and accessible by road
* No rock climbing is involved
* Selected by an experienced Scottish walker
* Each route includes a peak of over 2000 feet
* All Highland regions are included
* All walks can be completed in one day
* Each route has a detailed sketch map and ratings for technical difficulty, type of terrain and conditions in adverse weather

'An inspired selection in the Highlands and Islands which includes some standard favourites'
Yorkshire Post

'The book's value lies in its accessibility, and ideal for the "where do you fancy climbing this weekend" approach'
Glasgow Herald

'This book begs to be picked up and thumbed through . . . it will stimulate walkers to head for the hills'
Times Educational Supplement

Warner now offers an exciting range of quality titles by both established and new authors which can be ordered from the following address:

Little, Brown and Company (UK),
P.O. Box 11,
Falmouth,
Cornwall TR10 9EN.

Alternatively you may fax your order to the above address. Fax No. 0326 376423.

Payments can be made as follows: cheque, postal order (payable to Little, Brown and Company) or by credit cards, Visa/Access. Do not send cash or currency. UK customers and B.F.P.O. please allow £1.00 for postage and packing for the first book, plus 50p for the second book, plus 30p for each additional book up to a maximum charge of £3.00 (7 books plus).

Overseas customers including Ireland, please allow £2.00 for the first book plus £1.00 for the second book, plus 50p for each additional book.

NAME (Block Letters) ....

....

ADDRESS ....

....

....

☐ I enclose my remittance for _____

☐ I wish to pay by Access/Visa Card

Number ☐☐☐☐☐☐☐☐☐☐☐☐☐☐☐☐

Card Expiry Date ☐☐☐☐